ORGANISATIONAL BEHAVIOUR

VOLUME–1

N.K. JAIN

ATLANTIC®
PUBLISHERS & DISTRIBUTORS

Published by

ATLANTIC®

PUBLISHERS & DISTRIBUTORS

B-2, Vishal Enclave, Opp. Rajouri Garden,
New Delhi-110027
Phones : 25413460, 25429987, 25466842

Sales Office
7/22, Ansari Road, Darya Ganj,
New Delhi-110002
Phones : 23273880, 23275880, 23280451
Fax : 91-11-23285873
web : www.atlanticbooks.com
e-mail : info@atlanticbooks.com

ISBN 81-269-0500-X Vol. I
ISBN 81-269-0501-8 Vol. II
ISBN 81-269-0502-6 Set

Printed in India
at Nice Printing Press, Delhi

PREFACE

Organisational Behaviour is the study of human behaviour, individual differences, and performances in organisational settings. This study, complex as it is, has acquired new dimensions with the dynamic social and technological changes of the past two decades. The matter contained in the book has been organised along the context of definition of the field of organisational behaviour which involves the individual behaviour and the factors that affect such behaviour, group behaviour and group dynamics relative to individuals within the group and the group interface with the organisation and the structure of organisation itself. Changing demographics, cultural diversity, more educated workforce and awareness of rights and privileges has prompted a new look at the entire organisation structure and systems.

Organisational Behaviour prompted us to expand the management horizons and approach the subject from various angles and various viewpoints in an in-depth and exhaustive manner. It is an interdisciplinary field, drawing on concepts from a variety of areas. While writing this book, several questions arose in my mind as to what competences, knowledge and skills in organisational effectiveness will be needed by the users of this book, both today and in the future. I recognise that many readers of this book may never become managers in the traditional sense of the word but are likely to be members and leaders of teams. Thus, even if you do not aspire to become a manager, this edition is filled with insights, needed skills, and concepts that will assist you in becoming an effective employee, whatever your role in the organisation maybe. I have used models and research to help you enhance your understanding and skills.

Organisational Behaviour is the study of individual and group behaviour in work settings. Time and again, we see employees and managers who work hard and have all the necessary technical skills. But because of the lack of organisational effectiveness, competences, knowledge and skills, they never reach their full potential to contribute most effectively to the organisation. The book introduces students to the concept of organisation, organisational behaviour and how the managers fit in such organisational environment. It also describes various interdisciplinary forces that affect the complexity of human behaviour. This book has been prepared to cover extensively various facets—both micro as well as macro—of the field of Organisational Behaviour. The language of presentation is highly communicative so that it become interesting and comprehensive.

I designed this book to be used flexibly, so chapters need not necessarily be studied in the same sequence as presented. Within the framework of twenty chapters, the book describes about the Introductory Approaches to Organisational Behaviour, various Theories, Structure and Design, Motivation, Morale, Leadership Theories, Interpersonal Communication, Personality, Learning, Perception, Stress, Power and Authority, Organisational Change, Organisational Development, and Conflicts and Negotiations. All the contents of the syllabus have been described and analysed—each Chapter meant for a specific topic of the syllabus. Each Chapter starts with a scheme of discussion, wherein all the contents of the chapter have been specified in a planned manner to help the reader have an overview of the entire chapter in advance; and subsequently guiding him/her in grasping the chapter contents systematically without confusing one aspect of discussion with others. At the end of the each chapter review questions and references have been given for the students for better understanding of the subject and towards quick revision for examination purposes. Sufficient number of diagrams and comparative tables and appendices have been provided throughout the book for a better appreciation of typical business concepts. Accordingly, this book is much more comprehensive in its elaboration of introduction, and concepts of organisational behaviour. This book has been specially designed for MBA and other professional courses. I hope that the present book will prove more useful to the students and the teachers of the subject. Suggestions and constructive criticisms for improving and making it more useful and informative will be highly appreciated. I am also grateful to all those whose expert opinion and erudite scholarship is cited or substantially reproduced. My near and dears deserve all appreciation for their help and patience.

The preface of the book will not be complete without expressing a great sense of gratitude to Sh. Manish Kumar Gupta, CEO and Sh. Ashish Kumar Gupta, General Manager of Atlantic Publishers and Distributors, New Delhi, for their very kind acceptance to publish this book of mine for the benefits of students and teachers of this subject. Further, I extend my sincere thanks to the management staff of my publishers for their help and mutual cooperation for bringing out this edition in a very short span of time.

And last, but not the least, thanks to my family, who put up with the stresses throughout my writing work and enabled me to complete it within the stipulated time.

N.K. Jain

CONTENTS

1st

CHAPTER

OVERVIEW

Introductory Approaches of Organisational Behaviour

- ***After reading this chapter, you should be able to know:***

- What is an Organisation
- Managers in Organisations
- Managerial Functions
- Managerial Roles
- Managerial Skills
- Organisations Good or Bad
- Material Reasons of Organisation
- Importance of Organisation
- Organisations and the Need for Management
- What is Behaviour
- Organisational Behaviour
- Nature and Scope of Organisational Behaviour
- Contributing Disciplines to the Organisation Behaviour Field
- Some General Guidelines about Behaviour
- Significance of Organisational Behaviour
- Various Approaches of Organisational Behaviour
- Properties of Modern Organisations
- The Dependent Variables
- The Independent Variables
- Interdisciplinary Studies
- Foundations of Individual Behaviour
- Biological Foundation of Behaviour
- Inherited Characteristics
- Learned Characteristics
- Sensation
- Beliefs
- Significance of Beliefs
- Development of Beliefs
- The Future of Organisational Behaviour

1

Introductory Approaches of Organisational Behaviour

WHAT IS AN ORGANISATION

Organisation is the pattern of ways in which large numbers of people, too many to have intimate face to face contact with all others, and engaged in a complexity of tasks, relate themselves to each other in the conscious, systematic establishment and accomplishment of mutually agreed purposes. The term "organisation" is a word that can be used in a number of ways. We can speak of organisation as the activity that is an important function of management. We may speak of organisation the thing: people who are united by a common purpose. In the words of *Mooney* and *Reiley* "organisation is the form of every human association for the attainment of a common purpose." In other words, organisation is simply people working together for a common goal.

According to *Prifiner* and *Sherwood,* "The organisation is the rational co-ordination of the activities of a number of people for the achievement of some common explicit purpose or goal, through division of labour and function, and through a hierarchy of authority and responsibility."

According to *Sckeim E.H. and Bakke E.W.*, however gives a more elaborate definition of organisation. They defines it as "a continuing system of differentiated and co-ordinated human activities utilising, transforming and wedding together a specific set of human, material, capital and natural resources into a unique problem solving whole engaged in satisfying particular human needs in interaction which other systems of human activities and resources in its environment."

According to *Gary Johns*, "Organisations are social invention for accomplishing goals through group efforts." This definition, though simple, covers a wide variety of groups such as businesses, schools, hospitals, fraternal groups, religious bodies, government agencies and the like.

MANAGERS IN ORGANISATIONS

No *organisation*—whether it be economic, social, religious or political—can survive without *management*. Principles of management are now universally used not only for managing business organisations, but for managing various other types of organisations like educational, social, military and government. Management is thus the same process in all forms of organisation although it may vary widely in its complexity with the size of the organisation. The management of a big multinational company, though differing in detail from that of a small partnership firm, follows the same general pattern.

Management is perhaps the most influential element in the design of organisations. It is the element that coordinates current organisational activities and plans future ones. It allocates resources, arbitrates disputes, and provides leadership. If it is dynamic and progressive, the organisation is likely to fare well. If it is reactionary and static, the organisation is likely to stagnate, especially if confronted with changes in the environment. Management adapts the organisation to its environment and often shapes the environment to make it more suitable to the organisation.

MANAGERIAL FUNCTIONS

Lyndall Urwick divides management functions into his categories, viz., Forecasting, Planning, Organising, Command, Coordination and Control. Besides these he considers investigation (or research) and communication as important functions of management. *Luther Gulick* coined the word POSDCORB to indicate the principal functions of management. The POSDCORB stands for Planning (P), Organising (O), Staffing (S), Directing (D), Coordination (CO), Reporting (R), and Budgeting (B). Of these, Reporting is covered by the controlling function and budgeting represents both planning for controlling. *R.C. Davis* has identified only three functions of management, i.e., Planning, Organising, and Controlling. *J.L. Massie* classifies management functions into :

(i) Decision-making,
(ii) Organising,
(iii) Staffing,
(iv) Planning,
(v) Controlling,
(vi) Communicating, and
(vii) Directing.

Earnest Dale has given Innovating as a distinct and separate function of management. According to him, management involves introduction of new systems, procedures, methods, techniques, products and services and all these could be well described by the term Innovating. However, Planning of change is a part of the planning function.

It will be observed from the various classifications of functions of management given above, that the mangers are primarily responsible for:

(i) Planning,
(ii) Organising,
(iii) Staffing,
(iv) Directing, and
(v) Controlling.

Management functions are closely inter-linked and interwoven in character. The top executives in the management, hierarchy are usually entrusted with the basic functions in that order and the

lower-ranking executives are given the responsibility of executing the subsidiary functions of management. It is the organisational set up which helps such a distinction if the enterprise is scientifically organised with such of foresightedness and effective planning. Generally speaking, the functions of management can be classified into two broad categories:

1. Operative functions constituting of:

(i) Purchasing,
(ii) Production,
(iii) Marketing,
(iv) Financial,
(v) Personnel etc.

2. Managerial functions constituting of:

(i) Planning,
(ii) Organising,
(iii) Staffing,
(iv) Directing,
(v) Co-ordinating, and
(vi) Controlling.

The controlling functions comprises of coordinating, reporting and budgeting, and hence the controlling functions can be broken into these three separate functions. Based upon these seven functions *Luther Gullick* coined the word "POSDCORB".

I. Planning

Planning is future oriented and determines an organisation's direction. It is a rational and systematic way of making decisions today that will affect the future of the company. It is a kind of organised foresight as well as corrective hindsight. It involves the predicting of the future as well as attempting to control the events. It involves the ability to foresee the effects of current actions in the long run in the future. *Peter F. Drucker* has defined planning as follows:

"Planning is the continuous process of making present entrepreneurial decisions systematically and with best possible knowledge of their futurity, organising systematically the efforts needed to carryout these decisions and measuring the results of these decisions against the expectations through organised and systematic feedback."

An effective planning programme incorporate the effect of both external as well as internal factors. The external factors are shortages of resources, both capital and material, general economic trend as far as interest rates and inflation are concerned, dynamic technological advancements, increased governmental regulation regarding community interests, unstable international political environments etc. The internal factors that affect planning are limited growth opportunities due to saturation requiring diversification, changing patterns of work-force, more complex organisational structure, decentralisation etc.

II. Organising

Organised effort is essential for success of any enterprise. The process of organising consists of dividing activities, assigning duties and delegating authority for effective operation and achievement of goals. Bigger the organisation, more complex will be the job of organising people and their work as face to face communication becomes difficult. The organising process in general involves the following steps :

(i) Identification of activities keeping in view the objectives to be achieved.
(ii) Dividing activities into convenient groups.
(iii) Allocating activities of different departments and assigning duties.
(iv) Delegation of authority and fixing of responsibility for performance.
(v) Coordination of these activities throughout the organisation.

III. Staffing

Staffing is the function of hiring and retaining a suitable work-force for the enterprise both at managerial as well as non-managerial levels. It involves the process of recruiting, training, developing, compensating, and evaluating employees, and maintaining this work-force with proper incentives and motivations. Since the human element is the most vital factor in the process of management, it is important since people differ in their intelligence, knowledge, skills, experience, physical condition, age and attitudes, and this complicates the function. Hence, management must understand, in addition to the technical and operational competence, the sociological and psychological structure of the work-force.

IV. Directing

Leaders matter in all types of organisations. The countries are identified with their leaders such as Gandhi's India, Kennedy's America and Stalin's Russia, etc. Business organisations and their products too are identified with their leaders such as Ford's motors, Tata's steel, Birla's cars and Public Sector HMT watches, etc. In progressively managed business organisations the leadership is provided by the Board and the top executives. The responsibility of guiding the supervising the activities and operations falls on managers at different levels. Merely the planning, organising and staffing are not sufficient to set the tasks in motion. People maintaining the organisation have to be guided, motivated and supervised by managers to get the results.

Directing process in business was identified by Henry Fayol, with command. Management thinkers of today, however, include the following functions in it :

(i) Communication,
(ii) Motivation, and
(iii) Leadership.

V. Controlling

The function of control consists of those activities that are undertaken to ensure that the events do not deviate from the pre-arranged plans. The activities consist of establishing standards for work-performance and comparing it to these set standards and taking corrective actions as and when needed, to correct any deviations.

VI. Coordinating

Some authorities view coordination as a separate function of management. Henry Fayol, for instance, included coordination amongst one of the elements of management. Management thinkers of today, however, feel that coordination is all-pervasive and permeates every function of the management process. Thus planning, organising, staffing, direction and controlling, all help managers to achieve proper coordination. In planning process, for instance, departmental plans are integrated into a master plan, ensuring adequate coordination. Similarly the primary purpose of organising is to secure coordination, particularly inter-departmental and inter-personal. Coordination is also secured through proper direction of the human efforts by the exercise of effective leadership, guidance, motivation, supervision communication, etc. The control process also requires coordination. For instance, cost control is not possible without cooperation of all people concerned. Similarly performance evaluation is done correctly only when the departments and people cooperate in providing adequate data, facts and figures in time.

All these functions of management are closely inter-related. However, these functions are highly indistinguishable and virtually unrecognizable on the job. It is necessary, though , to put each function separately into focus and deal with accordingly. The following are the main *advantages* of a better co-ordination:

(i) The whole enterprise presents a picture of unified approach to the problems of the enterprise.
(ii) Splintering efforts do not spoil the working atmosphere in the enterprise.
(iii) Cross purpose working yields to better understanding and efficient working.
(iv) Inter-personnel and departmental conflicts seldom raise their ugly heads.
(v) Commonness of purpose is achieved.

MANAGERIAL ROLES

Henry Mintzberg has studied the work roles of the Chief Executive and has categorised these roles into three areas. These areas are interpersonal relationships, information processing and disseminating, and decision-making. Each of these areas are further subdivided into various roles. Those roles are:

I. Interpersonal Relationships

(i) *Manager's role as a figurehead.* Managers act as symbolic figureheads performing social or legal obligations. These duties include greeting visitors, signing legal documents, taking important customers to lunch, attending a subordinate's wedding or speaking at functions in schools and churches etc.

(ii) *Manager's leadership role.* Since a manager is responsible for the activities of his subordinates he must motivate them to perform better. He must be an exemplary leader so that his subordinates follow his directions and guidelines with respect and dedication.

(iii) In addition to their constant contact with their own subordinates and peers, the managers must maintain a network of outside contacts in order to assess the external environment of competition, social changes or changes in governmental rules and regulations. This can be achieved by attending meetings, professional conferences, personal phone calls, through mail etc.

II. Information Processing

(iv) *Manager's role as a monitor.* The managers are constantly monitoring their environment, collecting and studying information regarding their organisation and outside environment affecting their organisation. This can be done by reading reports and periodicals and through personal contacts.

(v) *Manager's role as a disseminator of information.* They transmit the information regarding changes in policies or other matters to their subordinates, their peers, and to other members of the organisation. This can be done through memos, phone calls or group or individual meetings.

(vi) *Manager's role as a spokesman.* The manager has to be a spokesman for his unit and represents his unit in either sending information to people or making some demands on behalf of his unit. This can be done through meetings and phone calls.

III. Decision-Making

(vii) *Manager's role as an entrepreneur.* The manager are constantly on the lookout for new ideas for product improvement or product addition. Thy initiate feasibility studies, arrange for capital for new products if necessary, and ask for suggestions from the employees for ways to improve the organisation in any way. This can be achieved through suggestion boxes, holding strategy meetings with project manager and Research and Development personnel.

(viii) *Manager's role as a conflict handler.* The managers are constantly involved as arbitrators in solving differences among the subordinates or the employees' conflicts with the management. These conflicts may arise due to demands for higher pay or other benefits. These conflicts may involve outside forces such as vendors increasing their prices or visits by governmental inspectors. Managers try to resolve these problems and take corrective action.

(ix) *Manager's role as resource allocator.* Managers make budgetary allocations to different activities of the organisation. They assign personnel to jobs, they allocate their own time to different activities and they allocate funds for new equipment, advertising, pay raises etc.

(x) *Manager's role as negotiator.* They negotiate contracts with the unions. The sales managers may negotiate prices with prime customers. The purchasing managers may negotiate prices with the vendors etc.

MANAGERIAL SKILLS

The various types of skills required by the managers - technical human conceptual and decision-making skills. The relative use of this skills appears to differ when the job of management is studied on a level of level basis. Conceptual skill deals with ideas, technical skill with things and human skill with people. While both conceptual and technical skills are needed for good decision-making, human skill is necessary for a good leader.

I. Technical Skills

Technical skills encompass the ability to apply specialised knowledge or expertise. When you think of the skills held by professionals such as civil engineers or oral surgeons, you typically focus on their technical skills. Through extensive formal education, they have learned the special knowledge and practices of their field. Of course, professionals do not have a monopoly on technical skills, and not all technical skills have to he learned in schools or formal training programs. All jobs required some specialised expertise, and many people develop their technical skills on the job.

II. Interpersonal Skills

Interpersonal skill is the ability to work with other people amicably. It involves patience, trust and genuine involvement in interpersonal relationships. It is the ability to lead and motivate and effectively interact with others. This will create an environment in which the workers work together as a team with a sense of belonging and dedication and this is truly conducive to high morale which is necessary for organisational success.

III. Human Skills

The ability to work with, understand, and motivate other people, both individually and in groups, describes human skills. Many people are technically proficient but interpersonally incompetent. They might be poor listeners, unable to understand the needs of others, or have difficulty managing conflicts. Since managers get things done through other people, they must have good human skills to communicate, motivate, and delegate.

IV. Diagnostic Skills

Diagnostic skill refers to manager's analytical ability where a manager can logically and objectively investigate and analyse a problem and an opportunity and use scientific approaches to arrive at a feasible and optimal solution. It is important however that a manager gets to the root cause of the problem so that the solution is the real and permanent one rather than simply a cosmetic one.

This skill overlaps with other skills because a manager may need to use technical, human, conceptual, or political skills to solve the problem that has been diagnosed.

V. Conceptual Skills

Managers must have the mental ability to analyse and diagnose complex situations. These tasks require conceptual skills. Decision-making, for instance, requires managers to spot problems, identify alternatives that can correct them, evaluate those alternatives, and select the best one. Managers can be technically and interpersonally competent yet still fail because of an inability to rationally process and interpret information.

VI. Political Skills

Political skill can be described as the ability to get your own way without seeming to be selfish or self-oriented. It is the ability to get your share of power and authority and use it without fear of losing it. It is the most complex skill in the sense that it is required to establish the right connections and impressing the right people and then skilfully using these connections to your own advantage. Political skill is most important at the middle management level because middle managers always aspire to reach the top levels of management.

VII. Communicational Skills

Communication skills are basic to all other skills and are important at all levels of management. A manager's best ideas will have little impact if they cannot be communicated effectively. Good communication is the foundation of sound management. Proper communications eliminates delays, misunderstanding, confusion, distortions and conflicts and improves coordination and control. Accordingly, communicational skill plays an important role in all walks of human life as well as organisational life.

ORGANISATIONS GOOD OR BAD

The topic whether organisations are good or bad has been kicked around a lot by management thinkers and practitioners frequently. "Organisations whether big or small, private or public, are not necessarily good or bad in themselves, even though at times it has been fashionable to criticise them vehemently."

Human beings are need-fulfilling and goal-achieving entities. They create various types of strategies to fulfil their needs and to achieve their goals. One of the important strategies is to organise themselves. *C.I. Barnard* cited a situation in which a person wanted to move a stone but could not. Either the stone was too big for the man or the man was too small for the stone. So he hired men and got it removed. Thus, came into existence an organisation, though only for a short while organisations are designed, essentially, by people to overcome individual limitations. In addition to these biological limitations, individuals suffer from limited cognitive capacities. In modern organisations, it is virtually impossible for an individual to be knowledgeable in a large number of diverse fields. The only way to enhance his capacities is to divide tasks into specialities and assign them to others. Organisations are the only instruments available for individuals to overcome their biological and psychological limitations. According to *Argyris*, organisations are usually formed to satisfy objectives "that can best be met collectively". Organisations are social inventions or tools developed by men to achieve things otherwise not possible. Organisations are contrived social instruments through which society, or portions of it obtain things that either could not be obtained at all or could not be had as easily or cheaply. Organisations provide warmth and support for individuals. They provide social satisfactions to members. People are by nature, gregarious beings, they always want relationships with others. Organisations enable individuals to satisfy their needs for interaction, companionship and belonging and contribution to common purpose.

MATERIAL REASONS OF ORGANISATION

According to *Hicks* and *Gullett*, people organise for three material reasons: to enlarge abilities, to compress the time required to accomplish an objective and to take advantage of the accumulated knowledge of previous generations.

I. Enlarge Abilities

Organisations help individuals enhance their capacities. Organisations permit individuals to associate their efforts with others in a fruitful way. Many things in the world could be achieved only through organised efforts. Examples like launching a space craft, building a gigantic warship, explorations in Antarctica etc. bear ample testimony to the fact that organisations are the only effective instruments available for individuals to enhance their limited abilities; only means for enjoying a better standard of living. Organisations also help individuals realise the full benefits of specialisation. Division of labour and specialisation enables an individual specialise in the job in which he has got proficiency leading to a better utilisation of resources.

II. Compress Time

Organisations compress the time needed to accomplish an objective. Often the time factor might receive a 'premium' when weighed against cost factor in respect of a crash programme like sending men to space or a planet like Mars. For example the alternative to land a man on a planet in 1986 at a phenomenal cost might be favourably considered in preference to an alternative to land a man on the planet in 1992 at a very reasonable cost. In such cases reducing the total elapsed time is more important than ordinary efficiency. Organisations compress the total elapsed time in order to realise an extremely important objective and enable individuals to priorities objectives on the basis of the time value assigned.

III. Accumulated Knowledge

Every organisation stores up knowledge and experience from time to time as to progress. The individuals who have contributed to its outstanding success might have been respectfully laid aside but their knowledge and invaluable experience is passed on to successive generations for further refinement. Organisations allow individuals to take advantage of the experience and insights of those who have gone before.

IMPORTANCE OF ORGANISATION

According to *L.A. Allen* sound organisation can contribute greatly to the continuity and success of the enterprise in the following ways:

I. Facilitates Administration

If the organisation plan is ill-designed, if it is merely a makeshift arrangement, then management is rendered difficult and ineffective. Poor organisation leads to waste motion and expensive overlap in work. Important work may be subordinated or may be overlooked totally. Sound organisation allows management to relate resource flows continually to overall objectives; it provides an appropriate platform from where management can perform the functions of planning, direction controlling etc. in a smooth way.

II. Facilitates Growth and Diversification

Sound organisation permits organisational elaboration. Under the traditional functional organisations growth and diversification of activities is facilitated by clear division of work, proper delegation of authority etc. As the organisation balloons to a reasonable proportion the functional type can be replaced by a more flexible decentralised organisation.

III. Permits Optimum Use of Resources

Sound organisation structure permits optimum use of technical and human resources. The organisation can take note of the latest technological improvements and incorporate for example computers, electronic data processing machines wherever necessary. Similarly, sound organisation structure permits optimum use of human efforts through specialisation. Right persons are placed in the right positions on the basis of their knowledge and experience. It also develops people by creating appropriate training and promotion opportunities. An ideal organisation plan, in short, would give a company the greatest possible strength for meeting predicted needs-changing conditions.

IV. Stimulates Creativity

Specialisation provides individuals with well-defined duties, clear lines of authority and responsibility. Where there is no sound organisation, work is divided by force and aggressiveness affecting the morale of the employees seriously. Sound organisation structure enables managers to turn over routine and repetitive jobs to supporting positions and concentrate an important issues where they can exploit their potential better.

However, sound organisation structure by itself does not guarantee success. It is not a sure bet. In the words of *Drucker* "good organisation structure does not by itself produce good performance just as a good constitution does not guarantee great presidents, or good laws or a moral society. But a poor organisation structure makes good performance impossible, no matter how good the individuals may be". *Alvin Brown* had discussed about the weaknesses of poor organisation structure in his article in *Advanced Management* under the following heads:

— Failure to act

— Wrong actions,

— Lack of quantity of effort,
— Lack of quality of effort,
— Waste of effort,
— Excessive quantity of effort, and
— Excessive quality of effort.

ORGANISATIONS AND THE NEED FOR MANAGEMENT

For most of our lives, we are members of one organisation or another—a college, a sports team, a musical or theatrical group, a religious or civic organisation, a branch of the armed forces, or a business. Some organisations, like the army and large corporations, are structured very formally. Others, like a neighbourhood basketball team, are more casually structured. But all organisations, formal or informal, are put together and kept together by a group of people who see that there are benefits available from working together toward some common goal. So a very basic element of any organisation is a goal or purpose. The goal will vary—to win a league championship, to entertain an audience, to sell a product—but without a goal no organisation would have a reason to exist.

All organisations also have some program or method for achieving goals—a plan. The plan might be to practice playing skills, to rehearse a certain number of times before each performance, or to manufacture and advertise a product. Whatever it is, without some plan for what it must do, no organisation is likely to be very effective.

Managers get things done through other people. They make decisions, allocate resources, and direct the activities of others to attain goals. Managers do their work in an organisation. This is consciously coordinated social unit, composed of two or more people, that functions on a relatively continuous basis of achieve a common goal or set of goals. On the basis of this definition, manufacturing and service firms are organisations and so are schools, hospitals, churches, military units, retail stores, police departments, and local, state, and federal government agencies. The people who oversee the activities of others and who are responsible for attaining goals in these organisations are managers (although they are sometimes called administrators, especially in not-for-profit organisations).

WHAT IS BEHAVIOUR ?

Behaviour is a way of action. It is basically goal oriented. In other words our behaviour is generally motivated by a desire to attain a goal. The specific goal is not always consciously known by the individual. Many times we wonder "why did I do that?"

The reason for our action is not always apparent to the conscious mind. The drives that motivate distinctive individual behavioural patterns are to a considerable degree subconscious and therefore not easily susceptible to examination and evaluation.

The basic unit of behaviour is an activity. In fact, all behaviour is a series of activities. As a human being, we always do something: walking, talking, sleeping, etc. and sometimes we do more than one activity at a time. Sometimes, we decide to change from one activity to another. Why do we do so? Or why do people engage in one activity and not another? A manager must understand, predict and control the activities of a person at a given moment. To predict behaviour, manager must know which motives or needs of people evoke a certain action at a particular time.

ORGANISATIONAL BEHAVIOUR

Organisational behaviour (OB) is concerned with the study of what people do in an organisation and how that behaviour affects the performance of the organisation. And because organisation behaviour is specifically concerned with employment-related situations, you should not be surprised to find that it emphasises behaviour as related to jobs, work, absenteeism, employment turnover, productivity, human performance, and management.

There is increasing agreement as to the components or topics that constitute the subject area of organisation behaviour. Although there is still considerable debate as to the relative importance of each, there appears to be general agreement that organisation behaviour includes the core topics of motivation, leader behaviour and power, interpersonal communication, group structure and processes, learning, attitude development and perception, change processes, conflict, work design, and work stress.

We can also think of organisation as a process; the process of identifying and grouping the work to be performed, defining and delegating responsibility and authority and establishing relationships for the purpose of enabling people to work most effectively together in accomplishing objectives. One result of this process will be an organisation structure which provides members a place to be and to work for organisational goals. Rightly *Litterer* pointed out that organisations are intervening elements between wants and their satisfactions and must be established before the wants are satisfied.

Organisational behaviour is an academic field of study which seeks to understand and describe human behaviour in organisational settings. From the conceptual standpoint, observes *Luthans*, "organisational behaviour is the result of interaction and interdependency between formal organisation and the human factors variables."

The formal organisation variable consists of three basic interdependent and interacting elements: *structure*, *processes* and *technology*.

The human factors variable also consists of three elements: *biological-physiological structure*, *psychological processes* and *personality*.

These variables are distinct but highly complex and interdependent. The interaction between human factors and formal organisation variable leads to organisational behaviour. Further, the organisational behaviour is revealed in organisational dynamics, conflict, change and adaptation. These variables of organisation behaviour and its manifestations are discussed here:—

I. Formal Organisation Variables

These include—*organisational structure, management processes* and *technology*.

The formal organisation variable consists of the *structure* which acts as a skeleton for it. The structure permits the management processes and technology elements to work. *Weber's* bureaucratic model exemplifies the classical organisation structure. Unity of command, equal authority and responsibility, limited span of control and allied concepts also play a significant part in a classical organisational structure. The classical structure extends itself to the neoclassical structure. Neoclassical concept represent the intermediate stage of theoretical and practical development of an organisational structure and include centralisation-decentralisation, departmentation, line and staff, etc. The modern organisational structures purport to meet the challenges of growth, complexity, conflict and change.

Management processes, as an integral element of the formal organisation variable, are interdependent and interacting with the organisational structure. Management processes include *decision-making*, *communication* and *control*.

Decision-making has been defined as choosing between alternatives. Its processes largely involve techniques for narrowing choices. *Communication* relates to application of symbols to transfer the meaning of informations. It forms a measure to influence others.

According to *Henry Fayol*, the process of *control* relates to verification as to whether everything in respect of things, people and actions is consistent with the plan visualised, the instructions given and principles adapted with a view to indicating shortcomings and mistakes as a measure to correct and prevent them.

In addition to human relations bias, the modern viewpoint on *control process* is also influenced by other motivating factors. For instance, detailed control, reports may be sent to operating people to accomplish prompt responsive action and budgeting may be on participative basis largely to meet information needs. It has been indicated, although not largely, that the new science of modern management will have a recentralised effect.

The element of *technology* includes both the techniques and the total human knowledge employed to attain the goals of an organisation. As a vital element of the formal organisation, it influences as well as is influenced by the organisational structure and management processes.

II. Human Factors Variables

These variables are *biological-physiological structure, psychological processes* and *personality*. These are analogous to the three elements of the formal organisation.

The *biological-physiological structure* is to human factor as the structure is to the formal organisation. This structure consists of heredity and incorporates the nervous system, sense organs, muscles and glands. The nervous system has a vital role to play in determining human behaviour and acts as a connector for sense organs, muscles and glands. The biological-physiological structure is the key for understanding human behaviour. *Psychological processes* which are analogous to the management processes of the formal organisation include perception, learning and motivation. These processes are of a great significance for the understanding of organisational behaviour. *Personality* relates to the human factor as technology relates to formal organisation. The study of development and structure of personality occupies great importance in organisational behaviour.

III. The Manifestations of Organisational Behaviour

The study and analysis of organisational behaviour forms the integrating theme for behavioural approach to management. It seeks to help the manager understand why individuals behave as they do in organisational settings, to enhance his expertise in predicting their future behaviour and in directing, changing and controlling this behaviour. Organisational behaviour *manifests* itself in organisational dynamics, conflict, change and adaptation. Organisational dynamics is the result of interaction between human factors and the formal organisation in the forms of groups and informal organisations. When the human factor interacts with the formal organisation, it becomes an integral part of the organisation itself. When an analysis of organisational behaviour indicates that the interaction between the human factor and formal organisation has resulted in the satisfaction of human needs and attainment of goals, a positive adaptation can be inferred. Motivation, leadership and organisational development techniques are employed to attain this adaptation. However, when the formal organisation goes against the human factors the organisational behaviour may result in frustration, goal or role conflict or resistance to change.

NATURE AND SCOPE OF ORGANISATIONAL BEHAVIOUR

The field of organisation behaviour is bewilderingly complex. To understand 'WHYS' of behaviour it is essential to problem deep into the organisational relationship, patterns of behaviour, etc. It is necessary to document the organisational factors influencing workers, it is necessary to understand the nature of this 'soft' discipline, its strengths, its weaknesses etc.

(i) Organisation behaviour is a rational thinking, not an emotional feeling about people. The major goals of OB are to explain and predict human behaviour in organisations. It is action-oriented and goal-directed.

(ii) Organisation behaviour seeks to balance human and technical values at work; it seeks to achieve productivity by building and maintaining employee's dignity, growth and satisfaction, rather than at the expense of these values.

(iii) Organisation behaviour is not a discipline in the usual sense of the term but rather an eclectic field of study that integrates behavioural sciences (psychology, sociology, anthropology, and social psychology etc.). It is a part of the social sciences.

(iv) Organisation behaviour is both a science and an art. The knowledge about human behaviour in organisations lies toward the science end of the continuum; the skill is applying that knowledge clearly lens toward being an art, recognising that individual differences in managerial style can vary considerably.

(v) Organisation behaviour is an inexact science. This is perhaps due to the fact that it is a young field of enquiry (in terms of the use of scientific techniques); comparatively little progress has been made in providing specific answers to specific organisational problem was such very little can be prescribed and it is very difficult to consistently predict the behaviour of people in organisations. It is possible to predict relationships between variables on a broad scale but it is difficult to apply predictive models on an individual basis.

(vi) Organisation behaviour exists at multiple levels. Behaviour occurs at the individual, the group, and the organisational systems level. Behaviour that is attributable to each of these levels can be both identified and isolated. But at the same time these three levels interact with each other and OB being affected by the behaviour of individuals, group level behaviour is affected by the organisational level phenomena and so on.

(vii) Organisation behaviour does not exist in vacuum. Organisations are made-up of both social and technical components and therefore characterised as socio-technical systems. The operational implication of this is that any approach to looking at behaviour must also take into account the technical component of organisation—especially such issues as the nature of the work and the technology. Organisations at the same time, must take into account the constraints of the working environment—for example the extent to which the market is changing, the extent to which the product is changing etc.

CONTRIBUTING DISCIPLINES TO THE ORGANISATION BEHAVIOUR FIELD

Organisational behaviour is an applied behavioural science that is built upon contributions from a number of behavioural disciplines. The predominant areas are psychology, sociology, social psychology, anthropology, and political science. As we shall learn, psychology's contributions have been mainly at the individual or micro level of analysis; the other four disciplines have contributed to our understanding of macro concepts such as group processes and organisation.

I. Psychology

Psychology is the science that seeks to measure, explain, and sometime change the behaviour of humans and others animals. Psychologists concern themselves with studying and attempting to understand individual behaviour. Those who have contributed and continue to add to the knowledge of OB are learning theorists, personality theorists, counselling psychologists, and, most important, industrial and organisational psychologists.

Early industrial and organisational psychologists concerned themselves with problems of fatigue, boredom, and other factors relevant to working conditions that could impede efficient work performance. More recently, their contributions have been expanded to include learning, perception, personality, training, leadership effectiveness, needs and motivational forces, job satisfaction, decision-making processes, performance appraisals, attitude measurement, employee selection techniques, work design, and job stress.

II. Sociology

Whereas psychologists focus on the individual, sociologists study the social system in which individuals fill their roles; that is, sociology studies people in relation to their fellow human beings. Specifically, sociologists have made their greatest contribution to OB through their study of group behaviour in organisations, particularly in formal and complex organisations. Some of the areas within OB that have received valuable input from sociologists are group dynamics, design of work teams, organisational culture, formal organisation theory and structure, organisational technology, communications, power, conflict, and inter-group behaviour.

III. Social Psychology

Social psychology is an area within psychology, but it blends concepts from psychology and sociology. It focuses on the influence of people on one another. One of the major areas receiving considerable investigation from social psychologists have been change—how to implement it and how to reduce barriers to its acceptance. In addition, social psychologists are making significant contributions in the areas of measuring, understanding, and changing attitudes; communication patterns; the ways in which group activities can satisfy individual needs; and group decision-making process.

IV. Industrial Psychology

Industrial psychology helps to understand the individual reactions to industrial environment. It involves selection and placement of individuals into particular jobs through psychological tests, study of mental health as affected by physical industrial environment, impact of organisational structure on human performance and the types of job affecting safety, and morale of workers.

V. Anthropology

Anthropology is the study of societies to learn about human beings and their activities. Anthropologists' work of cultures and environments, for instance, has helped us understand differences in fundamental values, attitudes, and behaviour between people in one's own countries and within different countries and different organisations. Much of our current understanding of organisational culture, organisational environments, and differences between national cultures is the result of the work of anthropologists or researchers using their methodologies.

VI. Political Science

Although frequently overlooked, the contributions of political scientists are significant to the understanding of behaviour in organisations. Political science studies the behaviour of individuals and groups within a political environment. Specific topics of concern include structuring of conflict, allocation of power, and how people manipulate power for individual self-interest.

Thirty years ago, little of what political scientists were studying was of interest to students of organisational behaviour. But times have changed. We have become increasingly aware that organisation are political entities; if we are to be able to accurately explain and predict the behaviour of people in organisations, we need to bring a political perspective to our analysis.

VII. Economics

Economics aids in the understanding of economic conditions at a given time, economic policies of the government, allocation of scarce resources to different competing alternatives, and all these factors affect the organisational climate. Organisational behaviour has learned a great deal from such economic factors as labour market dynamics, cost-benefit analysis, marginal utility analysis, human resource planning and forecasting and decision-making.

VIII. Engineering

Engineering, especially the industrial engineering branch, has contributed significantly in the areas of time and motion study, work measurement, work flow analysis, job design and wage and salary administration. Each of these areas has some impact on organisational behaviour.

IX. Semantics

Semantics, one of the more recent disciplines, helps in the study of communications within the organisation. Misunderstood and misdirected communication or simply lack of communication creates many behavioural problems. Accordingly, total, right and properly understood communication is very important in effective and efficient performance as per directives.

X. Medicine

Medicine is perhaps the newest field affecting organisational behaviour. The primary area of interest is work related stress, tension and depression. The study of causes and consequences of stress and use of medicinal drugs to reduce stress is fast becoming an area of study within the organisational setting.

SOME GENERAL GUIDELINES ABOUT BEHAVIOUR

You have already developed some generalisations that you find helpful in explaining and predicting what people do and will do. But how did you arrive at those generalisations? You did so by observing, sensing, asking, listening, and reading. That is, your understanding comes either directly from your own experience with things in the environment, or second hand, through the experience of others.

How accurate are the generalisations that you hold? Some may represent extremely sophisticated appraisal of behaviour and may prove highly effective in explaining and predicting the behaviour of others. However, most of us also carry with us a number of beliefs that frequently fail to explain why people do what they do. To illustrate, let's consider the following statements about work-related behaviour:—

(i) Happy workers are productive workers.

(ii) All individuals are most productive when their boss is friendly, trusting, and approachable.

(iii) The best leaders are those that exhibit consistent behaviour, regardless of the situations they face.

(iv) Interviews are effective selection devices for separating job applicants who would be high-performing employees from those who would be low performers.

(v) Everyone wants a challenging job.

(vi) You have to scare people a little to get them to do their jobs.

(vii) Because specific goals intimidate people, individuals work harder when asked just to do their best.

(viii) Everyone is motivated by money.

(ix) Most people are much more concerned with the size of their own salaries than with the size of other people's salaries.

(x) The most effective work groups are devoid of conflict.

How many of these statements do you think are true? For the most part they're all false. But whether these statements are true or false is not really important at this time. What is important is that many of the views you hold concerning human behaviour are based on intuition rather than fact. As a result, a systematic approach to the study of behaviour can improve your explanatory and predictive abilities.

SIGNIFICANCE OF ORGANISATIONAL BEHAVIOUR

The formal study of organisational behaviour began around 1948 to 1952. This still emerging field attempts to help managers understand people better so that productivity improvements, customer satisfaction, and a better competitive position can be achieved through better management practices.

The behavioural sciences—especially *psychology*, *sociology*, and *cultural anthropology*—have provided the basic framework and principles for the field of organisational behaviour. Each behavioural science discipline provides a slightly different focus, analytical framework, and theme for helping managers answer questions about themselves, non-managers, and environmental forces (e.g., competition, legal requirements, and social-political changes). Our multidisciplinary definition of organisational behaviour illustrates a number of points:

(i) Organisational behaviour is a way of thinking. Behaviour is viewed as operating at individual, group, and organisational levels. This approach suggests that when studying OB we must identify clearly the level of analysis-individual, group, and /or organisational–being used.

(ii) Organisational behaviour is multidisciplinary: it uses principles, models, theories, and methods from other disciplines. The study of OB isn't a discipline or a generally accepted science with an established theoretical foundation. It's a field that only now is beginning to grow and develop in stature and impact.

(iii) There's a distinctly humanistic orientation within organisational behaviour. People and their attitudes, perceptions, learning capacities, feelings, and goals are important to the organisation.

(iv) The field of organisational behaviour is performance oriented.

(v) The external environment is seen as having significant impact or organisational behaviour.

(vi) Since the field of organisational behaviour relies heavily on recognised disciplines, the scientific method is important in studying variables and relationships. As the scientific method has been applied to research on organisational behaviour, a set of principles and guidelines on what constitutes good research has emerged.

(vii) The field has a distinctive applications orientation; it concerns providing useful answers to questions that arise in the context of managing operations.

VARIOUS APPROACHES OF ORGANISATIONAL BEHAVIOUR

There are various approaches of organisational behaviour. Some of them are discussed below:

I. The Behavioural Approach

Like the other approaches to management, the behavioural approach has evolved gradually over many years. Advocates of the behavioural approach to management point out that people deserve to be the central focus of organised activity. They believe that successful management depends largely on a manager's ability to understand and work with people who have a variety of backgrounds, needs, perceptions, and aspirations. The progress of this humanistic approach from the human relations movement to modern organisational behaviour has greatly influenced management theory and practice.

II. The Human Relations Movement

The human relations movement was a concerted effort among theorists and practitioners to make managers more sensitive to employee needs. It came into force being as a result of special circumstances that occurred during the first half of this century. The human relations movement was supported by three very different historic influences: (i) the threat of unionisation, (ii) the Hawthorne studies, and (iii) the philosophy of industrial humanism.

(i) The Threat of Unionisation

To understand why the human relations movement evolved, one needs first to appreciate its socio-political background. From the late 1800s to the 1920s, American industry grew by leaps and bounds as it attempted to satisfy the many demands of a rapidly growing population. Cheap immigrant labour was readily available, and there was a seller's market for finished goods. Then came the Great Depression in the 1930s, and millions stood in bread lines instead of pay lines. Many held business somehow responsible for the depression, and public sympathy swung from management to labour. Congress consequently began to pass prolabour legislation. When the Wagner Act of 1935 legalised union-management collective bargaining, management began searching for ways to stem the tide of all-out unionisation. Early human relations theory proposed an enticing answer: satisfied employees would be less inclined to join unions. Business managers subsequently began adopting morale-boosting human relations techniques as a union-avoidance tactic.

(ii) The Hawthorne Studies

As the socio-political climate changed, a second development in industry took place. Behavioural scientists from prestigious universities began to conduct on-the-job behaviour studies. Instead of studying tools and techniques in the scientific management tradition, they focused on people. Practical behavioural research such as the famous Hawthorne studies stirred management's interest in the psychological and sociological dynamics of the workplace.

The Hawthorne studies began in 1924 in a Western Electric Plant near Chicago as a small-scale scientific management study of the relationship between light intensity and productivity. Curiously, the performance of a select group of employees tended to improve no matter how the physical surroundings were manipulated. Even when the lights were dimmed to moonlight intensity, productivity continued to climb. Scientific management doctrine could not account for what was taking place, and so a team of behavioural science researchers, headed by *Elton Mayo*, was brought in from *Harvard* to conduct a more rigorous study. By 1932, when the Hawthorne studies ended, over twenty thousand employees had participated in one way or another. After extensive interviewing of the subjects, it became clear to researchers that productivity was much less affected by changes in work conditions than by the attitudes of the workers themselves. Specifically, relationships between members of a work group and between workers and their supervisors were found to be more significant. Though the experiments and the theories that evolved from them are criticised today for flawed methodology and statistical in accuracies, the Hawthorne studies can be credited with turning management theorists away from the simplistic "economic man" model to a more humanistic and realistic view, the "social man" model.

(iii) The Philosophy of Industrial Humanism

Although unionisation prompted a search for new management techniques and the Hawthorne studies demonstrated that people were important to productivity, a philosophy of human relations was needed to provide a convincing rationale for treating employees better. *Elton Mayo*, *Mary Parker Follett*, and *Douglas McGregor*, although from very different backgrounds, offered just such a philosophy.

Born in Australia, *Elton Mayo* was a Harvard professor specialising in psychology and sociology when he took over the Hawthorne studies. His 1933 book, *The Human Problems of an Industrial Civilization*, inspired by what he had learned at Hawthorne, cautioned managers that emotional factors were a more important determinant of productive efficiency than physical and logical factors were. Claiming that employees create their own unofficial yet powerful workplace culture complete with norms and sanctions, *Mayo* urged managers to provide work that fostered personal and subjective satisfaction. He called for a new social order designed to stimulate individual cooperation.

Mary Parker Follett's experience as a management consultant and her background in Law, Political Science, and Philosophy produced her strong conviction that managers should be aware that each employee is a complex collection of emotions, beliefs, attitudes, and habits. To get employees to work harder, she believed, managers had to recognise the individual's motivating desires. Accordingly, *Follett* urged managers to motivate performance rather than to simply demand it. Cooperation, a spirit of unity, and self-control were seen as the keys to both productivity and a democratic way of life. Historians credit *Follett*, who died in 1933, with being decades ahead of her time in terms of behavioural and systems management theory.

A third philosophical rallying point for industrial humanism was provided by an American scholar named *Douglas McGregor*. In his 1960 classic, The Human Side of Enterprise, *McGregor* outlined a set of highly optimistic assumptions about human nature. Some historians have credited *McGregor* with launching the field of organisational behaviour.

III. Organisational Behavioural Approach

Organisational behaviour is a modern approach to management that attempts to determine the causes of human work behaviour and translate the results into effective management techniques. As such, it has a strong research orientation. Organisational behaviourists have borrowed an assortment of theories and research techniques from all of the behavioural sciences and applied them to people at work in modern organisations. The result is an interdisciplinary field in which psychology predominates. In spite of its relatively new and developing state, organisational behaviour has had a significant impact on modern management thought by helping to explain why employees behave as they do. Because human relations has evolved into a practical how-to-do-it discipline for supervisors, organisational behaviour amounts to a scientific extension of human relations.

Lessons from the Behavioural Approach

Above all else, the behavioural approach makes it clear to present and future managers that people are the key to productivity. According to advocates of the behavioural approach, technology, work rules, and standards do not guarantee good job performance. Instead, success depends on motivated and skilled individuals who are committed to organisational objectives. Only a manager's sensitivity to individual concerns can foster the cooperation necessary for high productivity. On the negative side, traditional human relations doctrine has been criticised as vague and simplistic. According to these critics, relatively primitive on-the-job behavioural research does not justify such broad conclusions. For instance, critics do not believe that supportive supervision and good human relations will lead automatically to higher morale and hence to better job performance. Also, recent analysis of the Hawthorne studies, using modern statistical techniques, have generated debate about the validity of the original conclusions. Fortunately, organisational behaviour, as a scientific extension of human relations, promises to fill some of the gaps left by human relationists while at the same time retaining an emphasis on people. Today, organisational behaviourists are trying to piece together the multiple determinants of effective job performance in various work situations and across cultures.

IV. The System Approach

A system is a collection of parts operating interdependently to achieve a common purpose. Working from this definition, the systems approach represents a marked departure from the past; in fact, it requires a completely different style of thinking. Universal process, scientific management, and human relations theorists studied management by taking things apart. They assumed that the whole is equal to the sum of its parts and can be explained in terms of its parts. Systems theorists, in contrast, study management by putting things together and assume that the whole is greater than the sum of its parts. The difference is analytic versus synthetic thinking. According to one management systems expert, "analytic thinking is, so to speak, outside-in thinking; synthetic thinking is inside-out." Neither negates the value of the other, but by synthetic thinking we can gain understanding that we cannot obtain through analysis, particularly of collective phenomena. Systems theorists recommend synthetic thinking because management is not practiced in a vacuum. Managers affect, and are in turn affected by, many organisational and environmental variables. Systems thinking has presented the field of management with an enormous challenge: to identify all relevant parts of organised activity and to discover how they interact. Two management writers predicted that systems thinking offers "a basis for understanding organisations and their problems which may one day produce a revolution in organisations comparable to the one brought about by *Taylor* with scientific management."

Chester I. Barnard's Early System Perspective

One sense, *Chester I. Barnard* followed in the footsteps of *Henry Fayol*. Like *Fayol*, *Barnard* established a new approach to management on the basis of his experience as a top-level manager. But the former president of New Jersey Bell telephone's approach differed from Fayol's. Rather than isolating specific management functions and principles, *Barnard* devised a more abstract systems approach. In his landmark 1938 book, *The Functions of the Executive*, *Barnard* characterised all organisations as cooperative systems. A cooperative system is a complex of physical, biological, personal, and social components which are in a specific systematic relationship by reason of the co-operation of two or more persons for at least one definite end.

According to *Barnard*, willingness to serve, common purpose, and communication are the principal elements in an organisation (or co-operative system). He felt that an organisation did not exist if these three elements were not present and working interdependently. As illustrated in Barnard viewed communication as an energising force that bridges the natural gap between the individual's willingness to serve and the organisation's common purpose. *Barnard's* systems perspective has encouraged management and organisation theorists to study organisations as complex and dynamic wholes instead of piece by piece. Barnard opened a promising door in the evolution of management thought.

General Systems Theory

General systems theory is an interdisciplinary area of study based on the assumption that everything is part of a larger, interdependent arrangement. According to *Ludwig von Bertalanffy*, a biologist and the founder of general systems theory, 'In order to understand an organised whole we must know the parts and the relations between them'. This interdisciplinary perspective was eagerly adopted by Barnard's followers because it categorised levels of systems and distinguished between closed and open systems.

Levels of Systems : Envisioning the world as a collection of system was only the first step for general systems theorists. One of the more important recent steps has been the identification of hierarchies of systems, ranging from very specific systems to general ones. Identifying of hierarchies of systems, ranging from very specific systems to general ones. Identifying systems at various levels has helped translate abstract general systems theory into more concrete terms.

Closed versus Open Systems : In addition to identifying hierarchies of systems, general systems theorists have distinguished between closed and open systems. A closed system is a self-sufficient entity, whereas an open system depends on the surrounding environment for survival. In reality, these two kinds of systems cannot be completely separated from each other. The key to classifying a system as relatively open or relatively closed system; after the battery is in place, it runs without help from the outside environment. In contrast, a solar-powered clock is a relatively open system; it cannot operate without a continuous supply of outside energy. They human body is a highly open system because life depends on the body's ability to import oxygen and energy and to export waste. In other words, the human body is highly dependent on the environment for survival. Along the same lines, general systems theorists tell us that all organisations are open systems because organisational survival depends on interaction with the surrounding environment. Just as no person is an island, no organisation or organisational subsystem is an island, no organisation or organisational subsystem is an island, according to this approach.

V. The Contingency Approach

A comparatively new line of thinking among management theorists has been labelled the contingency approach. Contingency management advocates are attempting to take a step away from universally applicable principles of management and toward situational appropriateness. In the words of *Fred Luthans*, a noted contingency management writer, 'The traditional approaches to management were not necessarily wrong, but today they are no longer adequate. The needed breakthrough for management theory and practice can be found in a contingency approach.' Formally defined, the contingency approach is an effort to determine through research which managerial practices and techniques are appropriate in specific situations. Imagine using Taylor's approach with a college educated computer engineer. Different situations require different managerial responses, according to the contingency approach.

Generally, the term contingency refers to the choice of an alternative course of action. For example, roommates may have a contingency plan to move their party indoors if it rains. Their subsequent actions are said to be contingent (or dependent) on the weather. In a management context, contingency has become synonymous with situational management. As one contingency theorist put it, 'The effectiveness of a given management pattern is contingent upon multitudinous factors and their interrelationship in a particular situation.' This means the application of various management tools and techniques must be appropriate to the particular situation because each situation presents to the manager its own problems. A contingency approach is applicable in intercultural dealings in which customs and habits cannot be taken for granted. In real-life management, the success of any given technique is dictated by the situation. For example, researchers have found that rigidly structured organisations with many layers of management function best when environmental conditions are relatively stable. Unstable surroundings dictate a more flexible and streamlined organisation that can adapt quickly to change. Consequently, traditional principles of management that call for rigidly structured organisations, regardless of the situation, have come into question.

Contingency Characteristics

Some management scholars are attracted to contingency thinking because it is a workable compromise between the systems approach and what can be called a purely situational perspective. The systems approach is often criticised for being to general and abstract, although the purely situational view, which assumes that very real-life situation requires a distinctly different approach, has been called hopelessly specific. Contingency advocates have tried to take advantage of common denominators without getting trapped into simplistic generalisation. Three characteristics of the contingency approach are: (a) an open-system perspective, (b) a practical research orientation, and (c) a multivariate approach.

(a) An open-system perspective

Open-system thinking is fundamental to the contingency view. Contingency theorists are not satisfied with focusing on just the internal workings of organisations. They see the need to understand how organisational subsystems combine to interact with outside social, political, and economic systems.

(b) A practical research orientation

Practical research is that which ultimately leads to more effective on-the-job management. Contingency researchers attempt to translate their findings into tools and situational refinements for more effective management.

(c) A multivariate approach

Traditional closed-system thinking prompted a search for simple one-to-one causal relationships. This approach is called bivariate analysis. For example, the traditional human relations assumption that higher morale leads automatically to higher productivity was the result of bivariate analysis. Only one variable, morale, was seen as the sole direct cause of changes in a second variable, productivity. Subsequent multivariate analysis has shown that many variables, including the employee's personality, the nature of the task, rewards, and job and life satisfaction, collectively account for variations in productivity. Multivariate analysis is a research technique used to determine how a combination of variables interacts to cause a particular outcome. For example, if an employee's personality is authoritarian, the task highly structured, and the individual highly satisfied with his or her life and job, then analysis might show that productivity could be expected to be high.

PROPERTIES OF MODERN ORGANISATIONS

A formal organisation is an economic and social entity in which a number of persons perform a variety of tasks in order to attain a common goal. It is an effective instrument that helps individuals accomplish personal objectives that they cannot achieve alone. It is a system of clearly defined structure of activities consciously designed to allow organisational participants to work effectively toward common goals. It is characterised by "being well-defined, bound by delegation, and relatively stable".

I. Social Entities

Organisations exist to serve the needs of people. They exist to combine human efforts in order to achieve certain goals. They perform some activity that creates something of value for the individuals and/or groups. An organisation, in fact, comes into being when (1) there are persons able to communicate with each other, (2) who are willing to contribute action and, (3) to accomplish a common purpose. The vitality or organisations lies in the willingness of individuals to contribute forces to the cooperative system. Thus, people are fundamental to the study of organisations. No organisation can exist without people, ghost villages and towns become uninhabited because they were no longer able to attract and hold people.

II. Goal Directed

All organisations are goal directed. They are designed for a purpose and much of the behaviour within and between organisations reflects that goal. Objectives legitimise the existence of an organisation. When objectives are not accepted by external constituencies or when the resource flows are not properly related to objectives, the organisation is labelled illegitimate or ineffective. Those organisations that consistently relate resource flows to goals will be more effective than those that do not.

III. Relatively Permanent

One basic feature of organisations is that they are relatively permanent social entities. They are created to last a long time. This characteristic allows organisations to continue their existence and operations even while changing their structure, their membership, their objectives and their top managers. Permanency does not mean that organisations are static always: "the regularity or persistence of some aspects of organisations can make them appear fixed and static. Closer examination reveals that there is much activity and often considerable adjustment to keep these manifestations so constant." This view is supported by *McFarland* also. According to him, organisations must be viewed dynamically, the structure changes as managers do their work.

IV. Structure

One fundamental feature of organisations is that they have structures, in which the stated role of each member is expressed in some detail. The tasks are deliberately subdivided into separate departments and sets of operations. Organisations are created basically to capitalise on specialisation. Because of this division of labour, there is need to coordinate and integrate the work performed and the resources employed by various departments/persons so that they effectively contribute to objectives.

V. Openness

An organisation operates as an open system. It both consumes resources and exports resources to the environment. It must interact with the environment to survive. Organisational performance, in other words its survival and continuance, is assessed in terms of how well it serves the constituencies in the environment.

THE DEPENDENT VARIABLES

Dependent variables are the key factors that you want to explain or predict and that are affected by some other factor. What are the primary dependent variables in OB? Scholars tend to emphasise *productivity, absenteeism, turnover,* and *job satisfaction.* Because of their wide acceptance, we shall use those four as the critical dependent variables in an organisation's human resources effectiveness. However, there is nothing magical about these dependent variables. They merely show that OB research has strongly reflected managerial interests over those of individuals or of society as a whole. Let's review those terms to ensure that we understand what they mean and why they have achieved the distinction of being OB's primary dependent variables.

I. Productivity

An organisation is productive if it achieves its goals and does so by transferring inputs to outputs at the lowest cost. As such, *productivity* implies a concern for both *effectiveness* and *efficiency.*

A hospital, for example, is *effective* when it successfully meets the needs of its clientele. It is *efficient* when it can do so at a low cost. If a hospital manages to achieve higher output from its present staff by reducing the average number of days a patient is confined to a bed or by increasing the number of staff-patient contacts per day, we say that the hospital has gained productive efficiency. A business firm is effective when it attains its sales or market share goals, but its productivity also depends on achieving those goals efficiently. Measures of such efficiency may include return on investment, profit rupee of sales, and output per hour of labour.

II. Absenteeism

It is obviously difficult for an organisation to operate smoothly and to attain its objectives if employees fail to report to their jobs. The work flow is disrupted, and often important decisions must be delayed. In organisations that rely heavily upon assembly-line production, absenteeism can be considerably more than a disruption; it can result in a drastic reduction in quality of output, and, in some cases, it can bring about a complete shutdown of the production facility. But levels of absenteeism beyond the normal range in any organisation have a direct impact on that organisation's effectiveness and efficiency.

Are *all* absences bad? Probably not! Although most absences have a negative impact on the organisation, we can conceive of situations in which the organisation may benefit by an employee's voluntarily choosing not to come to work. For instance, illness, fatigue, or excess stress can significantly decrease an employee's productivity. In jobs in which an employee needs to be alert—surgeons and airline pilots are obvious examples—it may well be better for the organisation if the employee does not report to work rather than show up and perform poorly. The cost of an accident in such jobs could be prohibitive. Even in managerial jobs, where mistakes are less spectacular, performance may be improved when managers absent themselves from work rather than make a poor decision under stress. But these examples are clearly atypical. For the most part, we can assume that organisations benefit when employee absenteeism is low.

III. Turnover

A high rate of *turnover* in an organisation results in high recruiting, selection, and training costs. How high are those costs? A high rate of turnover can also disrupt the efficient running of an organisation when knowledgeable and experienced personnel leave and replacements must be found and prepared to assume positions of responsibility.

All organisations, of course, have some turnover. In fact, if the "right" people are leaving the organisation—the marginal and submarginal employees—turnover can be positive. It may create the opportunity to replace an under-performing individual with someone who has higher skills or motivation, open up increased opportunities for promotions, and add new and fresh ideas to the organisation. In today's changing world of work, reasonable levels of employee-initiated turnover facilitate organisational flexibility and employee independence, and they can lessen the need for management initiated layoffs.

But turnover often involves the loss of people the organisation doesn't want to lose. For instance, one study covering 900 employees who had resigned their jobs found that 92 per cent earned performance ratings of "satisfactory" or better from their superiors. So when turnover is excessive, or when it involves valuable performers, it can be a disruptive factor, hindering the organisation's effectiveness.

IV. Job Satisfaction

The final dependent variable we will look at is *job satisfaction,* which we define simply, at this point, as the difference between the amount of rewards workers receive and the amount they believe they should receive. Unlike the previous three variables, job satisfaction represents an attitude rather than a behaviour. Why, then, has it become a primary dependent variable? For two reasons: its demonstrated relationship to performance factors and the value preferences held by many OB researchers.

The belief that satisfied employees are more productive than dissatisfied employees has been a basic tenet among managers for years. Although much evidence questions that assumed causal relationship, it can be argued that advanced societies should be concerned not only with the quantity of life—that is, concerns such as higher productivity and material acquisitions—but also with its quality. Those researchers with strong humanistic values argue that satisfaction is a legitimate objective of an organisation. Not only is satisfaction negatively related to absenteeism and turnover, but, they argue, organisations have a responsibility to provide employees with jobs that are challenging and intrinsically rewarding. Therefore, although job satisfaction represents an attitude rather than a behaviour, OB researchers typically consider it an important dependent variable.

THE INDEPENDENT VARIABLES

What are the major determinants of productivity, absenteeism, turnover, and job satisfaction? Our answer to that question brings us to the *dependent variables.* Consistent with our belief that organisational behaviour can best be understood when viewed essentially as a set of increasingly complex building blocks, the base, or first level, of our model lies in understanding individual behaviour.

I. Individual-level Variables

It has been said that "managers, unlike parents, must work with used, not new, human beings—human beings whom others have gotten to first". When individuals enter an organisation, they are a bit like used cars. Each is different. Some are "low-mileage"—they have been treated carefully and have had only limited exposure to the realities of the elements. Others are "well-worn," having been driven over some rough roads. This metaphor indicates that people enter organisations with certain characteristics that will influence their behaviour at work. The more obvious of these are personal or biographical characteristics such as age, gender, and marital status; personality characteristics; values and attitudes; and basic ability levels. These characteristics are essentially intact when an individual enters the workforce, and, for the most part, there is little management can do to alter them. Yet they have a very real impact on employee behaviour.

There are four other individual-level variables that have been shown to affect employee behaviour: *perception*, *individual decision making*, *learning* and *motivation*.

II. Group-level Variables

The behaviour of people in groups is more than the sum total of all the individuals acting in their own way. The complexity of our model is increased when we acknowledge that people's behaviour when they are in groups is different from their behaviour when they are alone. Therefore, the next step in the development of an understanding of OB is the study of group behaviour.

III. Organisation System Level Variables

Organisational behaviour reaches its highest level of sophistication when we add formal structure to our previous knowledge of individual and group behaviour. Just as groups are more than the sum of their member groups. The design of the formal organisation, work processes, and jobs; the organisation's human resource policies and practices (that is, selection processes, training programs, performance appraisal methods); and the internal culture all have an impact on the dependent variables.

INTERDISCIPLINARY STUDIES

Numerous studies conducted throughout the world were published and reported in professional journals including Human Relations, Personnel Psychology and Personnel, etc. In India, for example, great interest was shown by the academic research workers for conducting studies in this respect. This is particularly true of some universities, and of psychological units at the Indian Institute of Technology at Kharagpur and Kanpur. Organisations like ATIRA (Ahmedabad Textile Industries Research Association), SITRA (South Indian Textile Research Association) and SRC (Shri Ram Centre for Industrial Relations) were established to conduct researches, often of interdisciplinary nature into the social and psychological problems of industrial workers. The establishment of different management institutes has further given momentum of interdisciplinary researches on human problems in industry. Of special significance was the Ahmedabad Experiment by Rice conducted in the Ahmedabad Manufacturing and Calico Printing Company and published by the Tavistock Institute of Human Relations, London, under the title "*Productivity and Social Organisation*" in 1958.

The indirect-action component of the external environment affects organisations in two ways. First, forces may dictate the formation of a group that eventually becomes a stockholder. Second, indirect-action elements create a climate—rapidly changing technology, economic growth of decline, changes in attitudes toward work—in which the organisation exists and to which it may ultimately have to respond.

Social Variables

Fahey and *Narayanan* divide social variables into three categories : demographics, lifestyle, and social values. *Demographic* and *lifestyle changes* affect the composition, location, and expectations of an organisation's labour supply and customers. Social values underlie all other social, political, technological, and economic changes and determine all the choices that people make in life.

Social Values

In recent years, changing social values have affected out commitment to equality of opportunity and the regulation of industry, altered our assessments of the costs and benefits of new technology such as life-support systems for the seriously ill, and increased the social and economic expectations of consumers, women, and minorities.

Economic Variables

Obviously, general economic conditions and trends are critical to the success and the market conditions under which they are sold. Each is an economic variable.

Common economic indicators measures national income and product, savings, investment, prices, wages, productivity, employment, government activities, and international transactions. All these factors vary over time, and managers devote much of their organisations' time and resources to forecasting the economy and anticipating changes. Because economic change is now the norm rather than the exception, this task has become more complicated.

Political Variables

Will a government agency adopt a rigorous or a lenient stance toward the management of a company with which it is dealing? Will antitrust laws be rigidly enforced or ignored? Will government policy inhibit or encourage management's freedom to act? These sorts of questions concern political variables, and their answers depend largely on the nature of the political process and on the current political climate. The political process involves competition between different interest, groups, each seeking to advance its own values and goals. For example, out of the general political debate about the environment, groups emerged which had a direct impact on McDonald's products and services.

Technological Variables

Technological variables include advance in basic sciences such as physics, as well as new developments in products, processes, and materials. The level of technology in a society or a particular industry determines to a large extent what products and services will be produced, what equipment will be used, and how operations will be managed.

Major changes are on the horizon in the field of biotechnology, and Japanese corporations are mounting a powerful new challenge to American dominance in biotechnology products. Although we are only beginning to see the applications of this new technology, it is already a multibillion-dollar industry, with products ranging from genetically improved farm animals and grains to cancer treatments and biodegradable plastics.

FOUNDATIONS OF INDIVIDUAL BEHAVIOUR

Human behaviour, a complex phenomenon as it is, most difficult to define in absolute terms. It is primarily a combination of responses to external and internal stimuli. These responses would reflect psychological structure of the person and may be a result of a combination of biological and psychological processes. It is a system by which a human being senses external events and influences, interprets them, responds to them in an appropriate manner and learns from the result of these responses.

Psychologist *Kurt Levin* has conducted considerable research into the human behaviour and its causes. He believes that people are influenced by a number of diversified factors, both genetic and environmental, and the influence of these factors determines the pattern of behaviour. He called his conception of these influences "the field theory" and suggested that:

$$B = F(P, E)$$

So that behaviour (B) is a function (F) of the person (P) and environment (E) around him. It is important to recognise the effect of the "person" and that of environment individually as well as their interaction and dependence upon each other in order to understand the pattern of behaviour. These two factors are highly linked with each other. Any one of these two factors individually cannot explain fully the behaviour characteristics. An individual's behaviour may change due to a change in the same environment or exposure to a different environment. For example, a person who loses a well paying job may behave differently when he is unemployed. Similarly, just the environment in itself cannot be the cause of or explain a given behaviour. Different people behave differently in the same or similar environment. However, when the situation demands, the environment may change the behaviour of an individual. For example, certain training programs or rehabilitation programs have changed the human attitudes and behaviour. Sometimes a sudden and unexpected turn of events or a shock can also influence significant and permanent changes in the human behaviour. For example, there are a number of stories in the Indian religious scriptures where a known killer or a dacoit came to a temple and his whole personality and outlook changed. Thus the environment can change the individual in his or her behaviour. Similarly, the individuals can also change the environment by setting goals and standards and by determination and motivation

BIOLOGICAL FOUNDATION OF BEHAVIOUR

The general biological characteristics of the human system, especially as laid down in heredity and revealed during the subsequent period of development of the individual, influence the ways in which he tends to sense external event data, interpret them, respond to them and learn from his own past experience. Obviously, the human infant possesses behind him a long biological history and in front of him is a wide future of biological development. He tends to grow and develop through the course of time and this process of his development exerts great impact on his subsequent behaviour as revealed in the form of psychological processes.

What is Inherited?

The individual inherits a similarity to other individuals as well as a *uniqueness* in the form of genes and chromosomes. In addition, he inherits the physical traits and the ability to learn and behave intellectually which have a wide impact on his behavioural patterns. These inherited traits interact with the environmental factors in several ways to cause the unique patterns of adjustment of an individual.

How Does the Development Take Place?

The motor, language, and emotional developments of the individual reveal a normal sequence, although at varied rates. The growth of the individual is markedly influenced by the functioning of the ductless glands including the pituitary, the thyroid, the adrenals and the gonads. The extent of maturity of the individual determines the limit of what he can learn and what he cannot learn. The childhood sensory and perceptual experiences contribute markedly towards the magnitude of maturity of the sensory and perceptual abilities. Individuals who are deprived of love and affection during their early days of childhood, tend to reveal personality difficulties in their day-to-day behaviour. There is adequate evidence to support the view that the child-parent relationships influence the development of an individual's personality considerably.

The Role of the Nervous System

The structures of the nervous system play a significant part in bringing about the integration of human behaviour and personality. Some psychologists interpret human behaviour exclusively in terms of neural activity while others ignore the nervous system altogether in studying the overt behaviour. There is a consensus of opinion that a study of the neurophysiological process can enhance our understanding of the human system. Integration of human behaviour takes place because of the constant functioning of receptors, effectors and connectors. Here, the nervous system is primarily involved in the connecting process.

The numerous *receptor cells* attached to the individual's sense organs tend to convert physical and chemical events from the environment into neural events while the several *effector cells* attached to the muscles and glands convert these neural events into responses. The human behaviour ranges from the simple reflex action to the complex problem-solving activity involving various levels of integration. The structural unit of the nervous system is the nerve cell or neuron. As soon as a nerve is stimulated and the stimulation exceeds the neuron's threshold, it sends neural impulses along its fibre and across a synapse.

(i) The Components of Nervous System

The nervous system consists of central and peripheral components. The entire system can further be classified into a somatic system and an automatic system. The somatic system incorporates 31 spinal and 12 cranial nerves while the automatic system consists of the sympathetic system and the parasympathetic system which are responsible for internal adjustments. The sympathetic system functions in emotional situations while the parasympathetic system operates in routine maintenance. The central nervous system consists of the spinal cord and the brain and has several parts such as the thalamus, the hypothalamus, the cerebral cortex etc. which are of great significance. Obviously, the human being is characterised by great cortical control over all lower neural processes. The cortex consists of relatively specific areas of motor as well as sensory projection. Direct stimulation of specific areas causes muscular movement and their injury causes paralysis.

(ii) Recent Research Results

Recently, the vertical and concentric analyses both of structure and function have been emphasised in the study of the nervous system. It has been shown that the individual does not function well unless incoming sensory impulses arouse the brain and that he actively seeks arousal when input is below a certain minimum level and that sensory deprivation causes disturbance of the mental function. Obviously, these research results throw adequate new light on motivation and emotional processes.

INHERITED CHARACTERISTICS

Some of the inherited characteristics which may or may not be changed by external forces and may or may not be important determinants of performance are:

I. Physical Characteristics

Some of these characteristics relate to physical height, slim body, vision, dexterity and stamina, and have some bearing on performance. Manual dexterity, for example, results in quality performance in such jobs that require artistic manoeuvring. Similarly, tall and slim people are expected to dress well and behave in a sophisticated manner, and fat people are assumed to have a jovial nature.

II. Intelligence

Intelligence is primarily an inherited trait, even though children of some very intelligent parents have turned out to be less intelligent and vice-versa. It is also known that intelligence can be enhanced by proper environment or by proper motivation. *Einstein* was not considered very intelligent during his earlier years. In any case, intelligence as a trait is related to certain behaviours. Intelligent people are easy to convince if the point is right and they can be expected to be much more stable and predictable.

III. Sex

Being a male or female is genetic in nature and can be considered as an inherited characteristic. However, it is highly debatable whether being a male or a female in itself is indicative of any behavioural patterns. Man is expected to be tough while a woman is expected to be gentle. Men "never cry" and women are highly emotional, are some of the stereotyped assumptions that have no basis in genetic influences. These behaviours are developed, if at all due to differences in treatment that boys and girls receive in the family environment.

Even though some work roles are assumed to be the exclusive domain of woman, such as nurses or airline stewardnesses, these roles are being modified to accommodate men in these positions. As far as the administration of the management process is concerned, women in general do not differ from men in their operative behaviours.

IV. Age

Since age is determined by the date of birth, it is a kind of inherited characteristic. The age may affect the behaviour in physiological as well as psychological ways. Psychologically, young people are expected to be more energetic, innovative, risk taking and adventurous, while old people are supposed to be conservative and set in their ways. Physiologically, with age, older people experience waning of some of their faculties such as memory, stamina, coordination etc., and hence the related behaviours change as well. According to *Lehman*, the peak of creative ability is among people between the ages 30 and 40.

V. Religion

Religion and religiously based cultures play an important role in determining some aspects of individual behaviour, specially those that concern morals, ethics and a code of conduct. Highly religious people have high moral standards and usually do not tell lies or talk ill of others. They are highly contented and thus strive for the goal of achievement and self-fulfilment. Additionally, the religion and culture also determine attitudes towards work, and towards financial incentives.

LEARNED CHARACTERISTICS

Some of the behavioural characteristics that account for enormous diversity in human behaviour are a product of our exposure to various situations and stimuli, both within the family and the outside environment. These characteristics are acquired by learning where learning is defined as a "relatively permanent change in behaviour resulting from interactions with the environment."

These characteristics involve an individual's attitudes, values and perceptions about the environment around him. They are the result of the parental values and expectations and the values and norms of our cultures and sub-cultures. The children learn the need and values of being honest and truthful and the value of love and affections from the family environment. If the parents are always fighting, if the father is always drunk or if the mother resents the child, it is most likely that the child will grow up lacking the closeness of love and respect. Similarly, a loving family instills certain positive values about life in the minds of the children.

The physical environment itself has a profound effect on the individual behaviour. Persons who have come through the rigorous routine of the armed forces or students who have been active sportsmen may have learned the spirit of competition as well as cooperation. Similarly, students who have studied in religious schools and convents may have learned different values about truth and human decency.

Since inherited behavioural characteristics are more difficult to change or modify, it is the learned characteristics that the managers want to study, predict and control, but, a brief familiarity with this factor is necessary here. Some of these learned characteristics are:

I. Perception

Perception is the process by which information enters our minds and is interpreted in order to give some sensible meaning to the world around us. It is the result of a complex interaction of various senses such as feeling, seeing, hearing etc. Sayings and proverbs like "things are not what they seem" or "all that glitters is not gold", reflect a sense of perception. "One man's meat is another man's poison," is in a psychological sense an indication that different people see and sense the same thing in different ways.

Perception plays an important part in human as well as organisational behaviour. For example, if a manager perceives a subordinate's ability as limited, he will give him limited responsibility, even if the subordinate, in fact, is an able person. Similarly, we lose a lot of good friends due to our changed perceptions about them.

II. Attitude

Attitude is a perception with a frame of reference. It is a way of organising a perception. In other words, it is more or less a stable tendency to feel, think, perceive and act in a certain manner towards an object or a situation. It is a tendency to act in a certain way, either favourably or unfavourably concerning objects, people or events. For example, if I say that "I like my job," I am expressing my attitude about work.

Attitude has three elements in it that leads to measurable outcomes. These are feelings, thoughts and behaviours. Feelings and thoughts can be measured by simply asking individuals about their feelings and opinions. Behaviours can be measured either by actual overt actions or simply by asking the person how he would act in a certain situation. By measuring and integrating these three elements, a person's attitude towards a given situation can be established.

In general, a person may have a positive attitude which is good outlook of life, or negative attitude which means continuous complaining about problems in life. Organisationally speaking, an employee's negative attitude about work may be reflected by sub-standard work performance, excessive absenteeism, excessive complaining about work environment or disobedience to rules or authority. These attitudes can be changed either by simple persuasion or by training and coaching. *Kelman* has identified three processes that act as instruments of change. The first is *compliance* which is application of subtle pressure either through reward or punishment in order to change the behaviour, and expecting this change to be lasting.

The second process is that of *identification* with the person who is affecting the change and is acting as a change agent. This change agent could be a close friend who wants you to change and you respect and love him enough to do so to please him. In marriage, for example, both the husband and the wife make a lot of sacrifices and change their behaviours to please each other. The third process is the process of *internalisation,* which is more permanent in nature. This means that the new attitude is integrated with the other attitudes and becomes a part of the person's total personality. This change may occur through internal soul searching and the desire to change that comes from within.

III. Personality

When we describe people as quiet and passive or loud and aggressive or ambitious, we are portraying an aspect of their personality. Personality is a set of traits and characteristics, habit patterns and conditioned responses to certain stimuli that formulate the impression an individual makes upon others. This personality may come out as warm and friendly, or arrogant and aggressive. Many psychologists contend that personality traits develop in the early childhood years and very few personality changes can be made after the childhood years. Some personality characteristics such as physical build and intelligence are biological in nature, but most traits such as patience, open mindedness, extrovertness or introvertness, etc. are learned.

Some of these personality traits are highly influential in certain organisational operations from organisational behaviour point of view. For example, people who are open minded seem to work out better in bargaining agreements than people who are narrow minded. Similarly, people who are extroverts and outgoing are more likely to be successful as managers than those who are introverts.

IV. Values

Values, according to *Milton Rokeach*, represent basic convictions that "a specific mode of conduct or end-state of existence is personally or socially preferable to an opposite or converse mode of conduct or end-state of existence." They generally identify a person's moral structure on which the concept of good or bad and right or wrong is based. Values are emotionally charged priorities and are passionately defended. Values and behaviour are highly correlated. The values indicate behaviour pattern and while they do not necessarily and accurately predict behaviour, when behaviour occurs, it is likely to be in line with the values on holds. Value system, according to *Prof. A. Dasgupta,* "is a framework of personal philosophy which governs and influences the individual's reactions and responses to any situations." These reactions and responses direct individuals in a society to selectively attend to some goals and to subordinate other goals. In other words, value systems represent a prioritising of individual values in relation to their relative importance. This value system develops from the cultural environment in which the individual is brought up, the concept of nuclear family, religious influences or his code of conduct, respect for traditional concepts of ethics and morality, and degree of faith in the socially inherited religious elements and beliefs. These values are highly stable and enduring and once a value is internalised, it becomes, consciously or subconsciously a standard or criterion for defining action, for developing and maintaining attitudes towards relevant objects and situations, for justifying one's own and other's actions and attitudes, for morally defining self and others and for comparing self with others.

The value system also determines the form of social organisation in terms of family, groups or community and the role and status positions of individuals within the community. This will also determine the decision-maker in the family or the opinion leader in the community or the leader in the organisations.

Values are important in relation to the study of organisational behaviour because an organisation is a composite of attitudes, perceptions, personalities and individual behaviours of managers as well as workers. Values determine what is right and what is wrong where right or wrong is interpreted in terms of perceived values of the decision-maker. Values sometimes overpower even objectivity and rationality. For example, in order to open a profitable manufacturing plant in a developing country, it may be necessary to bribe a government official for granting of the license. This bribe may be customary and routinely accepted and rationally, it could be justified. However, the value system of the management may be such as to consider bribery unethical and hence the value system would overpower rationality.

SENSATION

The motivated individual senses the world, interprets it, responds to it and reacts to the results of his own responses. In order to survive, the motivated individual must be able to do so. It would not be possible for him to accomplish his motives unless his senses allow an intimate touch with the environment in which he lives. Obviously, when the individual is motivated, he tends to make adjustive changes in the external world. The complexity of his adjustment is determined by his capacity to sense his surroundings. He is equipped with the capacity to register vibration of air, light stimulus, smell, taste, touch, pressure, pain, temperature and movement.

Factors of Sensation

The factors of sensation include a stimulus, a specialised receptor and central nervous system.

The stimulus of sound varies in frequency, amplitude and complexity and is initiated by a series of condensations and refinements of particles at the eardrum. The auditory receptors include hair cells located in the inner ear. The auditory structures consists of the external ear, the middle ear and the inner ear and their maloperation can cause either conduction deafness or discrimination deafness. The pitch, loudness and timbre form the principal psychological dimensions of auditory sensation. The absolute threshold for intensity varies in terms of the wavelengths of stimulus.

The stimulus of vision is formed of electromagnetic waves and varies in wavelength, amplitude and complexity. It is because of the existence of two eyes which create retinal disparity that an individual is able to perceive three dimensions. The receptors for vision are the rods and cones located in the retina. Like a camera, the structures of the eye focus light waves on the retina. Structural maloperation causes near-sightedness, foresightedness or astigmatism. The individual can make visual discriminations of hue, brightness, saturation and form. In situations of dark adaptation, the sensitivity of the eye enhances by 100,000 times.

The stimuli to smell include molecules stemming from volatile chemical substances. The olfactory receptors include specialised structures in the top region of the nasal passage. Perhaps the process of smelling involves infrared radiation.

The individuals can sense pressure, warmth and cold with the aid of receptors located in the skin and underlying tissues. The sense of active movement or kinesthesis is the result of pressure caused by bunching and stretching of muscles. In addition, there are numerous sensory messages stemming from the organic processes in the body itself. However, the details of these sensory structures and functions are not analysed, hitherto.

BELIEFS

The logic behind the above discussion is that individual behaviour in organisations is explicable in terms of motivational, emotional, perceptual and learning processes. However, it cannot be described, analysed and predicted by reference to these basic processes considered singly. Rather, it is dynamic result of these processes operating simultaneously. Moreover, it is also a function of disposition such as belief.

Krech and Crutchfield define *belief* as an enduring organisation of perceptions and cognitions about some aspect of the individual's world. It is a pattern of meanings of a thing and the totality of the individual's cognition about the things. Since a perception or a cognition is in itself an organisation, a belief is an organisation of organisations. For example, an individual believes that the earth is spherical. Here, his belief involves several different types of related cognitions. Thus, he may hold that to travel in a straight line in any direction on its surface would eventually lead him to his starting point. Likewise, he also 'knows' that if he were to be placed far enough out in space away from the earth, he would see it to be spherical in shape like a ball.

Krech and *Crutchfield* use the term belief in a generic sense to embrace knowledge opinions and faith. Although there exist, observable differences among knowledge, opinions and faith, there is a common set of factors which govern and characterise them.

Beliefs *versus* Facts

There does not exist one-to-one correlation between beliefs and objectives facts. However, beliefs which reveal a discrepancy with the objective facts are as strong and certain as those which accurately correspond with the real situations. For example, an individual who believes that women are poor managers, may be as certain of this "fact" as he is certain that the sun will rise in the east. Of course, the strength of the belief is not a function of the extent of correspondence with the objective facts. Thus, it appears that an individual is not an altogether irrational begin if rationality is assessed in terms of the relationship between his beliefs and perceived facts.

Beliefs *versus* Attitudes

As *Krech* and *Crutchfield* further observe, while all attitudes incorporate beliefs, all beliefs do not form a part of attitudes. Although beliefs are motivationally relatively neutral, they are subject to special dynamic pressures when embedded in attitudes–an enduring organisation of motivational, emotional, perceptual and cognitive processes with respect to some aspect of the individual's world.

SIGNIFICANCE OF BELIEFS

Beliefs provide continuity to the personality of an individual. They assign meaning to his day-to-day perceptions and activities and serve in his attempted solutions of varied goals.

An individual's beliefs also exert a vital impact on his motivation in two ways. First, he must believe that he is capable of performing the acts which the organisation expects of him. If he does not believe that effective performance is even possible, his motivation is bound to be low. Second, he must believe that performance of acts desired by the organisation will have positive outcomes for him personally. Unless he believes that some personal benefits will follow from performing effectively, he is least likely to be motivated.

Limitations of Beliefs

Beliefs in the form of superstitions, delusions, prejudices and stereotypes pose varied human relations problems because of their wide divergence from the real situations. To understand and cure individuals of these beliefs, there is need to determined why there is such discrepancy.

DEVELOPMENT OF BELIEFS

Both cultural environment and the functional factors (those unique to the individual) exert impact on the growth of beliefs. Divergence in cultural (including family) environments causes differences in beliefs. However, exposure to a characteristic and defined set of stimulation does not lead to the growth of a uniform set of beliefs. Indeed, because of functional factors (i.e., needs, demands and emotions of the individual) beliefs develop selectively within the possible range. This partly accounts for the individual differences in beliefs.

While cultural environment provides most of the facts for beliefs, the functional factors are largely responsible for the manner in which these facts are incorporated. In addition, the following factors influence the direction of the self-preservation of the developing beliefs; the selective nature of perception, the operation of the constancy effect, the withdrawal behaviour induced by beliefs and the social support which many beliefs receive.

Change of Beliefs

Notwithstanding the self-operative forces embodied in beliefs, efforts may be made to change them. The following strategies can be used in a programme for belief change and control: (1) There may be differing objectives for change which must be specified; (2) There must be adequate safeguards to avoid the errors in diagnosing the needs, emotions, contents and the social support involved in beliefs; (3) As change in only one factor may have limited impact, there must be adherence to an integrated approach in the action programme; and (4) There is need to use a social approach by creating new group identifications and taking advantage of the divergence in cultural patterns.

Measurement of Beliefs

A number of methods and techniques can be used to measure beliefs by utilising an individual's behaviour and immediate experience.

Back-drop from Indian Culture

One of the major qualities of Indian culture is a strong belief in sacredness. As Sheila Dhar observes in her book *This India,* "You will see this very clearly in our villages. Think of the *pipal* tree, the river, the village well, the work-man's took, the plough, the grain of rice, the harvest, the kitchen, a certain plant or leaf or seed, a musical instrument, a piece of cloth, a fruit, a pen. Another long list, but any one of these things of daily use could be thought of as sacred in our villages. This sense of the sacred runs right through our society. Even Indian children in cities would perhaps not put their feet on a book, or kick a tree. Indians respect age and wisdom, anything that gives energy, and that is good. They are very ready to regard such things as holy. The big dams and factories that we have in India today are a sign that we are becoming more modern. But even these have been called *'temples of the new age'* by one of our great leaders."

THE FUTURE OF ORGANISATIONAL BEHAVIOUR

Fortunately, some identifiable trends have emerged in organisational behaviour. First, it can be said that organisational behaviour has truly arrived as an identifiable field of academic study, with definite implications for the effective management of human resources in today's organisations. This recognition of organisational behaviour as a legitimate academic and applied field should become even greater in the future.

Second, there is now a clear distinction between organisational behaviour and such other areas as general management and human resource management. For example, organisational behaviour is concerned with human behaviour in organisations, while human resource management is recognised as a strategy of the organisation and as an applied function concerned mainly with topics such as selection, compensation, and labour relations. The field of organisational behaviour is very broad, and both theorists and professional managers recognise that "organisations as we know them are the people in them." There is now considerable evidence that effective management of these people leads not only to increased productivity but also to a positive impact on the organisation's long-term financial performance. "This empirical support provides welcome guidance as well as a continuing challenge of implementation, as managers seek to a achieve sustained competitive advantage." The field of organisational behaviour is meeting this challenge with the better understanding and effective management of this most central dimension, the human behaviour dimension, of today's organisations.

In addition to organisational behaviour being recognised as an important and identifiable field of study and application, the micro-macro split in the topics and conceptual framework for organisational behaviour, which was at first thought to be getting wider (even in the past editions of this text), now seems to be lessening. Recognition is given to the important role of macro structural variables and the environment in the social learning theoretical framework. Macro variables play a major role, although still not as proportionately great a role as micro variables, in this edition and in the field in general.

Third, the topical coverage of the field of organisational behaviour will continue to move away from the traditional specialised topics in behavioural science and toward topics more identified with organisational behaviour *per se* (organisational culture, job stress, job design, goal setting, job satisfaction, organisational commitment, organisational behaviour modification, work teams, job conflict, organisational power and politics, informal organisation, managerial roles, interpersonal communication, managerial leadership, organisation development, and behavioural decision-making). The exceptions here are the mainstays of experimental psychology—attitudes, motivation, and learning. These latter topics continue to be very important areas in organisational behaviour.

Finally—and this, of course, most students and practitioners will be happy to hear—the trend toward making the organisational behaviour approach more understandable and applications-oriented should continue. Although there is a definite trend away from simple answers to complex organisational behaviour problems at all levels of analysis—individual, group, and organisational—in order to be considered useful, it must be both understandable and applicable to the real world. The successive editions of this text have given evidence of this trend. The organisational behaviour approach is clearly aimed at the more effective management of people. With emphasis on areas such as coping with organisational culture, international management, job stress, job design, goal setting, organisational behaviour modification, negotiation skills, teams, political strategies, leadership styles, organisation development, and decision-making techniques, this aim at applications should become clearer and more likely to hit the target of more effective management of human resources in the years to come.

The future of organisations will continually change at such a rate that it may be intimidating, if not downright scary, to many people. For example, well-known management futurist Charles Handy predicts :

> . . . a withering of the "employment organisation." A lot of scripts will need to be rewritten, including the script that includes job security in a corporation followed by a comfortable retirement. A lot of us will become "portfolio workers"—selling our skills to a variety of clients. And all of us will be looking beyond work to finding meaning and identity.

Like the management of change in the real world, organisational behaviour scholars and practicing managers must anticipate such changes and study/research them, in the case of academics, and manage them, in the case of practitioners, rather than ignoring or resisting these types of changes—which are sure to come.

The future of the field of organisational behaviour looks very bright and exciting. Although there will be some shifting emphasis in conceptual framework and topical coverage, the "bottom line" is that the study and application of the areas covered in this text will help make better, more effective managers of the most important and underutilised resource in any organisation: people. The effective management of people (both others and oneself), so that everyone can reach his or her full potential, is really what organisational behaviour is all about.

REVIEW QUESTIONS

1. Describe various schools of management thought prevalent from time to time.
2. Briefly explain the different kinds of skills needed by managers to perform the task of management in an organisation.
3. Discuss the various levels of management.
4. Explain the Taylor's contributions to the science of management.
5. "The principles of scientific management makes the beginning of management movement" — (Fayol). Describe.
6. Bring out clearly the broad principles of scientific management.
7. "The work of Taylor and Fayol essentially complementary". Discuss this statement. Also make a comparison between Taylor and Fayol.
8. Differentiate between the concept of Taylor and Mayo.
9. Describe the various schools of management thoughts in detail.
10. Describe the contributions and limitations of the human relations School.
11. What do you understand by system? Also explain the characteristics of system.
12. Write a detail note on the modern organisational theory.
13. Make a critical evaluation of :
    (a) Contingency approach
    (b) Classical approach
    (c) Neo-classification approach.
14. What do you understand by the term "organisation"? How does this organisation relate to the field of organisational behaviour?
15. Define organisational behaviour and give some generalisation about the behaviour.
16. Write full note on "Hawthorne Study".
17. Are organisations good or bad? Comment. Also give the importance of organisation.
18. Write short notes on:
    (a) Contingency approach
    (b) Interdisciplinary studies.
19. Organisational behaviour is result of interaction and interdepending between formal organisation and the human factor variables. Explain.
20. Behaviour is considered to be a function of the person and his environment. Explain in short.
21. What do you understand by "biological foundations of behaviour"? Is behaviour really founded on "biological" manipulations ? Explain your reasons.
22. Describe some of the inherited characteristics of behaviour.
23. Explain some of the learned characteristics of behaviour.
24. Write short notes on:
    (a) Sensation (b) Beliefs.

REFERENCES

1. Herbert G. Hicks and C. Ray Gullett, "Organisations Theory and Behaviour", McGraw Hill Book Company.
2. W.G. Scott and Mitchell, op cit.
3. John Kotter, "Organisational Dynamics : Diagnosis and Intervention", Addison-Wesley Publishing Company, Inc, 1978.
4. Katz and Georgopulos, Organiastion in a Changing World.
5. Fred Luthans "Introduction to Management: A Contingency Approach", McGraw Hill Company, New York.
6. William R. Dill, "Environment as an Influence on Managerial Autonomy?" Administrative Science Quarterly, Vol. 2.
7. Fred Luthans, op cit.
8. William L. Zwerman, "New Perspectives on Organisation Theory", Greenwood Publishing Corporation, West Port, Conn, 1970.
9. Henry C. Metcalf and Urwick eds. "Dynamic Administration: The Collected Papers of Mary Parder Follett", New York.
10. Norbert Weiner, "Cybernetics", MIT, Cambridge, Mass, 1948.
11. Phillip Selznick "Foundations of the Theory of Organisation", American Sociological Review, **Feb.** 1948.
12. George Homans, "The Human Group", Barcourt, Brace and Wood Inc, New York, 1950.
13. Charles Perrow, "The Short and Glorious History of Organisation Theory", Organisational Dynamics, Summer, 1973.
14. D.C. Phillips "Systems Theory: A Discredited Philosophy", Abacus, 5th Sept., 1969.
15. Bardley, D.F. and M. Calvin, "Behaviour: Imbalance in a New-work of Chemical Transformations: General Systems", Yearbook of the Society for the Advancement of General System Theory, 1956.
16. Hall and Fagun, Definition of System.
17. Kae H. Chung and Leon C. Megginson, "Organisational Behaviour: Developing Managerial Skills", Harper and Row Publishers, New York, 1981.

2nd

CHAPTER

OVERVIEW

PERCEPTION

• ***After reading this chapter, you should be able to know:***

- Introduction
- Factors Influencing Perception
- Perceptual Process
- Perceptual Selection
- Factors Influencing Perceptual Selectivity
- Perceptual Organisation
- Interpersonal Perception
- Impression Management
- Barriers to Perceptual Accuracy
- Attribution Theory
- Attributions Process
- Attributions of Success and Failure
- Difference between Perception and Sensation

2

PERCEPTION

INTRODUCTION

Why is perception important in the study of organisational behaviour? Simply because people's behaviour is based on their perception of what reality is, not on reality itself. *The world as it is perceived is the world that is behaviourally important.* "Perception refers to interpretation of sensory data. In other words, sensation involves detecting the presence of a stimulus whereas perception involves understanding what the stimulus means. For example, when we see something, the visual stimulus is the light energy reflected from the external world and the eye becomes the sensor. This visual image of the external thing becomes perception when it is interpreted in the visual cortex of the brain. Thus, visual perception refers to interpreting the image of the external world projected on the retina of the eye and constructing a model of the three dimensional world."

Perception is the process through which the information from outside environment is selected, received, organised and interpreted to make it meaningful to you. This input of meaningful information results in decisions and actions. It is a result of a complex interaction of various senses such as feeling, seeing, hearing, thinking and comparing with known aspects of life in order to make some sense of the world around us. The quality or accuracy of a person's perception is an important factor in determining the quality of the decision and action.

Perception is presented as an important cognitive process in understanding organisational behaviour. The environment (both antecedent and consequent) and other psychological processes, such as learning, motivation, and the whole of personality, are also important. However, although much of the material on perception is basic knowledge in the behavioural sciences, it has been largely overlooked or not translated for use by those in the organisational behaviour field.

FACTORS INFLUENCING PERCEPTION

How do we explain that individuals may look at the same thing, yet perceive it differently? A number of factors operate to shape and sometimes distort perception. These factors can reside in the *perceiver,* in the object or *target* being perceived, or in the context of the *situation* in which the perception is made.

I. Perceiver

When an individual looks at a target and attempts to interpret what he or she sees, that interpretation is heavily influenced by personal characteristics of the individual perceiver. Have you ever bought a new car and then suddenly noticed a large number of cars like yours on the road? It's unlikely that the number of such cars suddenly expanded. Rather, your own purchase has influenced your perception so that you are now more likely to notice them. This is an example of how factors related to the perceiver influence what he or she perceives. Among the more relevant personal characteristics affecting perception are attitudes, motives, interests, past experiences, and expectations.

'X' likes small classes because she enjoys asking a lot of questions of her teachers. 'Y', on the other hand, prefers large lectures. He rarely asks questions and likes the anonymity that goes with being lost in a sea of bodies. On the first day of classes this term, 'X' and 'Y' find themselves walking into the university auditorium for their introductory course in psychology. They both recognise that they will be among some 800 students in this class. But given the different attitudes held by 'X' and 'Y', it shouldn't surprise you to find that they interpret what they see differently. 'X' sulks, while 'Y's smile does little to hide his relief in being able to blend unnoticed into the large crowd. They both see the same thing, but they interpret it differently. A major reason is that they hold divergent *attitudes* concerning large classes.

Unsatisfied needs or *motives* stimulate individuals and may exert a strong influence on their perceptions. This fact was dramatically demonstrated in research on hunger. Individuals in the study had not eaten for varying numbers of hours. Some had eaten an hour earlier; others had gone as long as 16 hours without food. These subjects were shown blurred pictures, and the results indicated that the extent of hunger influenced the interpretation of the blurred pictures. Those who had not eaten for 16 hours perceived the blurred images as pictures of food far more frequently than did those subjects who had eaten only a short time earlier.

This same phenomenon has application in an organisational context as well. It would not be surprising, for example, to find that a boss who is insecure perceives a subordinate's efforts to do an outstanding job as a threat to his or her own position. Personal insecurity can be transferred into the perception that others are out to "get my job," regardless of the intention of the subordinates. Likewise, people who are devious are prone to see others as also devious.

It should not surprise you that a plastic surgeon is more likely to notice an imperfect nose than a plumber is. The supervisor who has just been reprimanded by her boss for the high level of lateness among her staff is more likely to notice lateness by an employee tomorrow than she was last week. If you are preoccupied with a personal problem, you may find it hard to be attentive in class. These examples illustrate that the focus of our attention appears to be influenced by our *interests*. Because our individual interests differ considerably, what one person notices in a situation can differ from what others perceive.

Just as interests narrow one's focus, so do one's *past experiences.* You perceive those things to which you can relate. However, in many instances, your past experiences will act to nullify an object's interest.

Objects or events that have never been experienced before are more noticeable than those that have been experienced in the past. You are more likely to notice a machine that you have never seen before than a standard filing cabinet that is exactly like a hundred others you have previously seen. Similarly, you are more likely to notice the operations along an assembly line if this is the first time you have seen an assembly line. In the late 1960s and early 1970s, women and minorities in managerial positions were highly visible because, historically, those positions were the province of white males. Today, women and minorities are more widely represented in the managerial ranks, so we are less likely to take notice that a manager is female, African-American, Asian-American, or Latino.

Finally, *expectations* can distort your perceptions in that you will see what you expect to see. If you expect police officers to be authoritative, young people to be unambitious, personnel directors to "like-people," or individuals holding public office to be unscrupulous, you may perceive them as such regardless of their actual traits.

II. Target

Characteristics of the target that is being observed can affect what is perceived. Loud people are more likely to be noticed in a group than are quiet ones. So, too, are extremely attractive or unattractive individuals. Motion, sounds, size, and other attributes of a target shape the way we see it. Because targets are not looked at in isolation, the relationship of a target to its background influences perception, as does our tendency to group close things and similar things together.

Objects that are close to each other will tend to be perceived together rather than separately. As a result of physical or time proximity, we often put together objects or events that are unrelated. Employees in a particular department are seen as a group. If two people in a four-member department suddenly resign, we tend to assume that their departures were related when, in fact, they may be totally unrelated. Timing may also imply dependence when, for example, a new sales manager is assigned to a territory and, soon after, sales in that territory skyrocket. The assignment of the new sales manager and the increase in sales may not be related—the increase may be due to the introduction of a new product line or to one of many other reasons—but there is a tendency to perceive the two occurrences as related.

Persons, objects, or events that are similar to each other also tend to be grouped together. The greater the similarity, the greater the probability that we will tend to perceive them as a common group. Women, blacks, or members of any other group that has clearly distinguishable characteristics in terms of features or colour will tend to be perceived as alike in other, unrelated characteristics as well.

III. Situation

The context in which we see objects or events is important. Elements in the surrounding environment influence our perceptions. For example, I may not notice a 25-year old female in an evening gown and heavy make-up at a nightclub on Saturday night. Yet that same woman so attired for my Monday morning management class would certainly catch my attention (and that of the rest of the class). Neither the perceiver nor the target changed between Saturday night and Monday morning, but the situation is different. Similarly, you are more likely to notice your subordinates goofing off if your boss from the head office happens to be in town. Again, the situation affects your perception. The time at which an object or event is seen can influence attention, as can location, light, heat, or any number of situational factors.

PERCEPTUAL PROCESS

Perception is the selection and organisation of environmental stimuli to provide meaningful experiences for the perceiver. Perception involves searching for, obtaining, and processing information. It represents the psychological process whereby people take information from the environment and make sense of their worlds.

The key words in the definition of perception are *selection* and *organisation*. Different people often perceive a situation differently, both in terms of what they selectively perceive and how they organise and interpret the things perceived. People receive stimuli from the environment through the five senses: taste, smell, hearing, sight, and touch. Everyone selectively pays attention to some aspects of the environment and selectively ignores other aspects at any particular time. For example, an apartment dweller may listen expectantly for a friend's footsteps in the hall but ignore sounds of the people upstairs. In an office, a secretary ignores the bell announcing the arrival of the elevator but jumps at the sound of the coffee cart's bell. These are examples of a selection process involving both external and internal factors that filters sensory perceptions and determines which will receive the most attention. The individual then organises the stimuli selected into meaningful patterns.

Perception is a process consisting of several sub-processes. We can take an input-throughput-output approach to understand the dynamics of the perceptual process. This approach emphasises that there is input which is processed and give output. The stimuli in the environment-subjects, events, or people-can be considered as the perceptual inputs. The actual transformation of these inputs through the perceptual mechanisms of selection, organisation, and interpretation can be treated as the throughputs, and the resultant opinions, feelings, attitudes, etc., which ultimately influence or behaviour, can be viewed as the perceptual outputs.

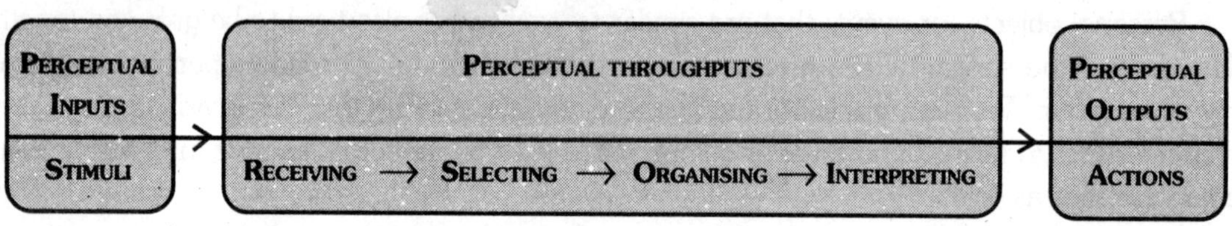

Fig. 1. *Simplified Process of Perception.*

Fig.1 is a simplified version of perception process. It does not present the whole factors which go in input-throughput-output process of perception. Figure presents a comprehensive view of process of perception.

Fig.1 of perception process presents three basic sub processes or elements of perception. These are existence of stimuli, perception mechanism, and perceptual outputs. Perceptual outputs along with other determinants of human behaviour affect and shape behaviour.

A person's interpretation of sensory stimuli will lead to a response, either overt (actions) or covert (motivation, attitudes and feelings), or both. Each person selects and organises sensory stimuli differently and thus has different interpretations and responses. Perceptual differences help to explain why people behave differently in the same situation. People often perceive the same things in different ways, and their behavioural responses depend, in part, on these perceptions.

PERCEPTUAL SELECTION

The phone is ringing, your television is blaring, a dog is barking outside, your PC is making a strange noise, and you smell coffee brewing. Which of these stimuli will you ignore? Which well you pay attention to?

Perceptual selection refers to the tendency to select certain objects from the environment for attention such that these objects are consistent with our existing beliefs, values and needs. Without this ability of selection the individuals will not be able to consider all available information necessary to initiate behaviour. This selectivity is enhanced by two related processes. First, it is believed that our senses are activated only by a certain type of stimuli so that some stimuli may go unnoticed if these are not strong, bright or loud enough to activate our senses. The second process, known as "sensory adaptation" relates to our ability to tune out certain stimuli to which we have been continuously exposed. For example, a new home owner near an airport might be excessively bothered by the noise, but such noise does not bother those who have been living there for a long time and have been exposed to this noise over this long period. *Perceptual selection* is the process by which people filter out most stimuli so that they can deal with the most important ones. Perceptual selection depends on several factors, some of which are in the external environment and some of which are internal to the perceiver.

FACTORS INFLUENCING PERCEPTUAL SELECTIVITY

The factors that influence *perceptual mechanism* are of various kinds—external, internal factors.

I. External (exogenous) Factors

External perception factors are characteristics that influence whether the stimuli will be notice. The following external factors may be stated as principles of perception :

(i) Size

The larger the size of an external factor, the more likely it is to be perceived. A hiker is far more likely to notice a fully grown fir tree than a seedling. For example, the maintenance engineer may pay more attention to a big machine than to a smaller one, even though the small machine costs the same as the big machine.

(ii) Intensity

The more intense an external factor, the more likely it is to be perceived (bright lights, loud noises, and the like). Even the language in a memo from a boss to an employee can reflect the intensity principle. A memo that reads "Please stop by my office at your convenience" would not fill you with the same sense of urgency as a memo that reads "Report to my office immediately"!

(iii) Status

Perception is also influenced by the status of the perceiver. High status people can exert influence on perception of an employee than low status people. For example, when we are introduced to the divisional manager and foreman, we are likely to remember the name of the divisional manager than the name of the foreman.

(iv) Contrast

External factors that stand out against the background or that are not what people expect are the most likely to be perceived. In addition, the contrast of objects with others or with their background may influence how they are perceived.

(v) Movement

A moving factor is more likely to be perceived than a stationary factor. Soldiers in combat learn this principle very quickly. Video games also illustrate the principle that motion is quickly detected.

(vi) Novelty and familiarity

Either a familiar or a novel factor in the environment can attract attention, depending on circumstances. People quickly notice an elephant walking along a city street. (Both novelty and size increase the probability of perception.) You are likely to first perceive the face of a close friend among a group of people walking toward you. A combination of these or similar factors may be operating at any time to affect perception. In combination with certain internal factors of the person doing the perceiving, they determine whether any particular stimulus is more or less likely to be noticed.

(vii) Frequency

The frequency principle states that a repeated external stimulus is more attention-getting than a single one. "A stimulus that is repeated has a better chance of catching us during one of the periods when our attention to a task is waning. In addition, repetition increases our sensitivity or alertness to the stimulus". Thus the greater the frequency with which a sensory stimulus is presented, the greater the chances we select it for attention. Repetition is one of the most frequently used technique in advertising and is the most common way of getting our attention. Repetition aids in increasing the awareness of the stimulus. But it has certain limitations. Repeating the confusing information increases confusion. Secondly, if stimulus is presented an excessive number of times you may choose to filter it out completely to avoid becoming irritated. And finally, frequency no doubt increases the probability of selection of stimulus by the receivers but it is no way connected to the accuracy of the interpretation of the information. Frequency simply results in making people aware of the stimulus.

(viii) Order

According to *Second* and *Backman*, the order in which the objects or stimuli are presented is an important factor in influencing selective attention. Sometimes, the first piece of information among many pieces received, receives the most attention, thus making the other pieces of information less significant. Sometimes, the most important piece is left to the end in order to heighten the curiosity and perceptive attention. For example, a writer of a communication may intentionally build up to a major point by proceeding through several smaller and less important points.

II. Internal or Personal Factors

Internal perception factors are aspects of the perceiver that influence perceptual selection. Some of the more important internal factors include personality, learning and perception, and motivation.

(i) Personality

Personality has an interesting relationship to perception. In part, perception shape personality; in turn, personality affects what and how people perceive.

An aspect of the personality called field dependence/independence provides a specific example of the relationship between personality and perception. A field-dependent person tends to pay more attention to external environmental cues, whereas a field-independent person relies mostly on bodily sensations. For example, in a test where a subject has to decide whether an object is vertically upright, a field-dependent individual will rely on cues from the environment, such as the corners of rooms, windows, and doors. A field-independent individual will rely mostly on bodily cues, such as the pull of gravity, to make the same judgement. A field–dependent person needs more time to find hidden figures embedded in complex geometrical designs than does a field-independent person. A field-dependent person is influenced more by the background or surrounding design than is a field-independent person. Field dependence/independence has some implications for organisational behaviour. For example, in comparison to a field-dependent employee, a field independent employee interacts more independently with others in the organisation. That is, a field-independent employee relies less on cues from others (such as a team leader or supervisor) to identify appropriate interpersonal behaviour. In addition, a field-independent employee seems to be more aware of important differences in others' roles, status, and needs.

(ii) Learning and Perception

Another internal factor affecting perceptual selection is learning, which can lead to the development of perceptual sets. A perceptual set is basically what a person expects from the stimuli on the basis of his learning and experience relative to same or similar stimuli. This is also known as cognitive awareness by which the mind organises information and forms images and compares them with previous exposures to similar stimuli.

In organisations, 'managers' and 'employees' past experiences and learning strongly influence their perceptions. For example, imagine an architect, a lawyer, and a real estate appraiser—all employed by the international design and engineering firm CRSS-approaching a tall office building in Toronto. These three individuals may notice distinctly different things about the building. The architect may first the architectural style and the construction materials used in the building. The lawyer may quickly perceive that the size and placement of advertising on the building violates a zoning regulation. The appraiser may focus on the general condition of the building and of the surrounding area, factors that would influence the building's price and salability. Each person pays attention to a different aspect of the same general stimulus because of the individual's training and work experiences. The culture into which a person is born determines many life experiences, and learned cultural differences influence the perceptual process.

(iii) Motivation

Motivation also plays an important role in determining what a person perceives. In general, people perceive thing that promise to help satisfy their needs and that they have found rewarding in the past. They tend to ignore mildly disturbing events (a barking dog) but will perceive dangerous ones (the house being on fire). Summarising an important aspect of the relationship between motivation and perception is the pollyanna principle, which states that people process pleasant stimuli more efficiently and accurately than unpleasant stimuli. For example, an employee who receives both positive and negative feedback during a performance appraisal session with her boss may more easily, clearly, and pleasantly remember the positive statements rather than the negative statements.

PERCEPTUAL ORGANISATION

Perceptual organisation is the process by which people group environmental stimuli into recognizable patterns. In the perceptual process, following selection, organisation takes over. The stimuli selected for attention now appear as a whole. For example, most people have a mental picture of an object with the following properties: Wood, four legs, a seat, a back, and armrests. This is our image of a chair. When people see an object that has all these properties, they recognise it as a chair. They have organised the incoming information into a meaningful whole.

I. Perceptual Grouping

A great deal remains to be learned about how the human mind assembles, organises, and categorises information. However, certain factors in perceptual organisation, such as perceptual grouping, are helpful in understanding perceptual organisation. Perceptual grouping is the tendency to form individual stimuli into a meaningful pattern by means such as closure, proximity, and similarity.

(i) Closure

Closure is the tendency to complete an object and perceive it as a constant, overall form. In other words, it is the ability to perceive a whole object, even though only part of the object is evident. People can organise their perceptions in terms of the closure principle when dealing with ideas and information . For example, a manager facing a complex decision may be able to develop a fairly accurate understanding of the issues even though her information isn't complete. Based on her experience and imagination, she "fills in the missing pieces" needed in order to make a decision.

(ii) Proximity

The proximity principle states that a group of objects may be perceived as related because of their nearness to each other. Employees often perceive other employees working together in a department as a team or unit because of their physical proximity. Suppose that four people on the third floor of a large office building quit their jobs. Even if they did so for completely unrelated reasons, the human resources department may perceive the resignations as a problem on the third floor and examine morale, pay, and working conditions there is an attempt to determine what is wrong.

(iii) Similarity

The similarity principle states that the more alike objects (or ideas) are, the greater is the tendency to perceive them as a common group. Similarity is very important in most team sports-thus the use of different colours of uniforms by the opposing teams. In football, for example, the quarterback must be able to spot an open receiver without a moment's hesitation, which would be extremely difficult (if not impossible) if both teams wore uniforms of the same colour. Many organisations, especially those in buildings with open floor plans, colour code the partitions and other accessories of each department to define separate functions and responsibilities usually. A company might require visitors to its plant to wear yellow hard hats and employees to wear white hard hats. Employees can then easily identify people who are unfamiliar with everyday safety precautions and routines when they are in the work area.

II. Figure-Ground

People tend to organise information on what is known as the figure-ground principle. This involves that in perceiving stimuli or phenomena, the tendency is to keep certain phenomena in focus and other phenomena are in background. More attention is paid to phenomena which have been kept as figure and less attention to phenomena kept in background. For example, while reading a book, the letters printed are treated as figure while the page on which the letters have been printed is taken as ground. The perception may change if certain stimuli are changed from figure to ground.

These principles and, in general, the ways that individuals organise their perceptions to make sense of their worlds are not something that managers and organisations can safely ignore.

INTERPERSONAL PERCEPTION

Person perception is the process by which individuals attribute characteristics or traits to other people. It is closely related to the attribution process. In general, the factors influencing person perception are the same as those that influence perceptual selection. That is, both external and internal factors affect person perception. However, we may usefully categorise factors that influence how a person perceives another as :

I. Characteristics of the perceiver.

II. Characteristics of the person being perceived.

III. Characteristics of the situation.

The characteristics of the perceiver include such factors as *needs, values, experience* and *attitudes*. The characteristics of the perceived include the *appearance, communication* and *personal behaviour* and the characteristics of the situation include *physical location, social setting* and *organisational setting.*

I. Characteristics of the Perceiver

A person's needs, habits, impact of past experience, ethics and values, attitudes and personality, all influence the perception process. For example, a person with strong ego needs would look at other people or situations either as ego satisfying or ego threatening, thus, perhaps making the perceptions, inaccurate. Similarly, less secure people often find faults with others. Secure persons tend to see others as warm and friendly.

Our ethics and values and our cultural upbringing also play an important role in our perception about others. A non-smoker may prejudge a smoker. Similarly, it is difficult to perceive the personality of a person raised in another culture, because our judgement is based upon our own values.

As an example, a negative attitude towards unions may inhibit the manager towards honest and straightforward talks with the unions during labour-management negotiations. Similarly, a personnel manager who is biased against women, minorities or handicapped person will be very sensitive to them during an employment interview. This happens because when we don't like a person, then we always look for negative aspects of that person.

Our attitudes towards others is also influenced by our previous experiences with them. For example, if an employee was promised a bonus or a promotion on certain accomplishments and did not receive the promised rewards inspite of such accomplishments, then he would perceive the manager with distrust.

II. Characteristics of the Person being Perceived

It may defy logic and objectivity, but we cannot deny that our perceptions about others are influenced by their physical characteristics such as appearance, facial expressions, age, gender, manner of communication as well as personality traits and other forms of behaviours. For example, when we see a person who appears to be assertive and confident, we assume him to be an executive or a leader. People dressed in business suits are generally thought to be professionals while people dressed in ordinary work clothes are assumed to be lower level employees.

Both verbal and non-verbal communication affect our perception about others. The choice of words and precision of language can form impressions about the education and sophistication of the person. The tone of voice sometimes indicates the mood of the person at a given time. The depth of conversation and choice of topics provide clues of people's intelligence. The body language or expressive behaviour such as how people sit and the movement of their eyes or a smile can indicate whether people are nervous or self confident.

Similarly, the status or occupation of a person creates an impression in our minds. We are awed by people of fame, wealth or professional status. We tend to behave in a more respectful way when we are introduced to a president of a large corporation or a judge of the Supreme Court or a movie celebrity. When we meet a person who is described to us as warm and friendly, we treat him differently as compared to meeting a person who is known to be cold and calculating.

III. Characteristics of the Situation

Physical, social and organisational settings of the situation or event can also influence perceptions. For example, if you meet some lady for the first time and she is with another person whom you respect and admire, you will create a favourable image about her in your mind as compared to a situation in which you see her with a person whom you intensely dislike. Of course, these initial impressions may change over the period of time, but the saying that the "first impression is the last impression" is very valid. Location of a given event is also an important factor in determining behaviour. You will behave with your boss differently at a social function than in the office. In an organisational setting where people are given an opportunity to interact in a friendly and sociable work situation, they become more trustworthy and less defensive.

IMPRESSION MANAGEMENT

Whereas social perception is concerned with how one individual perceives other individuals, impression management (sometimes called "self-presentation") is the process by which people attempt to manage or control the perceptions other forms of them. There is often a tendency for people to try to present themselves so as to impress others in a socially desirable way. Thus, impression management has considerable implications for areas such as the validity of performance appraisals (is the evaluator being manipulated into giving a positive rating?) and is a pragmatic, political tool for one to climb the ladder of success in organisation.

I. The Process of Impression Management

As with other cognitive processes, impression management has many possible conceptual dimensions and has been researched in relation to aggression, attitude change, attributions, and social facilitation, among other things. Most recently, however, two separate components of impression management have been identified—impression motivation and impression construction. Especially in an employment situation, subordinates may be motivated to control how their boss perceives them. The degree of this motivation to impression-manage will depend on such factors as the relevance the impressions have to the individual's goals, the value of these goals, and the discrepancy between the image one would like others to hold and the image one believes others already hold.

Impression construction, the other major process, is concerned with the specific type of impression people want to make and how they go about doing it. Although some theorists limit the type of impression only to personal characteristics, others include such other things as attitudes, physical states, interests, or values. Using this broader approach, five factors have been identified as being especially relevant to the kinds of impressions people try to construct: the self-concept, desired and undesired identity images, role constraints, target's values, and current social image. Although there is considerable research on how these five factors influence the type of impression that people try to make, there is still little known of how they select the way to manage others' perceptions of them. For example, do they directly tell their boss things such as "I'm really competitive and want to get ahead" or do they make indirect statements such as "I really like racquet ball; it is really competitive." There is also recent research evidence indicating that managers who are high self-monitors (regulate and control themselves based upon situational and interpersonal cues) are more sensitive and responsive to adjusting their self-presentations or impressions. These high self-monitors were found to be more likely to be promoted, but they are also more likely to change employers or to make a job-related move to a different state or country.

II. Employee Impression Management Strategies

There are two basic strategies of impression management that employees can use. If employees are trying to minimise responsibility for some negative event or to stay out of trouble, they may employ a demotion-preventative strategy. On the other hand, if they are seeking to maximise responsibility for a positive outcome or to look better than they really are, then they can use a promotion-enhancing strategy. The demotion-preventative strategy is characterised by the following :

(i) *Accounts*. These are employees attempts to excuse or justify their actions. Example excuses are not feeling well or not getting something done on time because of another higher-priority assignment.

(ii) *Apologies*. When there is no logical way out, the employee may apologise to the boss for some negative event. Such an apology not only gives the impression that the individual is sorry but also indicates that it will not happen again. The employee is big enough to face up to a problem and solve it.

(iii) *Disassociation*. When employees are indirectly associated with something that went wrong (for example, they are members of a committee or work team that made a bad decision), they may secretly tell their boss that they fought for the right thing but were overruled. Employees using this approach try to remove themselves both from the group and from responsibility for the problem.

The promotion-enhancing strategies involve the following :

(a) *Entitlements*. Under this approach, employees feel that they have not been given credit for a positive outcome. They make sure that it is known through formal channels. Or

they may informally note to key people that they are pleased their suggestions or efforts worked out so well.

(b) *Enhancements.* Here, employees may have received credit, but they point out that they really did more and had a bigger impact than originally thought. For example, their effort or idea not only served a customer well or met a difficult deadline, but can be used in the future to greatly increase profits.

(c) *Obstacle disclosures.* In this strategy, employees identify either personal (health or family) or organisational (lack of resources or cooperation) obstacles they had to overcome to accomplish an outcome. They are trying to create the perception that because they obtained the positive outcome despite the big obstacles, they really deserve a lot of credit.

(d) *Association.* Here, the employee makes sure to be seen with the right people at the right times. This creates the perception that the employee is well connected and is associated with successful projects.

The above strategies help construct impressions or perceptions. The motivation on the part of employees may or may not be a deliberate attempt to enhance themselves in terms of political power, promotions, and monetary rewards. Managers should be aware of deliberate manipulation of perceptions when making evaluations of their people. By the same token, such impression management could be used to get ahead in an organisation or keep good relations with customers. Here are some guidelines that have been offered for organisational members that will help them recognise various impression management tactics and the motives behind them :

(i) One should be on the lookout for high-probability impression management strategies. For example, recruiters should be careful to separate pure self-promotion and legitimate claims of competence, and those in positions of power or status should be aware of subordinates' efforts to ingratiate themselves ("buttering up the boss" and "apple-polishing").

(ii) There should be an attempt to minimise personal, situational, and organisational features that faster undesirable impression management. For example, organisations in which task performance is ambiguous and/or resources are scarce tend to generate relatively high levels of ingratiation.

(iii) One should look for ulterior motives and avoid being every influenced by impression management. For example, a manager who is able to distinguish between pure self-promotion and true competence is less likely to be biased by an invalid claim when appraising a staff member's performance.

In total, there is no question that deliberately employing an impression management strategy can have a positive impact on performance evaluations and getting ahead in an organisation. Even something as simple as dressing for success can have an impact on both an individual's and even an organisation's outcomes.

In conclusion, probably the best advice is that offered by *William Gardner* at the end of his analysis of impression management. He states : *"When selecting an image, never try to be something you're not. People will see through the facade. In sum, make every effort to put your best foot forward—but never at the cost of your identity or integrity!"*

BARRIERS TO PERCEPTUAL ACCURACY

Human beings, as complex as they are, cannot be absolutely objective about their judgements regarding their environment. There are a number of factors which taint our judgements about other people and situations. Since the success of our efforts and decisions is contingent upon the accuracy of the information, as well as the accuracy of impressions, it is necessary to know what the barriers to perceptual accuracy are, so that these can be considered in our judgements or can be eliminated, if possible. Some of these barriers are:

I. Stereotyping

It is perhaps one of the most common barriers in accurately perceiving others. In order to simplify matters, we often tend to classify people and events into already known or perceived general categories. As an example, suppose you get into an executive's office and notice a man and a woman talking to each other beside a secretary's desk. Our first reaction would generally be to assume that the woman is the secretary and the man is the executive even though the case may be just the opposite. This reaction is based upon our stereotyped impressions that the secretaries tend to be women and executives tend to be men.

In our minds we have established certain categories with certain characteristics or attributes. For example, the category of teenagers would have such attributes as independence, *parental defiance*, sexual liberation and so on. Then we infer that all persons who fit in that category exhibit the attributes that are associated with that category. Similarly, people associate some positive attributes when they meet a doctor, a judge, a company president or a college professor and negative attributes when they meet a school dropout, a drug addict or an alcoholic, even though, not all people strictly fit into these categories.

Stereotyping is particularly critical when meeting new people, since so little about them is known to us and we tend to characterise them according to certain categories on the basis of age, sex, occupation, religion and ethnic background. From organisational point of view, some of the more established stereotypes are:

(i) Sex Role Stereotypes

Both men and women have been stereotyped into separately perceived categories. Men have been considered as tough with leadership ability, self-confidence, competitiveness ambitiousness and analytical ability, while women are stereotyped as emotional, impulsive and submissive. Studies conducted by *Bartol* and *Butterfield* found that in interpersonal relations, female managers were rated as more effective and in task accomplishments, male managers were rated as more effective.

An interesting anecdote relating to classic sex role stereotype appeared in the *Wall Street Journal*. A part of it is reproduced below:

"Your secretary came outside to inspect the no-parking signs we put up at the drive-in teller," the police lieutenant told Martin Hartman, an assistant branch manager from Continental bank. "Hey, that was no secretary", objected Mr. Hartman, "that was my boss".

This example illustrates the traditional perspective that managerial positions are the domain of males and not females. Some of the other stereotype categories in which women workers are traditionally placed are: nurses, airline stewardesses, waitresses and some of the male stereotypes categories are: policemen, firemen, truck drivers, managers and so on.

(ii) Age Stereotypes

Age is another stereotype which presents problems in the organisational environment. Such capabilities as physical, psychological and intellectual are sometimes presumed on the basis of the age of the person. Studies conducted by *Rosen* and *Jerdee* found that some business students have clear stereotypes of older employees. The older employees are thought to be:

- More resistant to organisational change.
- Less creative.
- Less likely to take calculated risks.
- More conservative in nature.
- Lower in physical capacity.
- Less interested in learning new techniques.
- Less capable of learning new techniques.

Not all impressions about older people have a negative connotation. On the positive side, they are considered more experienced for consulting positions. They also tend to be perceived as more honest, dependable and trustworthy. These stereotype impressions affect business decisions regarding hiring, promotions and career development training programs.

II. Halo Effect

The halo effect refers to the tendency of judging the person entirely on the basis of a single trait which may be favourable or unfavourable. Sometimes, we judge a person by our first impression about him or her. A charming smile may create a favourable impression about the person. Similarly, if we are conscious of how a person is dressed, then a poorly dressed person will create a negative impression on us and a well dressed person would impress us positively. The halo effect can colour a person's image of others with regard to many other "unrelated" attributes based upon the impression regarding one attribute. In studies conducted by *Asch*, two sets of personality traits of the same person were given to two groups of people. The two lists were the same except that one list contained the trait "warm" and the other list contained the trait "cold". This one word difference led to significantly different evaluations of the person. The group with the list containing the word "warm" described the person as friendly, humorous, imaginative and intelligent and the group with the list containing the word "cold" described him aloof, serious and without many friends.

The halo effect is also likely to be related to our own self image. A manager who is always at work on time would view his subordinates who are habitually punctual more favourably than those who are not. This one trait of punctuality can influence a supervisor's rating of the employee's productivity and quality of his product more favourably, even if the actual performance is not up to the mark.

In our social interaction, we sometimes change our impressions about our long term friends on the basis of single act of our disliking. Many marriages have ended in divorce on the basis of a single unlikable trait of the partner.

III. Expectancy Effect

Expectancy is a tendency to perceive people, objects or events on the basis of what we expected them to be in the first place. It is sometimes referred to as "pygmallion effect". Pygmallion was a mythical Greek sculptor who made a statue of a girl that he wanted and made her come to life so that what came out was what he expected. Through expectancy, you may create certain things in the work situation that you expect to find to start with. This aspect is also known as "self-fulfilling prophecy". For example, if you have become a member of an important committee and you have been told that the committee is a high-level committee with a membership of intellectuals, you would meet the committee members with certain perceptions and would try to find in the membership what you expect to find based upon these perceptions. On the other hand, if you were told that the committee was set up under pressure for political reasons, you would have different perceptions about the membership of the committee. Now, even if the behaviour of the members was similar, it would be interpreted according to your own preconceived perceptions.

IV. Perceptual Defence

Perceptual defense is the mental process by which we tend to protect ourselves from such objects, situations or stimuli that are emotionally disturbing or perceptually threatening. We tend to ignore such disturbing part of our environment that does not require confrontation. For example, people who live near rail-road tracks may not even hear the trains, because they tend to become unaware or tend to ignore such happenings. Thus, through our perceptual defenses, we tend to distort or ignore information or stimuli that is culturally unacceptable or is in conflict with our established beliefs.

In a study conducted by *Haire* and *Grunes*, some college students were provided with a description of some factory workers. Included in the list of characteristics was the word "intelligent". Since the word "intelligent" is perceived to be contrary to the established belief about factory workers, the students choose to reject the description by using conceptual defenses. Four types of rejections were reported:

- *Denial*. Some of the students outrightly rejected the notion that factory workers could be intelligent.
- *Modification and distortion*. This was one of the most common forms of defense in which intelligence was accepted but the common modification was "not intelligent enough" or no initiative to rise above the group to which they belonged.

- *Change in perception.* Some students changed their perception of the worker because of the intelligence traits, though not very enthusiastically.
- *Recognition, but refusal to change.* Some students stated that they recognised the conflict about what they knew about the factory workers and what was told to them regarding the trait of intelligence.

V. Projection

Projection refers to the tendency of the people to see their own traits in other people, meaning that when they make judgements about others, they project their own characteristics into others. For example, while in America, an Indian person meeting another person from India would presume certain cultural characteristics in him that would be similar to his own characteristics. Similarly, when a professor meets another professor, he would make the same assumptions. As the saying goes, "to an honest man, every body is honest."

In the case of undesirable or threatening circumstances, projection can serve as a perceptual defense. A person who Cheats on his income tax return can justify this action by thinking that "every body is doing it". The dishonest worker may say "sure, I steal from the company, but so does every body else".

ATTRIBUTION THEORY

Our perceptions of people differ from our perceptions of inanimate objects such as desks, machines, or buildings because we make inferences about the actions of people that we don't make about inanimate objects. Nonliving objects are subject to the laws of nature, but they have no beliefs, motives, or intentions. People do. The result is that when we observe people, we attempt to develop explanations of why they behave in certain ways. Our perception and judgment of a person's actions, therefore, will be significantly influenced by the assumptions we make about that person's internal state.

Attribution theory has been proposed to develop explanations of the ways in which we judge people differently, depending on what meaning we attribute to a given behaviour. Basically, the theory suggests that when we observe an individual's behaviour, we attempt to determine whether it was internally or externally caused. That determination, however, depends largely on three factors: (i) distinctiveness, (ii) consensus, and (iii) consistency. First, let's clarify the differences between internal and external causation and then we will elaborate on each of the three determining factors.

Internally caused behaviours are those that are believed to be under the personal control of the individual. *Externally* caused behaviour is seen as resulting from outside causes; that is, the person is seen as having been forced into the behaviour by the situation. If one of your employees is late for work, you might attribute his lateness to his partying into the wee hours of the morning and then oversleeping. This would be an internal attribution. But if you attribute his arriving late to a major automobile accident that tied up traffic on the road that this employee regularly uses, then you would be making an external attribution.

Distinctiveness refers to whether an individual displays different behaviours in different situations. Is the employee who arrives late today also the source of complaints by co-workers for being a "goof-off"? What we want to know is whether this behaviour is unusual. If it is, the observer is likely to give the behaviour an external attribution. If this action is not unusual, it will probably be judged as internal.

If everyone who is faced with a similar situation responds in the same way, we can say the behaviour shows *consensus*. Our late employee's behaviour would meet this criterion if all employees who took the same route to work were also late. From an attribution perspective, if consensus is high, you would be expected to give an external attribution to the employee's tardiness, whereas if other employees who took the same route made it to work on time, your conclusion as to causation would be internal.

Finally, an observer looks for *consistency* in a person's actions. Does the person respond the same way over time? Coming in ten minutes late for work is not perceived in the same way for the employee for whom it is an unusual case as it is for the employee for whom it is part of a routine pattern. The more consistent the behaviour, the more the observer is inclined to attribute it to internal causes.

The key elements in attribution theory. It would tell us, for instance, that if your employee—Kiran generally performs at about the same level on other related tasks as she does—on her current task (low distinctiveness), if other employees frequently perform differently—better or worse—than Kiran does on that current task (low consensus), and if Kiran's performance on this current task is consistent over time (high consistency), you or anyone else who is judging Kiran's work is likely to hold her primarily responsible for her task performance (internal attribution).

One of the more interesting findings from attribution theory is that there are errors or biases that distort attributions. For instance, there is substantial evidence that when we make judgements about the behaviour of other people, we have a tendency to underestimate the influence of external factors and overestimate the influence of internal or personal factors. This is called the *fundamental attribution* error and can explain why a sales manager is prone to attribute the poor performance of her sales agents to laziness rather than to the innovative product line introduced by a competitor. There is also a tendency for individuals to attribute their own success to internal factors such as ability or effort while putting the blame for failure on external factors such as luck. This called the *self-serving bias* and suggests that feedback provided to employees in performance reviews will be predictably distorted by recipients depending on whether it is positive or negative.

Are these errors or biases that distort attributions universal across different cultures? We can't answer that question definitively, but there is some preliminary evidence that indicates cultural differences. For instance, a study of Korean managers found that, contrary to the self-serving bias, they tended to accept responsibility for group failure "because I was not a capable leader" instead of attributing it to group members. Attribution theory was developed largely in the United States on the basis of experiments with Americans. But the Korean study suggests caution in making attribution theory predictions outside the United States, especially in countries with strong collectivist traditions.

ATTRIBUTIONS PROCESS

The attribution process refers to the ways in which people come to understand the causes of others' (and their own) behaviours. Attributions play an important role in the process of person perception. Attributions made about the reasons for someone's behaviour may affect judgments about that individual's fundamental characteristics or traits (what he or she is "really like").

Basically, people make attributions in an attempt to understand the behaviour of other people and to make better sense of the environment. Individuals do not consciously make attribution in all circumstances (although they may do so unconsciously much of the time). However, under certain circumstances, people are likely to make causal attributions consciously. For example, causal attributions are common in the following situations:

(i) The perceiver has been asked an explicit question about another's behaviour. (Why did X do that?)

(ii) An unexpected event occurs. (I've never seen him behave that way. I wonder what's going on?)

(iii) The perceiver depends on another person for a desired outcome. (I wonder why my boss made that comment about my expense account?)

(iv) The perceiver experiences feelings of failure or loss of control. (I can't believe I failed my mid-term exam!).

Fig. 2. presents a basic model of the attribution. People infer "causes" to behaviours they observe in others, and these interpretations often largely determine their reactions to those behaviour. The perceived causes of behaviour reflect several antecedents:

(i) The amount of information the perceiver has about the people and the situation and how that information is organises by the perceiver;

(ii) The perceiver's beliefs (implicit personality theories, what other people might do in a similar situation, and so on); and

(iii) The motivation of the perceiver (for example, the importance to the perceiver of making an accurate assessment). Recall our discussion of the internal factors influencing perception-learning, personality, and motivation. In the attribution process, you can see another example of the influence of these internal factors. The perceiver's information and beliefs depend on previous experience and are influenced by the perceiver's personality. Based on information, beliefs, and motives, the perceiver often distinguishes between internal and external causes of behaviour; that is, whether people did something because of a real desire or because of the pressure of circumstances. The assigned cause of the behaviour—whether internal or external-helps the perceiver attach meaning to the event and is important for understanding the subsequent consequences for the perceiver. Among the consequences of this attribution process are the subsequent behaviour of the perceiver in response to the behaviour of others, the impact on feelings or emotions (how the perceiver now feels about events, people, and circumstances) and the effects on the perceiver's expectations of future events or behaviour.

ATTRIBUTIONS OF SUCCESS AND FAILURE

In terms of task performance, the attributions that employees and managers make regarding success or failure are very important. Managers may base decisions about rewards and punishments on their perceptions of why subordinates have succeeded or failed in performing some task. In general, individuals often attribute their own (and others') success or failure to four causal factors: ability, effort, tasks difficulty, and luck.

* I succeeded (or failed) because I had the skills to do the job (or because I did not have the skills to do the job). Such statements are ability attributions.
* I succeeded (or failed) because I worked hard (or because I did not work hard). Such statements are effort attributions.
* I succeeded (or failed) because it was easy (or because it was too hard). Such statements are attributions about task difficulty.
* I succeeded (or failed) because I was lucky (or unlucky). Such statements are attributions about luck or the circumstances surrounding the task.

Causal attributions of ability and effort are internal, and causal attributions of task difficulty and luck are external. These attributions about success or failure reflect differences in self-esteem and locus of control. For example, individuals with high self-esteem and high internal locus of control are likely to assess their own performance positively and to attribute their good performance to internal causes. The organisational importance of these success and failure attributions is demonstrated by research in hospitals that examined the feedback provided to nurses by their managers. When the managers perceived that poor performance was the result of lack of effort, their feedback messages to nurses tended to be punitive or negative in tone. Their attributions

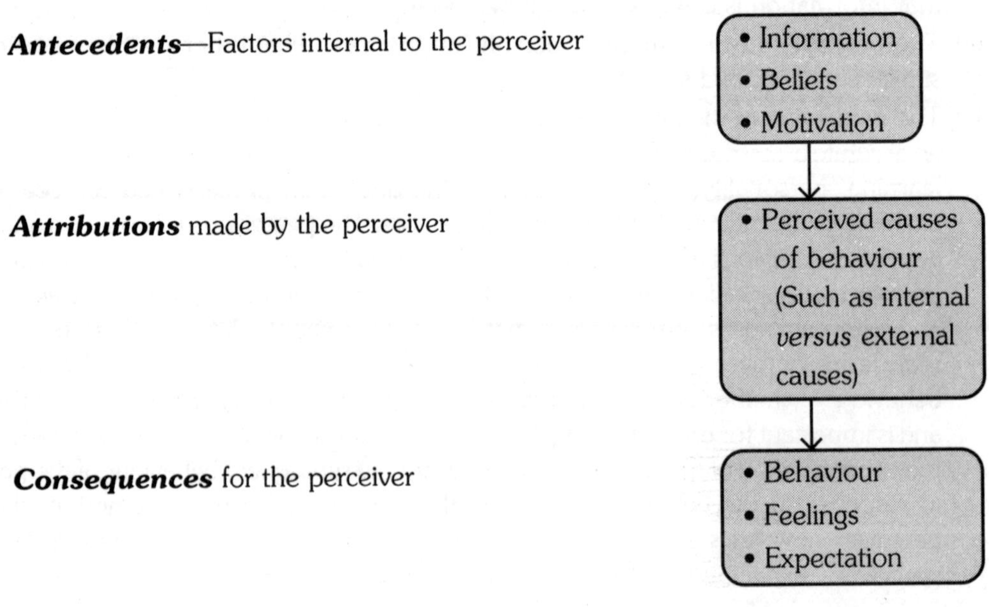

Fig. 2. *The Attribution Process.*

also affected the specific content of the feedback. For example, when the managers inferred that poor performance reflected lack of ability, their messages to nurses focused on instructions for doing the job better; when they thought that poor performance meant lack of effort, their messages to nurses tended to stress orders to be followed. Thus the managers' attributions about the reasons for performance failures by staff nurses influenced their communications behaviour , as suggested by the model of the attribution process shown in Fig. 2.

Not surprisingly, people have a strong tendency to attribute their success with a task to internal factors (ability or effort) and to attribute their failures to external factors (task difficulty or luck). This tendency is known as a self-serving bias. The tendency of employees to accept responsibility for good performance but to deny responsibility for poor performance often presents a serious challenge for managers and supervisors during performance appraisals. A self-serving bias may also create other types of problems. For example, it prevents an individual from accurately assessing his or her own performance and abilities and makes more difficult determining why a manager's course of action has failed. The general tendency to blame others for a person's own failures often is associated with poor performance and inability to establish satisfying interpersonal relationships at work and in other social settings.

DIFFERENCE BETWEEN PERCEPTION AND SENSATION

There has been a great deal of misunderstanding about the relationship between sensation and perception. The physical senses vision, hearing, touch, smell, and tastes, are different from perception. The sensation essentially deals with very elementary behaviour that is largely determined by physiological functioning. Perception on the other hand, is much more complex and broader than sensation. It is virtually a cognitive, psychological process of sensing, filtering, modifying the raw data. As sensation plays an important role of people in their private lives, perception plays a crucial part in organisational life. According to *Berelson* and *Steiner,* all knowledge of the world depends on the senses and their stimulation, but the facts of raw sensory data are insufficient to produce or explain the coherent picture of the world as experienced by the normal adults.

REVIEW QUESTIONS

1. What is perception? Explain the important factors affecting perception.
2. What are the various characteristics of the perceiver, those of the perceived and those of the situations which affect the perceptival process?
3. What is meant by perceptual selectivity? Briefly describe the factors which play a significant part in perceptual organisation.
4. What are the common barriers to perceptual accuracy?
5. Explain the various steps in the process of perception.
6. Write a short note on :
   (a) Contrast effect.
   (b) Employee loyalty.
   (c) Performance evaluation.

(d) Performance expectations.

(e) Attribution theory.

(f) Difference between perception and sensation.

REFERENCES

1. P.D. Knott, *"The Effects of Frustration and Magnitude of Rewards in Selective Attention, Size, Estimation and Verbal Evaluation", Journal of Personality, 39, 1971.*
2. *T.W. Costello and S.S. Zalking, "Psychology in Administration", Englewood Cliffs, NJ Prentice-Hall, 1963. also see, D.E. Hamachek, Encounters with the Self, New York, Hott, Rinhear and Winston, 1971.*
3. *Jerome S. Bruner and Leo Postman, Emotional Selectivity in Perception and Reaction, Journal of Personality, September, 1947.*
4. *Secord P.F., "Racial Features and Inference Processes in Interpersonal Perception", In R. Taguiri and L. Petrullo (ed.), Person Perception and Interpersonal Behaviour, Stanford, Calif; Stanford University Press, 1958.*
5. *Sheldon S. Zalking and T.W. Costello, 'Perception: Some Recent Research and Implications for Administration', Administrative Science Quarterly, Sept., 1962.*
6. *Blair J. Kolasa, Introduction to Behavioural Science for Business, Wiley Eastern Limited, New Delhi, 1978.*
7. *Edward Lawler III and John Grant Rhode, Information and Control in Organisations, Pacific Palisades, Calif; Goodyear Publishing, 1976.*
8. *Bernard Berrlson and Gary A. Steiner, Human Behaviour; Harcourt, Brace and World, Inc., New York, 87, 1964.*
9. *D.C. Dearborn and H.A. Simon, "Selective Perception: A Note on Departmental Identification of Executives", Sociometry, 21, 1958.*
10. *Leavitt, H.J., Managerial Psychology, University of Chicago Press, 1964.*
11. *Byron A. Grove and Willard A. Kerr, "Specific Evidence on Origin of Halo Effect in Measurement of Employee Morale", Journal of Social Psychology, August, 1951.*
12. *Mason Hairr, "Role Perception in Labour Management Relations: An Experimental Approach; Industrial and Labour Relations Review", January, 1955.*

3rd

CHAPTER OVERVIEW

PERSONALITY AND ATTITUDES

• ***After reading this chapter, you should be able to know:***

- Major Contributing Factors to Personality
- Personality Development and Socialisation
- Major Personality Attributes
- Theories of Personality
- Scale of Personality
- Organisational Implications
- Attitudes
- Determinants of Attitudes
- The Nature and Dimensions of Attitudes
- Functions of Attitudes
- Components of Attitudes
- Source of Attitudes
- Types of Attitudes
- Significance and Functions of Attitudes
- Changing Attitudes
- Attitudes and Consistency
- Cognitive Dissonance Theory
- Attitudes and Workforce Diversity
- Attitudes and Values
- Attitudes and Job Satisfaction

3

Personality and Attitudes

Personality is a concept that we use continuously in our day-to-day routine, when dealing with people. We talk about people as having a good personality or a bad personality or arrogant and aggressive personality. Sometimes we refer to disagreements among people as being due to personality conflicts. Personality can be reflected in a person's temperament and is a key factor influencing individual behaviour in organisations. Often the wrong type of personality of a superior proves disastrous in terms of worker unrest and protests. Sometimes the personality difficulties are the root cause of labour strikes. No matter how good the superior is in technical knowledge or other behavioural characteristics. It is the "temperament" of the superior that is crucial in cordial interaction with subordinates.

Personality is influenced by hereditary, cultural, and social factors. Regardless of how it's defined, however, psychologists generally accept certain principles:

(i) Personality is an organised whole; otherwise, the individual would have no meaning.

(ii) Personality appears to be organised into patterns that are to some degree observable and measurable.

(iii) Although personality has a biological basis, its specific development is also a product of social and cultural environments.

(iv) Personality has superficial aspects (such as attitudes toward being a team leader) and a deeper core (such as sentiments about authority or the Protestant work ethic).

(v) Personality involves both common and unique characteristics. Every person is different from every other person in some respects, while being similar to other persons in other respects.

These five ideas are included in this definition of personality:

An individual's personality is a relatively stable set of characteristics, tendencies, and temperaments that have been significantly formed by inheritance and by social, cultural, and environmental factors. This set of variables determines the communities and differences in the behaviour of the individual.

MAJOR CONTRIBUTING FACTORS TO PERSONALITY

There are various determinants of personality and these have been categorised in different ways. *McClelland* has categorised these factors into four fundamental theories—*traits* (acquired propensity to respond), *scheme* (beliefs, frame of reference, major orientations, ideas, and values), motives (inner drives), and *self-schema* (observation of one's own behaviour). Similarly, *Scott* and *Mitchell* have classified various determinants into *heredity*, *groups*, and *cultural factors*, both physiological and psychological which play important role in human personality. These factors are interrelated and interdependent. However, for the purpose of analysis, these can be classified into four broad categories:

(i) Biological Factors,
(ii) Family and Social Factors,
(iii) Cultural Factors, and
(iv) Situational Factors.

The impact of these factors on the personality may be seen from Fig. 1.

Out of the various factors of personality determinants, only biological factors have one-sided impact while other factors have interactive impact as the individual himself can also have some impact on these factors.

I. Biological Factors

(i) Heredity

Historically, the nature-nurture controversy in personality theory was a sharp disagreement about the extent to which genetic factors influence personality. Those holding the extreme nature position argued that personality is inherited. Those adhering to the extreme nurture position argued that a person's experiences determine personality. Current thinking is more balanced—both heredity (biology) and environment (experiences) are important, although some personality characteristics may be influenced more by one factor than the other. That is, some personality traits seem to have a strong genetic component whereas other traits seem to be largely learned (based on experiences). Deeply ingrained in many people's notions of personality is a belief in its genetic basis. Expressions such as "She is just like her father" and "He gets those irritating qualities from your side of the family, dear," reflect such beliefs. In fact, some personality theorists argue that heredity sets limits on the range of development of characteristics and that only within this range do environmental forces determine personality characteristics.

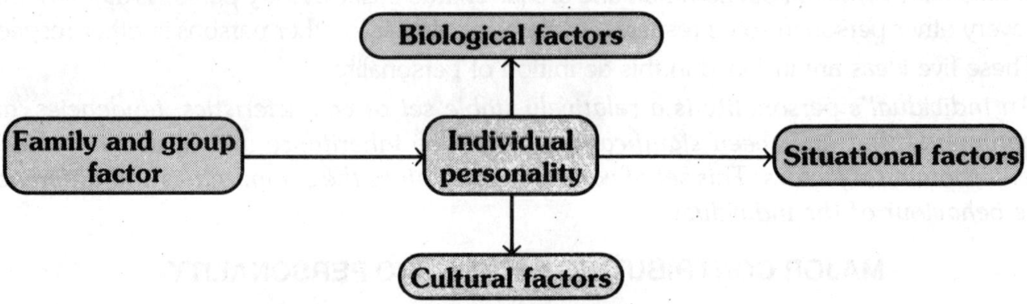

Fig. 1. *Sources of Personality.*

Recent studies of young children lend strong support to the power of heredity. Evidence demonstrates that traits such as shyness, fear, and distress are more likely caused by inherited genetic characteristics. This finding suggests that some personality traits may be built into the same genetic code that affects factors such as height and hair colour.

If personality characteristics were completely dictated by heredity, they would be fixed at birth and no amount of experience could alter them. If you were relaxed and easy-going as a child, for example, that would be the result of your genes, and it would not be possible for you to change those characteristics. But personality characteristics are not completely dictated by heredity.

(ii) Brain

Another biological factor that influences personality is the role of brain of an individual. Though some promising inroads are made by researchers, the psychologists are unable to prove empirically the contribution of human brain in influencing personality. Preliminary results from the electrical stimulation of the brain (ESB) research gives indication that better understanding of human personality and behaviour might come from the study of the brain.

(iii) Physical Features

Perhaps the most outstanding factor that contributes to personality i.e., the physical stature of an individual. An individual's external appearance is proved to be having a tremendous effect on his personality. For instance, the fact that a person is short or tall, fat or skinny, handsome or ugly, black or whitish will undoubtedly influence the person's effect on others and in turn, will affect the self-concept. According to *Paul H. Mussen* "... a child's physical characteristics may be related to his approach to the social environment, to the expectancies of others, and to their reactions to him. These in turn may have impacts on personality development." Similarly, a rapidly maturing girl or boy will be exposed to different physical and social situations and activities than will a slowly maturing boy or girl. Psychologists contend that the different rates of maturation will also influence the individual's personality.

II. FAMILY AND SOCIAL FACTORS

The development of the individual proceeds under the influence of many socialising forces and agencies, from nuclear family to more distant or global groupings. Family and social groups have most significant impact on personality development. These groups have their impact through socialisation and identification processes.

(i) Socialisation Process

The contribution of family and social group in combination with the culture is known as socialisation. In the words of *Mussen* "Socialisation is the process by which an individual infant acquires, from the enormously wide range of behavioural potentials that are open to him at birth, those behaviour patterns that are customary and acceptable according to the standards of his family and social group." It initially starts with the contact with mother and later on the other members of the family (father, sisters, close-relatives) and the social group plays influential role in shaping an individual's personality.

Socialisation is a process by which an individual infant acquires, from the enormously wide range of behavioural potentialities that are open to him at birth, those behaviour patterns that are customary and acceptable according to the standards of his family and social groups. Socialisation process starts with initial contact between mother and her new infant. Later on, other members of the family and social groups influence the socialisation process.

(ii) Identification Process

Identification process occurs when a person tries to identify himself with some person whom he feels ideal in the family. Generally a child in the family tries to behave like his father or mother. The identification process can be examined from three different perspectives. First, identification can be viewed is the similarity of behaviour (including feelings and attitudes) between child and model. Second, identification can be looked as the child's motives or desires to be like the model. Third, it can be viewed as the process through which the child actually takes on the attributes of the model. Apart from the socialisation and identification processes, the personality of an individual is influenced by the home environment. There is a substantial empirical evidence to indicate that the overall environment at home is created by parents is critical to personality development. Family background apart, social class also influences a person's perception, perception of self and others, and perception of work, authority and money, etc.

Socialisation and identification process is influenced by home environment, family members, and social groups.

(a) Environment

Many behavioural experts still believe that the environment plays a larger role in shaping personality than do inherited characteristics. Environmental components include culture, family, group membership and life experiences. Culture refers to the distinctive ways that different human populations or societies organise their lives. Anthropologists working in different cultures have clearly demonstrated the important role that future plays in personality formation. Individuals born into a particular culture are exposed to family and societal values and to their norms of acceptable behaviour. Culture also defines how the different roles in that society are to be performed. Culture helps determine broad patterns of behavioural similarity among people, but differences—at times extreme—in behaviour usually exist among individuals within a culture; that is, most cultures are not homogeneous. For example, the work ethic (hard work is valued, an unwillingness to work is sinful) usually is associated with western cultures. But this value doesn't influence everyone within those cultures to the same degree. Thus, although culture has an impact on the development of employees' personalties, not all individuals respond to cultural influences equally. Indeed, one of the most serious errors that managers can make is to assume that their subordinates are just like themselves.

(b) Family

The primary vehicle for socialising an individual into a particular culture is the person's immediate family. Both parents and siblings play important roles in personality development for most individuals. Members of an extended family—grandparents, aunts, uncles, and cousins also can influence personality formation. In particular, parents—or a single parent influence their children's development in three important ways:

- Through their own behaviours, they present situations that bring out certain behaviours in children.
- They serve as role models with which children often strongly identify.
- They selectively reward and punish certain behaviours.

The family's situation also is an important source of personality differences. Situational influences include the family's socio-economic level, size, race, religion, and geographic location; birth order within the family; parent's educational level; and so on. For example, a person raised in poor family simply has different experiences and opportunities than does a person raised in a wealthy family. Being an only child is different in some important respects from being raised with several brothers and sisters.

(c) Group Membership

The first group to which most individuals belong is the family. People also participate in various groups during their lives, beginning with their childhood playmates and continuing through teenaged schoolmates, sports teams, and social groups, and on into adult work and social groups. The numerous roles and experiences people have as members of groups represent another important source of personality differences. Although playmates and school groups early in life may have the strongest influences on personality formation, social and group experiences in later life continue to influence and shape personality. Understanding someone's personality requires understanding the groups—past and present—to which that person belongs.

III. Cultural Factors

Culture is traditionally considered as the major determinant of an individual's personality. The culture largely determines what a person is and what a person will learn. The culture within a person is brought up, is very important determinant of behaviour of a person. *Culture is the complex of these beliefs, values, and techniques for dealing with the environment which are shared among contemporaries and transmitted by one generation to the next*. Culture required both conformity and acceptance from its members. There are several ways of ensuring that members comply with the dictates of the culture. Such socialisation takes place through the early training given to the young of a culture, through establishing mores and through informal pressure to obey certain ways of behaving. The personality of an individual to a marked extend determined by the culture in which he is brought up. According to Mussen "each culture expects, and trains, its members to behave in the ways that are acceptable to the group." In spite of the importance of the culture on personality, researchers were unable to establish linear relationship between these two concepts 'personality' and 'culture'.

IV. Situational Factors

A third factor, the situation, influences the effects of heredity and environment on personality. An individual's personality, although generally stable and consistent, does change indifferent situations. The different demands of different situations call forth different aspects of one's personality. We should not, therefore, look at personality patterns in isolation.

It seems only logical to suppose that situations will influence an individual's personality, but a near classification scheme that would tell us the impact of various types of situations has so far eluded us. "Apparently we are not yet close to developing a system for clarifying situations so that they might be systematically studied." However, we do know that certain situations are more relevant than others in influencing personality.

Human personality is also influenced by situational factors. The effect of environment is quite strong. Knowledge, skill and language are obviously acquire and represent important modifications of behaviour.

PERSONALITY DEVELOPMENT AND SOCIALISATION

Study of, and research on, the development of personality has traditionally been an important area for understanding human behaviour. Modern developmental psychology does not get into the argument of heredity *versus* environment or of maturation (changes that result from heredity and physical development) *versus* learning. The human being consists of both physiological and psychological interacting parts. Therefore, heredity, environment, maturation, and learning all contribute to the human personality.

The study of personality has attempted to identify specific physiological and psychological stages that occur in the development of the human personality. This "stage" approach has been theoretical in nature. There are many well-known stage theories of personality development. However, as with most aspects of personality there is little agreement about the exact stages. In fact, a growing number of today's psychologists contend that there are no identifiable stages. Their argument is that personality development consists of a continuous process and the sequence is based solely upon the learning opportunities available.

I. Adult Life Stages

The work of *Daniel Levinson* on adult life stages has received attention. At first, he believed that "the life structure evolves through a relatively orderly sequence throughout the adult years," and, unlike other stage theories that were event-oriented (for example, marriage, parenthood, or retirement), his was age-based. In particular, he believed there was little variability (a maximum of two or three years) in four identifiable stable periods :

(i) Entering the adult world (ages twenty-two to twenty-eight).
(ii) Settling down (ages thirty-three to forty).
(iii) Entering middle adulthood (ages forty-five to fifty).
(iv) Culmination of middle adulthood (ages fifty-five to sixty).

He identified four transitional periods :

(i) Age-thirty transition (ages twenty-eight to thirty-three).
(ii) Mid-life transition (ages forty to forty-five).
(iii) Age-fifty transition (ages fifty to fifty-five).
(iv) Late adult transition (ages sixty to sixty-five).

Like historically significant stage theories of personality such as those of *Sigmund Freud* and *Erik Erikson*, *Levinson's* theory of adult life stages had a lot of intuitive and popular appeal, but, as is also the case with previous stage theories, the research evidence is quite mixed. For example, one study utilising longitudinal data found no support for *Levinson's* hypothesis that there should be greater variability in work attitudes during transitional as compared with stable developmental periods or that the greatest variability occurs during the mid-life transition. In other words, there may be such large individual differences among people that stage theories such as *Levinson's* don't really hold up. As a result, Levinson has reformulated his stages into what he now calls "eras" (early adult, mid-life, and late adult) and includes a transition-in period, a period of stability, and a transition-out period. In contrast to his earlier work discussed above, in which mobility or stability characterised whole stages of development, this new approach examines the interplay of mobility and stability within each life stage.

Hall has synthesised Levinson's theory and other adult stage theories (in particular the work of Erikson and Super) into an over all model for career stages. Figure 2 shows that there are four major career stages. During the first stage there is considerable exploration. The young employee is searching for an identity and undergoes considerable self-examination and role tryouts. This stage usually results in taking a number of different jobs and is, in general, a very unstable and relatively unproductive period in the person's career. In the second stage, establishment, the employee begins to settle down and indicates a need for intimacy. This is usually a growing productive period in the employee's career. The third stage of maintenance occurs when the person levels off onto a highly productive plateau and has a need for generativity (the concern to leave something to the next generation). This need often leads the person to assume a paternalistic or perhaps a mentor role with younger subordinates. As shown in Fig. 2, the person may either

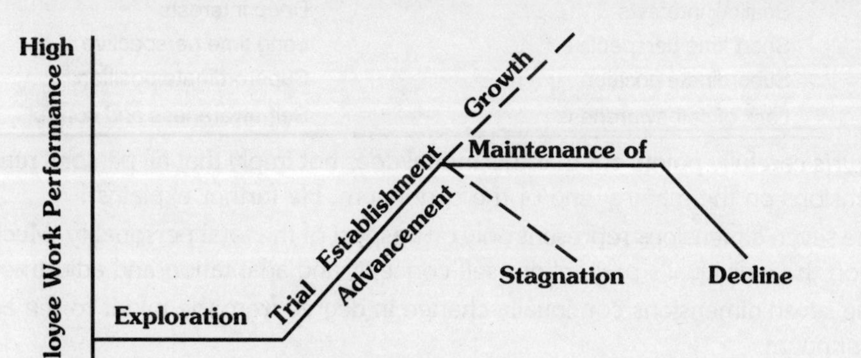

Fig. 2. *Douglas T. Hall's Career Stage Model.*

have a growth spurt or become stagnant and decline during this third career stage. The final stage, decline, is self-explanatory. The person indicates a need for integrity (that is the person needs to feel satisfied with his or her life choices and overall career). With the recent changes in mandatory retirement laws (there is no longer an upper age limit for mandatory retirement), better medical treatment, and the expectations of society concerning "gray power", this last stage may undergo drastic changes in the years ahead.

There is recent evidence that the heretofore assumed direct, linear relationship between age and job satisfaction may not be true. As Fig. 2 shows, toward the end of employees' careers, there may be a downturn in their satisfaction. This decline would agree with the career stage model, shown in Fig. 2, but may be happening at an earlier age. The decline may be the result of unmet expectations and the downsizing and "merger mania" that have left long-term employees feeling unwanted and with no sense of loyalty or belonging.

II. Immaturity to Maturity

In a departure from the strict stage approach, well-known organisational behaviour theorist Chris Argyris has identified specific dimensions of the human personality as it develops. Argyris proposes that the human personality, rather than going through precise stages, progresses along a continuum from immaturity as an infant to maturity as an adult. However, at any age, people can have their degree of development plotted according to the seven dimensions shown in Table.

Table 1 :

Immaturity Characteristics	Maturity Characteristics
Passivity	Activity
Dependence	Independence
Few ways of behaving	Diverse behaviour
Shallow interests	Deep interests
Short time perspective	Long time perspective
Subordinate position	Superordinate position
Lack of self-awareness	Self-awareness and control

Argyris carefully points out that this model does not imply that all persons reach or strive for all dimensions on the mature end of the continuum. He further explains :

(i) The seven dimensions represent only one aspect of the total personality. Much also depends upon the individual's perception, self-concept, and adaptation and adjustment.

(ii) The seven dimensions continually change in degree from the infant to the adult end of the continuum.

(iii) The model, being only a construct, cannot predict specific behaviour. However, it does provide a method of describing and measuring the growth of any individual in the culture.

(iv) The seven dimensions are based upon latent characteristics of the personality, which may be quite different from the observable behaviour.

In contrast to the classic stage theories of *Freud* and *Erikson, Argyris'* immaturity-maturity model of personality is specifically directed to the study and analysis of organisational behaviour. Argyris assumes that the personalities of organisational employees can be generally described by the mature end of the continuum. This being the case, in order to obtain full expression of employees' personalities, the formal organisation should allow for activity rather than passivity, independence rather than dependence, long rather than short time perspective, occupation of a position higher than that of peers, and expression of deep, important abilities. Argyris argues that too often the exact opposite occurs. The mature organisational participant becomes frustrated and anxious and is in conflict with the modern formal organisation. In other words. Argyris sees a basic incongruity between the needs of the mature personality and the nature of the formal organisation.

This incongruity premise is an important cornerstone for the entire conceptualisation of person-organisation structure interaction, which is discussed in relation to the organisational behaviour model used in this text. The fit between individual personality characteristics and organisational requirements is also frequently used today to explain job performance and work-related attitudes.

The Emerging Recognition of the Importance of Emotional Maturity, or EQ

Argyris recognised the important role that maturity may play in organisational behaviour many years ago. Very recently this concept has resurfaced in the popular press as emotional maturity or emotional intelligence or (as a takeoff from IQ) simply EQ. Based on research in both the neurological and behavioural sciences over the last ten years, it seems that a person's EQ may be a much better predictor of success (in school, in at least certain jobs, and in life) than the traditionally revered IQ (intelligence as measured by standardised tests). People with high EQ delay gratification (reason over impulsiveness), understand their own feelings, and, especially important in organisational behaviour, have a great deal of empathy for the feelings of others. This emotional maturity starts to develop at an early age and continues to develop both neurologically and through socialisation. Those who have developed high EQ know how to

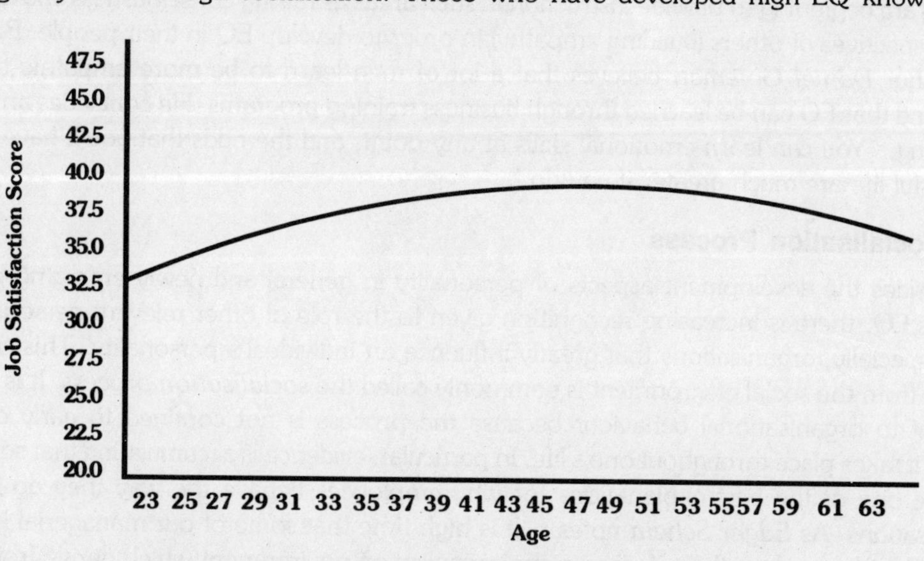

Fig. 3. *The Relationship between Age and Job-satisfaction.*

regulate their emotions, such as anger (the most difficult) or anxiety, in a way that enhances success on the job and in life.

EQ provides a way to operationalise the "people skills" that are considered so important in many careers. For example, *Seligman* designed a test of how people respond to setbacks (optimistically or pessimistically). He developed hypothetical questions to which the person was to choose the response most closely matching his or her own. Here are some sample questions :

(i) You owe the library $10 for an overdue book.
   (a) When I am really involved in what I am reading, I often forget when it's due.
   (b) I was so involved in writing the report, I forgot to return the book.

(ii) A friend says something that hurts your feelings.
   (a) He/she always blurts things out without thinking of others.
   (b) My friend was in a bad mood and took it out on me.

(iii) You are penalised for returning your income tax late.
   (a) I always put off doing my taxes.
   (b) I was lazy about getting my taxes done this year.

He found that sales people at the Metropolitan Life Insurance Company who answered with more b's than a's were better able to overcome bad sales days, recovered more easily from rejection, and changed jobs less frequently (major problems in the insurance industry). Also, EQ may be an overlooked dimension of predicting effective leadership. High-EQ leaders would seem to have empathy and graciousness as well as the uncanny ability to read a social situation (the great majority of emotional communication is nonverbal). Such characteristics may be more associated with effective leaders than are raw intelligence and technical skills.

To take advantage of this newly found personality attribute, human resources management trainers are beginning to provide instruction in such areas as raising consciousness and integrating the perspectives of others (building empathy) in order to develop EQ in their people. Best-selling EQ author *Daniel Goleman* believes that a lot of men learn to be more empathic from their wives and that EQ can be learned through business training programs. He concludes an interview by noting, "You can learn emotional skills at any point, and the odds that you'll have a happy, successful life are much greater if you do."

The Socialisation Process

Besides the development aspects of personality in general and newly emerging constructs such as EQ, there is increasing recognition given to the role of other relevant persons, groups, and, especially, organisations that greatly influence an individual's personality. This continuous impact from the social environment is commonly called the *socialisation process*. It is especially relevant to organisational behaviour because the process is not confined to early childhood; rather, it takes place throughout one's life. In particular, evidence is accumulating that socialisation may be one of the best explanations for why employees behave the way they do in today's organisations. As *Edger Schein* notes : "It is high time that some of our managerial knowledge and skill be focused on those forces in the organisation environment which derive from the fact that organisations are social systems which do socialise their new members. If we do not learn to analyse and control the forces of organisational socialisation, we are abdicating one of our primary managerial responsibilities." A recent study found that the socialisation tactics that organisations employ can have a positive, long-run impact on the adjustment of newcomers (i.e., lower role conflict and ambiguity, less stress, and higher job satisfaction and commitment).

Socialisation starts with the initial contact between a mother and her new infant. After infancy, other members of the immediate family (father, brothers, and sisters), close relatives and family friends and then the social group (peers, school friends, and members of the work group) play influential roles. Of particular interest is *Schein's* idea that the organisation itself also contributes to socialisation. He points out that the process includes only the learning of those values, norms, and behaviour patterns which, from the organisation's and the work group's points of view, are necessary for any new organisation member to learn.

The following are widely accepted characteristics of the organisational socialisation of employees :

(i) Change of attitudes, values, and behaviours.
(ii) Continuity of socialisation over time.
(iii) Adjustment to new jobs, work groups, and organisational practices.
(iv) Mutual influence between new recruits and their managers.
(v) Criticality of the early socialisation period.

Accordingly, organisation members must learn such things as not to drive a Ford if they are working for Chevrolet, not to criticise the company in public, and not to wear the wrong kind of clothes or be seen in the wrong kind of place. They must understand "who holds power and who does not, which informal networks of communication are reliable and which are unreliable, and what political manoeuvres they are likely to encounter in their department or unit. In short, if they wish to survive and prosper in their new work home, they must soon come to 'know the ropes'." The same is true for those in overseas assignments. They must be socialised into the correct conduct in dealing with the local culture.

Specific techniques of socialising new employees would include the use of mentors or role models, orientation and training programs, reward systems, and career planning. Specific steps that can lead to successful organisational socialisation would include the following :

(i) Provide a challenging first job.
(ii) Provide relevant training.
(iii) Provide timely and consistent feedback.
(iv) Select a good first supervisor to be incharge of socialisation.
(v) Design a relaxed orientation program.
(vi) Place new recruits in work groups with high morale.

Such deliberate socialisation strategies have tremendous potential impact on human resources management and organisational effectiveness.

MAJOR PERSONALITY ATTRIBUTES

According to the personality characteristics, there are four types of needs that people have at work. These are : needs for achievement, affiliation, autonomy, and dominance. Those who have high need for achievement engage themselves proactively in work behaviour in order to feel proud about their achievements and successes; those having high need for affiliation work co-operatively with others; those having high need for autonomy like to work in an environment with less close supervision; and those with high need for dominance are very effective in an environment where they can actively enforce their legitimate authority.

I. Machiavellianism

Machiavellianism refers to manipulation of others as a primary way of achieving one's goals. *Mach scale* measures the extent to which an individual tends to be machiavellian. People with high score on much scale, tend to be cool, logical in assessing the system around them, willing to twist and turn facts to influence others, and try to gain control of people, events, and situations by manipulating the system to their advantage.

II. Locus of Control

Locus of control refers to the extent to which individuals believe that they can control events affecting them. On the one hand, individuals who have a high internal locus of control (internals) believe that their own behaviour and actions primarily (but not necessarily totally) affect the events in their lives. On the other hand, individuals who have a high external locus of control (externals) believe that chance, fate, or other people primarily determine the events in their lives. Locus of control typically is considered to be a part of the conscientiousness factor.

Many differences between internals and externals are significant in explaining some aspects of behaviour in organisations and other social settings. Evidence indicates that internals control their own behaviour better, are more active politically and socially, and seek information about their situations more actively than do externals. Compared to externals, internals are more likely to try to influence or persuade others and are less likely to be influenced by others. Internals often are more achievement oriented than externals. Compared to internals, externals appear to prefer a more structured, directive style of supervision. A recent study showed that managers with a high internal locus of control adjusted more readily to international transfers than did managers with a high external locus of control. Recall that we are particularly interested in the relationship between these personality dimensions and behaviours.

III. Tolerance for Ambiguity

Based on personality characteristics, some people can tolerate high level of ambiguity without experiencing undue stress and still function effectively while people who have a low tolerance for ambiguity may be effective in structured work setting but it is almost impossible to operate effectively when things are rapidly changing and much information about the future turn of events is not available. Generally managers have to work in an environment full of uncertainty because of rapid change; therefore, they have to develop high level of tolerance for ambiguity.

IV. Introversion and Extraversion

In everyday speech, the labels introvert and extravert describe a person's congeniality: An introvert is shy and retiring, whereas an extravert is socially gregarious and outgoing. The terms have similar meanings when used to refer to a personality dimension. Introversion is a tendency to be directed inward and have a greater sensitivity to abstract ideas and personal feelings. Introverts are quiet, introspective, and emotionally unexpressive. Extraversion is an orientation toward other people, events, and objects, extraverts are sociable, lively, impulsive, and emotionally expressive.

Although some people exhibit the extremes of introversion and extraversion, most are only moderately introverted or extraverted or relatively balanced between the extremes Introverts and extraverts are widely distributed across educational levels, genders, and occupations. As might be expected, extraverts are well represented in managerial occupations because the manager's decisional role often involves identifying and solving problems with and through other people. Research even suggests that some extraversion may be essential to managerial success. However, either extreme extraversion or extreme introversion can interfere with an individual's effectiveness in an organisation. One of the most striking implications of the introversion-extraversion personality dimension involves task performance in different environments. The evidence suggests that introverts perform better alone and in a environment that is quiet, whereas extraverts perform better in an environment with greater sensory stimulation, such as a noisy office with many people and a high level of activity.

V. Work-ethic Orientation

People may have different work-ethic orientation. The extremely work-ethic-oriented people get greatly involved in the job and live up to being described as living, eating and breathing the job. For such people, work becomes the only consideration of satisfaction and they have very little outside interests. On the other hand, people with low work-ethic orientation try to do the minimum that is necessary to get without being fired on the job. For effective organisations, people with high work-ethic orientation are necessary as compared to extremely high or low work-ethic orientation because the extremely high work-ethic-oriented people will burn their energy too quickly creating lot of health problems, thus, affecting long-term organisational effectiveness adversely, while people with low work-ethic orientation will not be able to achieve anything meaningful for the organisation.

Based on the above discussion, some conclusions can be drawn about the desirable personality characteristics for effective managers. Apart from possessing the necessary managerial skills and abilities, managers need to have high level of self-concept, high level of tolerance for ambiguity, A type of personality good mix of needs for achievement, affiliation and power, internal locus of control, are relatively extroverts, and have high work-ethic orientation.

VI. Self-esteem

Self-esteem is the evaluation that an individual makes of himself or herself. People have opinions of their own behaviours, abilities, appearance, and worth. These general assessments, or judgments, of worthiness are affected somewhat by situations, success or failure, and the opinions of others. Nevertheless, they are stable enough to be widely regarded as a basic personality tradition or dimension. In terms of the big five personality factors, self-esteem most likely would be part of the adjustment factor.

Self-esteem affects behaviour in organisations and other social settings in several important ways. For example, self-esteem is related to initial vocational choice. Individuals with high self-esteem take risks in job selection, are attracted to high-status occupations, and are more likely to choose unconventional or nontraditional jobs than individuals with low self-esteem. A study of college students looking for a job reported that those with high self-esteem (i) received more favourable evaluation from organisational recruiters, (ii) were more satisfied with the job search, (iii) received more job offers, and (iv) were more likely to accept jobs before graduation than were students with low self-esteem. Self-esteem is related to numerous social and work behaviours. For example, individuals with low self-esteem are more easily influenced and individuals with high self-esteem are less easily influenced by the opinions of other workers. Further, individuals with high self-esteem place more value on actually attaining those goals than do employees with low self-esteem. Individuals with low self-esteem are more susceptible than are high self-esteem employees to adverse job conditions-stress, conflict, ambiguity, poor supervision, poor working conditions, and the like. In a general sense, self-esteem is positively related to attempts to achieve or a willingness to expend effort to accomplish tasks. Clearly, self-esteem is an important in individual difference in terms of effective work behaviour.

VII. Self Monitoring

A personality trait that has recently received increased attention is called self-monitoring. It refers to an individual's ability to adjust his or her behaviour to external, situational factors.

Individuals high in self-monitoring show considerable adaptability in adjusting their behaviour to external situational factors. They are highly sensitive to external cues and can behave differently in different situations. High self-monitors are capable of presenting striking contradictions between their public persona and their private self. Low self-monitors can't disguise themselves in that way. They tend to display their true dispositions and attitudes in every situation; hence, there is high behavioural consistency between who they are and what they do.

VIII. Risk Taking

People differ in their willingness to take chances. This propensity to assume or avoid risk has been shown to have an impact on how long it takes managers to make a decision and how much information they require before making their choice. For instance, seventy-nine managers worked on simulated personnel exercises that required them to make hiring decisions. High risk-taking managers made more rapid decisions and used less information in making their choices than did the low risk-taking managers. Interestingly, the decision accuracy was the same for both groups.

IX. Type A and B

Personality has been grouped into two categories denotes by alphabets A and B.

Type A's

(i) Are always moving, walking, and eating rapidly;
(ii) Feel impatient with the rate at which most events take place;
(iii) Strive to think or do two or more things at once;
(iv) Cannot cope with leisure time;
(v) Are obsessed with numbers, measuring their success in terms of how many or how much of everything they acquire?

In contrast to the Type A personality is the Type B, who is exactly opposite. Type B's are "rarely harried by the desire to obtain a wildly increasing number of things or participate in an endless growing series of events in an ever-decreasing amount of time."

Type B's

(i) Never suffer from a sense of time urgency with its accompanying impatience;
(ii) Feel no need to display or discuss either their achievements or accomplishments unless such exposure is demanded by the situation;
(iii) Play for fun and relaxation, rather than to exhibit their superiority at any cost;
(iv) Can relax without guilt.

Type A's operate under moderate to high levels of stress. They subject themselves to more or less continuous time pressure, creating for themselves a life of deadlines. These characteristics result in some rather specific behavioural outcomes. For example, Type A's are fast workers, because they emphasise quantity over quality. In managerial positions, Type A's demonstrate their competitiveness by working long hours and, not infrequently, making poor decisions because they make them too fast. Type A's are also rarely creative. Because of their concern with quantity and speed, they rely on past experiences when faced with problems. They will not allocate the time that is necessary to develop unique solutions to new problems. The rarely vary in their responses to specific challenges in their milieu; hence, their behaviour is easier to predict than that of Type B's.

THEORIES OF PERSONALITY

Many personality theorists, not only from the field of psychology but even from other fields dealing with human behaviour also, have carried on researches to find answers to the questions; What is personality? What does personality constitute? How is behaviour governed by personality? The various theorists, however, could not give the answers on which consensus could be reached; rather these have resulted into a number of theories of personality. Just as everyone has his own definition of personality, practically everyone has his own theory of personality. Thus, grouping the various theories and labelling the various categories becomes a difficult task. Each theorist cannot really be grouped with another, even though he may have operated from similar positions. However, the most logical grouping of personality theories seems to be into *Psychoanalytic, Type theories, Trait, and Self theories.*

I. PSYCHOANALYTIC THEORY

Psychoanalytic theory is based on the notion that man is motivated more by unseen forces than he is controlled by conscious and rational thought. Although *Sigmund Freud* is most closely related with this theory, others, such as *Carl Jung, Alfred Adler, Karen Korney*, and *Eric Fromm*, who all broke from *Freud*, made additional contributions. Clinical techniques were used primarily to develop psychoanalytic theory. *Freud* noted that his patients' behaviour could not always be consciously explained. This clinical finding held him to conclude that major motivating forces in man was unconscious framework. This framework contains three aspects, though interrelated but often conflicting. These are *id*, *ego* and *super ego*. They are so interrelated that they can only be artificially separated for individual study and analysis.

(i) The Id

It is the original and most basic system of human personality. It consists of everything psychologically that is inherited and present at the time of birth. At the base of the Freudian theory lies the id that is primitive, instinctual and governed by the principles of greedy and pleasure. Id represents a storehouse of all instincts, containing in its dark depths—all wishes, desires that unconsciously direct and determine our behaviour. Id is largely childish, irrational, never-satisfied, demanding and destructive of others. But id is the foundation upon which all other parts of personality are erected.

One notable characteristic of id is that it cannot tolerate uncomfortable levels of tension within it and seeks to release the tension as soon as it develops. The methods for dealing with tension by id are noteworthy. They are :

(i) Primary processes
(ii) Reflex actions.

The former attempts to discharge a tension by forming a mental image of desirable means of releasing the tension. But this kind of tension release is temporary and mental, and would not satisfy the real need. For instance, if a person is hungry the id deals with the situation by creating a mental image of desirable and good food that is palatable.

(ii) Ego

As an individual learns to separate the unreality from reality in childhood, the ego develops. The ego is reality-oriented part of thinking; it is largely practical and works in an executive capacity. Ego is rational and logical and in essence it is the conscious mediator between the realities of world and the id's demands. Its constantly works to keep a healthy psychological balance between id's impulsive demands and superego's restrictive guidance. Ego is rational master. The ego is said to be the executive part of the personality because it controls the gateway to action, selects the features of the environment to which it will respond, and decides what instincts will be satisfied.

One essential feature of ego is that it regulated and integrates the inner motives and conflicting demands, defends the person by using defense mechanism, and masters the person's goals. The ego develops by creating an effective perceptual mechanism that enables a person to adjust to the reality principle viz., tolerance of tension, expectation of punishment, awareness of things and associated inhibitions of actions. The most important characteristic of ego is that it has the ability to distinguish between mental images and actual sources of tension release, and it responds to the real sources of tension reduction. The ego performs this task by :

(a) Observing accurately what exists in the outside world (perceiving),
(b) Recording these experiences carefully (remembering), and
(c) Modifying the external world in such a way as to satisfy the instinctual wishes (acting).

Although ego contains no energy. *Freud* is of the view that it controls behaviour by means of the approach-avoidance conflict, turning the energy of id against itself. It governs how people act, what they say and think consciously. It attempts to find acceptable ways or solution to many demands and problems of an individual. If the ego succeeds, the individual is content, otherwise he will be dissatisfied and have a mental stress, ambivalence and burnout.

(iii) Superego

Superego represents noblest thoughts, ideals, feelings that are acquired by a person from his parents, teachers, friends, religion, organisation and colleagues etc. As a child grows and absorbs parental and cultural attitudes and values, he develops a superego. It is also labelled as "*ago-ideal*" that tells an individual what is acceptable. Superego is the moralistic segment of the human personality. The primary concern of superego is to determine whether the action proposed by "ego" is right or wrong so that the individual acts in accordance with the values and standards of the society. If people violate the prohibitions of superego they may feel guilty (by cursing themselves they have self-punishment).

Defence Mechanisms

The id, ego and superego will always be in conflict. Conflicts among the id (the pleasure seeking element), the superego (the noble and idealistic element) and the ego (the compromising element) results in defensive mechanisms that are necessary to reduce the tension and anxiety caused by conflict. These defence mechanisms may be—*aggression*, *repression*, *rationalisation*, *reaction*, *projection*, and *interjection*.

(a) Aggression

People become aggressive and attack a person or situation when conflict arises. A pure case of aggression results when the perceived source of tension and anxiety is attacked by the person who is affected. Sometimes, the aggression may be directed toward some innocent or uninvolved party. For instance, after confronting the dissatisfied customer, a manager may be aggressive toward a subordinate when he meets first after the aforesaid confrontation with the customer.

(b) Repression

Sometimes people resort to repression i.e., deliberately forgetting the issue. For instance, when a person is torn between the necessity of earning a living and the demands of a monotonous job would like to stay home from work. Through absenteeism he is avoiding at least a part of the threatening situation. But the problems cannot be solved by repressive defence, they simply be postponed.

Rationalisation. Here the individual resorts to redefinition of the situation that is anxiety or conflict producing. Ego tries to find excuses for the problem, and therefore, not conductive to problem-solving and personality development of the individual. For instance, a professor who is unable to deliver lecture effectively resorts to defensive mechanism by stating that there are some problems caused by non-serious students or may say "due to the unavailability of modern teaching aids I could not do much justice."

(c) Reaction formation

If an individual is uncomfortable with existing problem the ego may repress the problem and substitute it opposite. For instance, if an individual dislikes American lobby but is upset by this feeling, he may later on claim to like Americans.

(d) Projection

The ego denies sometimes that he has a particular emotions, feelings, actions especially when it causes the other person serious anxiety. Projection is a safely valve where ego blames something else without admitting the feelings or actions. Under projection a person imputes his feelings and actions to someone else.

(e) Interjection

Interjection, the opposite function, is one where ego takes in something from outside. (For example, my professor, my roommate, my bench-mate etc.) and sees it as a part of himself. Sociologists label this process "internalisation" which occurs when people start growing.

II. TYPE THEORIES

The type theories represent an attempt to scientifically describe personalities by classifying individuals into convenient categories. *Sheldon's* Physiognomy theory, *Carl Jung's* Extrovert and Introvert theory are some examples of type theories.

(i) Sheldon's Physiognomy Theory

William Sheldon has presented a unique body-type-temperamental model that represents a link between anatomical/psychological traits and characteristics of an individual with his behaviour. *Sheldon* identifies some relationship between the physique types of individuals and their personality temperaments. He identifies three body types—endomorph, mesomorph and ectomorph.

Endomorph. He is bulky and beloved. Sheldon contends that the endomorph to be rather fat, thick in proportion to his height. His personality temperament is viscertonic i.e., the person seeks comfort, loves fine food, eats too much, jovial, affectionate and liked-by-all person.

Mesomorph. He represents absolutely category two type person. He is basically strong, athletic and tough. His physique is appreciated by all. In fact, it is this personality all other "morphs" wish for. According to *Sheldon* he will tend to be somatotonic temperament i.e., he is fond of muscular activity; he tends to he highly aggressive, and self-assertive. He can run faster, smile brighter, and beats alone the other two 'morphs' together.

Ectomorph. The final category of people according to *Sheldon's* classification is the ectomorphs. These people are thin, long and poorly developed physically. Though physically weak, he leads the league in the intellectual department. His temperament is Cerebrotonic i.e., excessive inhibition, restraint, and avoidance of social contacts etc. He is labelled as absent-minded, shy, but brilliant university professor stereotype.

(ii) Carl Jung's Extrovert and Introvert Theory

Carl Jung, proposed his own two part theory of personality. Extroverts are optimistic, outgoing gregarious and sociable. Extrovert is basically objective, a reality-oriented individual who is much more doer than a thinker.

Introverts, by contrast, are more inward-directed people. They are less sociable, withdrawn and absorbed in inner life. Normally, a person who has few friends, avoids social contacts, and rarely speaks to others unless they speak first might be characterised as being introverted. Extroverts, on the other hand, are friendly, enjoy interaction with others, crave excitement and dislike solitude. Introverts, however, are being quite, retiring, enjoying solitude etc. According this theory, the personality has four dimensions :

- *Thinking* : It includes logical reasoning (rational, analytic)
- *Feeling* : It refers to the interpretation of a thing or event on a subjective scale (emotional, effect)
- *Sensation* : it deals with perception of thing in general sense (factual and concrete)
- *Intuition* : It is based on unconscious inner perception of the potentialities or events or things (associative or gestalt)

III. TRAIT THEORY

Trait theory visualises personality as a reflection of certain traits of the individual. Even though there are many traits that are common to most people, there are many other traits that are unique to a person and are not shared by other individuals. On the basis of the trait theory, people can be described as aggressive, loyal, pleasant, flexible, rumorous, sentimental, impulsive, cool and so on. Traits are the basic elements of personality and can be used to summarise behaviour. For example, if we saw people behaving in an extrovert and forceful manner in most situations, we could label their personality as aggressive. Similarly, if a person is observed in different situations as letting someone else take the initiative in deciding what to do, we could describe his personality trait as "submissive".

Cattel used groups of traits to describe the underlying structure of personality. He compiled a list of words that can be used to describe personality traits. He put these traits into two basic categories. These are the source traits and the surface traits. For example, stammering would be a surface trait resulting from the basic source trait of timidity. Some of the surface traits are : wise-foolish, sociable-exclusive, honest-dishonest and so on. Similarly, some of the source trait categories are : trustful-suspicious, forthright-shrewd, relaxed-tense, dominant-submissive, cheerfulness-depressed and so on.

(i) Allport's Trait Theory

One of the most exciting versions of trait theory is provided by *Allport* wherein he mentions common traits that are used to compare one personality with other. For such comparison he has identified six categories of values—social, political, religious, theoretical, economic, and aesthetic—in his theory. Besides these common traits Allport also made use of some unique traits the individuals possess. He calls these unique traits as personal dispositions. They can be cardinal (most pervasive), central (unique and limited in number) or secondary (periphery). Allport thus recognises the complexity of human personality.

Each individual has values that emphasise these six orientations (common traits). Some individuals may be high in economic and low in others. It is the profile of an individual's values that is useful in defining his personality.

(ii) Cattel's Trait Theory

From out of several different and sometimes overlapping words representing personality, *Cattel* has selected one hundred and seventy-one words that can be used to describe personality. Using the factor analytic approach, he has identified two categories of traits and labelled them 'surface traits' and 'source traits'. In all he identified thirty surface traits and ten source traits. A surface trait is something like a medical cause of the diverse symptoms. An example of surface trait is affectionate *versus* cold. An example of source trait is dominance *versus* submissiveness.

Evaluation of Trait Theories

When compared to type theories, trait theories have some sense. Instead of making unrealistic attempt to place personalities into discrete, discontinuous categories, trait theories give recognition to continuity of personalities. But the trait theories suffer from the following limitations :

(a) Traits may be too abstract. For example, the scale of 'measuring' 'anxiety' may be abstract.

(b) Traits approach focuses on isolated traits without specifying how these traits are organised within the personality. Without knowing which traits are more important and how they are related to other traits of an individual, it is not possible to make adequate description of an individual's personality. For instance an individual who scores high on a measure "compulsiveness" may engage in useless repetitive rituals, thereby interfering with the expression of other traits or show dogged determination to stay with a productive task, thus capturing advantage of other personality traits also.

(c) Another fundamental problem (or drawback) of trait theories is that they are essentially descriptive rather than analytical.

IV. SELF THEORY

Of many contemporary theories the one that has received the most recent emphasis is the self-theory of personality. Self theory rejects both psychoanalytic and behaviouristic conceptions of human nature as too mechanistic portraying people as creatures helplessly buffeted about by internal instincts or external stimuli. *Carl Rogers* is most closely associated with this approach of self-theory. Rogers and his associates have developed this personality theory that places emphasis on the individual as an initiating, creating, influential determinant of behaviour within the environmental framework. According to *Rogers* there are three basic ingredients of personality—the organism, the phenomenal field, and the self. To understand the *Roger's theory* we have to see :

(i) The self concept,
(ii) The organism and,
(iii) The development of self.

(i) Self-Concept

This theory is organised around the concept that personality and behaviour are largely determined by the individual himself. We tend to act in ways that are consistent with our own image of who we are. For example, a man known as a flirt would hardly stop at flirting. *Carl Rogers* is most closely associated with this theory. According to him, the best vantage point for understanding behaviour is from the internal frame of reference of the individual himself. An individual himself is the centre of experience. His self image is an integral of how he views himself and his perception of how others view him. This self-concept is a result of a person's interaction with his environment. This interaction in the form of learning experience helps us to develop, grow and mature, and we modify our self-concept as a result of these experiences. When we get positive feedback from others as a response to our behaviour, our self-concept is positively reinforced. On the other hand, when we get negative feedback from others, our self-regard is lowered, resulting in tension and anxiety.

From the point of view of organisational behaviour, the management must recognise that each individual's self-concept is unique and the application of various motivation, job enrichment and leadership styles will have different effects on different people. Thus, an employee with a self-concept of high intelligence, independence and confidence may not look for such reinforcement techniques as monetary rewards, job security or directive supervision. He may look for a challenging environment where he looks for recognition, responsibility and achievement. On the other hand, the monetary rewards and job security may be more effective on workers who have a self-concept of dependence, insecurity and who lack confidence in themselves.

There is yet another self in *Rogers self theory*. That is the ideal self. It represents the type of person an individual likes to be. This concept is similar to Freud's ego-ideal. If the ideal self is closer to the real self, then the individual will be more fulfilled and happy. On the other hand, if large discrepancy exists between these two then it results in an unhappy, dissatisfied individual.

(ii) The Organism

The organism is essentially the locus of all experience. The totality of experience is the phenomenal field. This field is known to the person himself and is frequently referred to as frame of reference. Behaviour of an individual is largely determined by the phenomenal field not by the stimulating conditions of event in the external field or environment.

The individual evaluates every experience in relation to his self-concept. The experiences may be symbolised or unsymbolised. When they are symbolised they become part of individual's consciousness. Conversely, when they are unsymbolised they remain outside the confines of the awareness or consciousness of an individual. The important thing here is that distorted symbolisation gives rise to inappropriate behaviour.

(iii) The Development of Self Personality

Rogers feels that the fundamental force motivating the human organism is self-actualisation i.e., "a tendency toward fulfilment, toward actualisation, toward the maintenance and enhancement of the organism." The tendency to self-actualisation of both the organism and the self is subject to the profound influence of the social environment, right from childhood. Actually, in the childhood itself, when the child's behaviour is evaluated continuously by their parents, he will be in a position to discriminate between thoughts and actions that are considered 'worthy' and 'unworthy'. He will be able to exclude the unworthy experiences from his self-concept.

Rogers maintains that the innate tendency toward self-actualisation often runs into conflict with two needs—the need for self-regard, and the need for positive reward. It is true that the latter need is universal whereas the former one is the internalisation of those actions and values that others approve. The regard may be conditional or unconditional. Ideally, the more completely the individual is given positive regard-acceptance that is not conditional to specific behaviours—the more congruence there will be between his self-concept and his actual experiences, as well as between his self-concept and ideal self.

Evaluation of the Self Theory

Self-concept is the result of one's perceptual process. It is a cognitive factor and maintained through thinking-related activities. The self-theory is appreciated on the ground that it is organised around the concept of self. It is the one in which personality and behaviour are largely determined by the individual whereas, in other theories, the individual is the only medium through which behaviour is elicited after having been acted on by elements over which he has no control.

Another positive point in favour of self theory is that the 'best advantage point for understanding is from the internal frame of reference of the individual himself. To Rogers the Individual is the centre of experience. To understand one's behaviour one should understand how that person views about himself.

In analysing organisational behaviour, it would be beneficial for the manager to understand the self-concept because this unique concept influences the way he should apply various reinforcement motivation and leadership techniques in the process of maintaining these required amount of output. For instance, monetary rewards for performance, authoritarian leadership style and motivational strategies when applied to an intelligent, independent, confident, workers may be ineffective. These techniques may prove to be effective when are applied to the unintelligent, insecure, indecisive workers.

The self theory focuses on the person's world as he perceives it. It is the individual's perception and interpretation of the experiences that determine behaviour. But the trouble with the self theory is that it vaguely defines the term such as self-actualisation, self concepts etc., and such vague concepts will not be of much value in making precise predictions of behaviour of individuals. Of several other troubling criticisms are the accurate measurements of subjective experiences and the revealing of self.

Similarities of Individuals

Every person is unique; no one else has the same body, no one else has had the same learning experiences. Even the identical twins upon closer observation tend to be different. But there are some similarities in individuals. The major similarities among individuals are as follows :

(i) *Intelligence.* Almost all human beings have intelligence. Difference is a matter of degree only. People can determine cause-and-effect relationships, deduce, infer, have fantasies, and make generalisations from insights and experiences. Almost all individuals apply intelligence to adapt to wide range of environmental conditions—such as climate, weather, new atmosphere, new topography etc.

(ii) *Self-reflexiveness.* Another apparently unique characteristic of all individuals is self-reflexiveness. People not only know so much, but they are also aware of their knowledge. It gives people the power of making choices; they can set goals and objectives and also can determine how they can reach the preset targets.

(iii) *Language.* Another interesting similarity of people is the communication. Human beings have by far the most effective audio languages and the only written ones. Communication is one of the major building blocks organisation. Though people make use of different languages, the purpose of all the languages is same, i.e., to communicate.

(iv) *Tool-making.* People have inherent innovative abilities. They have the power to make tools that are essential for their livelihood. From the viewpoint of an organisation, they innovate new systems to increase productivity and to maintain the complex exchange process in modern society. (For example, currency)

(v) *Externally registered gains.* Almost all people have the ability to carry forward the accumulated gains. This is how the whole fabric of civilisation is passed into new ones. Libraries are eloquent testimony of this ability.

(vi) *Miscellaneous.* People have family structures, social relations, they can bind and plan time. Many people try to understand their very existence through religion. People generally do not wait until random events produce what they want.

Difference among Individuals

People are alike, yet different. One undeniable fact in light of several decades of research on individual is that "individual differences moderate the way the people respond to various aspects of organisations and to the practice of organisations". With respect to field of work individuals differ in many respects :

(i) People differ in the importance they attach to intrinsic rewards to the job. People with different psychological make-ups to indeed respond differently to challenging *versus* routine jobs. Some people prefer challenging jobs that afford scope for the expression of higher-level and skilled abilities. Under this assumptions, sometime back, it was felt that job enrichment was touted as prescriptive panacea for increasing productivity and morale. In organisations, however, there exist a substantial minority of people who seek job security, routine operations in their jobs, material benefits from the jobs etc. Therefore, people in work organisations attach different degrees of importance to rewards for performance and the kind of job they would like to perform.

(ii) People differ in the style of supervision. In organisations, some people welcome opportunities for providing necessary input into important decisions and like to be their own boss to the maximum extent. Some individuals, on the other hand, may like to extend a helpful guiding hand to others if they are loaded with work.

(iii) People differ in the type of compensation plan they want or desire. Some people in work organisations prefer a straight salary system and appear to work hard and harder under such a system. Paradoxically, in organisation some other type of people respond enthusiastically to wage-incentive schemes based on piece-rate or quality of work etc.

(iv) People differ in their tolerance for stress, their need for stimulation. Some people cannot bear stress for long. Surprisingly some other people possess resistance power to tolerate the stress in task for longer periods.

(v) People differ in their preferred schedules of work hours. No two individuals are alike with respect to their preferred schedules of work. Some people, as we notice in day-to-day life, are early birds who start work as early as 6 A.M. and some other kind of people who become panic to work before 10 A.M. Similarly some people prefer doing serious studies during night time whereas some other people prefer doing it early in the morning. For instance, to take the real life example, the author of this book is an early bird who likes to start work before 6' O clock in the morning, the co-author likes to work midnight and panics at the thought of beginning the day before 11 A.M.

SCALE OF PERSONALITY

The two broad personality scales that are most widely accepted by psychologists as descriptive of personality structure are the large, ubiquitous, and virtually unavoidable dimensions of extraversion and anxiety H.J. Eysenck, professor of Psychology at London University, has developed the Eysenck Personality Inventory (E.P.I) which measures these and also has a lie scale. Validation shows that it provides an excellent measure of extraversion but is not as good at measuring anxiety.

A caution is perhaps appropriate at this stage. Experimental psychologists in the field of personality research are apparently unable to reach firm conclusions, convincing and acceptable to other psychologists, as to the nature of extraversion. A good illustration of this difficulty is provided by examination of the literature on extraversion and conditioning, which reveals many contradictory findings that present theory cannot explain. But these two basic dimensions, extraversion and neuroticism, are so widely established in the literature and common parlance that it would be extremely difficult to dispense with them.

Extraversion

The extravert is oriented towards the outside world. He is characteristically outgoing and spontaneously more concerned with restructuring his environment than with analysing its effects on his "inner being." The extravert seems to have the capacity to suppress negative feedback or criticism. He is strong in drive and zestfully involved in accomplishing things. He is sometimes described by psychologists as a sociophile, i.e., he prefers to be with people. He is assertive—even on occasions, aggressive.

There is probably a genetic basis to extraversion, in the sense that the extravert seems capable of mobilising sufficient energy to maintain a high level of drive, which is presumably a function of his basic metabolism. It is possible to argue that there must be neural correlates of the psychological process of suppression, which inhibits negative feedback. Leaving aside this speculation, it is nevertheless possible to assert that an extraverted adolescent seems more able, for example, to ask a question at a public meeting. On the positive side, his assertive temperament enables him to contribute; and his suppression of negative feedback (in this case, people turning to look at him) will facilitate his continuance.

The introvert, the obverse of the extravert, is oriented towards the inner world of the psyche; he tends to be shy, withdrawn and inhibited in social affairs. The introvert is usually introspective and as such is more interested in the world of ideas than practical affairs. The Bernreuter personality questionnaire results, when analysed, show a strong correlation between neuroticism and introversion. Modern research findings support the view that the extraversion-introversion dichotomy is a far from simple dimension of personality and is in fact made up of a number of components which are organised within the framework of a type.

Anxiety

Apparently few executives, if any, escape the feeling of anxiety which seems to be the dominant theme of modern life. A great number of people, including many executives, seem to suffer from a kind of cosmic hypochondria, marked by a diffuse anxiety neurosis and frequently coupled with a vague sense of futility.

Anxiety is characterised by diffusion of emotion in the sense that the cause may be difficult to specify and the choice of focus open. This leads to a situation where psychologists are inclined to treat individuals as if they have a "free floating pool of anxiety" which is continually searching for a focus. In the *Meaning of Anxiety*, *Rollo May* has defined anxiety as "the apprehension cued off by a threat to some value which the individual holds essential to his existence as a personality."

Although at one time it was customary for clinical psychologists to view any form of anxiety as unhealthy, the contemporary attitude is a little different and is based on the notion that a low level of anxiety may have some utility. However, it is usual to treat neurotic anxiety as irrational, in the sense that even a logical explanation of a subject's anxieties may not necessarily lead to their alleviation.

It is not uncommon in modern experiments on anxiety to allocate subjects into the three categories. Research with soldiers going into combat and patients going for surgery supports the proposition that those who admit to moderate and high levels of anxiety face stress less well than those who admit only slight anxiety. For example, both soldiers engaged in combat and patients after surgical operations appear to make a more effective adjustment to the difficult circumstances in which they find themselves if they admit to a low level of anxiety. Apparently a low level of anxiety enables the subject to mobilise his resources more effectively. Much the same can be said about the *performance* of university students. There is some evidence from British research work to support the belief that slightly neurotic but highly intelligent students seem to have a certain advantage over their better adjusted but equally intelligent fellows.

These findings in regard to the functional significance of a low level of anxiety are congruent with the research of *F.E. Fiedler* in regard to the superiority of the psychologically distant executive in certain circumstances. Apparently executives also function better with a modest level of anxiety.

Guilt and anxiety are intimately related; anxiety is characterised by a sense of dread—a feeling that something ominous is going to happen. When people talk about their feelings of guilt, they describe feelings of anxiety, in this case arising from infringement of moral rules or the value system and accompanied by the feeling that they ought to be punished. Guilt becomes a source of frustration because it blocks our need for self-esteem. Most normal people, in the process of growing up, experience a need for rules of behaviour within which they can operate and exercise discretion.

Brainwashing in part depends upon the exploitation of this feeling of guilt. This technique of persuasion apparently works best when the subject is left on his own to mull over his "sins". If he is denied the support of his primary group to resist, he may well come up with the desired formulas. This may lead to the experience of conversion. The primary working group plays a key part both in work and incombat situations. Breaking up this primary work group seems to be an integral part of the brainwashing process, Communist self-criticism groups, and T groups. To many disinterested parties, there are remarkable similarities.

ORGANISATIONAL IMPLICATIONS

The personality dimensions identified and discussed have important implications for organisational behaviour. Note that we identified specific relationships for each personality dimension. However, you must not conclude that managers or work groups should try to change or otherwise directly control employee personality, which, of course, is impossible anyway. Even if such control were possible, it would be highly unethical. Rather, the challenge for managers and employees is to understand the crucial role played by personality in explaining some aspects of human behaviour in the workplace. Knowledge of important individual differences provides managers, other employees, and students of organisational behaviour with valuable insights and a framework that they can use to diagnose evens and situations.

ATTITUDES

Attitudes are determinants of behaviour because they are linked with perception, personality, and motivation. An attitude is a positive or negative feeling or mental state of readiness, learned and organised through experience, that exerts specific influence on a person's response to people, objects, and situations. Each of us has attitudes on numerous topics—about unions, exercise, dieting, career goals, friends, and tax laws, for example. This definition of attitude has certain implications for managers. First, attitudes are learned. Second, attitudes define our predispositions toward given aspects of the world. Third, attitudes provide the emotional basis of our interpersonal relations and identification with others. And fourth, attitudes are organised and are close to the core of personality. Some attitudes are persistent and enduring; yet, like each of the psychological variables, attitudes are subject to change.

Attitudes are evaluative statements relating to objects, people or events and thus, reflect how one feels about something. When an individual says, "He likes his job", is expressing his attitude about work. They relate to a more or less stable set or predisposition of opinion, interest or purpose involving expectancy of certain kind of experience with an appropriate response.

Newcomb defines attitudes as a condition of readiness to be motivated. It is neither behaviour nor a cause of behaviour. It is an intervening predisposition. It indicates how an individual is likely to behave in a certain situation. It is "a set to action with an emotional overtone".

DETERMINANTS OF ATTITUDES

I. Affect

The emotional, or "feeling," component of an attitude is learned from parents, teachers, and peer group members. One study illustrates how the affective component can be measured. A questionnaire was used to survey the attitudes of a group of students toward the church. The students then listened to tape recordings that either praised or disparaged the church. As the tapes played, students' emotional responses were measured with a galvanic skin response (GSR) device. Both prochurch and antichurch students respond with greater emotion (displayed by GSR changes) to statements that contradicted their attitudes than to those that reflected their attitudes.

II. Cognition

The cognitive component of an attitude consists of the person's perceptions, opinions, and beliefs. It refers to the thought processes, with special emphasis on rationality and logic. An important element of cognition is the evaluative beliefs held by a person. Evaluative beliefs are manifested as the favourable or unfavourable impressions someone holds toward an object or person.

III. Behaviour

The behavioural component of an attitude refers to a person's tendency to act toward someone or something in a certain way (friendly, warm, aggressive, hostile, or apathetic, for example). Such actions could be measured or assessed to examine the behavioural component of attitudes.

Fig. 4, presents the three components of attitude in terms of work factors such as job design, company policies, and fringe benefits. These stimuli trigger affective (emotional), cognitive (thought), and behavioural responses. In essence, the stimuli result in the formation of attitudes, which then lead to one or more responses (affective, cognitive, or behavioural).

The theory of affective, cognitive, and behavioural components as determinants of attitudes and attitude change has a significant implication for managers. They must be able to demonstrate that the positive aspects of contributing to the organisation outweigh the negative aspects. Many managers achieve effectiveness by developing generally favourable attitudes in their employees toward the organisation and the job.

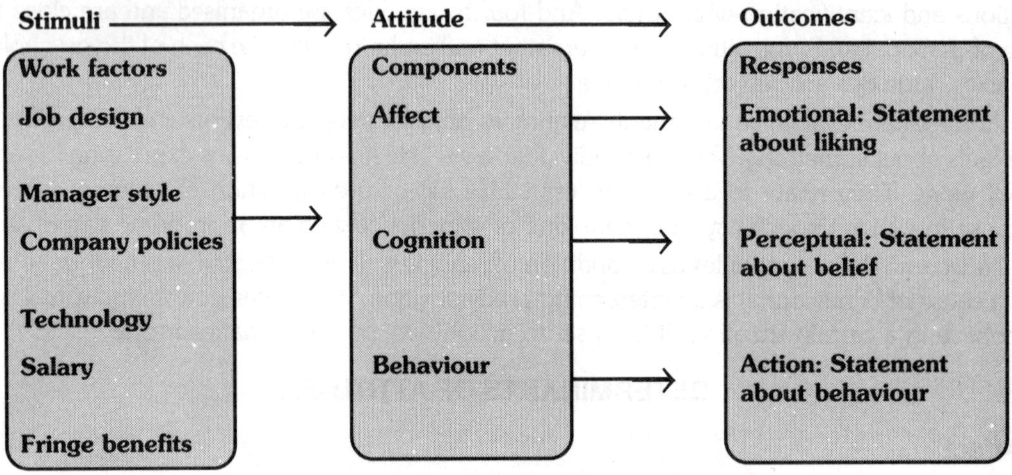

Fig. 4. *The Three Determinants of Attitude.*

Attitudes have many sources: family, peer groups, society, and previous job experiences. Early family experiences help shape individuals' attitudes. Young children's attitudes usually correspond to their parents. As children reach their teens, they begin to be more strongly influenced by peers. Peer groups influence attitudes because individuals want to be accepted by others. Teenagers seek approval by sharing similar attitudes or by modifying attitudes to comply with those of a group.

Culture, mores, and language influence attitudes. Attitudes of French Canadians toward France, of Americans toward people in Russia, and of Cubans toward capitalism are learned in society. Within the United States are subcultures—ethnic communities, ghetto communities, and religious groups—that help shape people's attitudes.

Through job experiences, employees develop attitudes about pay equity, performance review, managerial capabilities, job design, and work group affiliation. Previous experiences account for some individual differences in attitudes toward performance, loyalty, and commitment.

Individuals strive to maintain consistency among the components of attitudes. But contradictions and inconsistency often occur, resulting in a state of disequilibrium. The tension stemming from such a state is reduced only when some form of consistency is achieved.

The term ***cognitive dissonance*** describes a situation where there's a discrepancy between the cognitive and behavioural components of an attitude. Any form of inconsistency is uncomfortable so individuals attempt to reduce dissonance. Dissonance, then is viewed as a state within a person that, when aroused, elicits actions designed to return the person to a state of equilibrium. For example, the chief executive officer of a cigarette company may experience cognitive dissonance if she believes that she's honest and hardworking but that cigarettes contribute to lung cancer. She may think, "I'm a good human being, but I'm in charge of a firm producing a cancer-contributing product." These thoughts create inconsistency. Instead of quitting and giving up her successful career, she's more likely to modify her thoughts or cognitions. She could state, "Our firm has manufactured a cigarette that's now very safe and free of cancer-producing products." Or she may think that cigarette smoking actually improves smokers' mental well-being, that it helps them reduce or cope with stress. When inconsistency in attitudes arises, the person can attempt to work the problem out cognitively or behaviourally. Here the CEO used a cognitive process to reduce her dissonance.

Cognitive dissonance has important organisational implications. First, it helps explain the choices made by an individual with attitude inconsistency. Second, it can help predict a person's propensity to change attitudes. If individuals are required, for example, by the design of their jobs or occupations to say or do things that contradict their personal attitudes, they may change those attitudes to make them more compatible with what they have said or done.

THE NATURE AND DIMENSIONS OF ATTITUDES

Both personality and attitudes are complex cognitive processes. The difference is that personality usually is thought of as the whole person, while attitudes may make up the personality.

The term "attitude" frequently is used in describing people and explaining their behaviour. For example: "He has a poor attitude." "I like her attitude." "Our workers turn out poor-quality products because they have poor attitudes." More precisely, an attitude can be defined as a persistent tendency to feel and behave in a particular way toward some object. For example, George does not like working the night shift. He has a negative attitude toward his work assignment.

Attitudes can be characterised three ways. First, they tend to persist unless something is done to change them. For example, if George is transferred to the day shift, his attitude may become positive. Second, attitudes can fall anywhere along a continuum from very favourable to very unfavourable. At the present time, George's attitude may be moderately unfavourable. If he is transferred to the day shift, his attitude may change to highly favourable. Third, attitudes are directed toward some object about which a person has feelings (sometimes called "affect") and beliefs. In George's case this is the work shift. The following sections discuss the various dimensions of attitudes, including the basic components, antecedents, and functions, and, finally, how attitude can be changed.

Antecedents of Work-Related Attitudes

Traditionally, the situational determinants of attitudes received the most attention. In particular, Salancik and Pfeffer noted that the social context provide information to the employees to form their feelings, or affect (their job-related attitudes). More recently, personality traits or dispositions have been receiving increasing attention as antecedents of work-related attitudes. In particular, the dispositions of positive affectivity (PA) and negative affectivity (NA) have been found to be important antecedents to attitudes about one's job. As explained by George, NA reflects a personality disposition to experience negative emotional states; those with high NA tend to feel nervous, tense, anxious, worried, upset, and distressed. Accordingly, those with high NA are more likely to experience negative affective states—they are more likely to have a negative attitude toward themselves, others, and the world around them. Recent research supports this biasing effect of NA. Those with high PA have the opposite disposition and tend to have an overall sense of well-being, to see themselves as pleasurably and effectively engaged, and to experience positive attitudes. Such PA and NA states are important in understanding job satisfaction and work stress.

FUNCTIONS OF ATTITUDES

An understanding of the functions of attitudes is important to the study of organisational behaviour. Based on extensive review of surveys of employers, a recent analysis concluded that "the most important consideration in hiring and the biggest deficit among new workforce entrants are the attitudes concerning work that they bring with them to their jobs." Attitudes can help predict work behaviour. For example, if an attitude survey shows that workers are upset by a change in the work rules and the next week absenteeism begins to increase sharply, management may conclude that a negative attitude toward work rules led to an increase in worker absenteeism. An understanding of attitudes is also important because attitudes help people adapt to their work environment. Katz has noted that attitudes serve four important functions in this process.

I. The Adjustment Function

Attitudes often help people adjust to their work environment. When employees are well treated, they are likely to develop a positive attitude toward management and the organisation. When employees are berated and given minimal salary increases, they are likely to develop a negative attitude toward management and the organisation. These attitudes help employees adjust to their environment and are a basis for future behaviours. For example, if employees who are well treated are asked about management or the organisation, they are likely to say good things. Just the reverse would probably be true for those berated and given minimal salary increases.

II. The Ego-Defensive Function

Besides helping employees adjust, attitudes also help them defend their self-images. For example, an older manager whose decisions are continually challenged by a younger subordinate manager may feel that the latter is brash, cocky, immature, and inexperienced. In truth, the younger subordinate may be right in challenging the decisions. The older manager may not be a very effective leader and may constantly make poor decisions. On the other hand, the older manager is not going to admit this but will try to protect the ego by putting the blame on the other party. As a result, the older manager will have a negative attitude toward the younger one. The same is undoubtedly true for the younger manager, who will feel that the boss is not doing a good job. This attitude helps the younger person protect the ego. If the subordinate were to change this perception and believe that the boss was doing a good job, this individual would also have to stop criticising the boss. Quite obviously, this is something that the younger person does not want to do. So the attitude serves to justify the action and to defend the ego.

III. The Value-Expressive Function

Attitudes provide people with a basis for expressing their values. For example, a manager who believes strongly in the work ethic will tend to voice attitudes toward specific individuals or work practices as a means of reflecting this value. A supervisor who wants a subordinate to work harder might put it this way : "You have got to work harder. That's been the tradition of the company since it was founded. It helped get us where we are today, and everyone is expected to subscribe to this ethic." A company president who believes strongly in the need to support the United Way campaign might tell the top management team: "Everyone in this firm from top to bottom ought to support United Way. It's a wonderful organisation and it does a great deal of good for our community. I do not know where we'd be without it." In both these cases, attitudes serve as a basis for expressing one's central values.

IV. The Knowledge Function

Attitudes help supply standards and frames of reference that allow people to organise and explain the world around them. For example, a union organiser may have a negative attitude toward management. This attitude may not be based on fact, but it does help the individual relate to management. As a result, everything that managers say is regarded by the union organiser as nothing more than a pack of lies, a deliberate distortion of the truth, or an attempt to manipulate the workers. Regardless of how accurate a person's view of reality is, attitudes toward people, events, and objects help the individual make sense out of what is going on.

COMPONENTS OF ATTITUDES

Attitudes can be broken down into three basic components: *Emotional, Informational, and Behavioural.*

(i) *Emotional component* : The emotional component involves the person's feelings or affect—positive, neutral, or negative—about an object. In addition, the expression of emotions—either positive, like a customer service representative; negative like a bill collector or police officer; or neutral, like an academic administrator or public servant—is also important to work behaviour.

(ii) *Informational component* : The informational component consists of the beliefs and information the individual has about the object. It makes no difference whether or not this information is empirically real or correct. A supervisor may believe that two weeks of training is necessary before a worker can operate a particular piece of equipment. In reality, the average worker may be able to operate the machine successfully after only four days of training. Yet the information the supervisor is using (that two weeks is necessary) is the key to this attitude about training.

(iii) *Behavioural component* : The behavioural component consists of a person's tendencies to behave in a particular way toward an object. For example, the supervisor in the above paragraph may assign two weeks of machine training to all his new people.

It is important to remember that of the three components of attitudes, only the behavioural component can be directly observed. One cannot see another person's feelings (the emotional component) or beliefs (the informational component). These two components can only be inferred. For example, when the supervisor assigns a new employee to two weeks of training on the equipment, it is only inferred that :

(i) The supervisor has strong feelings about the length of training required, and

(ii) The individual believes that this length of training is necessary.

Yet understanding the antecedents of work-related attitudes is important in the study of organisational behaviour.

SOURCE OF ATTITUDES

Attitudes, like values, are acquired from parents, teachers, and peer group members. We are born with certain genetic predispositions. Then, in our early years, we begin modelling our attitudes after those we admire, respect, or maybe even fear. We observe the way family and friends behave, and we shape our attitudes and behaviour to align with theirs. People also imitate the attitudes of popular individuals and those they admire and respect. If the "right thing" is to favour eating at McDonald's, you are likely to hold that attitude.

In contrast to values, your attitudes are less stable. Advertising messages, for example, attempt to alter your attitudes toward a certain product or service: If the people at Ford can get you to hold a favourable feeling toward their cars, that attitude may lead to a desirable behaviour (for them)—you purchase of a Ford product.

In organisations, attitudes are important because they affect job behaviour. If workers believe, for example, that supervisors, auditors, bosses, and time-and-motion engineers are all in conspiracy to make employees work harder for the same or less money, then it makes sense to try to understand how these attitudes were formed, their relationship to actual job behaviour, and how they might be changed.

TYPES OF ATTITUDES

Robbins classifies attitudes in three categories: Job satisfaction, Job involvement and Organisational commitment.

(i) *Job satisfaction* : Relates to an individual's general attitude towards his job. It is a complex of several attitudes possessed by the worker. Blum defines job satisfaction as a general attitude which a worker has as a consequence of several specific attitudes in the following three areas: specific job factors, individual adjustment, and group relationships outside the job. Like motivation and morale, attitude and job satisfaction are scientific logical constructs or hypothetical processes.

An individual who has high level of job satisfaction, will reveal positive attitudes towards the job. Likewise, if he is dissatisfied with his job he will have negative attitudes towards it.

(ii) *Job involvement* : Relates to the extent to which an individual identifies with his job, actively participates in it and regards his performance important to his self-worth. An individual who reveals a high involvement in his job, is likely to be more productive, have higher satisfaction and he less prone to resign than the one with low involvement.

(iii) *Organisational commitment* : Indicates an individual's orientation toward the organisation and mobilises his loyalty towards, identification with and involvement in the organisation.

Indeed, an individual who reveals high commitment, may perceive his identity as closely associated with that of the organisation. It is more likely that a highly committed individual is a better performer and is less likely to disert his job than the one having a low level of commitment to the organisation.

SIGNIFICANCE AND FUNCTIONS OF ATTITUDES

In organisational settings, attitudes are of utmost significance in view of their vital roles in determining both satisfaction and performance of the individual. Indeed, job satisfaction and employee morale which form specific kinds of organisational attitudes, determine both the quality and quantity of performance, absenteeism and tardiness, accidents and grievances.

Attitudes are also called "frame of reference" and thus, provide the background against which facts and events are perceived. Attitudes provide a general context within which people tend to perceive specific aspects of their work life including pay, hours of work, nature of supervision, promotion avenues and allied factors.

As Pestonjee points out, attitudes perform at least four important functions in organisational settings: Determination of meaning, reconciliation of contradictions, organisation of facts and selection of facts:

(i) *Attitudes determine meaning of what is seen in the environment* : If an individual has a favourable attitude towards another individual, the former tends to judge the latter's actions as "good" or "superior". On the other hand, if he holds a negative attitude towards the other person, he may be prompt in disagreeing with him and fail to appreciate any good work done by him.

(ii) *Attitudes reconcile contradictions in the opinion of people* : With the help of a proper attitude as a background, it is possible for an individual to reconcile or rationalise the same actions which to another individual are obvious contradictions. Thus, when a worker takes a little rest during work-hours, his supervisor may consider this act a "loafing" or "relaxing" depending upon his attitude. Likewise, the worker may think that his supervisor is "spying" or "evaluating" him on the job depending on his own general attitude towards the management.

(iii) *Attitudes organise facts* : Accordingly, objective events can be perceived differently by different people with divergent attitudes. Thus, by changing the attitudes of workers, it is possible for an irresponsible union leader to cause misinterpretation of facts among them.

(iv) *Attitudes also facilitate the selection of facts* : An individual tends to select those facts and stimuli from the environment which are consistent with his cherished attitudes. Thus, attitudes act as a screen or filter. Usually, with a negative attitude towards union, several managers tend to enlist only its negative activities (i.e. sabotage, act of misconduct, etc.) and fail to pick up its positive behaviour (i.e. voluntary wage cut, new norms of productivity, etc.).

CHANGING ATTITUDES

Employee attitudes can be changed, and sometimes it is in the best interests of management to try to do so. For example, if employees believe that their employer does not take care of them, management would like to change this attitude. Sometimes attitude change is difficult to accomplish because of certain barriers. After the barriers are identified, some ways of overcoming them and effectively changing attitudes are examined.

I. Barriers to Changing Attitudes

There are two basic barriers that can prevent people from changing their attitude. One is called prior commitments, which occurs when people feel a commitment to a particular course of action and are unwilling to change. There is even theory and research support for escalation of commitment, the tendency for decision-makers to persist with failing courses of action.

The following scenario presents an example of escalation of commitment: The president of the company graduated from an Ivy League school and was personally instrumental in hiring the new head of the marketing department, who had graduated from the same school. Unfortunately, things are not working out well. The marketing manager is not very good. However, because the president played such a major role in hiring this manager, the chief executive is unwilling to admit the mistake. Using the ego-defensive function of attitudes, the president distorts all negative information received about the marketing manager and continues to believe that everything is going well and the right selection decision was made.

A second barrier is a result of insufficient information. Sometimes people do not see any reason to change their attitude. The boss may not like a subordinate's negative attitude, but the latter may be quite pleased with his or her own behaviour. Unless the boss can show the individual why a negative attitude is detrimental to career progress or salary raises or some other desirable personal objective, the subordinate may continue to have a negative attitude. This is particularly true when the attitude is a result of poor treatment by management. The worker will use the negative attribute to serve an adjustment function : "I can not respect a manager who treats me the way this one does."

II. Providing New Information

Fortunately, there are ways in which the barriers can be overcome and attitudes can be changed. One of these is by providing new information. Sometimes this information will change a person's beliefs and, in the process, his or her attitudes. In one classic study it was found that union workers had an anti management attitude. However, when some of the workers were promoted into the management ranks, their attitudes changed. They become aware of what the company was doing to help the workers, and, over time, this new information resulted in a change in their beliefs about managerial and in their attitude toward both the company and the union. They became more pro-company and less prounion.

III. Use of Fear

A second way of changing attitudes is through the use of fear. Some researchers have found that fear can cause some people to change their attitudes. However, the degree of fear seems to be important to the final outcome. For example, if low levels of fear arousal are used, people often ignore them. The warning are not strong enough to warrant attention. It moderate levels of fear arousal are used, people often become aware of the situation and will change their attitudes. However, if high degrees of fear arousal are used, people often reject the message because it is too threatening and thus not believable. They essentially dig in their heels and refuse to be persuaded. A good example is provided in the case of anti-smoking commercials. The Department of Health and Human Services found that when it ran ads using patients who were dying of cancer, the message was so threatening to smokers that they shut it out; they refused to listen. As a result, the commercials did not have the desired impact. Health officials found that commercials using only moderate fear arousal were the most effective ones.

IV. Resolving Discrepancies

Another way in which attitudes can be changed is by resolving discrepancies between attitudes and behaviour. For example, research shows that when job applicants have more than one offer of employment and are forced to choose, they often feel that their final choice may have been a mistake. However, this mild conflict, or dissonance, does not usually last very long. The theory of cognitive dissonance says that people will try to actively reduces the dissonance by attitude and behaviour change. Thus, when people take new jobs and begin working, they also start to have negative feelings toward the firms that were not chosen and positive ones toward the company that was chosen. The result may be that the new employees conclude they did indeed make the right choice.

V. Influence of Friends or Peers

Still another way in which attitude changes can come about is through persuasion by friends or peers. For example, if Joe Smith has been padding his expense account and finds out that his friends in sales have not, he is likely to change his own attitude. This assumes that Joe likes his coworkers and they have some persuasive control over him. On the other hand, if Joe believes that the other salespeople are all lazy and would pad their accounts if they only knew, how, he is unlikely to change his attitude toward doing so.

Additionally, it is important to remember that when a particular matter is of personal interest to people, they are likely to reject extreme discrepancies between their current behaviour and that of others. For example, if the other salespeople tell Joe that they never pad their expenses while he is padding his by several thousand dollars annually, Joe is unlikely to let them influence him. There are too many benefits to be achieved if he just keeps on doing what he has been doing. This is why unethical behaviour is so difficult to combat.

VI. The Co-opting Approach

A final way in which attitude changes often take place is by co-opting, which means taking people who are dissatisfied with a situation and getting them involved in improving things. For example, Nancy Jones feels that more needs to be done in improving employee benefits. As a result, the company appoints Nancy as a member of the employee benefits committee. By giving her the opportunity to participate in employee benefits decision making the company increases the chances that Nancy's attitude will change. Once she begins realising how these benefits are determined and how long and hard the committee works to ensure that the personnel are given the best benefits possible, she is likely to change her attitude.

ATTITUDES AND CONSISTENCY

Did you ever notice how people change what they say so it does not contradict what they do? Perhaps a friend of yours has consistently argued that the quality of American cars is not up to that of the imports and that he'd never own anything but a foreign import. But his dad gives him a late-model American-made car, and suddenly they are no so bad. Or, when going through sorority rush, a new freshman believes that sororities are good and that pledging a sorority is important. If she fails to make a sorority, however, she may say, "I recognised that sorority life is not all it's cracked up to be, anyway!"

Research has generally concluded that people seek consistency among their attitudes and between their attitudes and their behaviour. This means that individuals seek to reconcile divergent attitudes and align their attitudes and behaviour so they appear rational and consistent. When there is an inconsistency, forces are initiated to return the individual to an equilibrium state where attitudes and behaviour are again consistent. This can be done by altering either the attitudes or the behaviour, or by developing a rationalisation for the discrepancy.

For example, a recruiter for the ABC Company, whose job it is to visit college campuses, identify qualified job candidates, and sell them on the advantages of ABC as a place of work, would be in conflict if he personally believes the ABC Company has poor working conditions and few opportunities for new college graduates. This recruiter could, over time, Find his attitudes toward the ABC Company becoming more positive. He may, in effect, brainwash himself by continually articulating the merits of working for ABC. Another alternative would be for the recruiter to become overtly negative about ABC and the opportunities within the firm for prospective candidates. The original enthusiasm that the recruiter may have shown would dwindle, probably to be replaced by open cynicism toward the company. Finally, the recruiter might acknowledge that ABC is an undesirable place to work, but think that, as a professional recruiter, his obligation is to present the positive side of working for the company. He might further rationalise that no workplace is perfect; therefore, his job is not to present both sides of the issue, but rather to present a rosy picture of the company.

COGNITIVE DISSONANCE THEORY

Can we also assume from this consistency principle that an individual's behaviour can always be predicted if we know his or her attitude on a subject? If Mr. Jones views the company's pay level as too low, will a substantial increase in his pay change his behaviour, that is, make him work harder? The answer to this question is, unfortunately, more complex than merely a "Yes" or "No".

Leon Festinger, in the late 1950s, proposed the theory of cognitive dissonance. This theory sought to explain the linkage between attitudes and behaviour. Dissonance means an inconsistency. Cognitive dissonance refers to any incompatibility that an individual might perceive between two or more of his or her attitudes, or between his or her behaviour and attitudes. Festinger argued that any form of inconsistency is uncomfortable and that individuals will attempt to reduce the dissonance and, hence, the discomfort. Therefore, individuals will seek a stable state where there is a minimum of dissonance.

Of course, no individual can completely avoid dissonance. You know that cheating on your income tax is wrong, but you "fudge" the numbers a bit every year, and hope you are not audited. Or you tell your children to brush after every meal, but you do not. So how do people cope? Festinger would propose that the desire to reduce dissonance would be determined by the importance of the elements creating the dissonance, the degree of influence the individual believes he or she has over the elements, and the rewards that may be involved in dissonance.

If the elements creating the dissonance are relatively unimportant, the pressure to correct this imbalance will be low. However, say that a corporate manager—Mrs. Smita—believes strongly that no company should pollute the air or water. Unfortunately, Mrs. Smita, because of the requirements of her job, is placed in the position of having to make decisions that would trade off her company's profitability against her attitudes on pollution. She knows that dumping the company's sewage into the local river (which we shall assume is legal) is in the best economic interest of her firm. What will she do? Clearly, Mrs. Smita is experiencing a high degree of cognitive dissonance. Because of the importance of the elements in this example, we cannot expect Mrs. Smita to ignore the inconsistency. There are several paths that she can follow to deal with her dilemma. She can change her behaviour (stop polluting the river). Or she can reduce dissonance by concluding that the dissonant behaviour is not so important after all ("I've got to make a living, and in my role as a corporate decision maker, I often have to place the good of my company above that of the environment or society"). A third alternative would be for Mrs. Smita to change her attitude ("There is nothing wrong in polluting the river"). Still another choice would be to seek out more consonant elements to outweigh the dissonant ones ("The benefits to society from manufacturing our products more than offset the cost of society of the resulting water pollution").

The degree of influence that individuals believe they have over the elements will have an impact on how they will react to the dissonance. If they perceive the dissonance to be an uncontrollable result—something over which they have no choice-they are less likely to be receptive to attitude change. If, for example, the dissonance-producing behaviour is required as a result of the boss's directive, the pressure to reduce dissonance would be less than if the behaviour was performed voluntarily. While dissonance exists, it can be rationalised and justified.

Rewards also influence the degree to which individuals are motivated to reduce dissonance. High rewards accompanying high dissonance tend to reduce the tension inherent in the dissonance. The rewards act to reduce dissonance by increasing the consistency side of the individual's balance sheet.

These moderating factors suggest that just because individuals experience dissonance they will not necessarily move directly toward consistency, that is, toward reduction of this dissonance. If the issues underlying the dissonance are of minimal importance, if an individual perceives that the dissonance is externally imposed and is substantially uncontrollable by him or her, or if towards are significant enough to offset the dissonance, the individual will not be under greater tension to reduce the dissonance.

What are the organisational implications of the theory of cognitive dissonance? It can help to predict the propensity to engage in attitude and behavioural change. If individuals are required, for example, by the demands of their job to say or do things that contradict their personal attitude, they will tend to modify their attitude in order to make it compatible with the cognition of what they have said or done. Additionally, the greater the dissonance—after it has been moderated by importance, choice, and reward factors—the greater the pressures to reduce it.

Measuring the A-B Relationship

The early research work on attitudes assumed that they were causally related to behaviour; that is, the attitudes that people hold determine what they do. Common sense, too, suggests a relationship. It is not logical that people watch television programs that they say they like or that employees try to avoid assignments they find distasteful?

However, in the late 1960s, this assumed relationship between attitudes and behaviour (A-B) was challenged by a review of the research. Based on an evaluation of a number of studies that investigated the A-B relationship, the reviewer concluded that attitudes were unrelated to behaviour or, at best, only slightly related. More recent research has demonstrated that the A-B relationship can be improved by taking moderating contingency variables into consideration.

Moderating Variables

One thing that improves our chances of finding significant A-B relationships is the use of both specific attitudes and specific behaviours. It is one thing to talk about a person's attitude toward "preserving the environment" and another to speak of his or her attitude toward recycling. The more specific the attitude we are measuring, and the more specific we are in identifying a related behaviour, the greater the probability that we can show a relationship between A and B. If you ask people today whether or not they are concerned about preserving the environment, most will probably say "Yes". That does not mean, however, that they separate out recyclable items from their garbage. The correlation between a question that asks about concern for protecting the environment and recycling may be only +.20 or so. But as you make the question more specific—by asking, for example, about the degree of personal obligation one feels to separate recyclable items—the A-B relationship is likely to reach +.50 or higher.

Another moderator is social constraints on behaviour. Discrepancies between attitudes and behaviour may occur because the social pressures on the individual to behave in a certain way may hold exceptional power. Group pressures, for instance, may explain why an employee who holds strong anti-union attitudes attends pro-union organising meetings.

Still another moderating variable is experience with the attitude in question. The A-B relationship is likely to be much stronger if the attitude being evaluated refers to something with which the individual has experience. For instance, most of us will respond to a questionnaire on almost any issue. But is my attitude toward starving fish in the Amazon any indication of whether or not I'd donate to a fund to save these fish? Probably not! Getting the views of college students, with no work experience, on job factors that are important in determining whether or not they would stay put in a job in an example of an attitude response that is unlikely to predict much in terms of actual turnover behaviour.

Self-Perception Theory

Although most A-B studies yield positive results—that attitudes do influence behaviour—the relationship tends to be weak before adjustments are made for moderating variables. But requiring specificity, an absence of social constraints, and experience in order to get a meaningful correlation imposes severe limitations on making generalisations about the A-B relationship. This has prompted some researchers to take another direction—to look at whether or not behaviour influences attitudes. This view, called self-perception theory, has generated some encouraging findings. Let's briefly review the theory.

When asked about an attitude toward some object, individuals recall their behaviour relevant to that object and then infer their attitude from their past behaviour. So if an employee were asked about her feelings about being a training specialists at US West, she would likely think, "I've had this same job at US West as a trainer for ten years, so I must like it!" Self-perception theory, therefore, argues that attitudes are used, after the fact, to make sense out of an action that has already occurred rather than as devices that precede and guide action.

Self-perception theory has been well supported. While the traditional attitude-behaviour relationship is generally positive, it is also weak. In contrast, the behaviour-attitude relationship is quite strong. So what can be conclude? It seems that we are very good at finding reasons for what we do, but not so good at doing what we find reasons for.

ATTITUDES AND WORKFORCE DIVERSITY

Managers are increasingly concerned with changing employee attitudes to reflect shifting perspectives on racial, gender, and other diversity issues. A comment to a co-worker of the opposite sex, which 15 years ago might have been taken as a compliment, can today become a career-limiting episode. As such, organisations are investing in training to help reshape attitudes of employees.

A recent survey of US organisations with 100 or more employees found that 47 percent of them sponsored some sort of diversity training. Some examples; Police officers in Escondido, California receive 36 hours of diversity training each year. Pacific Gas & Electric Co. requires a minimum of four hours of training for its 12,000 employees. The Federal Aviation Administration sponsors a mandatory eight-hour diversity seminar for employees of its Western Pacific region.

What do these diversity programs look like and how do they address attitude change? They almost all include a self-evaluation phase. People are pressed to examine themselves and to confront ethnic and cultural stereo-types they might hold. Then participants typically take part in group discussions or panels with representatives from diverse groups. So, for instance, a Among man might describe his family's life in Southeast Asia, and explain why they resettled in California; or a lesbian might describe how she discovered her sexual identity, and the reaction of her friends and family when she came out.

Additional activities designed to change attitudes include arranging for people to do volunteer work in community or social service centres in order to meet face-to-face with individuals and groups from diverse backgrounds and using exercises that let participants feel what it's like to be different. For example, when participants see the film Eye of the Beholder, where people are segregated and stereotyped according to their eye colour, participants see what it's like to be judged by something they have no control over.

ATTITUDES AND VALUES

Values are linked to attitudes in that a value serves as a way of organising attitudes. Values are defined "as the constellation of likes, dislikes, viewpoints, shoulds, inner inclinations, rational and irrational judgments, prejudices, and association patterns that determine a person's view of the world." Certainly, a person's work is an important aspect of her world. Moreover, the importance of a value constellation is that, once internalised, it becomes (consciously or subconsciously) a standard or criterion for guiding one's actions. The study of values, therefore, is fundamental to the study of managing. There's evidence that values are also extremely important for understanding effective managerial behaviour.

Values affect the perceptions not only of appropriate ends but also of appropriate means to those ends. From the design and development of organisational structures and processes to the utilisation of particular leadership styles and the evaluation of the performance of subordinates, value systems are persuasive. An influential theory of leadership is based on the argument that managers can't be expected to adopt a leadership style that's contrary to their "need structures" or value orientations. Moreover, when managers evaluate subordinate's performance, he effects of the managers' values are noticeable. For example, one researcher reports that managers can be expected to evaluate subordinates with values similar to their own as more effective than subordinates with dissimilar values. The impact of values is more pronounced in decisions involving little objective information and, consequently, a greater degree of subjectivity.

Another aspect of the importance of values occurs when the interpersonal activities of managers bring them into a confrontation with different, and potentially contradictory, values. Studies have shown that assembly-line workers, scientists, and persons in various professional occupations are characterised by particular, if not unique, value orientations. Day-to-day activities create numerous situations in which managers must relate to others with different views of what's right or wrong. Conflicts between managers and workers, administrators and teachers, and line and staff personnel have been documented and discussed in the literature of management. The manner in which these conflicts are resolved is particularly crucial to the organisation's effectiveness.

IBM is often mentioned as a values model firm. This label is based on the fact that IBM managers practice management rooted in three tenets: commitment to excellence, respect for the individual and service for the customer. At IBM, the motto is to establish priorities and then attack them in an orderly fashion.

ATTITUDES AND JOB SATISFACTION

Job satisfaction is an attitude that individuals have about their jobs. It results from their perception of their jobs, based on factors of the work environment, such as the supervisor's style, policies and procedures, work group affiliation, working conditions, and fringe benefits. While numerous dimensions have been associated with job satisfaction, five in particular have crucial characteristics :

(i) *Pay.* The amount received and the perceived equity of pay.

(ii) *Job.* The extent to which job tasks are considered interesting and provide opportunities for learning and for accepting responsibility.

(iii) *Promotion opportunities*. The availability of opportunities for advancement.

(iv) *Supervisor.* The supervisor's abilities to demonstrate interst in and concern about employees.

(v) *Co-workers.* The extent to which co-workers are friendly, competent, and supportive.

In some studies, these five job satisfaction dimensions have been measured by the Job Descriptive Index (JDI). Employees are asked to respond yes, no, or ? (Can't decide) as to whether a word or phrase describes their attitudes about their jobs. The JDI attempts to measure a person's satisfaction with specific facets of the job. Other measures of job satisfaction, such as the Brayfield-Rothe measures, are more general.

A major reason for studying job satisfaction is to provide managers with ideas about how to improve employee attitudes. Many organisations use attitude surveys of determine levels of employee job satisfaction. National surveys have indicated that, in general, 75 to 80 percent of workers are satisfied with their jobs. Of course, though they are interesting, national surveys may not reflect the degree of job satisfaction in a specific department or organisation. Also, simply asking people how satisfied they are creates a problem; there's a bias toward giving a positive answer, since anything less indicates that the person is electing to stay in a dissatisfying job.

REVIEW QUESTIONS

1. How do you define personality? What are its major determinants that constitute the personality?
2. Explain various theories of personalities.
3. Explain similarities and differences among Individuals.
4. What are dimensions of personality? Explain.
5. Write short notes on:
   (a) Trait theory.
   (b) Type theory.
   (c) Cattel's trait theory.
6. What are the various stages in the life of a person relevent for personality development? What are the crises experienced by the person at each stage and the actions that he takes to develop a better personality?
7. How does immaturity-maturity continuum differ from stage theories of personality development? What are the organisational implications of this continuum?
8. Define attitude. How attitude affect behaviour?
9. Briefly explain the various types of attitudes. What are the functions of attitudes?

REFERENCES

1. *Clyde Kluckhohn and H.A. Murray, "Personality Formulation the Determinants", in C. Kluckhohn and B.A. Murray (ed.) Personality, Alfred A. Knopts Inc, New York, 1948*
2. *R. Stagner, Psychology of Personality, 2nd ed., New York, McGraw Hill, Book Company, 1948*
3. *Robert M. Liebert and Michael D. Spiegler, Personality, Homewood.*
5. *Paul H. Mussen, The Psychological Development of the Child Prentice Hall, Inc., Englewood Clieffs, NJ, 1963.*
6. *Floyd L. Ruch, Psychology of Life, 6th Ed. Scott, Foresman & Co., Chicago, 1963.*
7. *Sigmund Froud, The Metapsychology of Instincts, Repression and Unconscious, in Collected Papers of Sigmund Froud (ed.) Drnest Jones, New York, New American Library, 1955.*
8. *Stanley Milgram, "Some Conditions of Obedience and Disobedience to Authority, Human Relations, February, 1965.*
9. *Raymond Cattell, The Scientific Analysis of Personality, Chicago, Adinine, 1965.*
10. *R. Stagner, Psychology of Personality, 2nd ed., New York, McGraw Hill, Book Company, 1948.*
11. *D.E. James, Introduction to Psychology, Constable and Company Ltd., London, 1968.*
12. *Hamner and Organ, Organisational Behaviour: An Applied Psychologial Approach, Business Publications, Inc., Dallas, Texas, 1978.*
13. *Patric, E. Conor, Organisations: Theory and Design, Chicago: Science Research Associates, 1980.*
14. *Krech, D. Crutchfield, R.S. and Ballachey, E.L., "Individuals in Society", New York, McGraw Hill, 1962.*
15. *Bem, D.J., "Self-perception: An Alternative Interpretation of Cognitive Dissonance Phenomena", Psychological Review, 74, 1967.*
16. *Costello, T.W. and Zalking, S.S., Psychology in Administration, Englewood Cliffs, N.J. Prentice-Hall, 1963.*
17. *Blair J. Kolasa, op. cit., Newcomb T. and Svekla G., "Intrafamily Relationships in Attitude".*
18. *Adorno, T. Frenkel-Brunswik, E. Levinson D. and Sanford, R., The Authoritarian Personality, New York, Harper.*

4th

CHAPTER

OVERVIEW

WORK MOTIVATION

• ***After reading this chapter, you should be able to know:***

- Introduction
- Concept of Motivation
- Nature of Motivation
- Motivation Process
- Characteristics of Motivation Process
- Forms of Needs
- Theories of Motivation
- Content Theory
- Comparison of Maslow and Herzberg Models
- McClelland's Theory
- Alderfer's ERG Theory
- Process Theory of Motivation
- Vroom's Expectancy Theory of Motivation
- Contemporary Theories of Work Motivation
- Theory X and Theory Y
- Theory Z
- J. Stacy Adam's Equity Theory
- Financial and Non-Financial Incentives

4

WORK MOTIVATION

INTRODUCTION

Motivation refers to something dynamic which stems from within. As *Berelson* and *Steiner* observe, it refers to all those inner striving conditions which have been described as wishes, desires, drives, etc. It is an inner condition which activates or moves.

The word motivation stands for the term *movement*. We all know about motive power or an automotive (self-moving) vehicle. All these words have movement as their origin. The mechanism of motivation can be regarded as a movement towards a balance. This movement toward equilibrium is a *homeostatic mechanism.* Need is a starting point of this mechanism. A need is a lack or deficiency of something within the living system. When a lack or deficiency is caused in this system, it initiates a chain of events. Something taken place, some kind of activity happens, but it is not random activity. The individual who experiences a need does not engage in random behaviour or haphazard activity; rather, he engages himself in activity which is directed toward a goal. As soon as he reaches the goal, and the mechanism of motivation ends. Motivation, therefore, is initiated with the need and is ended with need satiation, with goal directed behaviour being the basic dynamic phase of the process.

Motivation is one of the most important factors affecting human behaviour. Motivation not only affects other cognitive factors like perception and learning but affects the total performance of an individual in organisational setting. This is the reason why managers attach great importance to motivation in organisation. In fact, *Likert* has called *motivation* as the core of management.

According to Viteles, "Motivation represents an unsatisfied need which creates a state of tension or disequilibrium, causing the individual to move in a goal directed pattern towards restoring a state of equilibrium, by satisfying the need".

CONCEPT OF MOTIVATION

In order to understand the concept of motivation, we have to examine three terms: *motive*, *motivating* and *motivation* and their relationship. Motive, based on the Latin word movere, motive (need) has been defined as follows:

"A *motive* is an inner state that energises, activates, or moves (hence motivation), and that directs behaviour towards goals." Motive has also been described as follows: "A motive is restlessness, a lack, a yen, a force. Once in the grip of a motive, the organism does something to reduce the restlessness, to remedy the lack, to alleviate the yen, to mitigate the force."

Here, we can differentiate between *needs* and *wants*. While *needs* are more comprehensive and include desires—both physiological and psychological, *wants* are expressed in narrow sense and include only those desires for which a person has money and also the desire to spend the money to satisfy the wants. There are many psychological needs, like social needs, recognition needs, etc. which do not fall under the category of wants.

Motivating. Motivating is a term which implies that one person, in the organisational context a manager, induces another, say employee, to engage in action (work behaviour) by ensuring that a channel to satisfy the motive becomes available and accessible to the individual. In addition to channelising the strong motives in a direction that is satisfying to both the organisation and the employees, the manager can also activate the latent motives in individuals and harness them in a manner that would be functional for the organisation.

Motivation. While a motive is energiser of action, motivating is the channelisation and activation of motives, motivation is the work behaviour itself. Motivation depends on motives and motivating, therefore, it becomes a complex process. For example, *Dubin* has defined motivation as follows :

"Motivation is the complex forces starting and keeping a person at work in an organisation. Motivation is something that moves the person to action, and continues him in the course of action already initiated."

According to *McFarland*, "Motivation refers to the way in which urges, drives, desires, aspirations, strivings, or needs direct, control or explain the behaviour of human beings."

The *concept* of motivation has three basic characteristics. These are:

- *Effort*. The amount of effort put into the activity identifies the strength of the person's work related behaviour. Hard work usually reflects high motivation. A student who works very hard to get top grades can be referred to as highly motivated.
- *Persistence*. Motivation is a permanent and an integral part of a human being. Its second characteristic is persistence in the efforts. Motivation is continuously goal directed so that once a goal is achieved, a higher goal is selected and efforts are exercised towards this higher goal.
- *Direction*. Persistent hard work determines the quantity of effort while direction determines the quality of the anticipated output. All efforts are to be directed towards the organisational goal. This would ensure that the persistent effort is actually resulting into accepted organisational outcomes.

NATURE OF MOTIVATION

In terms of its derivation, the work motivate means to move, to activate. In this general sense, anything, that initiates activity whether external or internal, is motivating. Today, the term means a lot more than this. Motivating is the work a manager performs to inspire, encourage and impel people to take required action. Some of the widely quoted definitions are given below:

(i) Motivation is a predisposition to act in a specific goal-directed way.

(ii) The immediate influences on the direction, vigour and persistence of action.

(iii) Steering one's actions toward certain goals and committing a certain part of one's energies to reach them.

(iv) How behaviour gets started, is energised, is sustained, is directed, is stopped and what kind of subjective reaction is present in the organism while all this is going on.

All these definitions contain three common aspects of the motivation process: What energises human behaviour? Who directs or channels such behaviour? How this behaviour is maintained or sustained?

MOTIVATION PROCESS

As an example, let us assume that a teacher has established a goal for himself to get a promotion and monetary raise in order to improve upon his standard of living. Thus the professor will shape his behaviour to achieve that goal. He will thus choose a course of action designed to obtain promotion. This course of action may be five published articles or one published book. He will be highly motivated and will put in persistent efforts in research and publish the desired number of articles or the book.

Once the promotion has been obtained the professor will re-evaluate his achievement relative to his initially established objective. If the pay raise is not adequate and there are grounds for further promotion and pay raise, the teacher will establish a higher goal and strive towards it. This example fits the basic motivational process as follows:

In the above example, if the motivator (publishing) does not serve the required purpose then the teacher will look at other alternatives as motivators such as service to the college and community, student guidance and curriculum development, good interactive relations with peers and superiors. Thus the *motivation process* involves the following steps:

(i) *Analysis of situation.* The situation that needs motivational inducement must be sized up so as to ascertain the motivational needs. From organisational behaviour point of view it must be recognised that since the needs of different employees differ both in nature as well as intensity, a composite view of the collective needs of the group is established with appropriate recognition of differences in individual needs.

(ii) *Selecting and applying appropriate motivators.* A list of all devices of motivation is drawn and a selection made of such motivators that motivate different types of people under different circumstances. Proper timing and the extent of motivation is also to be considered. The individual goals should be given adequate attention within the framework of group goals and the organisational goals.

(iii) *Follow-up.* It is important to know that the motivators selected are indeed providing the desired motivation. This can be accomplished by getting and evaluating the feedback. If these motivators are not showing the optimum effect, then alternative motivators should be selected and applied.

Characteristics of Motivation Process

The *process of motivation* is *characterised* by the following:

(a) *Motivation is an internal feeling.* Motivation points to energetic forces within individuals that drive them to behave in certain ways and to environmental forces that trigger these drives.

(b) *Motivation produces goal-directed behaviour.* Motivation has got a profound influence on human behaviour, it harnesses human energy to organisational requirements. There is the notion of goal orientation on the part of individuals, their behaviour is directed towards something.

(c) *Motivation contains systems orientation.* It considers in those forces in the individuals and in their surrounding environments that feedback to the individuals either to reinforce the intensity of their drive and the direction of this energy or to dissuade them from their cause of action and redirect their efforts.

(d) *Motivation can be either positive or negative.* Positive motivation or the carrot approach, offers something precious to the person in the form of additional pay, incentives, praise etc., for satisfactory performance. Negative motivation or stick approach emphasises penalties while controlling performance (reprimands, threat of demotion).

(e) *Motivation means bargaining.* Behaviour is what people DO. Motivation is WHY they do it. *Barnard* explained motivation in the form of 'inducements-contribution' theory. It focuses on workers and organisations endeavouring to find what payouts (inducements) to workers in exchange for what degree of cooperation (contributions) from workers will be satisfactory to both parties. The problem of motivation then becomes one of arriving at compensation to workers that will coax them the output that is required.

(f) *Motivation is a complete process.* Five reasons can be provided in support of this statement:-

  (i) First, motive is a hypothetical construct. It cannot be seen. Often we observe individuals putting a great deal of overtime. We cannot definitely state whether they are doing it because of additional income they receive or simply because they enjoy their work.

  (ii) Individuals may have a host of needs that are continuously changing, and, sometimes, in conflict with each other. As a result, it becomes exceedingly difficult to observe or measure motivation with certainty.

  (iii) People satisfy their needs in many different ways. A salesman may work hard to earn money; a second salesman may be spurred by his achievement motive and so on. By simply observing sales persons in action it is not easy to differentiate between these groups.

  (iv) Promoting an employee to a new and more challenging task may intensify the drive to work harder in anticipation of the next promotion. Thus, gratification of a particular need may gradually lead to an increase in its intensity.

  (v) Finally, goal-directed behaviour does not always lead to need satisfaction.

(g) *Motivation and satisfaction are related but not synonymous concepts.* Motivation is the drive to satisfy a want or goal. It is concerned with goal-directed behaviour. Satisfaction refers to the contentment experiences when a want is satisfied. The term 'satisfaction' is used to analyse outcomes already experienced by an employee. Satisfaction is a consequence of rewards and punishments associated with past experience.

FORMS OF NEEDS

Needs are deficiencies that an individual experiences at a particular point in time. Deficiencies may be *physiological* (e.g., a need for food), *psychological* (e.g. a need for self-esteem), or *sociological* (e.g., a need for social interaction). Needs are triggers of behavioural responses. The implication is that when needs (deficiencies) are present, the individual is more susceptible to managers' motivation efforts.

The basic objective behind classification of needs into different categories is to find out similarity and dissimilarity in various needs so that incentives are grouped to satisfy the needs falling under one category or the other. From this point of view, a meaningful classification of needs is based on the sources through which needs emerge. Needs may be a natural, biological phenomenon in an individual, or these may develop over the period of time through learning. Since these two types of needs emerge from two different sources, these may be satisfied by different types of incentives. Besides, there are certain needs which are neither purely biological nor these are completely learned but fall in between the two. Therefore, a separate category has to be provided for these. Thus, needs may be grouped into three categories:

(i) Primary needs,

(ii) Secondary needs,

(iii) General needs.

I. Primary Needs

Primary needs are also known as physiological, biological, basic, or unlearned needs. However, the term primary is more comprehensive as compared to other terms. Primary needs are animal drives which are essential for survival. These needs are common to all human beings, though their intensity may differ. Some of the needs are food, sex, sleep, air to breathe, satisfactory temperature, etc. These needs arise out of the basic physiology of life and are important to survival and preservation of species. These needs are also conditioned by social practices. According to the concept of 'economic man', these are the only wants of a human being and he attempts to satisfy them only. But researches in human behaviour show that psychological needs are equally rather more important for human beings.

II. Secondary Needs

As contrast to the primary needs secondary needs are not natural but are learned by the individual through his experience and interaction. Therefore, these are also called learned or derived needs. Emergence of these needs depends on learning. This is the reason why we find differences among need pattern of child and a matured individual. There may be different types of secondary needs like need for power, achievement, status, affiliation, etc.

III. General Needs

Though a separate classification for general needs is not always given, such a category seems necessary because there are a number of needs which lie in the grey area between the primary and secondary classifications. To be included in this category, a need must not be learned but at the same time, it is not completely physiological. In fact, there are certain such needs like need for competence, curiosity, manipulation, affection, etc.

Here, we have just mentioned the classification of various needs into different categories for providing an understanding of the way needs emerge. Their detailed description will be provided in various theories of motivation, particularly based on contents, as these theories try to explain the different needs which people seek to satisfy.

THEORIES OF MOTIVATION

I. Content Theory

Contents theories focus on the factors within the person that energise, direct, sustain and stop behaviour. They attempt to determine the specific needs that motivate people.

(i) Maslow's Hierarchy of Needs

The most widely recognised theory of motivation is the needs hierarchy theory. *Abraham Maslow* suggested that people have a complex set of exceptionally strong needs, which can be arranged in a hierarchy. Underlying this hierarchy are the following basic assumptions:

- A satisfied need does not motivate. However, when one need is satisfied, another need emerges to take its place, so people are always striving to satisfy some need.
- The needs network for most people is complex, with several needs affecting the behaviour of each person at any one time.
- In general, lower level needs must be satisfied before higher level needs are activated sufficiently to drive behaviour.
- There are more ways to satisfy higher level needs than lower level needs .

This theory states that a person has five primary types of needs: Physiological, security, affiliation, esteem, and self-actualisation. Fig. 1. shows these all five needs categories, arranged in *Maslow's* hierarchy.

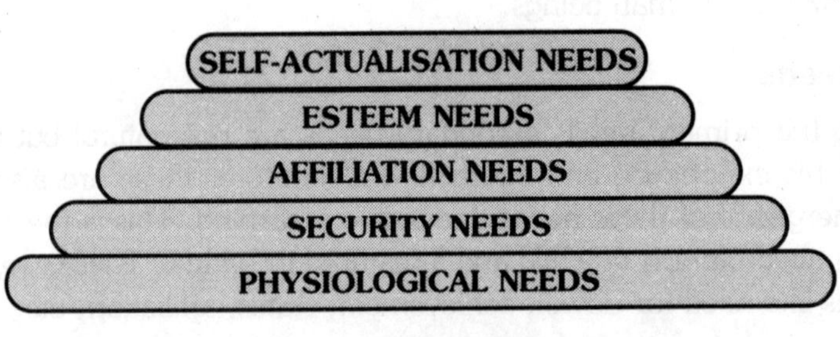

Fig. 1. *Maslow's Hierarchy of Needs.*

(a) Physiological needs

The needs for food, water, air, and shelter are all physiological needs and are the lowest level in *Maslow's* hierarchy. People concentrate on satisfying these needs before turning to higher order needs. Managers and others should understand that, to the extent that employees are motivated by physiological needs, their concerns do not centre on the work they are doing. They will accept any job that serves to meet their needs. Managers who focus on physiological needs in trying to motivate subordinates assume that people work primarily for money and are primarily concerned with comfort, avoidance of fatigue, and the like.

(b) Security needs

The needs for safety, stability, and absence of pain, threat, or illness are all security needs. Like physiological needs, unsatisfied security needs cause people to be preoccupied with satisfying them. People who are motivated primarily by security needs value their jobs mainly as a defence against the loss of basic need satisfactions. Managers who believe that security needs are most important focus on them by emphasising rules, job security, and fringe benefits. Such managers may not encourage innovation by employees and will not reward risk taking. Employees who are most concerned about security will follow rules strictly.

(c) Affiliation needs

The needs for friendship, love and a feeling of belonging are all affiliation needs. When physiological and sense that when affiliation needs are the primary source of motivation, people value the workplace as an opportunity for finding and establishing warm and friendly interpersonal relationships.

(d) Esteem needs

Personal feelings of achievement and self-worth and recognition or respect from others meet esteem needs. People with esteem needs want others to accept them for what they are and to perceive them as competent and able. Managers who focus on esteem needs try to motivate employees with public rewards and recognition for services. These managers may use lapel pins, articles in the company paper, achievement lists on the bulletin board, and the like to promote employee pride in their work.

(e) Needs for self-actualisation

Self-fulfilment comes from meeting self-actualisation needs. People who meet self-actualisation needs readily accept themselves and others and gain confidence in their problem-solving abilities. Managers who emphasise self-actualisation may involve employees in designing jobs, make special assignments that capitalise on employees' unique skills, or give employee teams leeway in planning and implementing work procedures. When *Ken Rosenthal* opened his first St. Louis Bakery/ Cafe, he achieved a measure of self-fulfilment.

Significance for the Workplace

Maslow's needs hierarchy theory implicitly states the goals that people value. It also suggests the types of behaviour that will help people meet various needs. The three lowest needs, physiological, safety, and social, are also known as deficiency needs. According to Maslow, unless these needs are satisfied, an individual will fail to develop into a healthy person, both physically and psychologically. In contrast, esteem and self-actualisation needs are known as growth needs. Satisfaction of these needs will help a person grow and develop to his or her potential.

(ii) Herzberg's Two-Factor Theory of Motivation

The motivator-hygiene theory is one of the most controversial theories of motivation because of two unique features. First, the theory stresses that some job factors lead to satisfaction, whereas others may prevent dissatisfaction but not be sources of satisfaction. Second, it states that job satisfaction and dissatisfaction do not exist on a single continuum.

Frederick Herzberg and his associates examined the relationship between job satisfaction and productivity in a group of accountants and engineers. Through the use of semistructured interviews, they accumulated data on various factors that these employees said had an effect on their feelings about their jobs. Two different sets of factors emerged: motivators and hygienes.

Motivator Factors

The first set of factors, motivator factors, includes the work itself, recognition, advancement, and responsibility. These factors are associated with an individual's positive feelings about the job and are related to the content of the job itself. These positive feelings, in turn, reflect the individual's experiences of achievement, recognition, and responsibility. The factors are predicated on lasting rather than temporary achievement in the work setting.

Motivators are intrinsic factors, or internal factors directly related to the job. Intrinsic factors (for example, a feeling of accomplishment after successful task performance) are largely internal

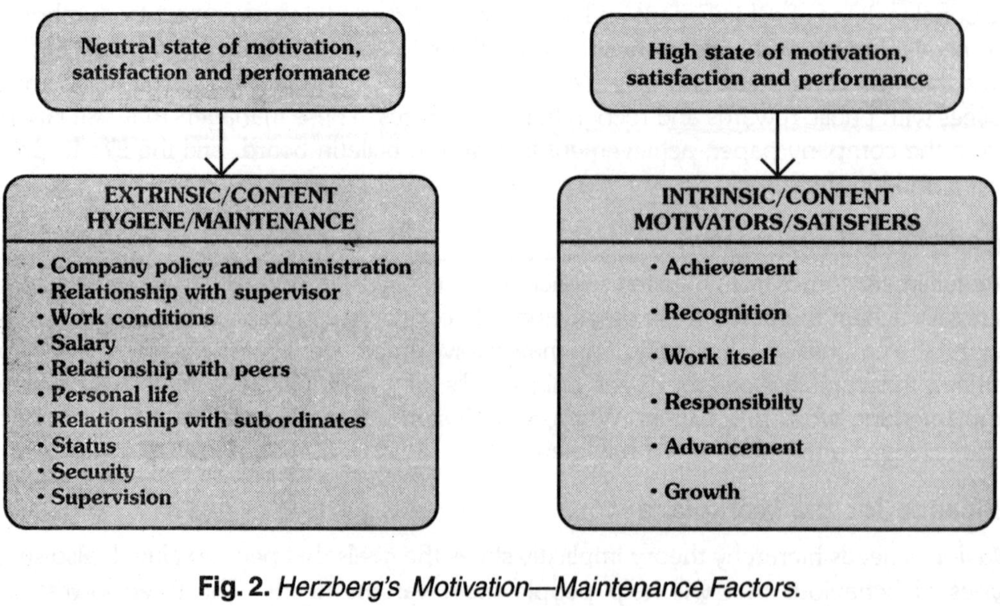

Fig. 2. *Herzberg's Motivation—Maintenance Factors.*

to the individual. The organisation's policies have only an indirect impact on them. Thus by defining exceptional performance, an organisation may enable individuals to feel that they have performed their tasks exceptionally well.

Hygiene Factors

Hygiene factors represent the need to avoid pain in the environment. They are not an intrinsic part of a job, but they are related to the conditions under which a job is performed. They are associated with negative feelings. They are environment related factors, hygienes. They must be viewed as preventive measures that remove sources of dissatisfaction from the environment. Like physical hygiene they do not led to growth but only prevent deterioration. Maintaining a hygienic work environment will not improve motivation any more than garbage disposal or water purification. Mr. Fictitious, who is in excellent health will not become any healthier by eating food but if he does not eat food he may become sick and die. Hygiene factors produce no growth in worker output but they prevent loss in performance caused by work restriction. *Herzberg* believed that hygienes create a zero level of motivation and if maintained at proper level prevent negative type of motivation from occurring. According to *Scott Myers* "maintenance factors are characterised by the fact that they inspire little positive sentiment when added, but incite strong negative reactions when removed."

Motivators

Motivators are associated with positive feelings of employees about the job. They are related to the content of the job. They make people satisfied with their job. If managers wish to increase motivation and performance above the average level, they must enrich the work and increase a person's freedom on the job. Motivators are necessary to keep job satisfaction and job performance high. On the other hand, if they are not present they do not prove highly satisfying.

(i) *Managerial implications.* Herzberg's theory casts new light on the content of work motivation. During the last thirty years employees have been paternalistically maintained too much and enthusiastically motivated too little. Managers have been focusing their attention on Hygiene factors often with poor results. They were preoccupied with the environment of work rather than work itself. The distinction of motivational and maintenance factors will help managers in spurring individuals to peak performance. The most basic implication of the motivation-maintenance theory is that in order to maximise human productivity it is absolutely necessary to satisfy employee's maintenance needs and provide the opportunity to gratify their motivation needs. The key to motivation lies in structuring meaningful jobs, jobs that are challenging and rewarding that provide increased opportunities for achievement, responsibility, growth and recognition. That is to say, in place of dull, boring and demotivating jobs, challenging jobs should be provided by the managers.

(ii) *Departure from the traditional view.* Traditionally, job satisfaction and dissatisfaction were viewed as opposite ends of a single continuum. When certain things are present on a job—good pay, opportunity for growth, healthy working environment—the employee will be satisfied. When they are absent, he is dissatisfied. The absence of dissatisfaction is satisfaction.

Herzberg's findings indicate that dissatisfaction is not simply the opposite of satisfaction or motivation. One can feel no dissatisfaction and yet not be satisfied. Satisfaction and dissatisfaction appear to be somewhat independent. They are not viewed as symmetrical items on a single scale, rather, they are viewed as attributes of different scales. The factors that cause dissatisfaction are different from those that result in satisfaction. Satisfaction is affected by motivators and dissatisfaction by hygiene factors.

Relation to Maslow's Need Hierarchy

Herzberg's theory is closely related to Maslow's need hierarchy. The hygiene factors are preventive and environmental in nature (see Table below), and they are roughly equivalent to *Maslow's* lower-level needs. These hygiene factors prevent dissatisfaction, but they do not lead to satisfaction. In effect, they bring motivation up to a theoretical zero level and are a necessary "floor" to prevent dissatisfaction, and they serve as a takeoff point for motivation. By themselves, the hygiene factors do not motivate. Only the motivators motivate employees on the job. They are roughly equivalent to Maslow's higher-level needs. According to Herzberg's theory, an individual must have a job with a challenging content in order to be truly motivated.

Table : Herzberg's Two-Factor Theory

Hygiene Factors	Motivators
Company policy and administration	Achievement
Supervision, technical	Recognition
Salary	Work itself
Interpersonal relations, supervisor	Responsibility
Working conditions	
Advancement	

Contribution to Work Motivation

Herzberg's two-factor theory casts a new light on the content of work motivation. Up to this point, management had generally concentrated on the hygiene factors. When faced with a morale problem, the typical solution was higher pay, more fringe benefits, and better working conditions. However, as has been pointed out, this simplistic solution did not really work. Management are often perplexed because they are paying high wages and salaries, have an excellent fringe-benefit package, and provide great working conditions but their employees are still not motivated. Herzberg's theory offers an explanation for this problem. By concentrating only on the hygiene factors, management are not motivating their personnel.

There are probably very few workers or managers who do not feel that they deserved the raise they received. On the other hand, there are many dissatisfied workers and managers who feel they did not get a large enough raise. This simple observation points out that the hygiene factors seem to be important in preventing dissatisfaction but do not lead to satisfaction. Herzberg would be the first to say that the hygiene factors are absolutely necessary to maintain the human resources of an organisation. However, as in the Maslow sense, once "the belly is full" of hygiene factors, which is the case in most modern organisations, dangling any more in front of employees will not motivate them. According to Herzberg's theory, only a challenging job that has the opportunities for achievement, recognition, responsibility, advancement, and growth will motivate personnel.

Critical Analysis of Herzberg's Theory

Although Herzberg's two-factor theory remains a very popular textbook explanation of work motivation and makes sense to practitioners, it also is true that from an academic perspective the theory oversimplifies the complexities of work motivation. When researchers deviate from the critical incident methodology used by Herzberg, they do not get the two factors. There seem to be job factors such as pay that lead to both satisfaction and dissatisfaction. For example, pay can be dissatisfying if not high enough, but also be satisfying as a form of achievement and recognition. These findings indicate that a strict interpretation of the two-factor theory is not warranted.

In spite of the obvious limitations, few would question that Herzberg has contributed substantially to the study of work motivation. He extended *Maslow's* need hierarchy concept and made it more applicable to work motivation. *Herzberg* also drew attention to the importance of job content factors in work motivation, which previously had been badly neglected and often totally overlooked. The job design technique of job enrichment is also one of *Herzberg's* contributions.

COMPARISON OF MASLOW AND HERZBERG MODELS

One of the main reasons for the popularity of the two factor theory is that it is compatible with *Maslow's* Need Hierarchy. *Maslow* and *Herzberg*—both tend to oversimplify the motivational process, emphasise the same set of relationships and deal with the same problem. Maslow formulated the theory in term of needs and Herzberg in terms of goals or rewards. However, *Herzberg* attempted to refine and hedge on the need hierarchy and cast a new light on the

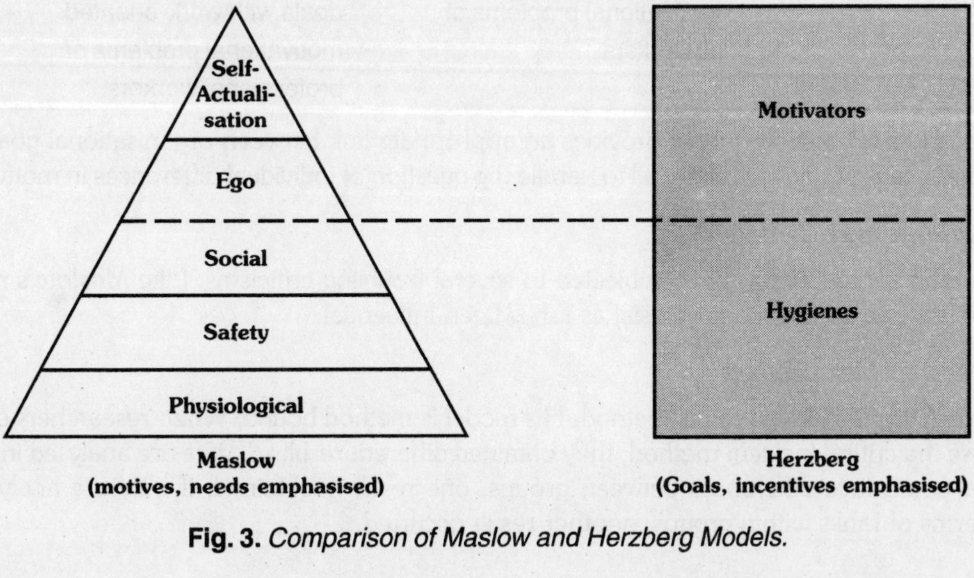

Fig. 3. *Comparison of Maslow and Herzberg Models.*

content of work motivation. Herzberg recommended the use of hygiene factors to help people to attain their lower level needs. Motivators are recommended to meet upper level needs. Whereas Maslow's construction implies a hierarchical (sequential) arrangement with greater force from unfulfilled needs and movement through the hierarchy in an ordered or 'cascade' fashion. According to *Maslow's* any unsatisfied need whether of lower order or higher order will motivate individuals.

Both models who marked similarities. As a result, the juxtaposition of the two models makes logical sense and is interesting to observe.

The hygiene factors are roughly equivalent to *Maslow's* lower order needs and the motivational factors are somewhat equivalent to higher order needs. Both models assume that specific needs energise behaviour.

Differences. Although there are marked similarities in the two models many differences exist.

Table : Comparison of Maslow and Herzberg Models

Issue	Maslow's Model	Herzberg's Model
Order of needs	Sequential arrangement of needs.	No such hierarchical arrangement.
Emphasis	Descriptive.	Prescriptive.
Essence of theory	Unsatisfied needs energise behaviour; this behaviour causes performance.	Gratified needs cause performance.
Motivator	Any need can be a motivator if it is relatively unsatisfied.	Only higher order needs serve as motivators.
Applicability	Takes a general view of the motivational problems of all workers.	Takes a micro-view and deals with work-oriented motivational problems of professional workers.

Unfortunately neither model provides an appropriate link between organisational goals and individual need satisfaction. Both fail to handle the question of individual differences in motivation.

Limitations and Criticism

Herzberg's theory has been subjected to several troubling criticisms. Like *Maslow's* model, *Herzberg's* has been as controversial as it has been influential.

(i) Research Methodology

(a) Herzberg is shackled to his method. His model is method bound. When researchers did not use the critical incident method, they obtained different results. If data are analysed in terms of percentage differences between groups, one result is obtained; if they are analysed in terms of ranks within groups, another result occurred.

(b) Actually the theory is limited by the 'critical incident' method used to obtain information. The subjects stated only extremely satisfying and dissatisfying job experiences. People tend to tell the interviewer what they think the individual would like to hear. So results obtained under the method may be a product of people's defensiveness than a correct revelation of objective sources of satisfaction and dissatisfaction. When things run smoothly, people tend to attribute the causes of satisfaction to their own achievements and accomplishments on the job. On the other hand, when things go wrong or poorly, they tend to attribute their dissatisfaction not to personal inadequacies or deficiencies but to factors in the work environment.

(c) Also, using the critical incident method may cause people to recall only the most recent experiences. The 'recovery of events' bias is embedded in the methodology.

(d) The method is fraught with procedural deficiencies also. The analysis of the responses derived from this approach is highly subjective, sometimes the researchers had to interpret the responses. The researcher evaluated the respondent's description of his previous behaviour. Herzberg type studies merely allow experimenter biases to creep in and interment the results.

(ii) Empirical Validity

(a) *King* noted that the model itself has five different theoretical interpretations and that the available research evidence is not consistent with any of these interpretations.

(b) The theory is most applicable to knowledge workers—managers, accountants, engineers. Most studies have shown that when the employees were professional in nature, the theory is applicable. Studies of manual workers are less supportive of the theory. *Herzberg's* study, hence, is not representative of the workforce in general.

(iii) Assumptions

(a) The assumption that the two sets of factors operate primarily in one direction is also not accurate. Critics questioned the mutual exclusiveness of the dimensions. In some cases 'maintenance factors' were found to be viewed as motivators by blue-collar employees. In one study it was found that hygiene factors were as useful in motivating employees as were his motivators. A clear distinction between factors that lead to satisfaction and those that lead to dissatisfaction cannot be maintained. Herzberg's model propagates a myth that hygienes are enough to motivate workers and motivators must be pressed into service while dealing with managers. This dichotomy is unfortunate because it perpetuates a chasm between subsystems of organisations that really should be integrated for effective performance. All are managers; all are workers.

(b) The theory focuses too much attention on 'satisfaction' or 'dissatisfaction' rather than on the performance level of the individual. Much importance is not given to such factors like status, pay, interpersonal relationship which are generally held as important determinants of satisfaction. Further, researchers have questioned the equation between satisfaction and motivation and also attacked the assumption that satisfaction leads to superior performance. Actually, motivation, satisfaction and performance are all separate variables and relate in indifferent ways from what was assumed by Herzberg.

In the words of *Dunnette, Campbell* and *Hackel,* the Herzberg's two factor theory is a grossly oversimplified portrayal of the mechanism by which job satisfaction or dissatisfaction comes about. Satisfaction or dissatisfaction can reside in the job content, the job context or both jointly.

Herzberg's Contribution

Despite these criticisms, Herzberg's two factor theory has made a significant contribution toward improving manager's basic understanding of human behaviour. He advanced a theory that was simple to grasp, based on some empirical data, and equally significant-offered specific action recommendation for managers to improve employee motivation levels. He drew the attention of managers to the importance of job content factors in work motivation which had been neglected previously. One of the most important contributions of *Herzberg's* work happens to be the tremendous impact it had in stimulating though, research and experimentation on the topic of motivation at work. Though he failed to provide a clear and comprehensive statement of the model, *Herzberg's*, probably, deserves the credit for acting as stimulus to other researchers who advanced alternative theories of work motivation.

In short, "the most meaningful conclusion that we can draw is that the two factor theory has now served its purpose and should be altered or respectfully laid aside. Theories are never true or false, but exhibit varying degrees of usefulness".

Job Enrichment

Job enrichment, as it is currently practised in industry, is a direct outgrowth of Herzberg's two factor theory of motivation. It is therefore based on the assumption that in order to motivate personnel, the job itself must provide opportunities for achievement, recognition, responsibility, advancement and growth. The basic idea is to restore to jobs the elements of interest that were taken away under intensive specialisation. At this stage it may be necessary to draw a distinction between job rotation, job enlargement and job enrichment.

The difference between there various terms have been depicted on a continuum of variety, responsibility and personal growth on the job. Under rotation the job duties to be performed are not changed. The worker is merely exposed to several jobs. He is taken off the boring job for a while and is allowed to take up a related task and so on. The problem with job rotation is that it does not change the basic characteristics of neither the job nor the individual. Monotony may be relieved temporarily, but the individual still returns to the same old boring job. Critics state that this approach involves nothing more than having people perform several boring and monotonous jobs rather than one. Job enlargement extends the worker's present job to include more tasks of a job i.e., horizontal loading of a job. However, horizontal loading does not enrich the task. Washing dishes, then silverware, and then pots and pans does no more to satisfy and provide an opportunity to grow than washing only dishes. Job enrichment tries to embellish the job with factors that Herzberg characterised as motivators : achievement, recognition, increased responsibilities, opportunities for growth, advancement, and increased competence. There is an attempt to build into jobs a higher sense of challenge and achievement.

(iii) McClelland's Theory

McClelland proposed three needs which are important in organisational settings for understanding motivation. These needs include achievement, power and affiliation and deserve attention because they have great significance in organisational settings.

(a) *The achievement motivation* has been intensively studied by *McClelland* and his associates and described in their treatise "The Achievement Motive". It has been defined as a desire to succeed in competitive situations based on a standard of excellence determined by others or one's own preceding standard.

The individual propelled by achievement motivation is constantly preoccupied with the desire for improvement and better performance in his position and tends to prefer situations where he can get quick and precise feedback on his performance. Individuals who are equipped with high achievement motivation are fond of taking calculated risks and search environments conducive to challenging opportunities, personal responsibility, autonomy and a sense of mastery. Such individuals derive greater excitement from the solving of a complex problem rather than the accompanying money or praise, and tend to make outstanding executives or entrepreneurs. The organisations which have a sizable number of such individuals make rapid progress.

It has also been demonstrated by McClelland in his empirical well-known work "The Achieving Society" that the *economic development* of a country has high positive correlation with the level of achievement motivation obtained in the population of that country. McClelland thinks that if attempts are made to detect *n* Ach in individuals or nations, this can facilitate faster economic development in underdeveloped countries like India.

He believes that *n* Ach in individuals or nations can be developed through *training courses*. He cites the results of a ten-day training course which was given to businessmen in India from Bombay and from a small city--Kakinada in the state of Andhra Pradesh to support this viewpoint. It was demonstrated statistically after two years that the individuals who took the course had done better than individuals who did not take the course or who took some other management course. As the Kakinada results showed, nine men, 18 per cent of the 52 participants, had revealed "unusual" enterprise in their business and 25 of the men, nearly 50 per cent, were unusually active during the 18 months following the course as compared to only 20 per cent in a control city. McClelland concludes that such methods of developing achievement motivation can help underdeveloped countries to move faster economically.

McClelland's theory implies that managers with high achievement motivation may set high standards of performance for themselves and their subordinates and are likely to be improvement and innovation minded in their positions.

(b) *The power motivation* has been extensively studied by *Adler*, *McClelland* and others. It has been defined as a desire to affect the behaviour of other individuals and to control and manipulate the surroundings. It has been assumed that power motivation becomes strong in people who feel themselves inadequate to achieve the respect and recognition from other individuals, and subsequently go out of their way to seek the attention of others. Individuals with high power motivation either emerge to be successful leaders or alcoholics. *McClelland* stresses that power motivation is closely related to managerial success. However, it is not certain which is the cause and which is the effect.

Power motivation may be in negative and unsocialised or positive and socialised forms. Thus, it appears that although the power motivation is not undesirable in itself, the ways it takes the form are significant. Such motivation is likely to energise and direct people to seek leadership roles. But it is also likely that in such roles individuals with high power motivation involving negative orientation may tend to adapt an exploitative autocratic style whereas those with low power motivation may resort to a *laissez-faire style*. Moderately high power motivation involving positive orientation leads to a participative or democratic leadership style.

(c) The *affiliation motivation* is a desire to interact with other individuals, to be liked by them, to belong to different groups, etc. Thus, it is related to social needs. *Schachter* in his treatise titled "The Psychology of Affiliation", has also analysed this motivation. He has assumed that individuals tend to seek affiliation to substantiate their beliefs and not merely to have good companionship. Such substantiation provides them with some kind of certainty in life-situations failing which there will be a lot of confusion, especially where one's beliefs are shattered.

Individuals tend to seek affiliation with those individuals who are exposed to identical situations. It is perhaps because of this fact that individuals tend to form informal organisations. The people who are unable to adjust to these organisations remain isolated and sometimes emerge as high producers. However, the number of such isolates is very small. Individuals also tend to engage themselves in social relations of their interdependence. They tend to interact and affiliate with those other individuals upon whom they depend for some resource or whom they perceive as a source of some gains. As soon as this dependence is declined, they are likely to minimise their interactions and affiliations with such individuals.

Basically, the affiliation motive is the desire to socialise as a goal in itself. People tend to seek good company, good family life, and popularity in groups just for its own sake leaders with high affiliation motivation are likely to be relations-oriented, warm, friendly and supportive while those with low affiliation motivation may be impersonal, bureaucratic and inaccessible in organisational settings. High affiliation motivation must, however, be accompanied by high achievement motivation in the leader, otherwise he is likely to sacrifice standards of performance for the sake of his popularity and be exploited by his subordinates.

McClelland's theory can be compared with *Maslow's* theory. The achievement motivation resembles self-actualisation need of *Maslow*. Affiliation motivation forms part of Maslow's social need. Lastly, power motivation as proposed by *McClelland* embraces safety, esteem and social needs embodied in Maslow's hierarchy.

(iv) Alderfer's ERG Theory

An extension of the Herzberg and, especially, the Maslow content theories of work motivation comes from the work of *Clayton Alderfer*. He formulated a need category model that was more in line with the existing empirical evidence. Like Maslow and Herzberg, he does feel that there is value in categorising needs and that there is a basic distinction between lower-order needs and higher-order needs.

Alderfer identified three groups of core needs : existence, relatedness, and growth (hence ERG theory). The existence needs are concerned with survival (physiological well-being). The relatedness needs stress the importance of interpersonal, social relationships. The growth needs are concerned with the individual's intrinsic desire for personal development. Figure shows how these groups of needs are related to the Maslow and Herzberg categories. Obviously, they are very close, but the ERG needs do not have strict lines of demarcation.

Alderfer is suggesting more of a continuum of needs than hierarchical levels or two factors of prepotency needs. Unlike Maslow and Herzberg, he does not contend that a lower-level needs has to be fulfilled before a higher-level need becomes motivating or that deprivation is the only way to activate a need. For example, according to ERG theory the person's background or cultural environment may dictate that the relatedness needs will take precedence over unfulfilled existence needs and that the more the growth needs are satisfied, the more they will increase in intensity.

There has not been a great deal of research on ERG theory. Although there is some evidence to counter the theory's predictive value, most contemporary analyses of work motivation tend to support Alderfer's theory over Maslow's and Herzberg's. Overall, ERG theory seems to include some of the strong points of earlier content theories but is less restrictive and limiting. The fact remains, however, that the content theories in general lack explanatory power regarding the complexities of work motivation and, with the possible exception of the implications for job design of Herzberg's work, do not readily translate to the actual practice of human resources management.

II. PROCESS THEORY OF MOTIVATION

Process theories try to describe and analyse how personal factors (internal to the person) interact to produce certain kinds of behaviour.

(i) Vroom's Expectancy Theory of Motivation

The expectancy theory of work motivation has its roots in the cognitive concepts of pioneering psychologists *Kurt Lewin* and *Edward Tolman*, and in the choice behaviour and utility concepts from classical economic theory. However, the first to formulate an expectancy theory directly aimed at work motivation was *Victor Vroom.* Contrary to most critics, Vroom proposed his expectancy theory as an alternative to content models, which he felt were inadequate explanations of the complex process of work motivation. At least in academic circles, his theory has become a popular explanation for work motivation and continues to generate considerable research.

Fig. 4, briefly summarises the Vroom model. As shown, the model is built around the concepts of valence, instrumentality, and expectancy, and is commonly called the *VIE theory.*

Meaning of the Variables

By valence, *Vroom* means the strength of an individual's preference for a particular outcome. Other terms that might be used include value, incentive, attitude, and expected utility. In order for

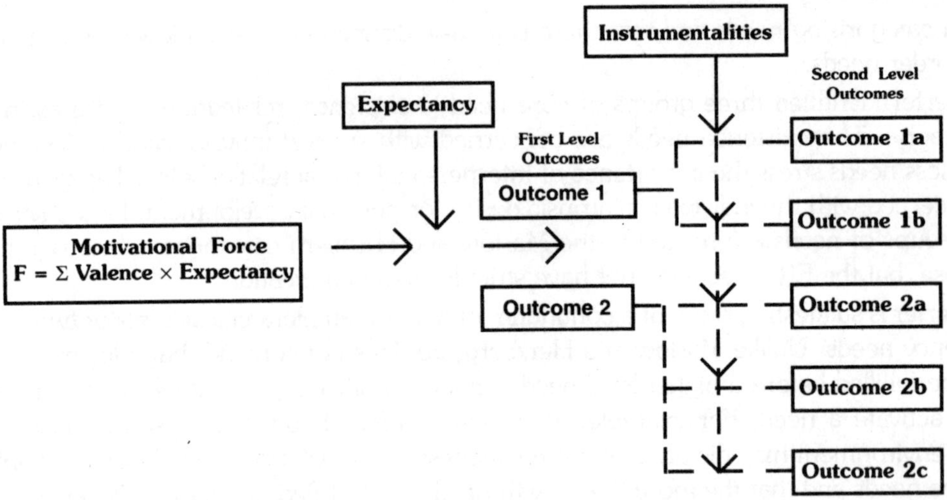

Fig. 4. *Vroom's Expectancy or VIE Theory of Work Motivation.*

the valence to be positive, the person must prefer attaining the outcome to not attaining it. A valence of zero occurs when the individual is indifferent toward the outcome; the valence is negative when the individual prefers not attaining the outcome to attaining it. Another major input into the valence is the instrumentality of the first-level outcome in obtaining a desired second-level outcome. For example, a person would be motivated toward superior performance because of the desire to be promoted. The superior performance (first-level outcome) is seen as being instrumental in obtaining a promotion (second-level outcome).

Another major variable in the Vroom motivational process is expectancy. Although psychological theorists all agree that expectancies are mental, or cognitive, states, there is little agreement about the nature of these states. Although at first glance the expectancy concept may seem to be the same as the instrumentality input into valence, it is actually quite different. Expectancy relates efforts to first-level outcomes (see Fig. 3.), while instrumentality relates first-level outcomes and second-level outcomes. In other words, expectancy in Vroom's theory is the probability (ranging from 0 to 1) that a particular action or effort will lead to a particular first-level outcome. Instrumentality refers to the degree to which a first-level outcome will lead to a desired second-level outcome. In summary, the strength of the motivation to perform a certain act will depend on the algebraic sum of the products of the valences for the outcomes (which include instrumentality) times the expectancies.

Implications of the Vroom Model for Organisational Behaviour

Vroom's theory departs from the content theories in that it depicts a process of cognitive variables that reflects individual differences in work motivation. It does not attempt to describe what the content is or what the individual differences are. Everyone has a unique combination of valences, instrumentalities, and expectancies. Thus, the Vroom theory indicates only the conceptual determinants of motivation and how they are related. It does not provide specific suggestions on what motivates organisational members, as the *Maslow*, *Herzberg*, and *Alderfer* models do.

Although the Vroom model does not directly contribute much to the techniques of motivating personnel in an organisation, it is of value in understanding organisational behaviour. It can clarify the relationship between individual and organisational goals. For example, suppose workers are given a certain standard for production. By measuring the workers' output, management can determine how important their various personal goals (second-level outcomes such as money, security, and recognition) are; the instrumentality of the organisational goal (the first-level outcomes, such as the production standard) for the attainment of the personal goals; and the worker's expectancies that their efforts and ability will accomplish the organisational goal. If output is below standard, it may be that the workers do not place a high value on the second-level outcomes; or they may not see that the first-level outcome is instrumental in obtaining the second-level outcomes; or they may think that their efforts will not accomplish the first-level outcome. Vroom feels that any one, or a combination, of these possibilities will result in a low level of motivation to perform. The model is designed to help management understand and analyse workers' motivation and identify some of the relevant variables; it does not provide specific solutions to motivational problems. Besides having an application problem, the model also assumes, as earlier economic theory did, that people are rational and logically calculating. Such an assumption may be too idealistic.

Importance of the Vroom Model

Probably the major reason Vroom's model has emerged as an important modern theory of work motivation and has generated so much research is that it does not take a simplistic approach. The content theories oversimplify human motivation. Yet the content theories remain extremely popular with practicing managers because the concepts are easy to understand and to apply to their own situations. On the other hand, the VIE theory recognises the complexities of work motivation, but it is relatively difficult to understand and apply. Thus, from a theoretical standpoints, the VIE model seems to help managers appreciate the complexities of motivation, but it does not give them much practical help in solving their motivational problems except simple prescriptions such as making sure employees know exactly what is expected of them.

In some ways Vroom's expectancy model is like marginal analysis in economics. Business people do not actually calculate the point where marginal cost equals marginal revenue, but it is still a useful concept for an economic theory of the firm. Likewise, the expectancy model attempts only to mirror the complex motivational process; it does not attempt to describe how motivational decisions are actually made or to solve actual motivational problems facing a manager.

(ii) The Porter-Lawler Model

Job satisfaction refer to the controversy over the relationship between satisfaction and performance that has existed since the beginnings of the human relations movement. The content theories implicitly assume that satisfaction leads to improved performance and that dissatisfaction detracts from performance. The Herzberg model is really a theory of job satisfaction, but still it does not adequately deal with the relationship between satisfaction and performance. The Vroom model also largely avoids the relationship between satisfaction and performance. Although satisfaction make an input into Vroom's concept of valence and although the outcomes have performance implications, it was not until *Porter* and *Lawler* refined and extended Vroom's model (for example, the relationships are expressed diagrammatically rather than mathematically, there are more variables, and the cognitive process of perception plays a central role) that the relationship between satisfaction and performance was dealt with directly by a motivation model.

Porter and Lawler start with the premise that motivation (effort or force) does not equal satisfaction or performance. Motivation, satisfaction, and performance are all separate variables and relate in ways different form what was traditionally assumed. Fig. 5, depicts the multivariable model used to explain the complex relationship that exists among motivation, performance, and satisfaction. As shown in the model, boxes 1, 2, and 3 are basically the same as the Vroom equation. It is important, however, that Porter and Lawler point out that effort (force or motivation) does not lead directly to performance. It is mediated by abilities and traits and by role perceptions. More important in the Porter-Lawler model is what happens after the performance. The rewards that follow and how these are perceived will determine satisfaction. In other words, the Porter-Lawler model is what happens after the performance. The rewards that follow and how these are perceived will determine satisfaction. In other words, the Porter-Lawler model suggests—and this is a significant turn of events from traditional thinking—that performance leads to satisfaction.

The model has had a fair degree of research support over the years. For example, a recent field study found that effort level and direction of effort are important in explaining individual performance in an organisation. Also, a comprehensive review of research verifies the importance of rewards in the relationship between performance and satisfaction. Specifically, it was concluded

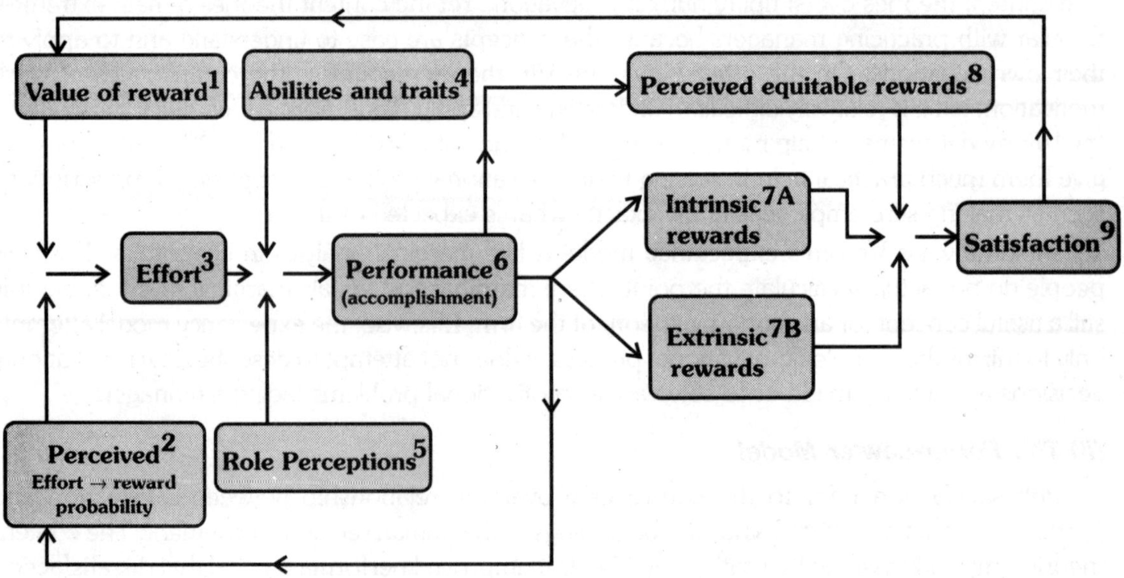

Fig. 5. *The Porter-Lawler Motivation Model.*

that performance and satisfaction will be more strongly related when rewards are made contingent upon performance than when they are not.

Implications for Practice

Although the Porter-Lawler model is more applications-oriented than the Vroom model, it is still quite complex and has proved to be a difficult way to bridge the gap to actual management practice. To Porter and Lawler's credit, they have been very conscientious of putting their theory and research into practice. They recommend that practicing managers go beyond traditional attitude measurement and attempt to measure variables such as the values of possible rewards, the perceptions of effort-reward probabilities, and role perceptions. These variables, of course, can help managers better understand what goes into employee effort and performance. Giving attention to the consequences of performance, Porter and Lawler also recommend that organisations critically re-evaluate their current reward policies. They stress that management should make a concentrated effort to measure how closely levels of satisfaction are related to levels of performance, and recently a practitioner-oriented article emphasised that the accuracy of role perceptions may be the missing link in improving employee performance. The inference here is that employees need to better focus their efforts on high-impact behaviours and activities that result in higher performance. However, both recent studies and comprehensive analyses continue to point out the complex impact that the cognitive process has in relation to rewards and other outcomes in organisations.

Contributions to Work Motivation

The Porter and Lawler model has definitely made a significant contribution to the better understanding of work motivation and the relationship between performance and satisfaction, but, to date, it has not had much impact on the actual practice of human resource management. Yet the expectancy models provide certain guidelines that can be followed by human resource management. For example, on the front end (the relationship between motivation and performance), it has been suggested that the following barriers must been overcome :

(i) Doubts about ability, skill, or knowledge.
(ii) The physical or practical possibility of the job.
(iii) The interdependence of the job with other people or activities.
(iv) Ambiguity surrounding the job requirements.

In addition, on the back end (the relationship between performance and satisfaction), guidelines such as the following have be suggested :

(i) Determine what rewards each employee values.
(ii) Define desired performance.
(iii) Make desired performance attainable.
(iv) Link valued rewards to performance.

The last point above is getting recognition in the management compensation plans of many big companies as indicated by the accompanying TQM in Action: Linking Managers' Rewards with Unit Performance.

III. CONTEMPORARY THEORIES OF WORK MOTIVATION

Although it is recognised that work-motivation theories are generally categorised into content and process approaches, equity and attribution theories have emerged in recent years and command most of the research attention. An understanding of these two theoretical developments is now necessary to the study of work-motivation in organisational behaviour.

(i) Theory X and Theory Y

The *Hawthorne* studies triggered a long series of studies. These threads were woven into a theoretical garment by *Prof. McGregor. McGregor* is credited as being the initiator of one of the most widely used and highly popular classification schemes for both the acceptable and unacceptable styles of today. This classification scheme was named, for want of better phraseology, Theory X and Theory Y, reflective of what he considered as two distinct perspectives of administrative action. Actually theory X and theory Y are attitudes or predispositions toward people. Theory X is negative, traditional and autocratic style while the theory Y is positive, participatory and democratic. Thus, these labels described contrasting set of assumptions about human nature.

Theory X

This is the traditional theory of human behaviour. In this theory, *McGregor* has certain assumptions about human behaviour. In his own words, these assumptions are as follows :

(i) Management is responsible for organising the elements of productive enterprises—money, materials, equipment, people—in the interest of economic ends.

(ii) With respect to people, this is a process of directing their efforts, motivating them, controlling their actions, modifying their behaviour to fit the needs of the organisation.

(iii) Without this active intervention by management, people would be passive—even resistant—to organisational needs. They must be persuaded, rewarded, punished, controlled, and their activities must be directed. This is management's task. We often sum it up by saying that management consists of getting things done through other people.

(iv) The average man is by nature indolent—he works as little as possible.

(v) He lacks ambition, dislikes responsibility, prefers to be led.

(vi) He is inherently self-centred, indifferent to organisational needs.

(vii) He is, by nature, resistant to change.

(viii) He is gullible, not very bright, the ready dupe of charlatan and the demagogue.

Of these assumptions, last five deal with the human nature and first three with managerial actions. These assumptions about human nature are negative in their approach, however much organisational processes have developed on these assumptions. Managers subscribing these views about human nature attempt to structure, control and closely supervise their employees. They feel that external control is most appropriate for dealing with irresponsible and immature employees. McGregor believes that these assumptions about human nature have not changed drastically though there is a considerable change in behavioural pattern. He argues that this change is not because of changes in the human nature, but because of nature of industrial organisation, management philosophy, policy, and practice.

Theory Y

The assumptions of Theory Y are described by *McGregor* in the following words:

(i) The expenditure of physical and mental effort in work is natural as play or rest. The average human being does not inherently dislike work. Depending upon controllable conditions, work may be a source of satisfaction or a source of punishment.

(ii) External control and the threat of punishment are not the only means for bringing about effort towards organisational objectives. Man will exercise self-direction and self-control in the service of objectives to which he is committed.

(iii) Commitment to objectives is a function of the reward associated with their achievement. The most significant of such awards, e.g., the satisfaction of ego and self-actualisation needs, can be direct product of effort directed towards organisational objectives.

(iv) The average human being learns under proper conditions not only to accept, but to seek responsibility. Avoidance of responsibility, lack of ambition, an emphasis on security are generally consequences of experiences, not inherent human characteristics.

(v) The capacity to exercise a relatively high degree of imagination, ingenuity, and creativity in the solution of organisational problems is widely, not narrowly, distributed in the population.

(vi) Under the conditions of modern industrial life, the intellectual potentialities of the average human being are only partially utilised.

The assumptions of Theory Y suggest a new approach in management. It emphasises on the cooperative endeavour of management and employees. The attempt is to get maximum output with minimum amount of control and direction. Generally, no conflict is visible between organisational goals and individual goals. Thus, the attempts of employees which are in their best interests are also in the interest of organisation.

Comparison of Theories X and Y

Both theories have certain assumptions about human nature. In fact, they are reverse sides of a coin, one representing head and the other representing tail. Thus, these assumptions seem to be mutually exclusive. The difference between two sets of assumptions can be visualised as follows:

(i) Theory X assumes human beings to be inherently distasteful towards work. Theory Y assumes that for human beings work is as natural as play.

(ii) Theory X emphasises that people do not have ambitions and try to avoid responsibilities in jobs. The assumptions under Theory Y are just the reverse.

(iii) According to Theory X, most people have little capacity for creativity while according to Theory Y, the capacity for creativity is widely distributed in the population.

(iv) In Theory X, motivating factors are the lower needs. In Theory Y, higher order needs are more important for motivation, though unsatisfied lower needs are also important.

(v) In Theory X, people lack self-motivation and require to be externally controlled and closely supervised to get maximum output from them. In Theory Y, people are self-directed and creative and prefer self-control.

(vi) Theory X emphasises scalar chain system and centralisation of authority in the organisation while Theory Y emphasises decentralisation and greater participation in the decision-making process.

(vii) Theory X emphasises autocratic leadership; Theory Y emphasises democratic and supportive leadership styles.

Implications of Theories X and Y

McGregor's assumptions in terms of Theory X and Theory Y are based on Maslow's need hierarchy model. In the beginning, when the concept of 'economic man' was accepted, some writers emphasised only on the satisfaction of physiological and safety needs. These were the basic constituents of the motivation model. However, because of changes in the value systems and social systems, higher-order needs were emphasised for human beings and these needs mostly replaced lower-order needs as constituents of motivation model. Similarly, assumptions under Theory X are being replaced by assumptions under Theory Y. This is being reflected in the managerial styles and techniques. Today we emphasise management by objectives, management by integration and self-control, supportive management, decentralisation, job enrichment. etc. These techniques are applicable in the organisations where self-motivated, self-controlled, mature, and responsible people work. McGregor believes that recent researchers in the behavioural sciences have shown that the assumptions of what he calls Theory Y may be more valid than the precepts of Theory X.

Theory Z

Of all the contemporary motivational theories in organisation theory literature the one that has received a great deal of attention is *Theory Z*. It is a new way of viewing the essential nature of man and the factors that motivate him. Theory Z has originated from the Japanese management philosophy. A notable feature of Japanese management is that managers seem to make better use of human capital. One reason why Japan has received utmost attention in the recent past by the organisational scientists is its success in many fronts. The rate of increment in productivity in Japan is roughly two to three times that of American firm over the past three decades, the absenteeism has been low, organisational commitment is high and turnover rate is half those of the America. Management experts in the recent past, had tried to analyse "how the companies in Japan are doing so exceptionally well" and the result of their analysis is the management style—Theory Z.

At the outset one can notice three apparent reasons for the relative success of Japanese system viz.—their technology, culture and the management system. The Japanese manufacturers have installed new and variegated technological equipment, but this is not radically different from the level of technology used in the rest of the world. Therefore the success of Japanese organisations goes beyond technology. As regards culture also Japanese employees do not possess significantly different traits when compared to their counterparts. This factor "culture" is also ruled out as effective contributor to productivity and success. For example, an average Japanese employee is less individualistic and more tolerant of excessive authority than is an average American. The most substantial explanation for the success of these organisations can therefore be in terms of their management system. Actually, their system is such that it integrates individual into the organisation to produce efficiency.

Organisational scientists who are working on exploring the realities of the "industrial miracle" of Japanese concerns have been responsible for this new theory called Theory Z. *William Ouchi* and *Alfred Jaeger* have been credited with studying and exploring the differences in styles of management of American and Japanese companies. Though the ideas of participation have appeared long back in Western literature it is Japan that has made the proper application of the concept of participation and got benefited by it. *William Ouchi* and *Jaeger* have identified seven major dimensions along which these American and Japanese companies differ. These dimensions can be presented thus:

(i) Period or Length of Employment

One important difference between both types of organisations (American and Japanese) is the length of employment of the people in organisation. It refers to the tenure of employees in the firm. American firms adapted to handle high rates of turnover of employees. Workers in this organisation are transient with no long term loyalty to their work group or employer and therefore management tries to minimise interdependencies between tasks. Moreover, an employee's specialised skills enable him to move between organisations. In type Z organisation the concept of employment is entirely different. Unlike A type organisations, in Z type organisations great stress is laid upon long-term employment. Long-term employment improves employee morale. It helps employees in getting familiar with coworkers and organisational workings. Further, the anticipation of a long career with a single organisation encourages a worker to become integrated into the organisation. Management, in turn can afford to take time and invest money in order to develop a talent bank within the organisation. Resignations are likely to be infrequent since employees are hired for a long time. Thus, an important factor in theory Z is the long-term employment. Similar to 'marriage', employment is also a permanent bondage of a worker with the organisation.

One praiseworthy feature of this type is that instead of hiring and firing people to suffer due to business cycles, organisations make certain adjustments to stabilise labour force. For example, during boom, employees are asked to do overtime instead of hiring people from outside. If the workload is too heavy the jobs can be dissected and may be subcontracted out to other firms. Similarly, during depression instead of laying off the labour force, the work week is typically shortened. For example, by cutting down the work week to twenty-five hours, every employee shares equally and no one needs to loose the job.

(ii) Decision-Making

It refers to the manner in which decisions are taken in the organisation. In the American type decisions are taken by individuals whereas in type Z organisation's decisions are participative. However, decision-making in Japan is not participative in the American sense of the term. It is not characterised by group meetings and discussions between superior and subordinates. In the typical Japanese model, the problem is exposed to all the members by the manager and is put to discussion in an informal way. When all are familiar with the proposal, then formal request for a decision will be made. The final outcome is not reflective of agreement but merely incorporation of decision input from any individual or group who or which will be quite likely to be affected. Another important point to observe in decision-making is regarding the punishment meted out for wrong decisions. Even in Japan heads roll when a decision turns out to be 'poor'. Punishment is more subtle and people in Japan will be demoted to less prestigious units.

(iii) Responsibility

In type A, since employees come and go frequently, they are required to assume individual responsibilities. On the other hand in type Z, it is virtually collective responsibility of all the members to see that the goals of organisation are accomplished.

(iv) Evaluation and Promotion

It refers to the frequency of employees' appraisal. In type A the evaluation process is frequent and rapid. Consequently promotions are also quick. In America ambitious employees can move up in their organisations frequently, if they perceive that their movement up the hierarchy is painfully slow, they can switch over to some other organisation where the prospects are brighter. In Japan life time employment means limited upward mobility. Evaluations are infrequent and promotions are slow, normally based on seniority. As a result employees are rather forcefully integrated into the culture of the organisation.

(v) Control

It refers to the methods of control wielded—whether employees are controlled with formal, explicit standards or implicit, informal standards. Control of employees through informal standards is advocated by the Japanese philosophy. The appraisal systems take into a number of factors apart from the current level of performance like personality traits, cooperation with co-workers etc. Occasional mistakes by members are considered part of the learning process and managers too, are willing to commit themselves to risky jobs because they do not have to show the results instantaneously say, for example, in one financial year. Control is exercised in American type organisations through formalisation—through rules, regulations and procedures.

(vi) Career Paths

It refers to whether employees have specialised skills in one particular area or expanding to several functional areas. Employees in type A seek job specialisation. In type Z instead of keeping people in their narrow areas of specialisation, employees are rotated laterally. This lateral movement gives employees job diversity and allows them to understand all parts of the organisation. Therefore, they pursue largely non-specialised career paths.

(vii) Concern

It refers to how that organisation views the employees. In type A there is segmented concern, i.e., employee is valued only during the time involved in the organisation (on the job). In type Z there is holistic concern. In other words the organisation's concern is oriented toward the total personal life of the employee. In fact, the major strategy used by the Japanese organisation is the socialisation process that indoctrinates the organisation's philosophy into every employee. Once hired, every employee undergoes an initial formal training programme running to six to eight months. In a sharp contrast to US employee, the Japanese employee is trained to socialise and committed to the organisation. His technical skills are secondary. When employees have no fear of being fired they will be willing to contribute something in the long interests of the organisation even if their skills become obsolete. He, in fact, becomes a typical proverbial 'organisation man'.

In summary, the type Z organisation retains the American cultural values of individualism but combines it with a collective approach to decision-making. Similarly explicit, formalised controls retained but are combined with implicit, informal social measurements. Further, career paths are moderately specialised. Finally, slow evaluations, slow promotions and long-term employment are associated with a comprehensive concern for employees including their families. The combination of these provide the framework for theory Z philosophy.

II. J. Stacy Adam's Equity Theory

Adam's Theory of Equity is one of the popular social exchange theories and is perhaps the most rigorously development statement of how individuals evaluate social exchange relationships. It is probably the clearest of the process theories. Basically the theory points out that people are motivated to maintain fair relationships with others and will try to rectify unfair relationships by making them fair. This theory is based on two assumptions about human behaviour.

1. Individuals make contributions (inputs) for which they expect certain outcomes (rewards). Inputs include such things as the person's past training and experience, special knowledge, personal characteristics etc. Outcomes include pay, recognition, promotion, prestige, fringe benefits etc.
2. Individuals decide whether or not a particular exchange is satisfactory, by comparing their inputs and outcomes to those of others in the form of a ratio. Equity exists when an individual concludes that his/her own outcome/input ratio is equal to that of other people.

Categories of Inequality

Schematically, inequity occurs when:

Overpayment inequity. The person gets more out of the job relative to what he puts in compared to another.

$$= \frac{\text{Person's outcomes}}{\text{Person's inputs}} > \frac{\text{Other's outcomes}}{\text{Other's inputs}}$$

Equity. In this situation both x and y obtain the same relative gain for their investments.

$$= \frac{\text{Person's outcomes}}{\text{Person's inputs}} = \frac{\text{Other's outcomes}}{\text{Other's inputs}}$$

Underpayment inequity. In this situation the person and the other do the same job but other gets paid more and the person experience dissonance.

$$= \frac{\text{Person's outcomes}}{\text{Person's inputs}} < \frac{\text{Other's outcomes}}{\text{Other's inputs}}$$

Adam states that "cognitive dissonance exists for person whenever his cognition of his job inputs and/or outcomes stand psychologically in over obverse relation to his cognitions of the inputs and/or outcomes of Other's."

How to Escape Inequity? (Inequity resolution strategies)

Suppose *A* and *B* are two typists who perform the same type of work in two different divisions of a company. Assume that *A* is paid Rs 3,000 a month and *B* is paid only Rs 2,800 a month. One day they meet and find out this unfortunate payment plan. According to equity theory both *A* and *B* will feel upset by this inequity. *A* will feel guilty for being paid more and *B* will resent the underpayment and will be frustrated. Now the question arises: how to bring about equity in their relationship ? For instance, *A* can do more or better work than *B* and *B* can do less or poorer work to equalise their ratios. This is termed as 'behavioural inequity resolution strategy'.

Another method to lower one's inputs is to remain absent from work. A and B can also attempt to adjust their outcomes to resolve inequity, for example A may refuse pay raises and B can demand for a raise. B may type for others against attractive remuneration in an attempt to raise his outcomes. If A lowers his outcomes and B raises his, they equalise their ratios and they may help to establish a fair relationship. Alternatively, they may decide to quit and get out of the relationship completely. Quitting a job, obtaining a transfer, absenteeism are common forms of leaving the field.

It is also possible to establish equity psychologically (psychological inequity resolution strategy). A and B can convince themselves that A actually works harder than B. Quite often inequitably paid workers convince themselves that they really are not working hard, thereby establishing equity between themselves and equitably paid workers. Thus, to restore equity, the person may alter the inputs or outcomes, cognitively distort the inputs or outcomes, leave the field, act on the other, or change the other.

The Major Postulates of the Theory

1. Perceived inequity creates tension in the individual.
2. The amount of tension is proportional to the magnitude of the inequity.
3. The tension created in the individual will motivate him/her to reduce it.
4. The strength of the motivation to reduce inequity if proportional to the perceived inequity.

In other words, the presence of inequity motivates the individual to change the situation through or psychological means to return to a condition of equity. Equity theory generally argues that it is the perceived equity of the situation that stimulates behaviour and satisfaction. Employee perception of the situation are more important here than objective 'reality'.

Equity Theory: Research Evidence

A large number of empirical studies have tested the components of equity theory under different conditions. The evidence supports most of the predictions of the theory. People paid on hourly basis who believes they are underpaid generally reduce both the quantity and quality of that which they are producing. Studies by *Arrowood* (1961), *Andrews* (1967), *Goodman* and *Friedman* (1968) supported the equity theory prediction: when two groups of subjects are paid on exactly the same basis those who view themselves as 'overpaid' perform substantially better. A recent study by *Pritchard*, *Dunnette* and *Jorgenson*, clearly reveal support for the theory: underpaid workers were less productive than equitably paid workers and overpaid workers were more productive than equitably paid workers.

Limitations

(i) It is somewhat narrow in its emphasis on visible rewards and overemphasizes conscious processes.

(ii) It is difficult to assess the perceptions (misperceptions) of employees. Hence, the difficulty in operationalising the concepts of the theory. In the words of *Dunham*, although easily understood the theory is complex and difficult in application.

(iii) How does person choose the Comparison Other? The process by which individuals decide whom to compare themselves with is not clearly understood at present. According to *Hamner* and Organ 'one of the weakest elements of equity theory is its analysis of the process by which individuals choose a Comparison Other'.

(iv) Equity theory is not precise enough to predict which actions are most probable.

Inspite of these limitations equity theory is a promising motivation theory and has direct relevance for compensation practice.

FINANCIAL AND NON-FINANCIAL INCENTIVES

People spend a large and important part of their lives in the organisation for which they work. They work because they expect something out of it. With respect to individual motivation, managerial action constitutes the selection of appropriate strategies, structures and policies to encourage and support motivated people to achieve organisational goals. This includes establishment of incentive and reward schemes (or systems) which will be valued by the employees. Members of the organisation must be persuaded to contribute their efforts toward the achievement of organisational goals. The work they perform, quite often, may have a little inherent interest or challenge. In other words, many a time the work may be either unpleasant or monotonous. Inspite of unpleasant features, work must be performed and this necessitates incentives.

Incentives are the inducements placed along the course of ongoing activities, keeping the activities directed toward organisational goals rather than others. Incentives are what the working employee gets from his employment in the organisation for being productive. Incentives are tangible and form part of the working environment. Furthermore, incentives entail more than stimulation of minimum work performance; they are vital in keeping the employee in an organisation as well as keeping him productive while at work. David McClelland, in this connection, rightly points out "In real life, rewards or incentives are like punctuation marks. They break-up sequences or call attention to them. In psychological terms, they are attention getting, effect-producing mechanisms, rather than substitutes for something else." A major approach to more effective motivation has appeared in various forms of attention to incentives. A manager now-a-days engages himself in driving the employees toward work through numerous incentives. The goal of incentives is superb performance by all members of organisation.

Incentives may be financial or non-financial. The distinction between financial and non-financial incentives rests on the difference in terms of pay-off. Any incentive that pay-off either directly or indirectly in money is labelled as financial incentive (for example, wages, salaries, bonus, profit-sharing schemes, retirement pay, vacation pay, etc.). Non-financial incentive, on the other hand, may take the form of earning higher status, greater responsibility, and participation in decision-making, token rewards like mementos etc. Thus any incentive that is not expressed in monetary terms is coined as non-financial.

Some incentives, however, have both financial and non-financial aspects. For example, promotion is financial as well as non-financial. It is financial in the sense that higher pay is attached to it. It typically carries higher responsibility, authority and status and therefore it is non-financial also. *Robert Dubin* contends that people seek promotions because they pay-off in both financial and non-financial ways. The following table exhibits different kinds of incentives that are generally provided in organisations:

Financial incentives	Non-Financial incentives	Both (Financial and non-financial) incentives
Individual Incentives:		
Taylor's Differential piece-rate plan	Authority Responsibility.	Promotion.
Gantt's Bonus plan Halsey's plan	Status	Seniority standing.
Emerson's efficiency plan	Supervision	
Rowan's plan	Participation in management.	Recognition for merit.
Group Incentive Plans:		
Production plan	Job satisfaction.	Designation as a permanent employee.
Profit-sharing plan	Job security.	
	Making job pleasant and interesting.	

Financial Incentives

Finance is a magic word in present culture. The bedrock appeal for money stems from its ability to control the environment. The idea that money is a strong motivator is deeply rooted and still controls the first responses of managers who are having trouble-motivating employees. Many people believe that money can control their environment and these people do respond well to monetary incentives.

The use of financial incentives as important motivators has been overemphasised in the recent past. Money as a motivator, a special kind of reinforcer, has been criticised by academic researchers. Over the years research in human relations and behavioural sciences has shown that "whereas money incentives had not proven effective, psychic rewards worked." Money's reputation as a motivator has began to slip.

The researchers have criticised the merit system as being detrimental to motivation rather than enhancing motivation as it intended to *Herb Meyer*, after reviewing research on pay system in General Electric and other companies concludes that merit pay does not work with elegant simplicity. In practice, managers typically seemed inclined to make relatively small discrimination in salary treatment among individuals in the same jobs, regardless of perceived differences in performances. *Herzberg* rigidly maintains that pay is not a motivator but a hygiene. If the employees receive what they expect, there will be no change in behaviour. Payment above expectation will probably change behaviour as the employee attempts to reduce the dissonance associated with the increased pay. On the other hand, payments below expectation causes dissatisfaction and prevents a positive work environment from being established. The essence of this philosophy is that providing workers with what they expect will have no remarkable effect on their behaviour; it is only when expectations are not met, that behaviour is changed.

Studies of effectiveness of financial incentives have revealed many shortcomings. Although occasional examples of outstanding results have been discovered they are by no means universal. In fact, the more customary experience seems to involve unsatisfactory, only reasonably satisfactory results. Money is one, but only one, of the factors of importance to the worker. The major error in utilising such an approach is the attachment of undue importance to it. It is wrong to see financial incentives as the only goal of employee. In good many cases, it may not even be the primary motivating factor. In surveys, workers seldom place pay higher than fourth or fifth in the list of things that are important to their morale. It is not to deny the simple fact that money affects the way an employee works—how much and how well.

But the question remains why the pay and merit system has lost its effectiveness? Several reasons are advanced by scholars.

(i) *Pay is not perceived as being related to job performance.* There is found inconsistent relationship between pay and performance in organisations. For instance, in a survey of six hundred middle and lower level managers, *Lawler* found virtually no relationship between their pay levels and their rated performance. Where individual and group incentives are to be applied several steps can be taken, therefore, to cement the connection between pay and performance :

(a) Determine what extrinsic rewards employees want.

(b) Determine the chance of employees getting the rewards by trying for them.

(c) Determine whether the cost to employees, in the form of effort, unwanted results, and foregone alternatives appears to them to be worth the potential rewards.

(d) Determine whether the pay is linked to performance.

(e) Monitor job attitudes to see what people believe about pay and performance and whether the most satisfied workers are the best performers.

(ii) *Performance ratings are viewed as biased.* Though managers appreciate incentive-plan philosophy they are dissatisfied with the evaluation of their performance by their superiors. Similarly the employees may be dissatisfied with the evaluation of their performance by the managers etc. A merit plan is based on the assumption that managers can make objective distinction between poor and good performance. But most of the evaluations are subjective in nature and reminds the employee very clearly that he is dependent on the supervisor for rewards. Therefore, merit plan may be viewed as biased and the employees may feel they are at the mercy of their supervisor. Merit plan, in order to get rid of this problem, must be based on objective measures such as goal attainment, cost reduction per unit, increase in sales etc., rather than subjective measures such as potential of the employees, cooperation they render to the supervisor, the employee attitudes etc.

(iii) *Rewards are not viewed as rewards*. Another associated problem in administering a merit increase concerns manager's ability to communicate accurately to the employees the fact that pay increase represents the positive message. Otherwise, employees may have the tendency to view the pay increase negatively. In other words, management believes that it is communicating a positive message to the employee when the message being received by the employee is actually negative. The reward message may not be seen as a reward in positive sense because of three major reasons:

(a) Conflicting reward structures may be operating.

(b) Employees perceive inequity in pay.

(c) The merit increase may be perceived as threat to the employee.

Reward schedules may be quite often conflicting because the company may have a defect in the merit plan itself. For example, the individual rewards may be set up in such a way that cooperation with other managers is discouraged (the best manager will get a free trip to Hong Kong—and the provisions like this), or cost-reduction programme may be introduced at the expense of other departments' outputs. It is, of course, better to keep financial incentives to everyone in the organisation based on the total performance of the organisational unit.

The feeling of inequity in pay can come from two sources. Firstly, the individual may perceive a merit increase to be unfair relative to his own previous year's performance. In other words he may be totally dissatisfied with the performance evaluation. He may also feel that performance evaluation is fair but the manager is unable to reward him suitably. Secondly, the employee may perceive that others who are performing at lower levels (below his own performance) are receiving higher amounts. The perceived inequity in pay also poses problems and more essentially employees do not view the rewards as rewards.

The final problem with the merit plan is that it may act as a threat to the self-esteem of the managers. *Herb Meyer* concludes in his research at General Electric that "inconsistencies between the information of the merit rise and the manager's own evaluation of his performance will be a threat to his self-esteem and the manager may, cope with this threat by denying the importance of hardwork or disparaging the merit system itself."

(iv) *Trust and openness about merit increase are low.* A merit plan will be accepted only when managers actively administer a performance appraisal system, good human relations exist, or managers properly communicate the reasons for the pay increases etc. The organisation must, therefore provide an open climate with respect to pay as well as an environment in which work and efforts are valued. For example, Xerox Corporate Planning Model, in its recent report on compensation plan has stated that "if pay and satisfaction are to be high, pay rises must be according to job demands in such a way that each perceived increment in a job demand factor will lead to increased pay."

(v) *Some organisations view money as the primary motivator ignoring the importance of the job itself.* It is important to remember that incentive system is not the only factor to take into account. Skinner, in this connection contends "how pleasant work conditions are, how easy or awkward a job, how good or bad tools are—many things of that sort make an enormous difference in what a worker will do for what he receives". Skinner warns managers that to much dependence on force and poorly designed motivational reward system may actually reduce the performance.

Non-Financial Incentives

The production worker is very rarely driven by money motivation. He is not highly skilled and his background has not generally been victory after victory but rather tie after deadlock after standoff with life. His lack of progress may be due to lack of ability, lack of psychological drive and stamina, poor environmental factors etc. In the wake of socio-economic constraints, a production worker attaches a high priority to esteem and recognition and social approval. The psychic rewards and the rewards of enhanced status and position are general forms of non-financial incentives. Apart from the power, authority and status, people also derive job satisfaction. Job satisfaction is considered to be one of the rewards for people at work. *Dubin* rightly contends "people doing more different and more skilled tasks get more rewards from their work in the form of job satisfaction. In particular, they seem to enjoy the variety of work and sense of personal responsibility they have for doing it."

REVIEW QUESTIONS

1. What do you understand by the term 'motivation'? Discuss the importance and nature of the Motivation.
2. Explain the various theories of motivation in detail.
3. Give the salient feature of theory "X" and theory "Y".
4. Explain Adam's theory of motivation.
5. "Expectancy is one of the most complex intricate, and logical theories of motivation"? Examine the truth of this statement.
6. Write a detail note on theory Z.
7. Explain in detail Herzberg's two-factor theory of motivation.

8. Explain Adam's theory of motivation.
9. Explain the Porter-Lawler model of motivation.

REFERENCES

1. *J.L. Gray and F.A. Starke, Organisational Behaviour, Ohio, Charles E. Merrill Co., 1977.*
   W.E. Reif, D.N. Ferrazzi and R. Evans Jr., "Job Enrichment: Who Uses It and Why?" Business Horizons, Vol. 17, No. 1. Feb., 1974.
2. *P.F. Drucker, "Beyond the Stick and Carrot: Hysteria over the Work Ethic". Psychology Today, Nov., 1973.*
3. *D. Katz and R.L. Kahn, The Social Psychology of Organisations, New York, John Wiley and Sons, 1938.*
4. *A.H. Kurloff, "An Experiment in Management—Putting Theory Y to Test", Personnel, Nov-Dec., 1963.*
   P. Hersey and K. Blanchard, Management of Organisational Behaviour, New Delhi, Prentice-Hall, 1982.
   R. Gordon, op. cit.
3. *J.J. Morse and J.W. Lorsch, 'Beyond Theory Y', HBR, May-June, 1970.*
4. *G. Strauss, "Personality-Organisation Hypothesis" in R. Dubin. op. cit.*
   For a Summary of Equity Theory Research on Employee Reactions to Pay see Steers and Porter, Motivation and Work Behaviour, op. cit.
5. *R.D. Pitchard, M.D. Dunnette, D.O. Jorgenson, "Efforts of Perceptions of Equity and Inequity on Worker Performance and Satisfaction," Jl. of Applied Psychology, 56, 1972.*
6. *L. Porter, E.E. Lawler and J.R. Hackman, Behaviour in Organisations, New York, McGraw Hill, 1975.*
7. *L.W. Porter and EE. Lawler, Managerial Attitudes and Performance Homewood, II Irwin, 1968.*
8. *S.P. Robbins, Organisation Theory, Englewood Cliffs, New Jersey, 1983.*
9. *R.L. Daft, Organisation Theory and Design, Minnesota, West Publishing Co., 1983.*
10. *F.E. Kast and J.E. Rosenzweig, Organisation and Management, New York, McGraw Hill, 1979.*
11. *M.D. Richards and W.A. Hielander (ed.), Readings in Management, Bombay, D.B. Taraporevala and Sons, 1971.*
12. *S. Zedeck and M. Blood, Foundations of Behavioural Science Research Organisations Belmont, Calif. Wardsworth Publishing Co., 1974.*
13. *Behaviour is not Determined by Wants Alone. Environment Social Norms, Attitudes, Perception, Knowledge and Defense Mechanisms—All Affect Behaviour.*
14. *H.G. Hicks and C.R. Gullett, The Management of Organisations, Tokyo, McGraw Hill, 1976.*
15. *J.A.C. Brown, The Social Psychology of Industry, Baltimore, Penguin Books, 1954.*
16. *D.M. McGregor, "The Human Side of Enterprise", The Management Review, Nov., 1957.*
    "Notable in the Framework is the Development and Refinement of the Structure of Needs. Not Satisfied with a Crude Dichotomy like Physical and Social Needs, Maslow Sketches a List of Basic Needs which are Regarded as Connotive or Striving Needs" Blair J. Kolasa, Introduction to Behavioural Science for Business, New Delhi, Wiley Eastern Ltd. 1978.
17. *D.R. Hampton, Contemporary Management, New York, McGraw Hill, 1981.*
    As a Theory of Motivation, Maslow Utilised the Two Concepts of Deprivation and Gratification to Provide the Dynamic Forces that Linked Needs to General Behaviour. Heused the Deprivation Concept

to Establish 'Dominance' within His Hierarchy of Needs. He Postulated that Deprivation or Dissatisfaction of a Need of High Prepotency Will Lead to the Domination of This Need over the Organisation's Personality"—Wabha and Bridwell, op. cit.

18. *E.H. Burack, Organisational Analysis, illinois, The Dryden Press, 1975.*

    P.R. Lawrence and J.W. Lorsch, "The New Management Job: The Integrator", Harvard Business Review, Nov-Dec., 1967.

19. *J.L. Gray and F.A. Starke, Organisational Behaviour, Charles E. Merril Pub. Co., Ohio, 1977.*

5th

CHAPTER

OVERVIEW

POWER, AUTHORITY AND POLITICAL BEHAVIOUR

• ***After reading this chapter, you should be able to know:***

- Features of Power
- Authority
- Different Forms of Authority
- Factors of Authority
- The Distinction among Power, Authority, and Influence
- Different Forms of Interpersonal Power
- Structural Sources of Power
- Power Relationships
- Contingency Approaches to Power
- Upward Flow of Power
- The Effective Use of Power
- Power Tactics
- Coalitions
- Dependency
- Interdepartmental Power
- Empowerment
- Politics
- Main Feature of Politics
- Factors Contributing to Political Behaviour
- Political Behaviour
- Organisational Politics
- Research on Organisational Politics
- Political Tactics
- Antidotes to Political Behaviour
- Personality and Political Behaviour
- Dysfunctional Political Behaviour
- Playing Politics
- Some Devious Political Tactics
- Ethics, Power, and Politics

5

Power, Authority and Political Behaviour

INTRODUCTION

The term power may be applied to individuals, groups, teams, organisations and countries. People continually attempt to influence the behaviour of others in the normal course of everyday living. For example, people quite naturally attempt to *reinforce* the satisfying behaviours of family members and friends.

Power is social term, that is, an individual has power in relation to other people, a group or team has power in relation to other groups, and so on. The concept of power characterises interactions among people—more than one person must be involved for the concept to apply. Further, power is never absolute or unchanging. It is dynamic relationship that changes as situations and individuals change. *Nord* defines power as follows :

"Power is the ability to influence flows of the available resources towards certain goals as opposed to other goals. Power is assumed to be exercised only when these goals are at least partially in conflict with each other."

Power is easy to feel and happy to exercise but difficult to define. It is a force that cannot be seen, but its impact (effects) can be felt. Power is extremely difficult to identify and measure objectively. Researchers exhibit an aversion to deal with matters of power because it defies precise definition and quantification. Much difficulty is due to the multidimensional nature of power.

Robbins has defined power in more elaborate way when he says, *"Power refers to a capacity and A has to influence the behaviour of B, so that B does something he or she would not otherwise do.* This definition implies : (i) A potential that need not be actualised to be effective, (ii) A dependence relationship, and (iii) That B has some discretion over his or her own behaviour.

An oversimplified definition of power states that "power is the ability to get things done the way one wants them to be done." More essentially, power is an exchange process—a person who commands services needed by others exchange them for compliance with his or her requests. Power is a function of ties of mutual dependence in social relationships. Power is the ability of one to control the actions of others. In the organisational context, power is the ability of one person (or department) to influence the behaviour of others in the organisation to bring about desired outcomes for power-holders. From the above definitions the following points emerge:

(i) Power represents the capacity, ability or potential to influence the behaviour of other people to achieve a certain goal.

(ii) Power is based on the two-tier concept of influencing others and being influenced.

(iii) Power can be potential or enacted.

(iv) Power is neither completely formal nor informal. It is rather a judicious mixture of two.

(v) Leaders exercise power to accomplish goals of an organisation.

(vi) Leaders have only as much power as others allow them to have.

(vii) Sometimes appearing to be powerful is just as important as being powerful.

(viii) Power is the difference between the two probabilities—the probability of an event occurring given action by the power-holder, and the probability of event occurring without the power-holder's action.

Thus, power has been defined basically as the capacity to do something or get intended results from others.

FEATURES OF POWER

Power has the following features:

(i) Power is one of the means to influence others for getting results. It implies that influence can be exercised by other means too, like use of authority, leadership, and communication.

(ii) Influence process occurs in a particular way when it is attempted by the use of power.

(iii) Power is used not only in getting certain results achieved but it also includes negative decisions, or the action of non-decision. Thus, power is not only one's influence over the decision-making, but also one's capability of limiting the scope of actual decision-making.

(iv) Power is extra organisational in nature and any one in the organisation may have this type of influence through the use of power provided one is capable of doing so.

Another instructive way of looking at power is to distinguish between "power over" (ability to dominate), "power to" (ability to act freely), and "power from" (ability to resist the demands of others).

AUTHORITY

Simon defines authority as the power to make decisions which guide the actions of another. It relates to a relationship between two individuals—superior and subordinate. While the superior frames and transmits decisions with the expectation that they will be accepted by the subordinate, the latter expects such decisions and his conduct is determined by them. Thus, the relationship of authority involves a set of behaviours on the part of both superior and subordinate.

The behaviour pattern of the superior involves a command and an expectation that it will be accepted by the subordinate. The behaviour pattern of the subordinate is determined by a single indeterminate decision to comply with that alternative action which is initiated by the superior.

DIFFERENT FORMS OF AUTHORITY

Following *Weber*, *Dubin* distinguishes three types of authority:

(i) Rational,

(ii) Traditional, and

(iii) Charismatic—the gift of grace.

The *Rational Authority* is based on the belief by subordinate in the legality and propriety of the rules governing the organisation and the right of leaders to exercise commands under such rules.

The *Traditional Authority* is based on the belief by subordinates in the sanctity of time-honoured traditions and the legitimate right or status of those exercising authority over them.

The *Charismatic Authority* is based on the devotion of subordinates to an individual who is believed to have exceptional personal characteristics which set him apart from others.

FACTORS OF AUTHORITY

There are a number of specific factors which induce acceptance of authority in organisations. These factors are called "sanctions" or sanctions of authority and include the following:

I. The Social Sanctions

The society develops in the individual expectations of obedience in certain social situations. The individual who fails to perform his role, is likely to experience the social disapproval of his fellows. For example, insubordination by a subordinate may be embarrassing to him because of the social sanctions.

II. The Psychological Factors

There are certain psychological factors (i.e., personality types) which play a significant role in enforcing authority relationships.

III. The Purpose

The purpose forms an effective sanction of authority under certain conditions. For example, in voluntary organisations efforts are contributed largely by people because they are sympathetic to its purpose.

IV. The Relation between the Job and Economic Security and Status

Several formal sanctions are based on the relations between the 'job' and economic security and status in organisation. For example, obedience is the price which the individual pays for retaining his position, obtaining a higher salary and allied advantages.

V. Unwillingness or Disinclination to Accept Responsibility

In situations where assigned task is not excessively unpleasant, the individual may prefer being told what to do rather than being forced to make the decisions himself. This is particularly true when the decision in question falls outside the area of his experience and competence. Thus, simple unwillingness or disinclination to accept responsibility may form a major reason for the acceptance or decisions made by others.

THE DISTINCTION AMONG POWER, AUTHORITY, AND INFLUENCE

"Power" itself can be defined as the ability to get an individual or group to do something—to get the person or group to change in some way. The person who possesses power has the ability to manipulate or change others. Such a definition of power distinguishes it from authority and influence.

Authority legitimatizes and is a source of power. Authority is the right to manipulate or change others. Power need not be legitimate. In addition, the distinction must be made between top-down classical, bureaucratic authority and *Barnard's* concept of bottom-up authority based upon acceptance. In particular, Barnard defined authority as "the character of a communication (order) in a formal organisation by virtue of which it is accepted by a contributor to or 'member' of the organisation as governing the action he contributes."

Such an acceptance theory of authority is easily differentiated from power. *Grimes* notes : "What legitimises authority is the promotion or pursuit of collective goals that are associated with group consensus. The polar opposite, power, is the pursuit of individual or particularistic goals associated with group compliance."

Influence is usually conceived of as being broader in scope than power. It involves the ability to alter other people in general ways, such as by changing their satisfaction and performance. Influence is more closely associated with leadership than power is, but both obviously are involved in the leadership process. Thus, authority is different from power because of its legitimacy and acceptance, and influence is broader than power, but it is so conceptually close that the two terms can be used interchangeably. Authority has the following characteristics :

(i) It is vested in a person's position. An individual has authority because of the position that he holds, not because of any specific personal characteristics.

(ii) It is accepted by subordinates. The individual in a legal authority position exercise authority and can gain compliance because she has a legitimate right.

(iii) Authority is used vertically and flows the top down in the hierarchy of an organisation.

Influence is word we often come across when studying power. We agree with *Henry Mintzberg* and others that making a distinction between influence and power adds little to understanding.

In addition to exercising authority, an individual or group may be able to influence the behaviour of other people in an organisation for many other reasons. In general power sources in an organisation may be categorised as:

(i) Interpersonal Power.

(ii) Structural Power.

DIFFERENT FORMS OF INTERPERSONAL POWER

Any discussion of power usually begins and sometimes ends with the five categories of the sources of power identified by social psychologists *John French* and *Bertram Raven*. Describing and analysing these five classic types of power serves as a necessary foundation and point of departure for the entire chapter:

I. Legitimate Power

Legitimate power is a person's ability to influence because of position. A person at a higher level has power over people below. In theory, organisational equals (e.g., all first-line supervisors) have equal legitimate power. However, each person with legitimate power uses it with a personal flair. Legitimate power is similar to Weber's concept of authority.

Subordinates play a major role in the exercise of legitimate power. If subordinates view the use of power as legitimate, they comply. However, the culture, customs, and value systems of an organisation determine the limits of legitimate power. A company president who suggests that all employees should vote for a particular political candidate may find that only some people comply with the suggestion.

II. Reward Power

A person derives power from the ability to reward compliance. Reward power is used to back up the use of legitimate power. If followers value the rewards or potential rewards that the person can provide (recognition, a good job assignment, a pay raise, additional resources to complete a job), they may respond to orders, requests, and directions. For example, a sales manager who can reward sales people with cash bonuses, expanded client lists, or additional entertainment funds can exert reward power.

III. Coercive Power

The opposite of reward power is coercive power, the power to punish. Followers may comply because of fear. A manager may block a promotion or transfer of a subordinate for poor performance. These practices, and the fear that they'll be used, are coercive power. Although punishment may result in some unexpected side effects, it's a form of coercive power that's still used to bring about compliance or to correct nonproductive behaviour in organisations. Managers tend to use coercive power in situations where large numbers of employees are being supervised.

IV. Expert Power

A person with special expertise that's highly valued expert power. Experts have power even when their rank is low. An individual may possess expertise on technical, administrative, or personal matters. The more difficult it is to replace the expert, the greater the expert power she possesses.

Expert power is a personal characteristic, while legitimate, reward, and coercive power are largely prescribed by the organisation. A secretary who has a relatively low-level organisational position may have high expert power because he knows the details of operating the business—where every thing is or how to handle difficult situations.

V. Referent Power

Many individuals identify with and are influenced by a person because of the latter's personality or behavioural style. The charisma of the person is the basis of referent power. A person with charisma is admired because of his personality. The strength of a person's charisma is an indication of his referent power. Charisma is a term often used to describe the magnetic personalities of some politicians, entertainers, or sports figures. Some managers are also regarded by their subordinates as charismatic.

The five bases of interpersonal power can be divided into two major categories: organisational and personal. Legitimate, reward, and coercive power are primarily prescribed by the organisation, the position, formal groups, or specific interaction patterns. A person's legitimate power can be changed by transferring the person, rewriting the job description, or reducing the person's power by restructuring the organisation. In contrast, expert and referent power are very personal. A person has expertise, or he develops a set of credentials or the image characteristic or an expert. A person has or does not have charisma. It can't be tampered with, modified, or developed through training programs. It's a personal style that's quite individualised.

The five types of interpersonal power aren't independent. On the contrary, Managers can use these power bases effectively in various combinations in differing circumstances. Several studies have examined issues related to contextual uses of power. One study of organisations found that legitimate, expert, and referent power were the three most important reasons employees reported for doing what a peer or boss requested. Two other studies' findings determined a strong correlation between managers' levels and use of expert and referent power and employees' emotional involvement and commitment to their jobs. Legitimate power was found to be highly associated with compliance but negatively associated with employee satisfaction.

STRUCTURAL SOURCES OF POWER

Much of the attention directed at power in organisations tends to focus on the power of managers over subordinates. An additional perspective is that many aspects of a situation, in part, determine power. They include the design of the organisation, the type of departmental structure, the opportunity to influence, access to powerful individuals and critical resources, the nature of the position an individual holds, and so on. For example, the power associated with a particular position or job is affected by its visibility to upper management and its importance or relevance with respect to the organisation's goals or priorities. *Structural and situational sources of power* reflect the division of labour and membership in different departments, teams, and groups. These work assignments, locations, and roles naturally result in unequal access to information, resources, decision-making, and other people. Any of an almost infinite variety of specific situational factors could become a source of power in an organisation.

I. Knowledge as Power

Organisations are information processors that must use knowledge to produce goods and services. The concept of knowledge as power means that individuals, teams, groups, or departments that possess knowledge crucial to attaining the organisation's goals have power. People and groups in a position to control information about current operations, develop information about alternatives, or acquire knowledge about future events and plans have enormous power to influence the behaviour of others. Thus certain staff and support activities—a data processing centre, for example—sometimes seem to have influence disproportionate to their relationship to the organisation's major goals and activities.

The increased use of personal computers and computerised work stations is having a dramatic impact on access to and use of information—and thus on power relationships—in many organisations. Information is rapidly becoming more widely available to many employees. Greater access to information tends to flatten the hierarchy and make hoarding information by employees or departments more difficult. Information sharing has important implications for the quality of decision-making and other aspects of performance.

II. Resources as Power

Organisations need a variety of resources, including human resources, money, equipment, materials, supplies, and customers to survive. The importance of specific resources to a firm's success and the difficulty of obtaining them vary. The concept of resources as power suggests that departments, groups, or individuals who can provide essential or difficult-to-obtain resources acquire power in the organisation. Which resources are the most important depends on the situation, the organisation's goals, the economic climate, and the goods or services being produced. The old saying that "he who has the gold makes the rules" sums up the idea that resources are power.

III. Decision-Making as Power

Decisions in organisations often are made sequentially, with many individuals or groups participating. The decision-making process creates additional power differences among individuals or groups. The concept of decision-making as power means that individuals or groups acquire power to the extent that they can affect some part of the decision-making process. They might influence the goals being developed, premises being used in making a decision, alternatives being considered, outcomes being projected, and so on. The ability to influence the decision-making process is a subtle and often overlooked source of power. Decision-making power doesn't necessarily reside with the final decision-maker in an organisation.

IV. Networks as Power

The extensive use of computer networks is spreading and presetting management with both opportunities and challenges. These networks enables many employees to share information simultaneously. Further, computer networks provide workers with information that previously was available only to management. Networks also provide another access : the ability to join discussions of senior executives or other top managers. The existence of structural and situational power depends not only on access to information, resources, and decision-making, but also on the ability to get cooperation in carrying out tasks. Managers and departments that have connecting links with other individuals and departments in the organisation will be more powerful than those who don't. As suggested by Fig. 1, traditional superior-subordinate vertical relationships are important aspects of power. In addition, the horizontal linkages provided by both internal and external networks help explain power differences. The concept of networks as power implies that various affiliations, networks, and coalitions, both inside and outside the organisation, represent sources of power.

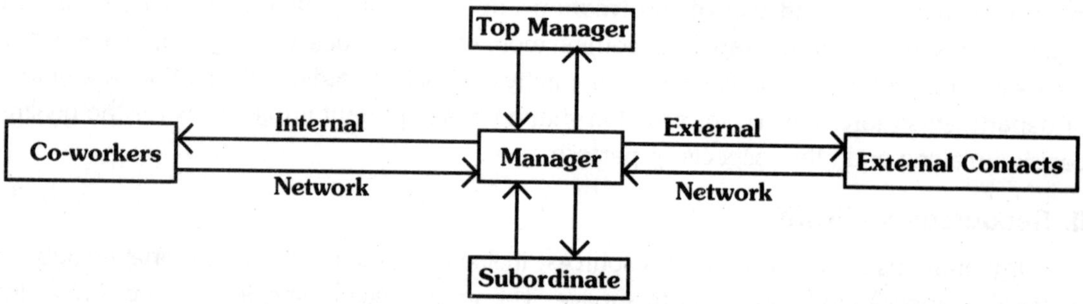

Fig. 1. *Work Relationships and Power.*

For example, power is provided by the following connecting links, each of which relates to the factors already discussed:

(i) *Information links* : To be effective, managers and employees must be "in the know" in both the formal and informal sense. (*Knowledge is power*.)

(ii) *Supply links:* Outside links provide managers with the opportunity to bring materials, money, or other resources into their departments or teams. (*Resources are power*.)

(iii) *Support links:* A manager's job must allow for decision-making discretion—the exercise of judgement. Managers must know that they can make decisions and assume innovative, risk-taking activities without each decision or action having to go through a stifling, multi-layered approval process. Managers and other professionals need the backing of other important figures in the organisation, whose support becomes another resource they bring to their own work unit. (Participation in decision-making is power and an important indicator of support links.)

Internal networks are key to understanding how the organisation gets work done. To identify and determine how they operate, managers and employees can undertake a network analysis, whereby they attempt to diagram important relationship networks within the organisation. For example, the advice network reveals employees that others depend on to solve problems and provide technical information. The trust network shows which employees share delicate political information with each other. The communication network indicates who talks to whom on a regular basis. By understanding these and other networks, managers can diagnose the informal, organisation and understand more about how work actually gets done (or fails to get done) in the organisation, as well as identify power differences among individuals and groups.

V. Lower Level Employee Power

Although we commonly think of power as something that managers have, lower level employees also may wield considerable power. Some sources of interpersonal power-expert power, in particular—may allow subordinates to influence their managers. For example, the secretary who can use a Windows spreadsheet has the power to influence her manager's decisions if the manager cannot personally use the spreadsheet and must rely on the secretary's expertise.

Although lower level employees may have some interpersonal power, their ability to influence other's behaviour more likely stems from structural or situational sources. Fig. 2. suggest that their power is a result of their positions in the organisation. Networks or affiliations with powerful individuals or groups may be yet another source of their power. Further, the expertise of employees and the amount of effort expended also influence the extent of their power. As Fig. 2, illustrates, whether expertise and effort increase employees' power depends, in part, on their superior's expertise and effort. For example, if an employee's manager has little knowledge about a certain task and the employee has considerable knowledge, the relative power of the employee increases. Employees also can acquire power by expending effort in areas where management puts little effort.

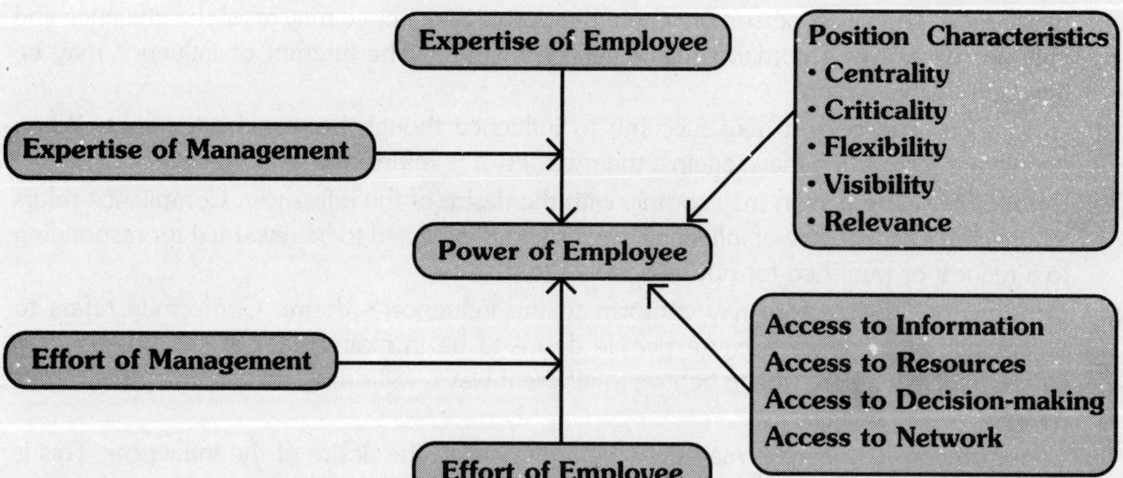

Fig. 2. *Model of Lower Level of Power.*

POWER RELATIONSHIPS

Power variable is a relational one. A person or group cannot have power is isolation; it has to be in relationship to other person or group. The parties involved in power relationship are tied to each other by mutual dependency. By virtue of mutual dependency, it is more or less imperative for each party to be able to control or influences other's conduct. It implies that each party to the power relationship is in a position to some degree to grant or deny facilities or hinder the other's gratification. Thus, the power to control or influence the other resides in control over things which other person values. This may be material things or abstract things like attitudes and ego support.

Dependency of some kind is the basic characteristic of all the modern organisations. Such dependency exists either among individuals or units and subunits. For example, the design of a bureaucratic organisation rests largely on the power. Variable with the intent of ensuring that each level in the organisation has sufficient power. This power however, is affected by informal patterns worked out over time and by personal differences in the exercise of the power available in a unit or subunit. Thus, various units may have power in varying amounts. For example, *Perrow* has concluded that in the industrial firms sales departments are overwhelmingly regarded as the most powerful units. The other subunits of the firm regard them in that way and behave accordingly.

In the mutual dependency, the power of a person over another depends on the amount of resistance the other person can put against the influence attempts by the person. Thus power is balanced if both have equal power and dependency upon each other. The relationship is imbalanced when either of them has more power or dependency than the other. This is the situation when power can be exercised. However, it does not mean that power always brings desired result.

(i) Resistance. The target person on whom the power is exercised may resist the influence and may not behave in accordance to influencer's wishes. The attempt of influence may be thwarted by the person.

(ii) Obedience. The person may succumb to influence though he would rather not. When people are forced to behave against their wishes, it is referred to as obedience.

(iii) Compliance. The person may comply with the desire of the influencer. Compliance refers to a person's acceptance of influence because he is expected to be rewarded for responding to a request or punished for not responding to it.

(iv) Conformity. The person may conform to the influencer's desire. Conformity refers to acceptance of influence because people desire to be in mainstream of social behaviour. Often, people who are free to behave in different ways, will simply do what they see others doing.

(v) Commitment. The person may show commitment to the desire of the influencer. This is the most desirable outcome from the use of power as there is enthusiastic release of energy and talent to satisfy the influencer's requests.

CONTINGENCY APPROACHES TO POWER

As in other areas of organisational behaviour and management, contingency approaches to power are beginning to emerge. For example, *Pfeffer* simply says that power comes from being in the "right" place. He describes the right place or position in the organisation as one where the manager has :

(i) Control over resources such as budgets, physical facilities, and positions that can be used to cultivate allies and supporters.

(ii) Control over or extensive access to information—about the organisation's activities, about the preferences and judgments of others, about what is going on, and who is doing it.

(iii) Formal authority.

There is some research support for such insightful observations, and there are also research findings that lead to contingency conclusions such as the following:

(i) The greater the professional orientation of group members, the greater relative strength referent power has in influencing them.

(ii) The less effort and interest high-ranking participants are willing to allocate to a task, the more likely lower-ranking participants are to obtain power relevant to this task.

Besides these overall contingency observations, there is increasing recognition of the moderating impact of the control of strategic contingencies such as organisational interdependence and the extent to which a department controls critical operations of other departments or the role of influence behaviours in the perception of power.

UPWARD FLOW OF POWER

Most people think of power as being exerted in a downward direction. Its true that individuals in positions at the lower end of the power hierarchy generally have less power than do individuals in higher-level positions. However, power can also be exercised up the organisation. In sociological terms, a person exerting power upward has personal power but no authority. The power sharing argument in the opening issue for Debate suggests that power should flow not only downward but also upward if optimal performance is to be accomplished.

The discussion of legitimate authority suggests that individuals in higher level positions (supervisors) can exert only as much power as individuals in lower-level positions (subordinates) accept. The concept of subordinate power can be linked to expertise, location, and information. Significant upward power or influence can sometimes be exerted by a relatively low-ranking secretary, computer programmer, or clerk who possesses expertise, is in a position to interact with important individuals, or has access to and control of important information. Expertise, location, and information control are important determinants of the power potential of employees at lower levels of the hierarchy.

Two important source of upward influence have been referred to as manipulative persuasion and manipulation. Manipulative persuasion is a person's direct attempt to disguise the true persuasion objective. This is the hidden agenda ploy. Through persuasive skill, the individual accumulates power to gain an objective. For example, a manager trying to have a poor worker transferred may present only the strengths of the worker to a project manager looking for people for a new assignment. Although the manager's true objective is to unload the worker on someone else, that objective is hidden within the manager's persuasive presentation of the employee's strengths.

Manipulation refers to the form of influence in which both the objective and the attempt are concealed. For example, instead of providing customer complaints to a manager as they're received, the clerk receiving the complaints may arrange them in such a way as to place other employees or a department in a more or less favourable light. If the clerk arranges the incoming complaints so that the manager in charge reprimands a departmental supervisor whom the clerk doesn't like the clerk's action would be considered manipulation in the upward direction.

THE EFFECTIVE USE OF POWER

When managers, employees, or teams face a situation in which they want to influence the behaviour of others, they must choose a strategy. Influence strategies are the methods by which individuals or groups attempt to exert power or influence others' behaviour. Table A lists various influence strategies that managers and employees use in the workplace.

Researchers and others are interested in identifying effective influence strategies and understanding the situations in which each might be used. For example, studies have indicated that the influence strategies of rational persuasion, inspirational appeal, and consultation shown in Table A often are the most effective in a variety of circumstances. Overall, the least effective strategies seem to be pressure, coalition, and legitimating. However, it is a mistake to assume that certain strategies always will work and that others won't. Differences in effectiveness occur when attempts to influence are downward rather than upward or lateral in the hierarchy and when they are used in combination rather than independently. In general, a manager or employee must take into account the power sources available, the direction of attempts to influence, and the goals being sought when selecting an influence strategy.

Table A—Influence Strategies

Influence Strategy	*Definition*
Rational persuasion	Use logical arguments and factual evidence
Inspirational appeal	Appeal to values, ideals, or aspirations to arouse enthusiasm
Consultation	Seek participation in planning a strategy, activity, or change
Ingratiation	Attempt to create a favourable mood before making request
Exchange	Offer an exchange of favours, share of benefits, or promise to reciprocate at later time
Personal appeal	Appeal to feelings of loyalty or friendship
Coalition	Seek aid or support of others for some initiative or activity
Legitimating	Seek to establish legitimacy of a request by claiming authority or by verifying consistency with policies, practices, or traditions
Pressure	Use demands, threats, or persistent reminders

Having the capacity to influence (power) the behaviour of others and effectively using this capacity aren't the same thing. Managers who believe that they can effectively influence the behaviour of others by acquiring enough power to simply order other people around generally are unsuccessful. In addition, the evidence indicates that the ineffective use of power has many negative implications, both for the individual and the organisation. For example, one study examined the consequences of over-reliance on assertiveness and persistence as an influence strategy (the "pressure" strategy in Table). Managers who were very assertive and persistent with others—characterised by a refusal to take no for an answer, reliance on repeated reminders, frequent use of face-to-face confrontations, and the like—suffered negative consequences. Compared to other managers studied, these aggressive managers (1) received the lowest performance evaluations, (2) earned less money, and (3) experienced the highest levels of job tension and stress.

In addition to selecting the correct influence strategy, effective influence in organisations often depends on an exchange process somewhat related to the "exchange" influence strategy shown in Table. The exchange process in power relationships is based on the "law of reciprocity"—the almost universal belief that people should be paid back for what they do. Imagine a situation in which an employee is asked by her manager to work through the weekend on an important project. The employee does so but receives no recognition, no extra time off, no extra pay—not even a "thank you." The employee later discovers that her manager took sole credit for the project, which was quite successful. This employee, and most observers, would agree that the manager has violated an important aspect of a good working relationship.

The expectation of reciprocal actions, or exchange, occurs repeatedly in organisations. In part, because people expect to be "paid back," influence becomes possible in many situations. The exchange process is particularly important in relationships, such as networks of peers or colleagues, where formal authority to compel compliance is absent. Power in the exchange process stems from the ability to offer something that others need. The metaphor of currencies provides a useful way to understand how the exchange process influences behaviour. Table B provides some interesting examples of the currencies.

Table B—Organisational Currencies Traded in the Exchange Process

Currency	*Example*
Resources	Lending or giving money, budget increases, personnel, space
Assistance	helping with existing projects or undertaking unwanted tasks
Cooperation	Giving task support, providing quicker response time, approving a project, or aiding implementation
Information	Providing organisational or technical knowledge
Advancement	Giving a task or assignment that can aid in promotion
Recognition	Acknowledging effort, accomplishment, or abilities
Network/contacts	Providing opportunities for linking with others
Personal support	Giving personal and emotional backing

The effective use of power is a difficult challenge for managers, employees, and organisations. The goal is to influence the behaviour of others in ways that are consistent with both the needs of the organisation and its employees. If the use of power isn't carefully managed, powerful individuals may exploit those with less power in the organisation and substitute their self-interests for the legitimate interests of the organisation.

Effective managers and employees often have the following five *characteristics*:

(i) They understand both the interpersonal and the structural sources of power and the most effective methods of using them to influence people. For example, professionals (e.g., research and development scientists, engineers, lawyers, or professors) tend to be more readily influenced by expertise than by other interpersonal sources of power. Effective managers and employees often recognise the structural and situational problems that exist in a power relationship and modify their own behaviour to fit the actual situation. As a result, they tend to develop and use a wide variety of power sources and influence strategies. Some ineffective managers rely too much on one or a few power bases or influence strategies.

(ii) They understand the nature of the exchange process underlying many successful attempts to influence others. They recognise that, over time, unless reciprocal exchanges are roughly equivalent and fair, hard feelings will result and their ability to influence others will decline.

(iii) They understand what is and what is not legitimate behaviour in acquiring and using power. The misuse or lack of understanding of a source of power can destroy its effectiveness. For example, individuals erode expert power if they attempt to demonstrate expertise in areas in which they do not have the required knowledge. Individuals may lose referent power by behaving in ways that are inconsistent with characteristics or traits that are attractive to others.

(iv) They tend to seek positions that allow the development and use of power. In other words, they choose jobs that immerse them in the crucial issues and concerns of an organisation. These jobs provide opportunities for and, indeed, demand influencing the behaviour of others. Successful performance in these positions, in turn, allows the individual to acquire power.

(v) They temper their use of power with maturity and self-control. They recognise that their actions influence the behaviours and lives of others. Although they are not necessarily reluctant or afraid to use their power-recognising that influencing the behaviour of employees is a legitimate and necessary part of the manager's role—they nevertheless apply power carefully. They do so in principled and fair ways that are consistent with organisational needs and goals.

POWER TACTICS

The power tactical dimensions or strategies are :

(i) *Reason.* Use of facts and data to make a logical or rational presentation of ideas.

(ii) *Friendliness.* Use of flattery, creation of goodwill, acting humble, and being friendly prior to making a request.

(iii) *Coalition.* Getting the support of other people in the organisation to back up the request.

(iv) *Bargaining.* Use of negotiation through the exchange of benefits or favours.

(v) *Assertiveness.* Use of a direct and forceful approach such as demanding compliance with requests, repeating reminders, ordering individuals to do what is asked, and pointing out that rules require compliance.

(vi) *Higher authority.* Gaining the support of higher levels in the organisation to back up requests.

(vii) *Sanctions.* Use of organisationally derived rewards and punishments such as preventing or promising a salary increase, threatening to give an unsatisfactory performance evaluation, or withholding a promotion.

The researchers found that employees do not rely on the seven tactics equally. However, the most popular strategy was the use of reason, regardless of whether the influence was directed upward or downward. Additionally, the researchers uncovered four contingency variables that affect the selection of a power tactic: the manager's relative power, the manager's objectives for wanting to influence, the manager's expectation of the target person's willingness to comply, and the organisation's culture.

A manager's relative power impacts the selection of tactics in two ways. First, managers who control resources that are valued by others, or who are perceived to be in positions of dominance, use a greater variety of tactics than do those with less power. Second, managers with power use assertiveness with greater frequency than do those with less power. Initially, we can expect that most managers will attempt to use simple requests and reason. Assertiveness is a backup strategy, used when the target of influence refuses or appears reluctant to comply with the request. Resistance leads to managers using more directive strategies. Typically they shift from using simple requests to insisting that their demands be met. But the manager with relatively little power is more likely to stop trying to influence others when he or she encounters resistance because he or she perceives the costs associated with assertiveness as unacceptable.

Managers vary their power tactics in relation to their objectives. When managers seek benefits from a superior, they tend to rely on kind words and the promotion of pleasant relationships; that is, they use friendliness. In comparison, managers attempting to persuade their superiors to accept new ideas usually rely on reason. This matching of tactics to objectives also holds true for downward influence. For example, managers use reason to sell ideas to subordinates and friendliness to obtain favours.

The manager's expectations of success guide his or her choice of tactics. When past experience indicates a high probability of success, managers use simple requests to gain compliance. Where success is less predictable, managers are more tempted to use assertiveness and sanctions to achieve their objectives.

Finally, we know that cultures within organisations differ markedly—for example, some are warm, relaxed, and supportive; others are formal and conservative. The organisational culture in which a manager works, therefore, will have a significant bearing on defining which tactics are considered appropriate. Some cultures encourage the use of friendliness, some encourage reason, and still others rely on sanctions and assertiveness. So the organisation itself will influence which subset of power tactics is viewed as acceptable for use by managers.

COALITIONS

Those "out of power" and seeking to be "in" will first try to increase their power individually. Why share the spoils if one doesn't have to? But if this proves ineffective, the alternative is to form a coalition. There is strength in numbers.

The natural way to gain influence is to become a power-holder. Therefore, those who want power will attempt to build a personal power base. But, in many instances, this may be difficult, risky, costly, or impossible. In such cases, efforts will be made to form a coalition of two or more "outs" who, by joining together, can combine their resources to increase rewards for themselves.

Historically, blue-collar workers in organisations who were unsuccessful in bargaining on their own behalf with management resorted to labour unions to bargain for them. In recent years, white-collar employees and professionals have increasingly turned to unions after finding it difficult to exert power individually to attain higher wages and greater job security.

What predictions can we make about coalition formation? First, coalitions in organisations often seek to maximise their size. In political science theory, coalitions move the other way—they try to minimise their size. They tend to be just large enough to exert the power necessary to achieve their objectives. But legislatures are different from organisations. Specifically, decision-making in organisations does not end just with selection from among a set of alternatives. The decision must also be implemented. In organisations, the implementation of and commitment to the decision is at least as important as the decision itself. It's necessary, therefore, for coalitions in organisations to seek a broad constituency to support the coalition's objectives. This means expanding the coalition to encompass as many interests as possible. This coalition expansion to facilitate consensus building, of course, is more likely to occur in organisational cultures where cooperation, commitment, and shared decision-making are highly valued. In autocratic and hierarchically controlled organisations, this search for maximising the coalition's size is less likely to be sought.

Another prediction about coalitions relates to the degree of interdependence within the organisation. More coalitions will likely be created where there is a great deal of task and resource interdependence. In contrast, there will be less interdependence among subunits and less coalition formation activity where subunits are largely self-contained or resources are abundant.

Finally, coalition formation will be influenced by the actual tasks that workers do. The more routine the task of a group, the greater the likelihood that coalitions will form. The more that the work that people do is routine, the greater their substitutability for each other and, thus, the greater their dependence. To offset this dependence, they can be expected to resort to a coalition. We see, therefore, that unions appeal more to low skill and nonprofessional workers than to skilled and professional types. Of course, where the supply of skilled and professional employees is high relative to their demand or where organisations have standardised traditionally nonroutine jobs, we would expect these incumbents to find unionisation attractive.

DEPENDENCY

Greater B's dependency on A, the greater the power A has over B. When you possess anything that others require but that you alone control, you make them dependent upon and, therefore, you again power over them. Dependency, then, is inversely proportional to the alternative sources of supply. If something is plentiful, possession of it will not increase your power. If everyone is intelligent, intelligence gives no special advantages. Similarly, among the superrich, money is no longer power. But, as the old saying goes, "In the land of the blind, the one-eyed man is king!" If you can create a monopoly by controlling information, prestige, or anything that others crave, they become dependent on you. Conversely, the more that you can expand your options, the less power you place in the hands of others. This explains, for example, why most organisations develop multiple suppliers rather than give their business to only one. It also explains why so many of us aspire of financial independence. Financial independence reduces the power that others can have over us. Dependency is increased when the resource you control is important, scarce, and nonsubstitutable.

I. Importance

If nobody wants what you've got, its not going to create dependency. To create dependency, therefore, the thing(s) you control must be perceived as being important. It's been found, for instance, that organisations actively seek to avoid uncertainty. We should, therefore, expect that those individuals or groups who can absorb an organisation's uncertainty will be perceived controlling an important resource. For instance, a study of industrial organisations found that the marketing departments in these firms were consistently rated as the most powerful. It was concluded by the researcher that the most critical uncertainty facing these firms was selling their products. This might suggest that during a labour strike, the organisations negotiating representatives have increased power. These inferences appear to be generally valid. Labour negotiators do become more powerful within the personnel area and the organisation as a whole during periods of labour strike. An organisation such as Intel, which is heavily technologically oriented, is highly dependent on its engineers to maintain its products' technical advantages and quality. And, at Intel, engineers are clearly a powerful group. These examples support not only the view that the ability to reduce uncertainty increases a group's importance and, hence, its power but also that what's important is situational. It varies between organisations and undoubtedly also varies over time within any given organisation.

II. Scarcity

As noted previously, if something is plentiful, possession of it will not increase your power. A resource needs to be perceived as scarce to create dependency.

This can help to explain how low-ranking members in an organisation who have important knowledge not available to high-ranking members gain power over the high-ranking members. Possession of a scarce resource—in this case, important knowledge—makes the high-ranking member dependent on the low-ranking member. This also helps to make sense out of behaviours of low-ranking members that otherwise might seem illogical, such as destroying the procedure manuals that describe how a job is done, refusing to train people in their jobs or even to show others exactly what they do, creating specialised language and terminology that inhibit others from understanding their jobs, or operating in secrecy so an activity will appear more complex and difficult than it really is.

The scarcity-dependency relationship can further be seen in the power of occupational categories. Individuals in occupations in which the supply of personnel is low relative to demand can negotiate compensation and benefit packages which are far more attractive than can those in occupations where there is an abundance of candidates. College administrators have no problem today finding English instructors. The market for corporate finance teachers, in contrast, is extremely tight, with the demand high and the supply limited. The result is that the bargaining power of finance faculty allows them to negotiate higher salaries, lighter teaching loads, and other benefits.

III. Nonsubstitutability

The more that a resource has no viable substitutes, the more power that control over that resource provides. Higher education again provides an excellent example. In universities where there are strong pressures for the faculty to publish, we can say that a department head's power over a faculty member is inversely related to that member's publication record. The more recognition the faculty member receives through publication, the more mobile he or she is. That is, since other universities want faculty who are highly published and visible, there is an increased demand for his or her services. Although the concept of tenure can act to alter this relationship by restricting the department head's alternatives, those faculty members with little or no publications have the least mobility and are subject to the greatest influence from their superiors.

INTERDEPARTMENTAL POWER

To this point, the primary focus has been on individual power and how its obtained. However, interdepartmental power is also important. Even though all vice-presidents of departments at the same level in the managerial hierarchy are supposed to have the same amount of power, this isn't usually the case. Some vice-presidents have more power than others by virtue of being in a particular unit or department. In an early study of subunit power, *Charles Perrow* surveyed managers in 12 industrial firms. He was concerned about power differences in the production, sales and marketing, research and development, and finance and accounting departments. Perrow's survey results indicated that sales and marketing units had the most power. The subunit rank ordering from most powerful to least powerful was (1) sales and marketing, (2) production, (3) finance and accounting, and (4) research and development.

The strategic contingency theory developed by *D.J. Hickson* focused on subunit power. A strategic contingency is an event or activity that's extremely important for accomplishing organisational goals. *Michel Crozier*, a French sociologist, provided insight into the idea of strategic contingencies. He studied the relationship between workers in the production and maintenance departments of French tobacco processing plants. Crozier found that the production workers enjoyed job security because of tenure, were protected against unfair disciplinary action, and weren't replaced or transferred arbitrarily. Production workers were less skilled than the maintenance workers. Maintenance workers were highly skilled; they were recruited and selected only after going through a rigorous screening process.

The production workers were dependent on the maintenance workers. This power differential was explained in terms of the control exercised by the maintenance workers over an important contingency. If machines were shut down, the entire plant came to a halt. Efficiently functioning machines were needed to accomplish output goals. Since they repaired machines at the request of the production workers, the maintenance workers possessed significant power.

When machines were down, production workers' job performance suffered. Stoppages totally disrupted their work flow and output. Crozier proposed that the maintenance workers controlled a strategically contingent factor in the production process. Crozier's study also stimulated other studies that eventually resulted in a strategic contingencies explanation of power differences.

Hinnings and associates studied the strategic contingency explanation of power in 28 subunits of seven manufacturing organisations in Canada and the United States. Engineering, marketing, production, and accounting departments were studied. Each subunit interacted with the three others. The researchers examined various indicators of power, such as substitutability (ability of the subunit to obtain alternative performance for its activities), work flow pervasiveness (the degree to which the work flows of a subunit were linked to the work flows of other subunits), uncertainty (the lack of information about future events), and work flow immediacy (the speed and severity with which the work flow of a subunit affected the final outputs of the organisation). Researchers found that only a combination of high values on all the power indicators gave a subunit dominant, first-rank power. Thus, being able to deal with uncertainty alone or possessing substitutability power alone does not provide a subunit with dominant power over other subunits.

Using the work of Crozier and of Hickson and associates, we can concisely explain strategic contingencies. The model in Fig. 3 suggests that subunit power, the power differential between subunits, is influenced by (1) the ability to cope with uncertainty, (2) the centrality of the subunit, and (3) the substitutability of the subunit.

I. Coping with Uncertainty

Unanticipated events can create problems for any organisation or subunit. Therefore, the subunits most capable of coping with uncertainty typically acquire power, *"Uncertainty itself does not give power; coping gives power. If organisations allocate to their various subunits task areas that vary in uncertainty then those subunits that cope most effectively with the most uncertainty should have the most power within the organisation."* Coping activities comprise three types :

In *coping by prevention*, a subunit works at reducing the probability that some difficulty will arise. For example, designing a new product to prevent lost sales because of new competition in the marketplace is a coping technique. Another example would be to hire two individuals when only one is actually needed, because of expected turnover.

Coping by information is another type. The use of forecasting is an example. Possessing timely forecasting information enables a subunit to deal with such events as competition, strikes, shortages of materials, and consumer demand shifts. Planning departments conducting forecasting studies acquire power when their predictions prove accurate.

Coping by absorption, the third type, involves dealing with uncertainty as it impacts the subunit. For example, one subunit might take a problem employee from another subunit and then attempt to retrain and redirect that employee. This is done as a favour, so that the other subunit does not have to go through the pain of terminating or continuing to put up with the employee. The subunit that takes in the problem employee gains the respect of other subunits, which results in an increase in power. Regarding the relation of coping with uncertainty to power, Hinnings said, "The more a subunit copes with uncertainty, the greater its power within the organisation."

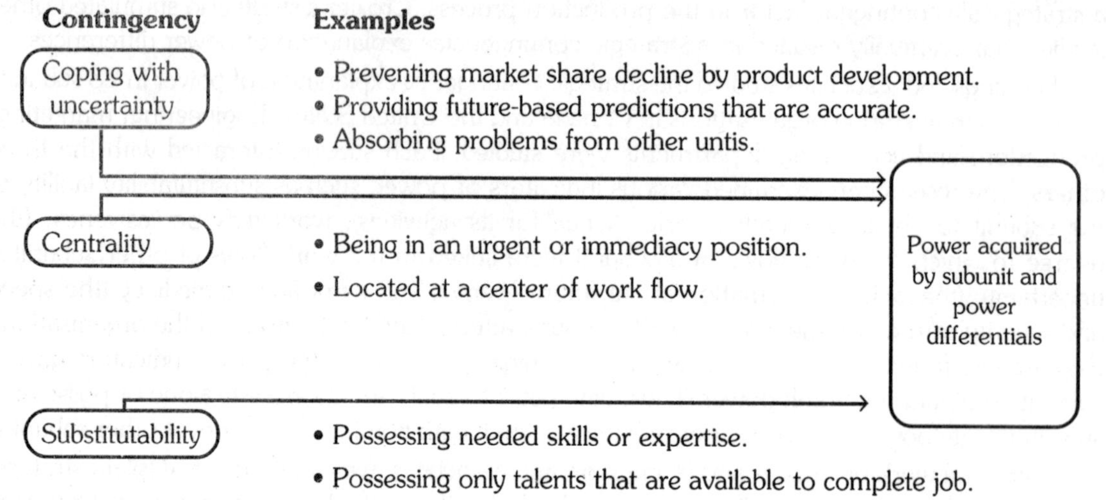

Fig. 3. *A Contingency Model of Subunit Power. (Interdepartmental Power).*

II. Centrality

The subunits most central to the flow of work in an organisation typically acquire power. No subunit has zero centrality since all are somehow interlinked with other subunits. A measure of centrality is the degree to which the work of the subunit contributes to the final output of the organisation. A subunit in a position to affect other subunits has some degree of centrality and, therefore, power. A subunit also possesses power if its activities have a more immediate or urgent impact than that of other subunits. The two main centrality propositions offered by *Hinnings* and *associates* are :

(a) The higher the pervasiveness of the work flows of a subunit, the greater is its power within the organisation.

(b) The higher the immediacy of the work flows of a subunit, the greater is its power with the organisation.

III. Substitutability

Substitutability refers to other subunits' ability to perform activities of a particular subunit. If an organisation has or can obtain alternative sources of skill, information, and resources to perform the job done by a subunit, the subunit's power is diminished. On one hand, training subunits lose power if training work can be done by line managers or outside consultants. On the other hand, a subunit with unique skills and competencies (e.g., the maintenance workers in Crozier's study) is hard to duplicate or replace; this increases the subunit's power over other subunits.

Changes in the labour market may result in changes in a subunits' power. Today, there's a shortage of robotic technical specialists. Since robotic technicians are difficult to replace, train, and substitute for, the robotic subunit of an organisation possesses inordinate power. Of course, other reasons exist for the emergence of powerful robotic subunits, such as their access to technical information, their centrality, and the productivity improvements that they bring about.

Hinnings and associates captured the importance of substitutability power when they proposed that the lower the substitutability of the activities of a subunit, the greater is its power within the organisation.

In summary, the first step a subunit may take to increase its power is to assume responsibility for activities critical to the organisation. The subunit may then seek to increase it pervasiveness, ability to cope with uncertainty, and/or non substitutability. Eventually, the subunit will possess enormous levels of power in relation to other subunits in the organisation.

EMPOWERMENT

Empowerment occurs when employees are adequately trained, provided with all relevant information and the best possible tools, fully involved in key decisions, and fairly rewarded for results. TQM advocate prefer to reorganise the typical hierarchy into teams of people from different specialities. Total Quality Management (TQM) as employee-drive. In other words, it empowers employees at all levels in order to tap their full creativity, motivation, and commitment. Frances *Hesselbe* in, a widely respected former head of the girl Scouts of the USA, offered this perspective: "The more power you give away, the more you have." This can be a difficult concept to grasp for traditional authoritarian managers who see empowerment *versus* no empowerment. Rather, the issue is how empowerment should take place.

POLITICS

It can be observed that every one plays some kind of politics at some point of time in the organisation. We can find references that define politics as one or more of the following: self-serving behaviour, acquisition of power, protection of one's own domain, building of support through group formation, or influence manoeuvring. In all these cases, politics involves acquisition of power or be around power and engage in self-serving behaviour. Therefore, politics can be referred to as actions for seizing, holding, extracting, and executing of power by individuals and groups for achieving personal goals. Because of organisational politics, organisational decisions are affected in such a way that they contribute to personal goals rather than organisational goals. *Tushman* has defined politics as follows :

"Politics refers to the structure and process of the use of authority and power to affect definition of goals, directions and the other major parameters of the organisation. Decisions are not made in a rational or formal way but rather through compromise, accommodation and bargaining."

This definition, though explains the process of politics and its effect on decision-making which does not remain rational does not specifically indicate self-serving behaviour of the people engaged in politics. *Miles* has included self-interest concept in defining politics. He says that :

"Organisational politics is the process whereby individuals or groups use whatever power they can a mass to influence organisational decisions in the direction of their own interests."

On the basis of the review of various definitions of organisational politics, *Drory* and *Romm* have arrived at the following definition of organisational politics:

"Organisational politics refers to intentional behaviours that are designed to enhance or protect a person's influence and self-interest."

There has been no shortage of definitions for organisational politics. Essentially, however, they have focused on the use of power to affect decision-making in the organisation or on behaviours by members that are self-serving and organisationally nonsanctioned. For our purposes, we shall define political behaviour in organisations as those activities that are not required as part of one's formal role in the organisation, but that influence, or attempt to influence, the distribution of advantages and disadvantages within the organisation.

This definition encompasses key elements from what most people mean when they talk about organisational politics. Political behaviour is outside one's specified job requirements. The behaviour requires some attempt to use one's power bases. Additionally, our definition encompasses efforts to influence the goals, criteria, or processes used for decision-making when we state that politics is concerned with "the distribution of advantages and disadvantages within the organisation." Our definition is broad enough to include such varied political behaviours as withholding key information from decision-makers, whistleblowing, spreading rumours, leaking confidential information about organisational activities to the media, exchanging favours with others in the organisation for mutual benefit, and lobbying on behalf of or against a particular individual or decision alternative.

A final comment relates to what has been referred to as the "legitimate-illegitimate" dimension in political behaviour. Legitimate political behaviour refers to normal everyday politics—complaining to your supervisor, bypassing the chain of command, forming coalitions, obstructing organisational policies or decisions through inaction or excessive adherence to rules, and developing contacts outside the organisation through one's professional activities. On the other hand, there are also illegitimate political behaviour that violate the implied rules of the game. Those who pursue such extreme activities are often described as individuals who "play hardball." Illegitimate activities include sabotage, whistleblowing, and symbolic protests such as wearing unorthodox dress or protest buttons, and groups of employees simultaneously calling in sick.

The vast majority of all organisational political actions are of the legitimate variety. The reasons are pragmatic: The extreme illegitimate forms of political behaviour pose a very real risk of loss of organisational membership or extreme sanctions against those who use them and then fall short in having enough power to ensure that they work.

MAIN FEATURE OF POLITICS

Based on the definition of politics, its main features can be described as follows:

(i) Political behaviour involves some kind of power either directly or indirectly. Power can be exercised by those who are informal positions and enjoy authority. It can also be influenced by other persons close to those who hold formal authority.

(ii) Politics involves behaviour that is self-serving. It suggests that either organisational resources are used for personal benefits or benefits to be given to one person are given to another. In both the cases, the decision is not rational from organisation's point of view.

(iii) Politics takes place when an individual recognises that achievement of his goals is influenced by the behaviour of others. In such a case, politicking involves the elimination of adversaries by the influential manoeuvres of a member of the organisation.

(iv) All self-serving behaviours which do not involve use of power or threat of use of power cannot be termed as politics. For example, an employee's asking for a rise in pay is not political behaviour, but the use of threat to unionise to obtain in pay rise amounts to political behaviour.

FACTORS CONTRIBUTING TO POLITICAL BEHAVIOUR

Not all groups or organisations are equally political. In some organisations, for instance, politicking is overt and rampant, while in others, politics plays a small role in influencing outcomes. Why is there this variation? Recent research and observation have identified a number of factors that appear to encourage political behaviour. Some are individual characteristics, derived from the unique qualities of the people the organisation employs; others are a result of the organisation's culture or internal environment.

I. Individual Factors

At the individual level, researchers have identified certain personality traits, needs, and other factors that are likely to be related to political behaviour. In terms of traits, we find that employees who are high self-monitors, possess an internal locus of control, and have a high need for power are more likely to engage in political behaviour.

The high self-monitor is more sensitive to social cues, exhibits higher levels of social conformity, and is more likely to be skilled in political behaviour than the low self-monitor. Individuals with an internal locus of control, because they believe they can control their environment, are more prone to take a proactive stance and attempt to manipulate situations in their favour. Not surprisingly, the Machiavellian personality—which is characterised by the will to manipulate and the desire for power—is comfortable using politics as a means to further his or her self-interest.

Additionally, an individual's investment in the organisation, perceived alternatives, and expectations of success will influence the degree to which he or she will pursue illegitimate means of political action. The more that a person has invested in the organisation in terms of expectations of increased future benefits, the more a person has to lose if forced out and the less likely he or she is to use illegitimate means. The more alternative job opportunities an individual has—due to a favourable job market or the possession of scarce skills or knowledge, a prominent reputation, or influential contacts outside the organisation—the more likely he or she is to risk illegitimate political actions. Finally, if an individual has a low expectations of success in using illegitimate means, it is unlikely that he or she will attempt to do so. High expectations of success in the use of illegitimate means are most likely to be the province of both experienced and powerful individuals with polished political skills and inexperienced and naive employees who misjudge their chances.

II. Organisational Factors

Political activity is probably more a function of the organisation's characteristics than of individual difference variables. Why? Because many organisations have a large number of employees with the individual characteristics we listed, yet the extent of political behaviour varies widely.

Although we acknowledge the role that individual differences can play in fostering politicking, the evidence more strongly supports that certain situations and cultures promote politics. More specifically, when an organisation's resources are declining, when the existing pattern of resources is changing, and which there is opportunity for promotions, politics is more likely to surface. In addition, cultures characterised by low trust, role ambiguity, unclear performance evaluation systems, zero-sum reward allocation practices, democratic decision-making, high pressures for performance, and self-serving senior managers will create breeding grounds for politicking.

When organisations downsize to improve efficiency, reductions in resources have to be made. Threatened with the loss of resources, people may engage in political actions to safeguard what they have. But any changes, especially those that imply significant reallocation of resources within the organisation, are likely to stimulate conflict and increase politicking.

Promotion decisions have consistently been found to be one of the most political in organisations. The opportunity for promotions or advancement encourages people to compete for a limited resources and to try to positively influence the decision outcome.

The less trust there is within the organisation, the higher the level of political behaviour and the more likely that the political behaviour will be of the illegitimate kind. So high trust should suppress the level of political behaviour in general and inhibit illegitimate actions in particular.

Role ambiguity means that the prescribed behaviours of the employee are not clear. There are fever limits, therefore, to the scope and functions of the employee's political actions. Since political activities are defined as those not required as part of one's formal role, the greater the role ambiguity, the more one can engaged in political activity with little chance of it being visible. The practice of performance evaluation is far from a perfected science. The more that organisations use subjective criteria in the appraisal, emphasise a single outcome measure, or allow significant time to pass between the time of an action and its appraisal, the greater the likelihood that an employee can get away with politicking. Subjective performance criteria create ambiguity. The use of a single outcome measure encourages individuals to do whatever is necessary to "look good" on that measure, but often at the expense of performing well on other important parts of the job that are not being appraised. The amount of time that elapses between an action and its appraisal is also a relevant factor. The longer the time period, the more unlikely that the employee will be held accountable for his or her political behaviours.

The more that an organisation's culture emphasises the zero-sum or win-lose approach to reward allocations, the more employees will be motivated to engage in politicking. The zero-sum approach treats the reward "pie" as fixed so that any gain one person or group achieves has to come at the expense of another person or group. If I win, you must lose! If $10,000 in annual raises is to be distributed among five employees, then any employee who get more than $2,000 takes money away from one or more of the others. Such a practice encourages making others look bad and increasing the visibility of what you do.

In the last 25 years, there has been a general move in North America and among most developed nations toward making organisations less autocratic. Managers in these organisations are being asked to behave more democratically. They're told that they should allow subordinates to advise them on decisions and that they should rely to a greater extent on group input into the decision process. Such moves toward democracy, however, are not necessarily embraced by all individual managers. Many managers sought their positions in order to have legitimate power so as to be able to make unilateral decisions. They fought hard and often paid high personal costs to achieve their influential positions. Sharing their power with others runs directly against their desires. The result is that managers, especially those who began their careers in the 1950s and 1960s, may use the required committees, conferences, and group meetings in a superficial way, as arenas for manoeuvring and manipulating.

The more pressure that employees feel to perform well, the more likely they are to engage in politicking. When people are held strictly accountable for outcomes this puts great pressure on them to "look good." If a person perceives that his or her entire career is riding on next quarter's sales figures or next months' plant productivity report, there is motivation to do whatever is necessary to make sure the numbers come out favourably.

Finally, when employees see the people on top engaging in political behaviour, especially when they do so successfully and are rewarded for it, a climate is created that supports politicking. Politicking by top management, in a sense, gives permission to those lower in the organisation to play politics by implying that such behaviour is acceptable.

POLITICAL BEHAVIOUR

Political behaviour of individuals and groups consists of their attempts to influence the behaviour of others and the course of events in the organisation in order to protect their self-interests, meet their own needs, and advance their own goals. Described in this way, almost all behaviour may be regarded as political. Labelling behaviour as political, however, usually implies a judgment that individuals or groups are gaining something at the expense of other employees, groups or the organisation. People often are self-centred and biased when labelling actions as political behaviour. For example, employees may justify their own behaviour as defending legitimate rights or interests yet call similar behaviour by others "playing politics."

ORGANISATIONAL POLITICS

Only in recent years has the topic of organisational politics (also known as impression management) begun to receive serious attention from management theorists and researchers. But as we all know from practical experience, organisational life is often highly charged with political wheeling and dealing. A corporate executive has underscored this point by asking:

Have you ever done a very satisfactory piece of work only to have it lost in the organisational shuffle? Have you ever come up with a new idea only to have your boss take credit for it? Have you ever faced a situation where someone else made a serious mistake and somehow engineered it so you got the blame?

Whether politically motivated or not, managers need to be knowledgeable about organisational politics because their careers will be affected by it. New managers, particularly, should be aware of the political situation in their organisation. As "new kids on the job" they might be more easily taken advantage of than other more experienced managers. Certain political manoeuvres also have significant ethical implications.

Organisational politics involves actions by individuals or groups to acquire, develop, and use power and other resources in order to obtain preferred outcomes when there is uncertainty or disagreement about choices. When people share power and differ about what must be done, many decisions and actions quite naturally will be the result of a political process.

What Does Organisational Politics Involve?

As the term implies, self-interest is central to organisational politics. In fact, organisational politics has been defined as "the pursuit of self-interest at work in the face of real or imagined opposition." Political manoeuvring is said to encompass all self-serving behaviour above and beyond competence, hard work, and luck. Although the term organisational politics has a negative connotation, researchers have identified both positive and negative aspects.

Political behaviours widely accepted as legitimate would certainly include exchanging favours, "touching bases," forming coalitions, and seeking sponsors at upper levels. Less legitimate behaviours would include whistleblowing, revolutionary conditions, threats, and sabotage.

Employees resort to political behaviour when they are unwielding to trust their career solely to competence, hard work, or luck. One might say that organisational politicians help luck along by relying on political tactics. Whether employees will fall back on political tactics has a lot to do with an organisation's climate or culture. For example, imagine yourself trying to climb the managerial ladder at Pepsi Co Inc., where political manoeuvring is said to be active amid a climate of "creative tension".

Managers are pitted against each other to grab more market share, to work harder, and to bring more profits out of their businesses. Because winning is the key value at Pepsi, losing has its penalties. Consistent runners-up find their jobs gone. Employees know they must win merely to stay in place—and must devastate the competition to get ahead....

The immediate past chairman set a constant example. He once resorted to using a snow mobile to get to work in a blizzard, demonstrating the ingenuity and dedication to work he expects from his staff. This type of pressure has pushed many managers out. But a recent survey shows that others thrive under such conditions.

One can only speculate about the value of such a highly political climate. In view of Pepsi's titanic battle with Coca-Cola, a strong competitive spirit seems appropriate. Of course, those who were forced out or had their toes stepped on might have a different view.

RESEARCH ON ORGANISATIONAL POLITICS

Researchers in widely cited study of organisational politics conducted structured interviews with eighty-seven managers employed by thirty electronics firms in southern California. Included in the sample were thirty chief executive officers, twenty-eight middle managers, and twenty-nine supervisors. Significant results included the following:

(i) The higher the level of management, the greater the perceived amount of political activity.
(ii) The larger the organisation, the greater the perceived amount of political activity.
(iii) Personnel in staff positions were viewed as more political than those in line positions.
(iv) People in marketing were the most political; those in production were the least political.
(v) "Reorganisation changes" reportedly prompted more political activity than any other type of change.
(vi) A majority (61 per cent) of those interviewed believed organisational politics helps advance one's career.
(vii) Fourty-five per cent believed that organisation politics distracts from organisational goals.

Regarding the last two findings, it was clear that political activities were seen as helpful to the individual. On the other hand, the interviewed managers were split on the question of the value of politics to the organisation. Managers who believed political behaviour had a positive impact on the organisation cited the following reasons: "gaining visibility for ideas, improving coordination and communication, developing teams and groups, and increasing esprit de corps...." As listed above, the most often cited negative effect of politics was its distraction of managers from organisational goals. Misuse of resources and conflict were also mentioned as typical problems.

POLITICAL TACTICS

As defined earlier, organisational politics takes in a lot of behavioural territory. The following six political tactics are common expressions of politics in the workplace:

(i) *Posturing*: Those who use this tactic look for situations in which they can make a good impression. "One-upmanship" and taking credit for other people's work are included in this category.
(ii) *Empire building*: Gaining and keeping control over human and material resources is the principal motivation behind this tactic. Those with large budgets usually feel more safely entrenched in their positions and believe they have more influence over peers and superiors.
(iii) *Making the supervisor look good*: Traditionally referred to as "apple polishing," this political strategy is prompted by a desire to favourably influence those who control one's career ascent. Anyone with an oversized ego is an easy target for this tactic.
(iv) *Collecting and using social IOUs*: Reciprocal exchange of political favours cab be done in two ways: (1) by helping someone look good or (2) by preventing someone from looking bad by ignoring or covering up a mistake. Those who rely on this tactic feel that all favours are coins of exchange rather than expressions of altruism or unselfishness.
(v) *Creating power and loyalty cliques*: Because there is power in numbers, the idea here is to face superiors and competitors as a cohesive group rather than alone.
(vi) *Destructive competition*: As a last-ditch effort, some people will resort to character assassination through suggestive remarks, vindictive gossip, or outright lies. This tactic also includes sabotaging the work of a competitor.

Obvious illegalities notwithstanding, one's own values and ethics and organisational sanctions are the final arbiters of whether or not these tactics are acceptable.

ANTIDOTES TO POLITICAL BEHAVIOUR

Each of the foregoing political tactics varies in degree. The average person will probably acknowledge using at least one of these strategies. But excessive political manoeuvring can become a serious threat to productivity when self-interests clearly override the interests of the group of organisation. Organisational politics can be kept within reasonable bounds by applying the following five tips:

(i) Strive for a climate of openness and trust.
(ii) Measure performance results rather than personalities.
(iii) Encourage top management to refrain from exhibiting political behaviour that will be imitated by employees.
(iv) Strive to integrate individual and organisational goals through meaningful work and career planning.
(v) Practice job rotation to encourage broader perspectives and understanding of the problems of others.

PERSONALITY AND POLITICAL BEHAVIOUR

So far, we have stressed the situational and structural determinants of political behaviour. Just as power has both personal and situational sources, some individuals appear more likely to engage in political behaviour than others. Several personality traits are related to a willingness to do so (and in some cases, a willingness to use power). We discuss four of them: the need for power, Machiavellianism, locus of control, and risk-seeking propensity.

I. Need for Power

The need for power is a motive, or basic desire, to influence and lead others and to control the current environment. As a result, individuals with a high need for power are likely to engage in political behaviour in organisations. Successful managers often have high needs for power. The desire to have an impact, to control events, and to influence others often is associated with effective managerial behaviours, equitable treatment of subordinates, and, hence, higher morale.

However, some aspects of strong power needs may not be particularly useful for effective management. The need for power may take two different forms: personal power and institutional power. On the one hand, managers who emphasize personal power strive to dominate others; they want loyalty to themselves, rather than to the organisation. When this type of manager leaves the organisation, the work group may fall apart, On the other hand, managers who emphasize institutional power demonstrate a more socially acceptable need for power. They create a good climate or culture for effective work, and their subordinates develop an understanding of and loyalty to the organisation. Interestingly, some research indicates that female managers often demonstrate greater needs for institutional power and lesser needs for personal power than their male counterparts.

II. Machiavellianism

Niccolo Machiavelli was a sixteenth-century Italian philosopher and statesman whose best-known writings include a set of suggestions for obtaining and holding governmental power. Over the centuries, Machiavelli has come to be associated with the use of deceit and opportunism in interpersonal relations. Thus Machiavellians are people who view and manipulate others for their own purposes.

As a personal style of behaviour toward others, Machiavellianism is characterised by (1) the use of guile and deceit in interpersonal relationships, (2) a cynical view of the nature of other people, and (3) a lack of concern with conventional morality. A person who scores high on a test to measure Machiavellianism probably agrees with the following statements:–

(i) The best way to handle people is to tell them what they want to hear.
(ii) Anyone who completely trusts anyone else is asking for trouble.
(iii) Never tell anyone the real reason you did something unless it is useful to do so.
(iv) It is wise to flatter important people.

Machiavellians are likely to be effective manipulators of other people. They often effectively influence others, particularly in face-to-face contacts, and tend to initiate and control social interactions. As a result, Machiavellianism can be associated with a tendency to engage in political behaviour. For example, a study that examined the relationship between a propensity to engage in political behaviour in organisations and a variety of individual differences reported that Machiavellianism was the strongest correlate of political behaviour among the variables investigated. The study concluded that Machiavellianism may be a good predictor of political behaviour in many organisational situations.

III. Locus of Control

Recall that locus of control refers to the extent to which individuals believe that they can control events that affect them. Individuals with a high internal locus of control believe that events result primarily from their own behaviour. Those with a high external locus of control believe that powerful others, fate, or chance primarily determine events. Internals tend to exhibit more political behaviours than externals and are more likely to attempt to influence other people. Further, they are more likely to assume that their efforts will be successful. The study of relationships among political behaviour and individual differences referred to in the preceding section also supported the notion that the propensity to engage in political behaviour is stronger for individuals who have a high internal locus of control than for those who have a high external locus of control.

IV. Risk-Seeking Propensity

Individuals differ (sometimes markedly) in their willingness to take risks, or in their risk-seeking propensity. Some people are risk avoiders, and others can be described as risk seekers. Negative outcomes (such as demotions, low performance ratings, and loss of influence) are possible for individuals and groups who engage in political behaviour in organisations. Engaging in political activity isn't risk free; to advocate a position and to seek support for it is to risk being perceived as opposing some other position. In many situations, risk seekers are more willing to engage in political behaviour, whereas risk avoiders tend to avoid such behaviour because of its possible consequences.

DYSFUNCTIONAL POLITICAL BEHAVIOUR

Organisations are political system where individuals try, first of all, to satisfy their wants. *Harold D. Lasswell* once rightly remarked "politics—who gets what, where, when, how". It is process where one acquired power, transfers and exercises it over others to satisfy his desires. In this process politics has a tendency of producing undesirable consequences called 'dysfunctions'. Any behaviour by an organisational member that is self-serving is called organisational politics. Self-aggrandisement, no doubt, is important but sometimes hinders the organisation in achieving its goals. Any activity or action by individuals that is at the cost of organisational goals and interests can be termed as dysfunctional. When organisation's and individual's interests interact the intersecting segment signifies functional behaviour and the rest is treated as dysfunctional. Diagrammatically, this can be seen in Fig. 4.

Therefore when the individual and organisational interests are not complementary, incongruent, then dysfunctional political behaviour inevitably sets in. Dysfunctional political behaviour can assume any of the following forms :

(i) Scapegoating.
(ii) Passing the buck.
(iii) Red-herring tactics.
(iv) Sabotage.
(v) Falsification or hiding the important information.
(vi) Discrediting others.
(vii) Indulging in deliberate bad bally-hoed techniques etc.

What Factors Contribute to Dysfunctional Politicking?

Andrew DuBrin has identified five fundamental factors that give rise to dysfunctional political behaviour. It should, however, be noted that there may be innumerable other factors which may be inexplicable.

(i) *Competition for Power.* As the resources in the organisation are scarce, power is also available in limited supply. Scarcity gives birth to competition. In the process of acquiring power people feel it rational to play games known as politics and many a time those activities have negative flavour and negative affect on the organisation in terms of poor performance by its members. Further, organisational members frequently involve in perpetual jockeying in the process of acquiring power.

Such competition develops some kind of ill-healthy atmosphere in the organisation that organisation cannot bear for long if go uncared.

(ii) *Subjective Evaluation of Performance.* It is very difficult to evaluate the performance of individual objectively. Therefore, managers frequently resort to subjective evaluation that

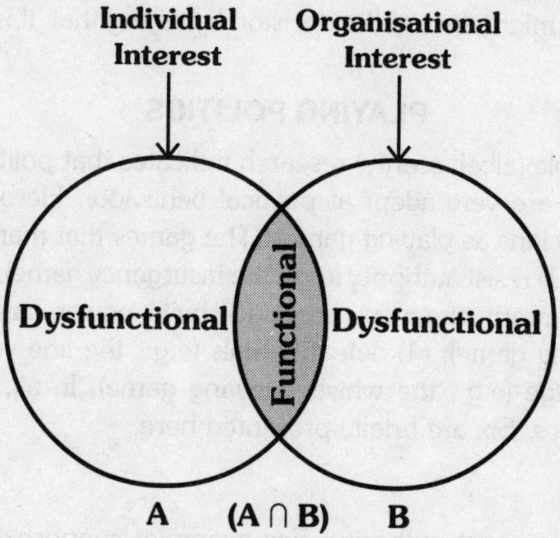

Fig. 4. *Functional Behaviour.*

may lead to undesirable consequences if the employees are dissatisfied with the boss. Whenever subjective kind of evaluation is existing, members may think some bias in supervisor's evaluation and cast doubt on the procedures. True, whenever employees think or perceive the evaluation to be inaccurate they may be forced into dysfunctional political activities. The less objectivity in defining and measuring performance evaluation criteria, the greater is the room for the individual to engage in dysfunctional political behaviour.

(iii) *Delay in Feedback*. There is, generally, time lag in the feedback system. The lag is so long that by the time an individual's actions are compared with outcomes he is likely to move to different positions in the organisations. People are moved, frequently, to another position or other positions before their contribution on the current job is actually assessed and fully appraised. By this they are sometimes forced to emphasise only visible actions, i.e., pseudo-performance, and get promotions by eye-wash tactics.

(iv) *Saturation in Promotions*. People work hard and win promotions. When they reach the maximum as per their talent and skills, they resort to dysfunctional politicking. Peter principle can be recalled here. That is to say, in a hierarchy every employee tends to rise to his levels of incompetence and he will have no other business than to engage in politics that have undesirable consequences. When individuals are promoted beyond their capabilities to perform, they are likely to indulge in unproductive politics at the cost of the company.

(v) *Employees' Participation in Decision-making*. Decentralisation has made the present day organisation autocratic. Power-hunger managers find it hard to share their power with employees and in order to retain their power and establish their supremacy, they constantly try to engage in manoeuvring and manipulating. Sometimes, an employee outclasses the manager by rendering valuable suggestions in decision-making and an intolerable manager resorts to politics and might discard the decision by saying that 'it is at the cost of company's welfare'.

PLAYING POLITICS

If anything, the available (albeit scanty) research indicates that politics exists in organisations and that some individuals are very adept at political behaviour. Herbert Mintzberg and others describe these adept politicians as playing games. The games that managers and non managers engage in are intended to (1) resist authority (e.g., the insurgency game), (2) counter the resistance to authority (e.g., the counterinsurgency game), (3) build power bases (e.g., the sponsorship game and coalition-building game), (4) defeat reveals (e.g., the line versus staff game), and (5) effect organisational change (e.g., the whistle-blowing game). In all, Mintzberg describes and discusses 13 political games. Six are briefly presented here.

I. Insurgency Game

This game is played to resist authority. For example, suppose that a plant supervisor is instructed to reprimand a particular worker for violating company policies. The reprimand can be delivered according to the supervisor's feelings and opinions about its worth and legitimacy. A reprimand delivered in a halfhearted manner will probably have no noticeable effect. However, if delivered aggressively, it may be effective. Insurgency in the form of not delivering the reprimand as expected by a higher-level authority would be difficult to detect and correct. Insurgency as a game to resist authority is practised in organisations at all levels.

II. Counterinsurgency Game

Often, a person in an authority position fights back when faced with insurgency. The supervisor's superior may have to carefully monitor whether policies concerning the reprimand are being followed. One tactic is to occasionally (not always) follow up requests given to subordinates with a detailed checking system. For example, the person with ultimate authority could ask the supervisor on occasion whether the reprimand had been given, when it was given, what the person's reaction was, and how the supervisor would make presentation improvements in the future. The superior could also check with the person reprimanded to determine when and how the reprimand was given. The purpose of periodic monitoring is to encourage the supervisor to deliver the reprimand according to company procedures.

III. Sponsorship Game

In this rather straightforward game, a person attaches herself to someone with power. The sponsor is typically the person's boss or someone else with higher power and status. Typically, individuals attach themselves to someone who is on the move. A few rules are involved in playing this game: First, the person must be able to show commitment and loyalty to the sponsor. Second, the person must follow each sponsor-initiated request or order. Third, the person must stay in the background and give the sponsor credit of everything. Finally, the person must be thankful and display gratitude to the sponsor. The sponsor is not only a teacher and trainer but also a power base. Some of the sponsor's power tends to rub off on the person through association.

The "Hard Work" Close-Up indicates that playing politics may help a manager sell an idea or get ahead in the organisation.

IV. Coalition-Building Game

A subunit such as a personnel/human resources department or a research and development department may be able to increase its power by forming an alliance, or coalition, with other subunits. The strength-in-numbers idea is encouraged by coalition building. When such alliances are formed within the organisation, common goals and common interests are emphasized. However, forming coalitions with groups outside the organisation can also enhance the power of a subunit.

The following example illustrates acquiring power by building an internal coalition. In most organisations, the personnel/human resources department typically has limited power. However, litigation involving employee relations and employee health problems associated with disability triggered by joy stress is becoming costly. Consequently, legal staffs in organisations have acquired power. These legal staffs don't have the information, daily contact with employees, and records needed to serve the firm's legal needs. Skills and information to cope with employee-based uncertainties are more in the domain of the personnel/human resources department would enhance both their power bases. The coalition would enable the organisation to effectively address legal issues.

V. Line *versus* Staff Game

The line manager versus the staff adviser game has existed for year in organisations. In essence, this game pits line authority to make operating decisions against staff advisers' expertise. There are also value differences and a clash of personality. On one hand, line managers are typically more experienced, more oriented to the bottom line, and more intuitive in reaching decisions. On the other hand, staff advisers tend to be younger, better educated, and more analytical decision-makers. These differences result in the two groups viewing the organisational world from slightly different perspectives.

Withholding information, having access to powerful authority figures, creating favourable impressions, and identifying with organisational goals are tactics used by line and staff personnel. The line *versus* staff clash must be controlled in organisations before it reaches the point at which, because of the disruption, organisational goals aren't being achieved.

VI. Whistle-blowing Game

This game is played to bring about organisational change. It takes place when a person in an organisation identifies a behaviour that violates his sense of fairness, moral, ethics, or law and them blows the whistle. Whistle-blowing means that the person informs someone—a newspaper reporter, a government representative, a competitor—about an assumed injustice, irresponsible action, or violation of the law.

The whistle-blower, who may come from level in the organisation, attempts to correct the behaviour or practice by bypassing the authority system within the organisation. This is viewed in a negative light by managers with position power. For example, when a pilot complained to management first and then to the public about defects in his plane's automatic pilot mechanisms, his complaints were attacked by management as being groundless. An engineer complained about the O-rings of the Challenger booster rockets—which later cracked, leading to the death of seven astronauts. The engineer's complaints weren't given a high priority to check out. In another example, a biologist reported to the Environmental Protection Agency that his consulting firm had submitted false data to the agency on behalf of an electric utility company; he was fired. In still another publicized case, an engineer at Ford complained about faulty design of the Pinto. Unfortunately, this whistle-blower was demoted. Many legal costs and settlements from Pinto crash victims might have been avoided if the whistle-blower's message has been taken seriously.

Although federal law protects whistle-blower's rights, some organisations continue to retaliate against an informant. A study found that identified whistle-blowers were as likely to experience retaliation after the law's passage as they were prior to passage. Often, whistle-blowing is done secretly to avoid retribution by the authority system.

SOME DEVIOUS POLITICAL TACTICS

Politics is considered as a dirty game for a simple reason that politicians would use any and all possible means; irrespective of their validity on ethical grounds, in order to obtain and retain their power base. While it is possible to acquire political strength through honest means such as expertise, seniority and integrity, there are other devious tactics which may be difficult to defend on moral grounds but nevertheless used extensively. Some of these techniques are :

(i) *Embrace or demolish*. Sometimes it becomes necessary to make decisions and take actions that are unpopular such as demoting or transferring some one. Such a person who is demoted or transferred against his will, is likely to become your political enemy. It may be politically advantageous move to have this person fired so that he will not be there to take revenge at a later date. This is specially significant during corporate takeovers. According to *Anthony Jay* : "The guiding principle is that senior men in taken-over firms should either be warmly welcomed and encouraged or sacked; because if they are sacked they are powerless, whereas if they are simply downgraded they will remain united and resentful and determined to get their own power back."

(ii) *Divide and rule*. If effective, this is the most successful and powerful tactic to retain political power. Historians have recorded the fact that the British ruled India by pursuing the policy of dividing the Indians on the basis of caste and religion and thus ruling India for a long time. The assumption underlying this strategy being that those who are divided will not form coalitions themselves thus making them weak in any confrontations. By encouraging bickering among possible rivals, it is possible to keep them continuously off balance so that they will never get together to mount a successful attack against you. However, it is a risky technique in that should the rivals become aware of your such devious schemes they can get together for the sole purpose of unseating you from your power base.

(iii) *Exclude the opposition.* Another technique of getting your own way is to make sure that any opposition is absent at important meetings where such oppositions block your desired outcomes. This could be done by holding such meetings at a time when rivals are away either on business trips or on vacation. With the opposition absent, it is possible to influence the decision-making process in your favour. One historically significant incident relating to this technique occurred at the United Nations during the Korean War. In order to send UN troops to Korea, it was necessary to have a unanimous decision to do so at the Security Council. However, the representative from the Soviet Union was holding out and was vehemently against this resolution. By keeping the heated discussion on, and by frustrating the efforts of the Soviet Union representative, it was made possible for him to walk out in anger and protest. Thus the opposition being absent, the resolution to send UN troops to Korea was passed.

ETHICS, POWER, AND POLITICS

Issues of power and politics often involve ethical issues as well. For example, if power is used within the formal boundaries of a manager's authority and within the framework of organisational policies, job descriptions, procedures, and goals, it's really nonpolitical power and most likely doesn't involve ethical issues. But use of power outside the bounds of formal authority, politics, procedures, job descriptions, and organisational goals is political in nature. When this occurs, ethical issue are likely to be present. Some examples might include bribing government officials, lying to employees and customers, polluting the environment, and a general "ends justify the means" mentality.

Managers confront ethical dilemmas in their jobs because they frequently use power and politics to accomplish their goals. Each manager, therefore, has an ethical responsibility. Recently, researchers have developed a framework that allows a manager to integrate ethics into political behaviour. Researchers recommend that a manager's behaviour must satisfy certain to be considered ethical.

(i) *Utilitarian outcomes*: The manager's behaviour results in the optimal satisfaction of people both inside and outside the organisation. In other words, it results in the greatest good for the greatest number of people.

(ii) *Individual right:* The manager's behaviour respects the rights of all affected parties. In other words, it respects basic human rights of free consent, free speech, freedom of conscience, privacy, and due process.

(iii) *Distributive justice:* The manager's behaviour respects the rules of justice. It treats people equitably and fairly, not arbitrarily.

What does a manager do when a potential behaviour cannot pass the three criteria? Researchers suggest that it may still be considered ethical in the particular situation if it passes the criterion of overwhelming factors. To be justified, the behaviour must be based on tremendously overwhelming factors in the nature of the situation, such as conflicts among criteria (e.g., the manager's behaviour results in both positive and negative results), conflicts within the criteria (e.g., a manager uses questionable means to achieve a positive result), and/or an incapacity to employ the first three criteria (e.g., the manager acts with incomplete or inaccurate information).

REVIEW QUESTIONS

1. What is power? Explain the characteristics of power.
2. Explain the various types of interpersonal sources of power.
3. Distinguish between power and authority.
4. Explain the structural sources of power in an organisation.
5. What do you mean by dependency? Explain the technical dimension or strategies.
6. What is coalition? What is it likely to develop?
7. Write short note on empowerment.
8. Write short notes on:
   (a) Upward flow of power.
   (b) Effective use of power.
   (c) Empowerment.
9. Define political behaviour. What factors contribute to political activity?
10. What do you understand by defensive behaviours? Explain the effects of defensive behaviours.
11. What is authority? Explain the types and factors of authority.
12. Briefly explain the concept of dysfunction political behaviour.

REFERENCES

1. *Judith R. Goron, A Diagnositc Approach to Organisational Behaviour, Massachusetts, Allyn Bacon Inc.*
2. *Hickson D.J. Kimmings C.R., Lee C.A., Schneck R.E., "Strategic Contingencies Theory of Intra-organisational Power", Administrative Science Quarterly, 1971.*
3. *Jerald G. Bachmann, C.G. Smith and J.A. Slesinger, "Control Performance, and Satisfaction: An Analysis of Structural and Individual Effort", Journal of Personality and Social Psychology, 1966.*
4. *M.L. Tushman, "A Political Approach to Organisations: A Review and Rationale", Academy of Management Review, 2, 1977.*
5. *C.W. Lachenmeyer, "Organisational Politicking: An Analysis", Pelham: New York Institute for Analysis, Evaluation and Design of Human Action, 1979.*
6. *Pffener and Sherwood, Administrative Behaviour.*
7. *D.L. Madison, R.W. Allen, L.W. Porter, P.A. Renwick and B.T. Mayes, "Organisational Politics: An Exploration of Managers' Perceptions", Human Relations, 1980.*
8. *Stephen P. Robbins, "Organisational Behaviour: Concepts and Controversies", Prentice-Hall, Englewood Cliffs, 1979.*
9. *Jeffrey Pfeffer, Organisational Design, Berkeley: University of California Press, 1970.*
10. *M.L. Tushman, "A Political Approach to Organisations: A Review and Rationale", Academy of Management Review, April, 1977.*

11. *P.M. Blau, Exchange and Power in Social Life, New York, John Wiley and Sons, 1964.*
12. *R.M. Emerson, "Power-dependence Relation", American Sociological Review, op. cit.*
13. *J.P. Kotter, "Power, Dependence and Effective Management", Harward Business Review, July-Aug., 1977.*
14. *B.H. Raven and W. Kruglanski, "Conflict and Power", in P.G. Swingle (ed.), The Structure of Conflict, New York, Academic Press, 1975.*
15. *John Scholper, "Social Power", in Advances in Experimental Social Psychology, Vol. 2, Leonard Brekoviet (ed.), Academic Press, New York, 1965.*

6th

CHAPTER

OVERVIEW

WORK STRESS

• ***After reading this chapter, you should be able to know:***

- Introduction
- A working Model of Stress and Work
- Sources of Stress
- Basic Forms of Stress: Frustration and Anxiety
- Stress and Job Performance
- The Effects of Stress
- The Causes of Stress
- Stress Management

6

WORK STRESS

INTRODUCTION

Although there are numerous definitions and much debate bout the meaning of job stress, *Ivancevich* and *Matteson* define stress simply as "the interaction of the individual with the environment," but then they go on to give a more detailed working definition, as follows: *Stress in an adaptive response, mediated by individual characteristics and/or psychological processes, that is a consequence of any external action, situation, or event that places special physical and/or psychological demands upon a person.*

Beehr and *Newman* define job stress as "a condition arising from the interaction of people and their jobs and characterised by changes within people that force them to deviate from their normal functioning." Taking these two definitions and simplifying them for the purpose of this chapter, "stress" is defined as an adaptive response to an external situation that results in physical, psychological, and/or behavioural deviations for organisational participants.

Stress is a term basically used in *physical sciences* which means pressure of one object on another. There are three terms which are used synonymously to denote this phenomenon : stress, strain, and pressure, however, there are thin differences in these terms. From *physical sciences*, the terms stress came to medical sciences and finally to *social science*. As per the medical explanation, the term *stress is the body's general response to environmental situations.*

Selye, who has done considerable research on stress, has viewed stress as the "non-specifically induced changes within a biological system." It is nonspecific because any adaptation to a problem faced by the body, irrespective of the nature of the problem, is included in stress.

In other words, stress can be viewed in a number of different ways and has been described as the most imprecise word in the scientific dictionary. The word "stress" has also been compared with the word "sin"; "Both are short, emotionally charged words used to refer to something that otherwise would take many words to say." After the definition of stress and the relation to burnout are discussed, some of the historical background is presented.

Stress is a dynamic condition in which an individual is confronted with an opportunity, constraint, or demand related to what he or she desires and for which the outcome is perceived to be both uncertain and important. This is a complicated definition. Let's look at its components more closely.

Stress is not necessarily bad in and of itself. While stress is typically discussed in a negative context, it also has a positive value. It is an opportunity when it offers potential gain. Consider, for example, the superior performance that an athlete or stage performer gives in "clutch" situations. Such individuals often use stress positively to rise to the occasion and perform at or near their maximum.

More typically, stress is associated with constraints and demands. The former prevent you from doing what you desire. The latter refers to the loss of something desired.

A Working Definition

Each interpretation of stress offers important insights. We define stress as an adaptive response, mediated by individual differences and/or psychological processes, that is a consequence of any external (environmental) action, situation, or event that places excessive psychological and/or physical demands on a person.

This definition portrays stress in a more negative light than do most definitions. We have, however, included the term excessive in our definition because, certainly, not all stress is negative. The stress that *Dr. Hans Selye*, the pioneer or stress research, referred to as eustress (from the Greek eu, meaning good, and in euphoria) is stimulating in a positive sense. Eustress is necessary in our lives.

Out definition allows us to focus attention on specific environmental conditions as potential sources of stress. Such conditions are called stressors. Whether stress is felt or experienced by a particular individual depends on that individual's unique characteristics. Furthermore, the definition emphasises an adaptive response. The vast majority of a person's responses to stimuli in the work environment don't require adaptation; thus, they are not really potential sources of stress.

Keep in mind that a variety of dissimilar situations—work effort, fatigue, uncertainty, fear, emotional arousal—can produce stress. Therefore, to isolate a single factor as the sole cause is extremely difficult.

A WORKING MODEL OF STRESS AND WORK

The distinction between stress at work and stress at home is artificial at best. For example, sources of stress at work spill over into a person's nonwork activities. As a consequence of stressors experienced at work, the individual may come home irritable, short-tempered, and fatigue and argue with the spouse. The resulting marital conflict may be a source of subsequent stress that in turn negatively affects job performance. Thus, stress at work and stress away from work are often interrelated. This chapter's main concern, however, is with stressors at work. To better understand the link between stressors, stress, and consequences, we have develop an integrative model of stress and work. A managerial perspective is used to develop the parts of the model in Fig. 1. The model divides stressors at work into four categories: physical environmental, individual, group, and organisational. The model also presents five potential categories of the

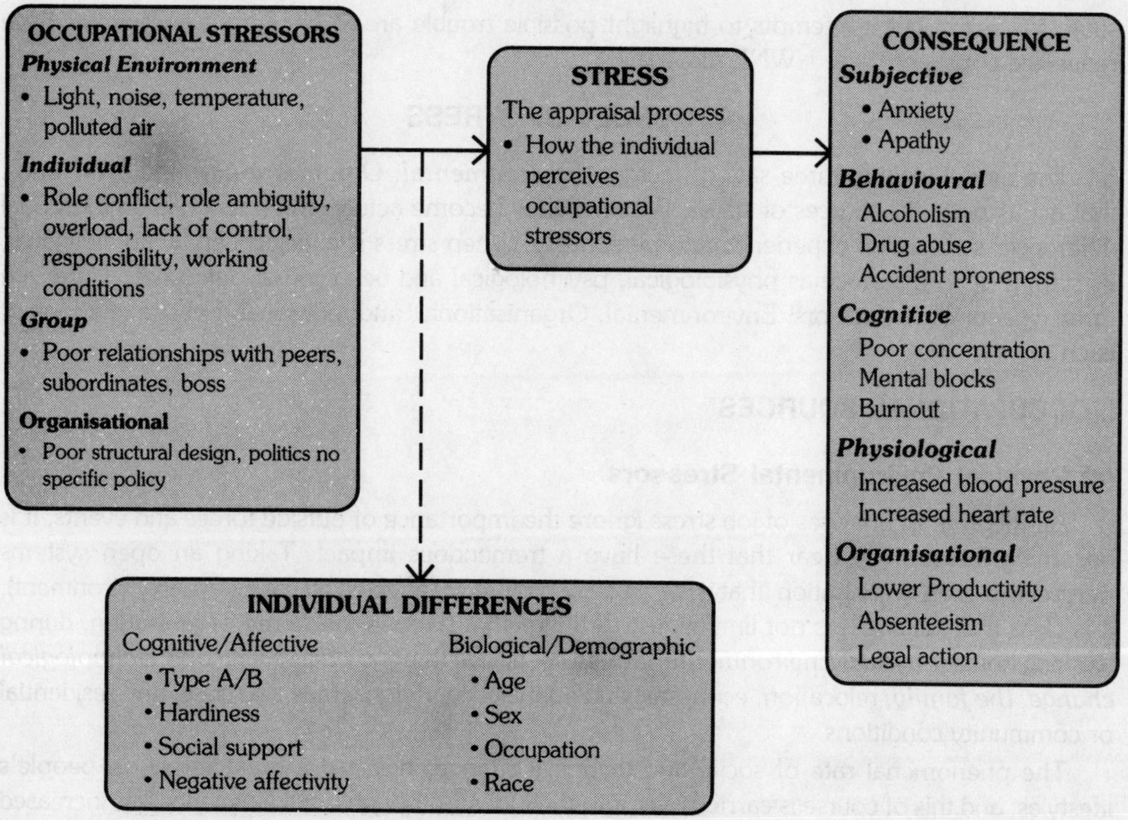

Fig. 1. *Strees and Work : A Working Model.*

effects of stress. In this book, we are concerned primarily with the effects that influence job performance.

The model introduces "individual differences" that can affect reactions to stress. Individual differences investigated by occupational stress researchers have included age, sex, work addiction, self-esteem, and community involvement. We will discus the individual differences that have received the most research attention: life events, Type A, hardiness, social support, and negative effectively.

Northwestern National Life Insurance Co. (NWNL) in Minneapolis conducted a national survey. The results indicated that 7 out of 10 workers experience stress often; respondents having multiple stress-related problems rose from 13 per cent in 1985 to 25 per cent in 1991. The study also revealed 26 stress producers and stress reducers. A stress test and booklet was developed from the survey results. For example, the NWNL workplace stress scale provides three stress points if downsizing occurs or if workloads vary greatly. On the stress reducer side, minus three points are given if management has developed a program to reduce stress and if employees are recognised and rewarded fairly for their contributions. The NWNL stress test, like any self-report scale, is subject to error, but it attempts to highlight possible trouble areas. Numerous companies have requested copies of these NWNL materials.

SOURCES OF STRESS

The model identify three sets of factors: *Environmental*, *Organisational*, and *Individual*, that act as potential sources of stress. Whether they become actual stress depends on individual differences such as job experience and personality. When stress is experienced by an individual, its symptoms can surface as physiological, psychological and behavioural outcomes. There are three categories of stressors: Environmental, Organisational, and Individual. Let's take a look at each.

I. OCCUPATIONAL SOURCES

(a) Physical Environmental Stressors

Although most analyses of job stress ignore the importance of outside forces and events, it is becoming increasingly clear that these have a tremendous impact. Taking an open systems perspective of an organisation (that is, organisation is greatly affected by the external environment), it is clear that job stress is not limited just to things that happen inside the organisation, during working hours. *Physical Environmental Stressors* include things such as *social and technological change*, *the family*, relocation, economic and financial conditions, race and class, and residential or community conditions.

The phenomenal rate of social and technical change, has had a great effect on people's lifestyles, and this of course is carried over into their jobs. Although medical science has increased the life spans of people and has eradicated or reduced the threat of many disease, the pace of modern living has increase stress and decreased personal *wellness*. The concept of wellness has been defined as "a harmonious and productive balance of physical, mental, and social well-being brought about by the acceptance of one's personal responsibility for developing and adhering to a health promotion program." Because people tend to get caught up in the rush-rush, mobile, urbanised, crowded, on-the-go lifestyle of today, their wellness in general has deteriorated, and the potential for stress on the job has increased.

A *family situation*—either a brief crisis, such as a squabble or the illness of a family member, or long-term strained relations with the spouse or children—can act as a significant stressor for employees.

Relocating the family because of a transfer or a promotion can also lead to stress. Some stress researchers define these personal life stressors as unresolved environmental demands requiring adaptive behaviours in the form of social readjustments.

Life's changes may be slow (getting older) or sudden (the death of a spouse). These sudden changes have been portrayed in novels and movies as having a dramatic effect on people, and medical researchers have verified that especially sudden life changes do in fact have a very stressful impact on people. They found a definite relationship between the degree of life changes and the subsequent health of the person. The more changes, the poorer the subsequent health. These life changes can also directly influence job performance.

Social variables such as race, sex and class can also become stressors. For professional women, the particular sources of stress have been identified as discrimination, stereotyping, the marriage/work interface and social isolation. In particular dual family and work roles frequently result in job stress. The same is true of the *local community or region* that one comes from. For example, one researcher identified the condition of housing, convenience of services and shopping, neighbourliness, and degree of noise and air pollution as likely stressors.

(b) Organisational Stressor

Besides the potential stressors that occur outside the organisation, there are also those associated with the organisation itself. Although the organisation is made up of groups of individuals, there are also more macro-level dimensions, unique to the organisation, that contain potential stressors. Fig. 1, shows that these macro-level stressors can be categorised into administrative policies and strategies, organisational structure and design, organisational processes, and working conditions.

One problem in the study of organisational stressors is identifying which stressors are most important. A major part of working within organisations for some individuals is participation in decision-making. Participation refers to the extent that a person's knowledge, opinions, and ideas are included in the decision process. Such participation can contribute to stress. Some people may be frustrated by the delays often associated with participative decision-making. Others may view shared decision-making as a threat to the traditional right of a supervisor or manager to have the final say.

Another stressor, organisational structure, has rarely been studied. One study of trade salespeople examined effects of tall (bureaucratically structured), medium, and flat (less rigidly structured) organisations on job satisfaction, stress, and performance. Researchers determined that salespeople in the least bureaucratically structured organisational experienced less stress and more job satisfaction and performed more effectively than did salespeople in medium and tall structures. We have considered only a small sample of the tremendous amount of behavioural and medical research on stressor, stress, and effects linkage. The information gathered, with other organisational research, is contradictory in some cases. However, the available research implies these important points:

(i) Stressors at work are related to physical, psychological, and emotional changes in individuals.

(ii) The adaptive responses to stressors at work have been measured by self-rating, performance appraisals, and biochemical tests. Much more research must be done in properly measuring stress at work.

(iii) There is no universally acceptable list of stressors. Each organisation has its own unique set.

(iv) Individual differences explain why a stressor that's disruptive and unsettling to one person is challenging to another person.

(c) Group Stressors

The effectiveness of any organisation is influenced by the nature of the relations among groups. Group characteristics can be powerful stressors for some individual. Behavioural scientists have suggested that maintaining good relationships among the members of a work group is a central factor in individual well-being. Poor relations include low trust, low supportiveness, and low interest is listening to any trying to deal with the problems that confront another employee. Studies in this area have reached the same conclusion: mistrust of co-workers is positively related to high role ambiguity, which leads to inadequate communications among people and low job satisfaction. These group stressors can be categorised into three areas:

(i) *Lack of group cohesiveness.* Starting with the historically famous Hawthorne studies, it has become very clear that cohesiveness, or "togetherness", is very important to employees, especially at the lower levels of organisations. If an employee is denied the opportunity for this cohesiveness because of the task design, because the supervisor does things to prohibit or limit it, or because the other members of the group shut the person out, the resulting lack of cohesiveness can be very stress-producing.

(ii) *Lack of social support.* Employees are greatly affected by the support of one or more members of cohesive group. By sharing their problems and joys with others, they are much better of. If this type of social support is lacking for an individual, the situation can be very stressful. There is even research indicating that the lack of social support is so stressful that it accounts for some health care costs.

(iii) *Intra-individual, interpersonal and intergroup conflict.* Conflict is conceptually very closely linked to stress. Conflict is normally associated with incompatible or hostile acts between intra-individual dimensions such as personal goals or motivational needs/values, between individuals within a group, and between groups.

(d) Individual Stressor

Stressors at the individual level have been studied more than any other category.

Role conflict occurs when two or more persons have different and sometimes opposing expectations of a given individual. Thus there are two or more sets of pressures on the individual so that it is not possible to satisfy all of them. In other words, role conflict occurs when contradictory demands are simultaneously placed upon an employee. For example, an architect may be expected to produce creative designs, while on the other hand, there may be time constraints put upon him, both roles being in conflict with each other. Similarly, a contractor may ask a carpenter to do something which may be different than what the city building codes prescribe, thus causing a role conflict.

Another type of role conflict is the *inter-role conflict* where an individual plays more than one role simultaneously in his life and the demands of these roles conflict with each other. For example, a father may know that his son has committed a crime but does not inform the police or a police officer may be invited to his brother's wedding party where the guests use drugs which is against the law.

Role ambiguity is a set of activities associated with a certain position in the organisation or in the society. According to Kahn, if these work activities are ill-defined, then the person who is carrying out these activities will not behave as others expect him to, because his role is not clearly defined. Thus when there is lot of uncertainty regarding job definitions or job expectations, then people experience role ambiguity. Role ambiguity is particularly strong among managerial jobs where responsibilities are more general in nature and role definitions and task specifications are not clear. This role ambiguity is specially prevalent among companies that have merged or acquired other companies while keeping the employees. Thus employees become uncertain of what exactly they are supposed to do and exactly whom they report to. This role ambiguity causes stress.

Role overload occurs when the work requirements are so excessive that employees feel that they do not have adequate time or ability to meet such requirements. Working under time pressure is specially stressful whether it is meeting a deadline for a report or studying near the exam period. The physiological symptoms of stress significantly prior to deadline and decrease sharply after the deadline has passed. The role overload can occur either when there is too much work to complete in a given time or when it is too difficult to accomplish because of lack of skills and ability.

Role underload occurs when a person's ability is underutilised so that either there is too little work or there is too little variety in the work. If a salesman with high interpersonal skills is given a job in a department store where there are not too many customers, then he will feel that this ability is not being properly utilised. Similarly, assembly line workers whose jobs are routine and highly monotonous also experience role underload.

Responsibility for people. Any type of responsibility can be a burden upon an individual. For example, organisational responsibility for such factors as budgets, equipment and projects can cause stress. However it is the responsibility for people working for you that is a cause for continuous concern.

Lack of participation. When the employees are invited to participate in decision making process in their areas of concern then the employees perceive to have more control over their own environment thus reducing the extent of role conflict and role ambiguity that causes stress. For example, in a work situation where high role conflict is created because of inconsistent demands from the superiors, the stress created by high role conflict is reduced if the subordinates and superiors can participate and work together in reducing such inconsistencies.

II. INDIVIDUAL DIFFERENCES

The Stress and Work model suggests that various factors moderate the relationship between stressors and stress. A moderator is a condition, behaviour, or characteristics that qualifies the relationship between two variables. The effect may be to intensify or weaken the relationship.

(a) Type A/B

Pattern of behaviour associated with research conducted on coronary heart disease. The type A person is an aggressive driver who is ambitious, competitive, task-oriented, and always on the move. Type A behaviour pattern (TABP) searching the medical literature, they found that traditional coronary risk factors such as dietary cholesterol, blood pressure, and heredity could not totally explain or predict coronary heart disease (CHD), the name given to cardio-vascular diseases characterised by an inadequate supply of oxygen to the heart. Type A's have more heart attacks than do Type B's.

Conversely, the individual with a *Type B behaviour pattern* generally feels no pressing conflict with either time or persons. The Type B may have considerable drive, want to accomplish things, and work hard, but a confident style allows him to work at a steady pace and not to race against the clock.

(b) Hardiness

Everyone has observed individual differences of people faced with stressors. Some people seem to go to pieces at the slightest provocation, while others seem unflappable in the face of extremely stressful situations. Those able to cope successfully with extreme stressors seem to have a *hardiness* disposition.

(c) Social Support

Some research indicates that social support reduces or buffers the adverse psychological impacts of exposure to stress and stressful situations. Interaction with another person or a group is sure to involve social support if it is perceived by the recipient as esteem enhancing or if it involves stress-related interpersonal aid. The term *perceived support* refers to a generalised evaluation individuals make in various situations that they are cared for and valued, that significant others are available to them in times of need, and that they are satisfied with their relationship.

BASIC FORMS OF STRESS: FRUSTRATION AND ANXIETY

Frustration is a form of behaviour which occurs when a person wishes to achieve a certain objective or pursue a certain course of action, but is prevented in doing so. It refers to an obstruction or impediment to goal-oriented behaviour. Examples of frustration include a salesman continuously failing to make a sale, a professor continuously applying for a promotion and failing to get it or to get subordinates to act according to our wishes. There are several factors that cause frustration. First is the unnecessary delay in achieving the goal, even when the goal is eventually available. Delay in getting a promotion, delay in finishing a report and even waiting for a friend after the due time can cause frustration. The second factor affecting frustration is the lack of resources. Sometimes the goals are not achieved because individuals lack the physical, personal or interpersonal resources. A professor who is burdened with administrative duties and does not get enough time to do research which is necessary for promotion may become frustrated because of such time constraints. The third cause of frustration may be the actual failure in achieving the goal. A lost client, a poor evaluation by superiors, failure in the exam or failure to get a promotion are all causes of frustration which are manifested in stress.

A second form of stress is the "anxiety" which is a feeling of inability and helplessness in formulating appropriate responses or plans for dealing with the anticipated negative outcomes. It occurs when a decision has to be made but the outcome of the decision could have positive as well as negative consequences. For example, should you cheat in the exam or not, not knowing whether you will get through or get caught? These are some anxious moments. Anxiety also occurs when all your options result in undesirable consequences. For example, if you are working with a company for a long time and have built roots in the community where you live and your company is moving to a different far off location and you have the choice of either moving with the company or losing the job. Both of these alternatives make you feel uncomfortable and hence become a cause of anxiety. What causes anxiety in work environment?

According to *Hammer* and *Organ*, "Differences in power in organisation which leave people with a feeling of vulnerability to administrative decisions adversely affecting them; frequent changes in organisations, which make existing behaviour plans obsolete; competition, which creates the inevitability that some persons lose "face", esteem and status; and job ambiguity (especially when it is coupled with pressure). To these may be added some related factors, such as lack of job feedback, volatility in the organisations' economic environment, job insecurity and high visibility of one's performance (success as well as failures). Obviously, personal non organisational factors come into play as well, such as physical illness, problems at home, unrealistically high personal goals and estrangement from one's colleagues or one's peer group".

Accordingly, there are a number of factors, both organisational as well as individualistic that cause frustration and anxiety.

STRESS AND JOB PERFORMANCE

One of the major concerns of management is the negative impact stress has on job performance. People under high stress tend to withdraw from the contact with the stressor in the form of turnover and absenteeism. In extreme cases it may result in sabotage. Workers sometimes create mechanical failures in order to take a break from strain of monotonous work. Any factor that causes negative effects on our physical and psychological wellbeing is also expected to affect our work behaviour. Exposure to strong and enduring stress influences important aspects of our behaviour at job thus affecting productivity.

The relationship between stress and performance appears to be rather complex. It is affected by the difficulty of the task being performed, the nature of the specific stressor involved and a wide range of personal and situational factors. However, in general, productivity is considered to be at peak with moderate level of stress. Performance is poor at low level of stress as well as at high level of stress. At low level of stress, the person may not be sufficiently energised and may not be wholeheartedly involved in his work, resulting in low productivity. As the level of stress increases from low levels to moderate levels, the performance level also increases to reach at the peak level. An optimum level of stress exists for any task. If the stress continues to increase from this level, the person becomes too agitated and frustrated, resulting in performance deterioration.

It has been believed that the relationship between stress and performance is curvilinear. It follows an inverted u-shaped curve as shown previously and reproduced here.

However, the validity of the clear-cut relationship is being questioned and some behaviour scientists believe that performance actually decreases when stress increases from low levels to moderate levels, even though the rate of decrease in performance is less than the rate of decrease when stress increases from moderate to high levels.

Stress also impairs the ability to make effective decision. People under stress are in a state of irritation and are unable to concentrate. They become impatient and they are more likely to avoid or postpone making decisions. They are less likely to seek new information and are more likely to forget some important pieces of available information. As a result, the quality of decisions they make suffers, and the cost of a wrong decision can be very high.

THE EFFECTS OF STRESS

As is pointed out in the introductory comments, stress is not automatically bad for individual employees or their organisational performance. In fact, it is generally recognised that low levels of stress can even enhance job performance. For example, one recent study found that mild stress, such as getting a new supervisor or being involuntarily transferred, may have the positive result of an increased search for information in the job. This may lead employees to new and better ways of doing their jobs. Also, mild stress may get employees' "juices" flowing and lead to increased activity, change, and overall better performance. People in certain jobs, such as in sales or creative fields (for example, newspaper journalists and television announcers who work under time pressures), would seem to benefit from a mild level of stress. People in other jobs, such as police officers or physicians, may not benefit from constant mild stress.

Research is also emerging that indicates that the level of difficulty, the nature of the task being performed, personal dispositions (such as Type A, personal control and learned helplessness, self-efficacy, and psychological hardiness) other psychological dispositions (such as negative affectivity), and neuroticism may affect the relationship between stress and performance. However, it is still safe to conclude that :

(i) The performance of many tasks is in fact strongly affected by stress.

(ii) Performance usually drops off sharply when stress rises to high levels.

Generally, stress is considered to be negative, thereby meaning that it has negative consequences. However, stress has neutral connotation; it is only the degree of stress which produces positive or negative consequences. From this point of view, stress can be classified as eustress or distress.

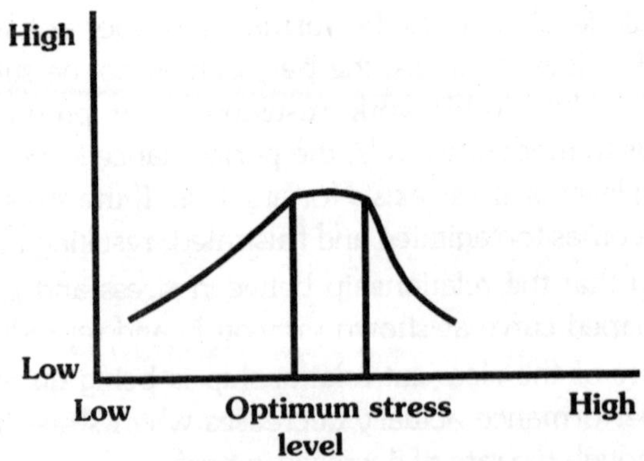

Fig. 2. *Level of Stress and Performance.*

Eustress. Eustress denotes the presence of optimum level of stress in an individual which contributes positively to his performance. This may lead employees to new and better ways of doing their jobs. In certain jobs such as sales, creativity (journalism, radio/television announcement where time pressure is significant), a mild level of stress contributes positively to productivity.

Distress. Distress denotes the presence of high level of stress in an individual which affects job performance adversely and creates many types of physical, psychological, and behavioural problems.

Fig. 2, shows varying degree of stress and their effect on performance. At the optimum level of stress (eustress), the performance is maximum. It is lower in the case of very low-level stress, and still lower in very high-level stress. Though optimum level of stress may be different for different individuals, each individual can determine how much stress is functional for him to operate in a productive manner. High level of stress (distress) causes physical, psychological, and behavioural problems.

I. Physical Problems due to Stress

Most of the attention and basic research over the years has been devoted to the impact that stress has on physical health. A high level of stress is accompanied by high blood pressure and high levels of cholesterol and may even result in heart disease, ulcers, and arthritis. There may even be a link between stress and cancer.

Obviously, such serious physical ailments have a drastic effect on the individual; not always so obvious, but just as serious, are the effects that physical problems such as heart disease can have on the organisation. *Ivancevich* and *Matteson* have provided the following worksheet for computing the costs of replacing employees lost to heart disease in a company employing 4,000 people.

1. Number of employees	4,000
2. Men in age range forty-five to sixty-five (0.25 x line 1)	1,000
3. Estimated deaths due to heart disease per year (0.006 x line 2)	6
4. Estimated premature retirement due to heart problems per year (0.003 x line 2)	3
5. Company's annual personnel losses due to heart disorders (sum of lines 3 and 4)	9
6. Annual replacement cost: the average cost of hiring and training replacements for experienced employees (line 5 x $4,300)	$38,700
7. Number of employees who will eventually die of heart disease if present rate continues (0.5 x line 1)	2,000

These figures are just estimates, but they dramatically illustrate how heart disease alone can affect costs and sheer numbers of employees in a typical organisation. Obviously, not all heart disease can be directly linked to stress; environmental conditions and the person's general state of health, heredity, and medical history also certainly contribute. However, there seems to be enough evidence that stress can and does contribute to this dreaded disease and to other physical problems as well.

II. Psychological Problems due to Stress

While considerable attention has been given to the relationship between stress and physical health, especially within the medical community, not as much has been given to the impact of stress on mental health. Yet, at least indirectly if not directly, the psychological problems resulting from stress may be just as important, if not more important, to day-to-day job performance as the physical problems.

High levels of stress may be accompanied by anger, anxiety, depression, nervousness, irritability, tension, and boredom. One study found that stress had the strongest impact on aggressive actions, such as sabotage, interpersonal aggression, hostility, and complaints. These types of psychological problems from stress, in turn, are especially relevant to poor job performance, lowered self-esteem, resentment of supervision, inability to concentrate and make decisions, and job dissatisfaction. These outcomes of stress can have a direct cost effect on the organisation. For example, the National Centres for Disease Control reported that psychological stress is the sources of numerous job-related insurance claims. Recent court cases have also brought stress-related problems stemming from employment under the employer's worker's compensation insurance. Experts are predicting that if the number of stress-related workers' compensation claims continues to grow at current rates, these claims will lead all other claims in this decade.

Of even greater significance, the outcomes of stress can have a subtle, but very real, effect on the styles and effectiveness of managers in key positions. For example, managers who are under constant stress may become very moody, and their subordinates soon learn not to disturb them, even with important information, because they will just "bite your head off". Such managers may also realise, at times, that they are acting this way; they may feel that they are not living up to the expectations of their important position and suffer a loss of self esteem. In this state they may also procrastinate and continue to put things off and not make needed decisions. And, finally they may resent their boss for trying to get them back on track and begin to hate the job in general. Co-workers, subordinates, and superiors may become very disgusted with such a manager and explain the behaviour away as being the result of a "rotten personality", when in fact the problems are the result of stress. If the manager had a heart attack, every one would feel sorry and say that he or she was under too much stress, but manager's moodiness, low self-esteem, inability to make a decision, and dissatisfaction with the boss and the job cause people to get angry and say that the manager is "no darned good" or "can't get along with anyone". Both a heart attack and a psychological problem may have the same cause (too much stress), and although people may react to them differently; the negative effect on performance is the same in the case of a psychological problem, or perhaps even worse.

III. Behavioural Problems due to Stress

As has been the case with other topics covered in this text the behavioural unit of analysis may be most helpful-in this case, in analysing the effects job stress. Direct behaviours that may accompany high levels of stress include underrating or overeating, sleeplessness, increased smoking and drinking, and drug abuse. When it is realized that 6 per cent of the population are alcoholics, that another estimated 10 per cent are problem drinkers, and that 6 billion doses of amphetamines and barbiturates are consumed annually, the potential problems for employee behaviour caused by alcohol and drug abuse become dramatically clear. For example, one company had such a problem with on-the-job drinking that it bought a breath-alcohol meter to test its employees. The president of the union in this firm stated : "There were a couple of people who came to work drunk everyday." Although the meter has not been used yet, one worker was overheard to say, "I guess I'll have to stop going to the bar at lunchtime." Besides being dangerous, as in this company, which is used a lot of saws and punches, these problems may be manifested in tardiness, absenteeism, and turnover.

There is some research evidence indicating a relationship between stress and especially absenteeism and turnover. For example, workers may experience stress and react by getting drunk and staying home from work the next day with hangover. They then feel bad about this drinking. They may feel that they are letting everyone down "the morning after" and eventually quit or be fired from the job. In the meantime the absenteeism rate climbs, and subsequently the turnover rate increases, both of which are very costly to the organisation in terms of filling in for absent workers and replacing those who have left. Staying away from a job that is causing stress or quitting the job is a "flight" reaction to the situation. Actually, this may be a healthier reaction than a "fight" reaction, in which the person may stay on the stress-producing job and become angry and/or aggressive.

Like the psychological problems resulting from stress, the behavioural problems are often not attributed to stress by co-workers or supervisors and generate little sympathy. But, also like the psychological and the physical symptoms of stress, the behavioural problems can be controlled, more effectively managed, and even prevented by the individual and the organization.

THE CAUSES OF STRESS

I. Extra Organisational Stressors

Although most analyses of job stress ignore the importance of outside forces and events, it is becoming increasingly clear that these have a tremendous impact. Taking an open systems perspective of an organisation (that is, organisation is greatly affected by the external environment), it is clear that job stress is not limited just to things that happen inside the organisation, during working hours. Extra organisational stressors include things such as societal/technological change, the family, relocation, economic and financial conditions, race and class, and residential or community conditions.

Although medical science has increased the life spans of people and has eradicated or reduced the threat of many disease, the pace of modern living has increase stress and decreased personal wellness. The concept of wellness has been defined as "a harmonious and productive balance of physical, mental, and social well-being brought about by the acceptance of one's personal responsibility for developing and adhering to a health promotion program." Because people tend to get caught up in the rush-rush, mobile, urbanised, crowded, on-the-go lifestyle of today, their wellness in general has deteriorated, and the potential for stress on the job has increased.

Life's changes maybe slow (getting older) or sudden (the death of a spouse). These sudden changes have been portrayed in novels and movies as having a dramatic effect on people, and medical researchers have verified that especially sudden life changes do in fact have a very stressful impact on people. They found a definite relationship between the degree of life changes and the subsequent health of the person. The more changes, the poorer the subsequent health. These life changes can also directly influence job performance. One psychologist, *Faye Crosby,* reports that divorce interferes with work more than any other trauma in a person's life. She says. "During the first three months after a spouse walks out, the other spouse—male or female—usually is incapable of focusing on work."

II. Organisational Stressors

Besides the potential stressors that occur outside the organisation, there are also those associated with the organisation itself. Although the organisation is made up of groups of individuals, there are also more macro-level dimensions, unique to the organisation, that contain potential stressors. Figure shows that these macro-level stressors can be categorised into administrative policies and strategies, organisational structure and design, organisational processes, and working conditions.

III. Group Stressors

The group can also be a potential source of stress. These group stressors can be categorised into three areas :

(i) *Lack of group cohesiveness.* Starting with the historically famous Hawthorne studies, it has become very clear that cohesiveness, or "togetherness", is very important to employees, especially at the lower levels of organisations. If an employee is denied the opportunity for this cohesiveness because of the task design, because the supervisor does things to prohibit or limit it, or because the other members of the group shut the person out, the resulting lack of cohesiveness can be very stress-producing.

(ii) *Lack of social support.* Employees are greatly affected by the support of one or more members of cohesive group. By sharing their problems and joys with others, they are much better of. If this type of social support is lacking for an individual, the situation can be very stressful. There is even research indicating that the lack of social support is so stressful that it accounts for some health care costs.

(iii) *Intra-individual, interpersonal and intergroup conflict.* Conflict is conceptually very closely linked to stress. Conflict is normally associated with incompatible or hostile acts between Intra-individual dimensions such as personal goals or motivational needs/values, between individuals within a group, and between groups.

STRESS MANAGEMENT

I. Organisational Coping Strategies

Organisational coping strategies are designed by management to eliminate or control organisational-level stressors in order to prevent or reduce job stress for individual employee.

In the structural area, steps would be taken to back away from high degrees of formalisation and specialisation. The same would be done in the areas of physical conditions (for example, safety hazards would be removed, and lighting, noise and temperature would be improved) and processes/functions (for example, communication and information would be improved, and ambiguous or conflicting goals would be clarified or resolved). In addition, the Association for Fitness in Business estimates that 12,000 companies today offer stress-coping programs, ranging from counselling services, lunchtime stress-management seminars, and wellness publications to elaborate company-run fitness centres where employees can sweat out the tension. There is also evidence that the number of stress management programs is increasing and they are being evaluated more rigorously.

In addition to working on each specific organisational stressors identified in fig., more generalised strategies might include the following :

(i) Create a supportive organisational climate

Even though an increasing number of firms today are moving toward a more horizontal, network type of structure, too many continue to be highly formalised, with accompanying inflexible, impersonal climates. This type of climate can lead to considerable job stress. A coping strategy would be to make the structure more decentralised and organic, with participative decision-making and upward communication flows. In theory, these structural and process changes would create a more supportive climate for employees, give them more control over their jobs, and prevent or reduce their job stress.

(ii) Enrich the design of tasks

As is brought out there, enriching jobs either by improving job content factors (such as responsibility, recognition, and opportunities for achievement, advancement, and growth) or by improving core job characteristics (such as skill variety, task identity, task significance, autonomy, and feedback) may lead to motivational states or experienced meaningfulness, responsibility, and knowledge of results. Presumably, these enriched tasks will eliminate the stressors found in more routine, structured jobs. However not all people respond favourably to enrich job designs; and therefore, at least with some people some of the time, the enriched job may actually lead to increased job stress. For example, an individual with low growth needs, low self-efficacy, lack of hardiness, and/or fear of failure may experience increased stress in an enriched job. However, a recent study found that innovative ways of managing task design may be an effective way to cope with stress.

(iii) Reduce conflict and clarity organisational roles

Role conflict or ambiguity was identified earlier as a major individual stressor. It is up to management to reduce the conflict and clarify organisational roles so that this cause of stress can be eliminated or reduced. Each job should have clear expectations and the necessary information and support so that the job-holder is not left with conflicting demands or an ambiguous understanding of what he or she is to do. A specific roles clarification strategy might be to have the person occupying a role obtain a list of expectations from each role definer (e.g., the boss).

This list would when be compared with the focal person's expectations, and any differences would be openly discussed to clarify ambiguities and negotiated to resolve conflict.

(iv) Plan and develop career paths and provide counselling

Traditionally, organisations have shown only passing interest in the career planning and development of their employees. Individuals are left to decide career moves and strategies on their own and, at most, get paternalistic advice once in a while from a supervisor. This situation is analogous to that of students at a large university who are simply names on an advisor's computer printout sheet, which contains the names of hundreds of advises. This situation obviously can be a source of considerable uncertainty and stress for both the students and the professor. The same is true for members of any large organisation; the stress is created by not knowing what their next move is or how they are going to make it.

Besides the generalised organisational coping strategies for all employees discussed above, because of the stress resulting from downswing in recent years, new concern is being given to both those who are let go and those who survive. For example, theoretical models are being created and basic researches being done on coping with job loss. One stream of research has examined the role that procedural justice (perceptions of fairness) plays on those affected by downsizing. In three studies (of those already laid off, survivors of a firm that had downsized, and those scheduled to be laid off), it was found that fair procedural justice had a positive impact.

II. INDIVIDUAL COPING STRATEGIES

Today, self-help remedies, do-it-yourself approaches, weight-loss clinics and diets, health foods, and physical exercise are being given much attention in the mass media. People are actually taking responsibility, or know they should be taking responsibility, for their own wellness. Individual coping strategies for dealing with stress make sense. In other words, most people don't have to be convinced of the value of taking charge and actually making a change in their lives.

Some specific techniques that individuals can use to eliminate or more effectively manage inevitable, prolonged stress are the following :

(i) Exercise

Today, it is not whether you win or lose, but whether you get some good exercise that counts. People of all ages are walking, jogging, swimming, riding bicycles, or playing softball, tennis, or racket ball in order to get some exercise to combat stress. Although this seems to make a great deal of sense and many laypeople and physicians swear by its, there still is no conclusive evidence that exercise will directly reduce the chances of heart disease or stroke. But there seems little doubt that it can help people better cope with stress, even if only as a result of the side effects, such as relaxation, enhanced self-esteem, and simply getting one's mind off work for a while.

(ii) Relaxation

Whether a person simply takes it easy once in a while or uses specific relaxation techniques such as biofeedback or mediation, the intent is to eliminate the immediately stressful situation or manage a prolonged stressful situation more effectively. Taking it easy may mean curling up with a good book in front of a fireplace or watching something "light" (not a violent program or a sports program) on television. Meditation involves muscle and mental relaxation; the person slowly repeats a peaceful phrase or word or concentrates on a mental picture in a quite location. There is some research evidence that much meditation can have a desirable physical and mental impact on people. Whether it can have a practical impact on job stress is yet to be determined. However, a number of firms are using it. For example, a stockbroker who regularly uses mediation recently stated : "It's widely known that this industry has a lot of stress. So where a lot of people drink alcohol, we meditate. It's not that we don't feel stress. It just doesn't hit us as much."

(iii) Behavioural Self-control

By deliberately managing the antecedents and the consequences of their own behaviour, people can achieve self-control. For example, sales managers who have a steady stream of customer complaints all day could change the antecedent by having an assistant screen all complaints and allow only exceptions to reach them. They could also manage the consequences by rewarding themselves with an extra break when they remain calm and collected after interacting with a particularly angry customer. Besides managing their own behaviour to reduce stress, people can also become more aware of their limits and of "red flags" that signal trouble ahead. They can avoid people or situations that they know will put them under stress. In other words, this strategy involves individuals' controlling the situation instead of letting the situation control them.

(iv) Cognitive Therapy

Besides behavioural self-control techniques, a number of clinical psychologists have entered the stress field in recent years with cognitive therapy techniques. Techniques such as Ellis's rational emotive model and Meichenbaums cognitive behaviour modification have been successfully used to reduce test anxiety and have recently been used as an individual strategy for reducing job stress. One study described the approach as follows:

Participants were taught that much of their experienced strain (anxiety, tension, etc.) is caused by their cognitions ("self-talks"). This part of the treatment program, then, consisted of off-line lectures and interactive discussions designed to help participants :

(a) Recognise events at work and what cognitions they elicit;

(b) Become aware of the effects of such cognitions on their physiological and emotional responses;

(c) Systematically evaluate the objective consequences of events at work; and

(d) Replace self-defeating cognitions that unnecessarily arouse strain (e.g., "I'm an incompetent worker who cannot handle the workload") with more adaptive appraisals (e.g., "I handle this workload as well as anyone else," or "the workload is too high and I should approach my supervisor").

When this coping strategy (combined with some simple relaxation techniques) was systematically evaluated by a field experimental design in a social service agency, it was found to have a positive impact on some of both the physiological (epinephrine, a hormone produced by the adrenal glands) and the psychological (depression) variables measured. However, they were no significant effects on some of the other variables measured, and the treatment effects were not replicated in a subsequent intervention on the original control group. Another study evaluated a similar cognitive therapy approach applied to policy academy trainees. This study found that in simulated exercises, those who used the cognitive strategy performed more effectively and exhibited greater self-control and less strain than those who did not use the approach. However, there were methodological flaws that probably prevent definitive conclusions at this point on the value of the cognitive approach to managing stress. Yet, as is true of the other strategies discussed so far, there is enough promise to continue its use in trying to cope with stress.

(v) Networking

One clear finding that has come out of social psychology research over the years is that people need and will benefit from social support. Applied as a strategy to reduce job stress, this would entail forming close associations with trusted empathetic coworkers and colleagues who are good listeners and confidence builders. These friends are there when needed and provide support to get the person through stressful situations. Today, such alliances, especially if deliberately sought out and developed, are called networks. Although the relationship between social support and stress reduction appears complicated, there is some research evidence that a networking strategy may be able to help people cope better with job stress and be more effective and successful managers.

REVIEW QUESTIONS

1. What do you understand by the term "stress"? Explain the potential sources of stress.
2. What individual difference variables moderate the relationship between potential stressors and experienced stress?
3. Explain fully the consequences of stress.
4. What are the basic forms of stress? Explain.
5. Explain the general adaptation syndrome.
6. Differentiate between role ambiguity and role conflict.

REFERENCES

1. *Sethi, Amarjit S., "Yoga for Coping with Organisational Stress", in Amarjit S. Sethi and Randall S. Schuler (eds), "Handbook of Organisational Stress Coping Strategies",*
2. *Ballinger Publishing Company; 1984.*
3. *Hammer, W.C. and D. Organ, "Organisational Behaviour: An Applied Psychological Approach",*
4. *Business Publications, 1978.*
5. *Kahn R.L., D.M. Wolfe, R.P. Quinn, J.D. Snoekand and R.A. Rosenthal, "Organisational Stress: Studies in Role Conflict and Ambiguity".*

6. *U.S. News and World Report, March 13, 1978, (Report Based Upon the Study Conducted by the National Institute for Occupational Safety and Health, Department of Health, Education and Welfare).*
7. *Shushan L. Find and Fred L. Otte, "Management Styles, Mediating Variables, and Stress among HRD Professionals," Human Resource Development Quarterly, Winter 1994.*
8. *Hans Selye, Stress without Distress, Philadelphia: Lippincott.*
9. *John M. Ivancevich and Michael T. Matteson, "Stress: Can We Cope," Time, June 6, 1983.*
10. *T.A. Beehr and J.E. Newman "Job Stress, Employee Health and Organisational Effectiveness: A Facet Analysis, Model and Literature Review," Personal Psychology, Winter 1978.*
11. *Thomas G. Cummings and Cary L. Cooper, "A Cybernetic Framework for Studying Occupational Stress," Human Relations.*

7th

BEHAVIOURAL APPROACHES TO GROUP

CHAPTER OVERVIEW

• ***After reading this chapter, you should be able to know:***

- Introduction
- Types of Group
- Why do People Join Groups?
- Factors of Groups Formation
- The Nature of Groups
- Features of a Mature Group
- Functions of Groups
- Stages of Group Development
- Group Structure
- Group Tasks
- Group Think
- Group Shift
- Types of Group Interaction
- Teams *versus* Groups
- Group Dynamics
- Internal Determinants of a Group Change
- External Determinants of a Group Change
- Theories of Group Formation
- Committee Groups
- Types of Committee Groups
- Benefits of Committees
- Limitations of Committees
- Group Decision-Making
- The Nature of Decision-Making
- Characteristics of Decision-Making
- Decision-Making Process
- Positive and Negative Aspects of Group Decision-Making
- Homans Model
- Participative Decision-Making Technique
- The Leadership Role in Group Decision-Making
- The Rational Decision-Making Process

7

Behavioural Approaches to Group

INTRODUCTION

The term group refers to two or more individuals who bear an explicit psychological relationship to one another. For each group member the other group members stand in somewhat immediate psychological form so as to extent the impact of their behaviour and their features on him. In general, a number of people together at a given place and given time can be considered as a group. People in a bus or the same compartment of a train or students in a class are all known as *groups*. A *group* is defined as two or more employees of the team interact with each other and influence each other's performance.

A group comprises people with shared goals who often communicate with one another over a period of time and are few enough so that each individual may communicate with all others person-to-person. For our purposes, a group is a small number of individuals who communicate person-to-person to achieve one or more common goals. Accordingly, we do not focus on large groups such as a political party, ethnic group, or occupational group.

Groups in organisations can alter the individual's motivations or needs, and can influence the behaviour of individuals in an organisational setting. Organisational behaviour is more than the logical composite of the behaviour of individuals. It is also the behaviour of groups that interact the activities within groups.

According to *David Horton Smith, 'a group is the largest set of two or more individuals who are jointly characterised by a network of relevant communications, a shared sense of collective identity and one or more shared dispositions with associated normative strength'*. In other words, a group is a collection of two or more people who have a common goal or interest and interact with each other to accomplish their objective, are aware of one another and perceive themselves to be a part of the group.

TYPES OF GROUP

Groups can be either formal or informal. It's possible to subclassify groups as command, task, interest, or friendship groups. Command and task groups are dictated by the formal organisation, whereas interest and friendship groups are informal alliances.

I. Formal Groups

In formal groups, the behaviours that one should engage in are stipulated by and directed toward organisational goals. The six members making up an airline flight crew are an example of a formal group. A group is formal when it is purposely designed to accomplish an organisation objective or task. It is created via a formal authority for some defined purpose.

A formal group can be a command group or a functional group which is relatively permanent and is composed of managers and their subordinates who meet regularly to discuss general and specific ideas to improve product or service. In business organisations, most employees work in such command groups.

The formal work groups usually work under a single supervisor, even though the structure of these groups may vary. For example, in one form of group such as in production, the members of the work group depend on each other as well as on the supervisor and in another form of group, such as sales force, the members of the group work fairly, independently and their common contact may be the district sales manager.

(i) Command Group

A *command group* is determined by the organisation chart. It is composed of the subordinates who report directly to a given manager. An elementary school principal and his/her twelve teachers form a command group, as do the director of postal audits and his five inspectors.

(ii) Task Groups

Task groups, also organisationally determined, represent those working together to complete a job task. However, a task group's boundaries are not limited to its immediate hierarchical superior. It can cross command relationships. For instance, if a college student is accused of a campus crime, it may require communication and coordination among the dean of academic affairs, the dean of students, the registrar, the director of security, and the student's advisor. Such a formation would constitute a task group. It should be noted that all command groups are also task groups, but because task groups can cut across the organisation, the reverse need not be true.

Types of Task Groups : Task groups may be classified on the basis of the relationships between group members. The three basic types of task groups are *counteracting, coaching,* and *interacting*.

(a) *Counteraction group* : A *counteraction group* exists when members interact to resolve some type of conflict, usually through negotiation and compromise. A labour-management negotiating group is one example of a counteracting group. Management and union representatives usually believe that at least some of their goals conflict.

(b) *Coaching group* : A *coaching group* exists when group members perform their jobs relatively independently in the short run. Relatively and in the short run indicate that, without interdependence over time, there would be no task group. For example, college students enrolled in the same course may participate relatively independently of each other in class discussions but act interdependently with others in undertaking a team project. Another example of a coaching, group is a bowling team where the team score is the sum of the team members' scores. Coaching groups are likely to be the effective when individual efforts do not require much coordination. For example, a regional sales manager may need to bring her sales representatives together quarterly to review common problems and issues. However, the day-to-day activities of each sales representative doesn't involve communication and coordination with the other sales representatives. In addition, the total regional sales and profits are primarily the sum of each sales representative's performance.

(c) *Interacting group* : An *interacting group* exists when a group or team cannot accomplish its goal(s) until all members have completed their shares of the task. For example, the assembly team of a large luggage manufacturer consists of about ten people who perform the separate jobs required to assemble a complete piece of luggage. If one job isn't done, the goal—the finished suitcase cannot be completed. Common forms of interacting groups include committees, task forces, teams, boards, advisory councils, work crews, review panels, and the like.

II. Informal Groups

In contrast, *informal groups* are alliances that are neither formally structured nor organisationally determined. These groups are natural formation in the work environment that appear in response to the need for social contact. Three employees from different departments who regularly eat lunch together are an example of an informal group.

Informal groups provide a very important service by satisfying their members' social needs. Because of interactions that result from the close proximity of workstations or task interactions, we find workers playing golf together, riding to and from work together, lunching together, and spending their breaks around the water cooler together. We must recognise that these types of interactions among individuals, even though informal, deeply affect their behaviour and performance.

Whereas formal groups are established by organisations to achieve some specific objectives, the informal groups are formed by the members of such groups by themselves. They emerge naturally in response to the common interests of organisational members. They are formed spontaneously, without any formal designation, and with common interests such as self-defence, work assistance and social interaction. They exist outside the formal authority system and without any set rigid rules. Though officially unrecognised, they exist in the shadow of the formal structure as a network of personal and social relations which must be understood and respected by the management.

The informal work groups are based upon socio-psychological support and reasoning and depend upon member's interaction, communication, personal likings and disliking and social contacts within as well as outside the organisation. How powerful are these informal groups can be seen from the fact that if one member of the group is fired, sometimes all workers go on strike in support of that member of the group. The bonds between members are very strong and these bonds bring in a sense of belonging and togetherness. This togetherness can have a powerful influence on productivity and job satisfaction, since employees motivate each other and share each other's burden by training those who are new and by looking up to old timers for guidance, advice, and assistance.

Informal groups generally result due to personal bonds and social interaction among people who work together at the same place and may have similarities as well as differences in their nature and their outlook. These groups have their own structure, sometimes parallel to the formal structure with their own leaders and followers, group goals, social roles and working patterns. They have their own unwritten rules and a code of conduct which every member implicitly accepts. Members trust and help each other. For example, in a department of a college, the departmental secretary may yield more authority in some areas then even the chairperson as in the case of typing exams and typing course outlines. Thus a professor who has a good rapport with the secretary, as a member of the informal group, would have the papers typed sooner than other.

(i) Interest Groups

People who may or may not be aligned into common command or task groups may affiliate to attain a specific objective with which each is concerned. This is an *interest group*. Employees who band together to have their vacation schedules altered, to support a peer who has been fired, or to seek improved working conditions represent the formation of united body to further their common interest.

(ii) Friendship Groups

Groups often develop because the individual members have one or more common characteristics. We call these formations *friendship groups*. Social alliances, which frequently extend outside the work situation, can be based on similar age or ethnic heritage, support for Tata football, or the holding of similar political views, to name just a few such characteristics.

III. Primary & Secondary Groups

Primary groups are characterised by small size, frequent face-to-face interactions and intimacy among members. The examples are *family groups*, *play groups* and *neighbourhood groups*.

Secondary groups called *reference groups*, are characterised by large size and an individual's identifications with values and beliefs prevailing in them rather than actual interactions. The examples are *occupational associations and ethenic groups*.

IV. In-and-Out Groups

In-groups represent a clustering of individuals holding prevailing values in a society, The *Out-gropus* from the masses viewed as subordinate or marginal in culture.

WHY DO PEOPLE JOIN GROUPS?

There is no single reason why individuals join groups. Because most people belong to a number of groups, it's obvious that different groups provide different benefits to their members. Summarises the most popular reasons people have for joining groups.

(i) *Security:* By joining a group, individuals can reduce the insecurity of "standing alone." People feel stronger, have fewer self-doubts, and are more resistant to threats when they are part of a group.

(ii) *Status:* Inclusion in a group that is viewed as important by others provides recognition and status for its members.

(iii) *Self-esteem:* Groups can provide people will-feelings of self-worth. That is, in addition to conveying status to those outside the group, membership can also give increased feelings of worth to the group members themselves.

(iv) *Affiliation:* Groups can fulfil social needs. People enjoy the regular interaction that comes with group membership. For many people, these on-the-job interactions are their primary source for fulfilling their needs for affiliation.

(v) *Power:* What cannot be achieved individually often becomes possible through group action. There is power in numbers.

(vi) *Goal achievement:* There are times when it takes more than one person to accomplish a particular task—there is a need to pool talents, knowledge, or power in order to complete a job. In such instances, management will rely on the use of a formal group.

FACTORS OF GROUPS FORMATION

Why do individuals form themselves into groups? What are the reasons for forming or joining a group and what are the benefits to such individuals who become a part of the group? There are many factors that influence the formation of the group, the most important being the individual need satisfaction. This means that the members expect affiliation with the group to satisfy a need. This need is primarily a social need for love, affection and friendship which is the third level need in Maslow's model of hierarchical needs. But the need could also be economic in nature because of economic group incentives which are generally financially more generous than individual incentives. Also being a member of a union is economically advantageous because unions can fight for higher pay and fringe benefits more effectively.

According to *George Homans,* there are three elements that form the foundations of groups. These are *activities*, *interactions* and *sentiments*. These three elements are interrelated. An improvement in one element will trigger an improvement in others.

One of the major purposes behind the formation of a group is the gratification of the members' needs. In order to survive a group must yield satisfactions to its members. The reason for group formation in relation to the following factors:

(i) Groups provide warmth and support for individuals. Man needs others to feel fulfilled. When individuals are "Solitaires" lacking that warmth and support, they suffer. Aloneness leads to a degree of insecurity. In fact, the harshest punishment that can be given a prisoner in the US Penal System is to be put in solitary confinement for a given period of time. Elton Mayo observed that employees who are isolated from each other because of plant layout find their jobs less satisfying than those group members who are able to socialise on the job.

(ii) Groups help employees satisfy their security needs or their need for power. They serve the important function of helping individuals cope with their environment. Most employees join groups (Unions for example) to protect themselves against what they perceive to be arbitrary or capricious acts by superiors. Under conditions of an oppressive boss, or a very difficult and demanding job, people join together to share sentiments and develop implicit or explicit tactics for dealing with the environment.

(iii) The work group is a primary source of recognition and esteem for many individuals. It gives an individual recognition status and further opportunity to relate to others. Joining a high status group can help an individual acquire esteem in the eyes of persons outside the group whether or not he is distinguished member of the group. Group membership provides opportunities for recognition and praise that are not available outside the group.

(iv) Economic reasons also cause group formation. In many instances groups from because individuals believe that they can derive greater economic benefits in their jobs if they form into groups.

(v) Another important fact or group formation involves the proximity of people to each other. The proximity makes it possible for people to learn about the characteristics of others and offers an excellent opportunity to exchange thoughts, ideas and attitudes regarding on-and-off-the-job activities. This leads to mutual interaction (relieves boredom) and helps in establishing and stabilising perceptions of the work place. Groups also serve as sources of information, help out when members are sick or absent.

(vi) Another reasons as to why a person joins a group is his feeling that the group can help him accomplish goals. Organisational tasks demand cooperative effort of a number of people. The formal or informal group can be extremely useful in solving specific work problems or in preventing the individuals from committing mistakes on the job.

THE NATURE OF GROUPS

No generally accepted definition of a group exists. Instead, we present a range of available views developed over many years in a variety of disciplines. From these different perspectives, we develop a comprehensive definition of a group.

(i) *A Group in Terms of Perception:* Many behavioural scientists believe that for a collection of individuals to be considered as a group, its members must perceive their relationships to others. For example, a small group is defined as any number of persons engaged in interaction with one another in a single face-to-face meeting or series of such meetings, in which each member receives some impression or perception of each other member distinct enough so that he can, either at the time or in later questioning, give some reaction to each of the others as an individual person, even though it may be only to recall that the other was present. This view points out that the members of a group must perceive the existence of each member as well as the existence of the group.

(ii) *A Group in Terms of Organisation:* Sociologists view the group primarily in terms of organisational characteristics. For example, according to a sociological definition, a group is an organised system of two or more individuals who are interrelated so that the system performs some function, has a standard set of role relationships among its members, and has a set of norms that regulate the function of the group and each of its members.

(iii) *A Group in Terms of Motivation:* A group that fails to aid its members in satisfying their needs has difficulty remaining viable. Employees who aren't satisfying their needs in a particular group will search for other groups to aid in important need satisfaction. This view defines a group as a collection of individuals whose existence as a collection is rewarding to the individuals.

(iv) *A Group in Terms of Interaction:* Some theorists assume that interaction in the form of interdependence is the core of "groupness." This view stresses interpersonal interactions. We mean by a group a number of persons who communicate with one another often over a span of time, and who are few enough so that each person is able to communicate with all of the others, not at second-hand through other people, but face-to-face.

All of these four views are important because they all point to key features of groups. Furthermore, if a group exists in an organisation, its members:

(a) Are motivated to join.

(b) Perceive the group as a unified unit of interacting people.

(c) Contribute in various amount to the group processes (i.e., some people contribute more time or energy to the group).

(d) Reach agreements and have disagreements through various forms of interaction.

FEATURES OF A MATURE GROUP

If and when a group takes on the following characteristics, it can be called a mature group:

(i) Member are aware of their own and each other's assets and liabilities vis-a-vis the group's task.

(ii) These individual differences are accepted without being labelled as good or bad.

(iii) The group has developed authority and interpersonal relationships that are recognised and accepted by the members.

(iv) Group decisions are made through rational discussion. Minority opinions and dissension are recognised and encouraged. Attempts are not made to force decisions or a false unanimity.

(v) Conflict is over substantive group issues such as group goals and the effectiveness and efficiency of various means for achieving those goals. Conflict over emotional issues regarding group structure, processes, or interpersonal relationships is at a minimum.

(vi) Members are aware of the group's processes and their own roles in them.

A hidden but nonetheless significant benefit of group maturity is that individuality is strengthened and not extinguished.

FUNCTIONS OF GROUPS

Organisational life is repeat with horror stories of how groups operate as 'demolition squads' cutting down organisational work to meaningless levels. In an effort to cut down such militant groups to size managers arrogantly try to impede group relationships by making frequent transfers, by assigning people who are known to be incompatible to the same work group or by erecting physical barriers between departments considered to be vulnerable 'spots' for group pressures.

Such efforts, though justifiable in extreme situations, back-fire, because, as we have seen, employees have a strong need for affiliation. Lack of social interaction is likely to lead to greater turnover, absenteeism, accidents, lower quality of work etc. Managers must understand that groups are an inevitable and useful feature of organisational life. Their essential job will be to manage organisational groups in such a way as to make them more productive and satisfying to their members. Groups perform three functions that are important to an enterprises success.

(i) *Socialisation of New Employees.* The work group teaches the new employee the work norms, that is, how to behave at work. It orients and educates the new employees into the enterprise's work rules and norms and helps him under control.

(ii) *Getting the Job Done.* The work group teaches the employee how to cope with the job. Truly speaking, it is the organisation that provides the necessary training for employees to do the job, but in practice it is the work groups within the organisation, that help the employees learn how to interact with the rest of the organisation and how to get the job done.

(iii) *Decision-Making.* Well established groups that are operating effectively can contribute to organisational members by turning out better decisions. Two heads are better than one.

STAGES OF GROUP DEVELOPMENT

Experts have identified six distinct stages in the group development process. During stages 1 through 3, attempts are made to overcome the obstacle of uncertainty over power and authority. Once this first obstacle has been surmounted, uncertainty over interpersonal relations becomes the challenge. This second obstacle must be cleared during stages 4 through 6 if the group is to achieve maturity. Each stage confronts the group's leader and contributing members with a unique combination of problems and opportunities.

Stage 1: Orientation. Attempts are made to "break the ice." Uncertainty about goals, power, and interpersonal relationships is high. Members generally want and accept any leadership at this point. Emergent leaders often misinterpret this "honeymoon period" as a mandate for permanent control.

Stage 2: Conflict and Challenge. As the emergent leader's philosophy, objectives, and policies become apparent, individuals or subgroups advocating alternative courses of action struggle for control. This second stage may be prolonged while members strive to clarify and reconcile their roles as part of a complete redistribution of power and authority. Many groups never continue past stage 2 because they get bogged down due to emotionalism and political infighting. Committees within the organisation are often the brunt of jokes because their frequent failure to mature beyond stage 2 prevents them from accomplishing their goals.

Stage 3: Cohesion. The shifts in power started in stage 2 are completed, under a new leader or the original leader, with a new consensus on authority, structure, and procedures. As "we" feeling becomes apparent as everyone becomes truly involved. Any lingering differences over power and authority are resolved quickly. Stage 3 is usually of relatively short duration. If not, the group is likely to stall.

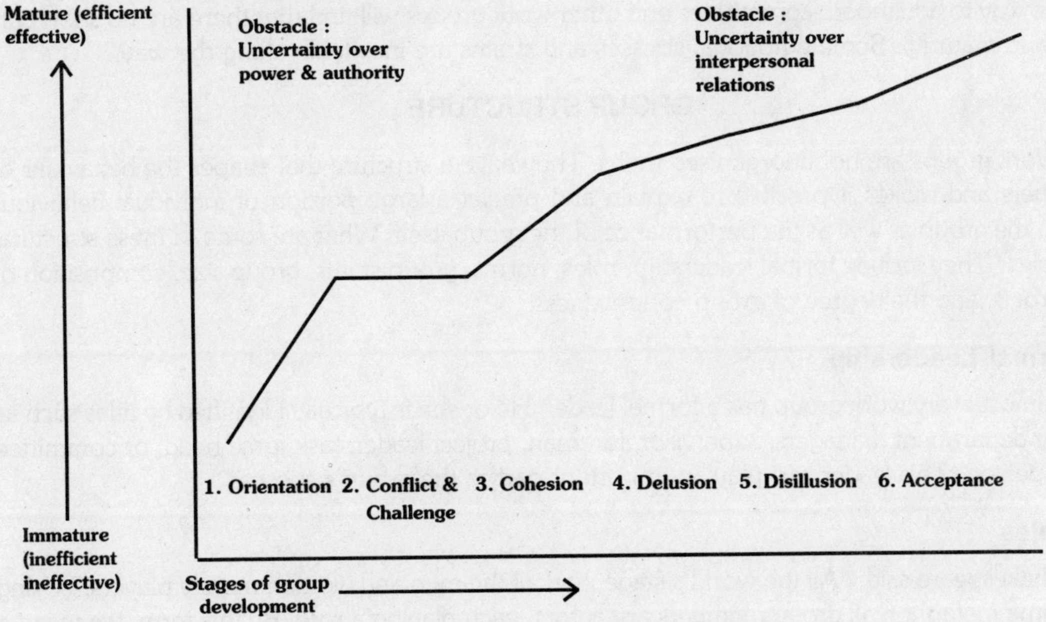

Fig. 1. *Stages of Group Development.*

Stage 4: Delusion. A feeling of "having been through the worst of it" prevails after the rather rapid transition through stage 3. Issues and problems that threaten to break this spell of relief are dismissed or treated lightly. Members seem committed to fostering harmony at all costs. Participation and camaraderie run high as members believe that all the difficult emotional problems have been solved.

Stage 5: Disillusion. Subgroups tend to form as the delusion of unlimited goodwill wears off, and there is a growing disenchantment with how things are turning out. Those with unrealised expectations challenge the group to perform better and are prepared to reveal their personal strengths and weaknesses if necessary. Others hold back. Tardiness and absenteeism are symptomatic of diminishing cohesiveness and commitment.

Stage 6: Acceptance. It usually takes a trusted and influential group member who is concerned about the group to step forward and help the group move from conflict to cohesion. This individual, acting as the group catalyst, is usually someone other than the leader. Members are encouraged to test their self-perceptions against the reality of how others perceive them. Greater personal and mutual understanding helps members adapt to situations without causing problems. Members' expectations are more realistic than ever before. Since the authority structure is generally accepted, subgroups can pursue different matters without threatening group cohesiveness. Consequently, stage 6 groups tend to be highly effective and efficient.

Time-wasting problems and inefficiencies can be minimised if group members are consciously aware of this developmental process. Just as it is impossible for a child to skip being a teenager on the way to adulthood, committees and other work groups will find that there are no short cuts to group maturity. Some emotional stresses and strains are inevitable along the way.

GROUP STRUCTURE

Work groups are not unorganised mobs. They have a structure that shapes the behaviour of members and makes it possible to explain and predict a large portion of individual behaviour within the group as well as the performance of the group itself. What are some of these structural variables? They include formal leadership, roles, norms, group status, group size, composition of the group, and the degree of group cohesiveness.

I. Formal Leadership

Almost every work group has a formal leader. He or she is typically identified by titles such as unit or department managers, supervisor, foreman, project leader, task force head, or committee chair person. This leader can play an important part in the group's success.

II. Roles

Shakespeare said, "All the world's stage, and all the men and women merely players." Using the same metaphor, all group members are actors, each playing a *role*. By this term, we mean a set of expected behaviour patterns attributed to someone occupying a given position in a social unit. The understanding of role behaviour would be dramatically simplified if each of us chose one role and "played it out" regularly and consistently. Unfortunately, we are required to play a number of diverse roles, both on and off our jobs.

Role Identity. There are certain attitudes and actual behaviours consistent with a role, and they create the *role identity*. People have the ability to shift roles rapidly when they recognise that the situation and its demands clearly require major changes. For instance, when union stewards were promoted to supervisory positions, it was found that their attitudes changed from prounion to promanagement within a few months of their promotion. When these promotions had to be rescinded later because of economic difficulties in the firm, it was found that the demoted supervisors had once again adopted their prounion attitudes.

Role Perception. One's view of how one is supposed to act in a given situation is a *role perception*. Based on an interpretation of how we believe we are supposed to behave, we engage in certain types of behaviour.

Where do we get these perceptions? We get them from stimuli all around us—friends, books, movies, television. Many current law enforcement officers learned their roles from reading Sidney Sheldon novels or watching Amitabh's movies. Tomorrow's lawyers will certainly be influenced by the actions of attorneys in the O.J. Simpson double-murder trial. Of course, the primary reason that apprenticeship programs exist in many trades and professions is to allow beginners to watch an "expert," so that they can learn to act as they are supposed to.

Role Expectations. Role expectations are defined as how others believe you should act in a given situation. How you behave is determined to a large extent by the role defined in the context in which you are acting. When role expectations are concentrated into generalised categories, we have role stereotypes.

In the workplace, it can be helpful to look at the topic of role expectations through the perspective of the *psychological contract.* There is an unwritten agreement that exists between employees and their employer. This psychological contract sets out mutual expectations—what management expects from workers, and vice versa. In effect, this contract defines the behavioural expectations that go with every role. Management is expected to treat employees justly, provide acceptable working conditions, clearly communicate what is a fair day's work, and give feedback on how well the employee is doing. Employees are expected to respond by demonstrating a good attitude, following directions and showing loyalty to the organisation.

Role Conflict. When an individual is confronted by divergent role expectations, the result is *role conflict*. It exists when an individual finds that compliance with one role requirement may make more difficult the compliance with another. At the extreme, it would include situation in which two or more role expectations are mutually contradictory.

All of us have faced and will continue to face role conflicts. The critical issue, from our standpoint, is how conflicts imposed by divergent expectations within the organisation impact on behaviour. Certainly, they increase internal tension and frustration. There are a number of behavioural responses one may engage in. For example, one can give a formalised bureaucratic response. The conflict is then resolved by relying on the rules, regulations, and procedures that govern organisational activities. For example, a worker faced with the conflicting requirements imposed by the corporate controller's office and his own plant manager decides in favour of his immediate boss—the plant manager.

III. Group Norms

Norms are the standards shared by the members of a group. They have certain characteristics that are important to group members. First, norms are formed only with respect to things that have significance for the group. They may be written, but they're often verbally communicated to members. In many cases, they are never formally stated, but somehow are known by group members. Second, norms are accepted in various degrees by group members. Some are accepted completely, others only partially. And third, norms may apply to every group member or to only some group members.

Both formal and informal groups may have a variety of norms. For example, most groups have loyalty norms fostering the development of a strong degree of loyalty and commitment from their members. Members are expected to do certain things (e.g., work late, accept transfers, help out other members) to prove they are loyal. Other groups have formal or informal dress norms. Company sales force members may all dress similarly to present the company's desired image to customers; people working in the operations centre of a bank away from customers, however, may come to work in very casual clothing. Finally, groups have resource allocation norms and performance norms. Resource allocation norms of a formal organisation relate to how status symbols, pay, and promotions should be allocated. Informal groups may also have allocation norms regarding such informal rewards as who works with whom or who gets helped and does the helping. Performance norms relate to evaluating satisfactory performance. Informal groups, this may be made relatively clear by management; but as we shall see, performance norms may not be accepted by the informal group. In fact, informal groups may have performance norms of their own.

Group norms are the informal guidelines of behaviour and a code of conduct that provides some order and conformity to group activities and operations. These rules are expected to be followed by all the group members. These norms and rules usually develop gradually and informally as group members learn as to what behaviours are necessary for the group to function effectively. These norms may include a code of dress for meetings or being on time for the meetings are behaving in a predictable manner both within and outside the group meetings. This predictability of behaviour also causes higher degree of cohesiveness within the group. Predictability reduces chaos, ambiguity and conflict. Discomfort would be high in a committee or a task group, if the group members are not sure as to how each member would behave. Norms also identify the values and ethics of the group members. They are establish on the basis of what is right and decent and expected of professionals. For example, some companies have vary rigorous dress standards, tolerating no deviation, such as Federal Bureau of Investigation (FBI). There are basically two types of norms. These are :

(i) *Behaviour Norms.* These are rules and guidelines defining the day-to-day behaviour of people at work. This behaviour pattern may include punctuality as a habit, completing any given assignments within the required time frame-work, not losing temper, showing respect for other member's opinions, not monopolising the conversation and so on. Certain professionalism is expected from all members and this professionalism is predictable form of behaviour.

(ii) *Work Norms.* Work norms regulate the performance and productivity of individual members. An overlay ambitious worker who produces more is considered as much a deviate from the norms as a worker who is under producer. Work norms usually put an acceptable level of productivity, within reasonable tolerances so that comparatively poor performers can also be accommodated and that they do not become a burden on their employers. Workers performing below the lower acceptable level are generally informally reprimanded and encouraged to produce more.

Group norms are generally reinforced if all members agree to abide by them and the members all age if they firmly believe that adherence to such norms will facilitate group goals achievement or ensure group survival and additionally, such norms do not conflict with individual values and principles. Also, the norms are reinforced if the members value their membership in the group and do not like the outcomes of violating them. The outcome of violating the group norms must be sufficiently consequential in order to discourage members to deviate from them. Did you ever notice that golfers don't speak while their partners are putting on the green or that employees don't criticise their bosses in public? Why? The answer is; "Norms!"

All groups have established *norms*, that is acceptable standards of behaviour that are shared by the group's members. Norms tell members what they ought and ought not to do under certain circumstances. From an individual's standpoint, they tell what is expected of you in certain situations. When agreed to and accepted by the group, norms act as a means of influencing the behaviour of group members with a minimum of external controls. Norms differ among groups, communities, and societies, but they all have them.

(i) Common Classes of Norms

A work group's norms are like an individual's fingerprints—each is unique. Yet there are still some common classes of norms that appear in most work groups. Probably the most common class of norms is *performance norms*. Work groups typically provide their members with explicit cues on how hard they should work, how to get the job done, their level of output, appropriate levels of tardiness, and the like. A second category encompasses *appearance norms*. This includes things like appropriate dress, loyalty to the work group or organisation, when to look busy, and when it's acceptable to goof off.

Another category concerns social *arrangement norms*. These norms come from informal work groups and primarily regulate social interactions within the group. With whom group members eat lunch, friendships on and off the job, social games, and the like are influenced by these norms.

A final category relates to *allocation of resources norms*. These norms can originate in the group or in the organisation and cover things like pay, assignment of difficult jobs, and allocation of new tools and equipment. Norms typically develop gradually as group members learn what behaviours are necessary for the group to function effectively. Most norms develop in one or more of the following four ways:

(i) *Explicit statements made by a group member*—often the group's supervisor or a powerful member.

(ii) *Critical events in the group's history*.

(iii) *Primacy*. The first behaviour pattern that emerges in a group frequently sets group expectations.

(iv) *Carry-over behaviours from past situations*.

But groups don't establish or enforce norms for every conceivable situation. The norms that the group will enforce tend to be those that are important to it. But what makes a norm important?

(i) *If It Facilitates the Group's Survival*. Groups don't like to fail, so they look to enforce those norms that increase their chances for success. This means that they'll try to protect themselves from interference from other groups or individuals.

(ii) *If It Increases the Predictability of Group Members' Behaviours*. Norms that increase predictability enable group members to anticipate each other's actions and to prepare appropriate responses.

(iii) *If It Reduces Embarrassing Interpersonal Problems for Group Members*. Norms are important if they ensure the satisfaction of their members and prevent as much interpersonal discomfort as possible.

(iv) *If It Allows Members to Express the Central Values of the Group and Clarify What is Distinctive about the Group's Identity*. Norms that encourage expression of the group's values and distinctive identity help to solidify and maintain the group.

Conformity. As a member of a group, you desire acceptance by the group. Because of your desire for acceptance, you are susceptible to conforming to the group's norms. There is considerable evidence that groups can place strong pressures on individual members to change their attitudes and behaviours to conform to the group's standard.

The results suggest that there are group norms that press us toward conformity. We desire to be one of the group and avoid being visibly different. We can generalise further to say that when an individual's opinion of objective data differs significantly from that of others in the group, he or she is likely to feel extensive pressure to align his or her opinions to conform with those of the others.

IV. Status

We live in a class-structured society. Despite all attempts to make it more egalitarian, we have made little progress toward a classless society. Even the smallest group will develop roles, rights, and rituals to differentiate its members. Status is an important factor in understanding human behaviour because it is a significant motivator and has major behavioural consequences when individuals perceive a disparity between what they believe their status to be and what others perceive it to be.

(i) How Status Develops in a Group?

Every work group has a status system. The various jobs into which the work of the group is subdivided have different prestige values in the eyes of workers. Status develops in a group because of particular individuals possesses or contributes values to the organisation that are highly regarded by the members. A number of research studies have shown that people can quickly identify status differences within groups. There are many cues and symbols : One's air, composer, dress, titles, even such things as parking space, number of tables etc., convey status.

(ii) How Status Structures Influence Group Behaviour?

A peon with college education would find his job very uncomfortable in a place where illiterates are recruited for such positions. Unless able to play down the educational attributes, he is likely to be labelled as a city guy or the college kid. It will be difficult to gain full acceptance. Status incongruence creates psychological tension and this state is unpleasant and dissatisfying. It is therefore, highly important for employees to believe that the organisation's formal status system is congruent. Status congruency is said to exist when all the status attributes are ranked equally by all members of a group. In other words, there is equity between the perceived ranking of an individual and the status accounterments he is given by the organisation. Status congruency provides for more consistent and predictable behaviour.

(i) Status incongruence can cause uncertainty and ambiguity. Low morale, high tension and high anxiety maybe the result. *William F. Whyte's* famous studies on human relations in restaurant industry indicated that tension and conflict often resulted in between cooks and employees who served food at the counter. A common factor in these instances of conflict was that lower-status employees were giving orders regularly to higher status persons, communication patterns tend to emerge along status lines. Persons of equal status tend to communicate with one another rather than with persons of different status.

(ii) Status structures may create excessive social distance between such personnel as physicians and nurses, professors and students who could benefit from closer interaction.

(a) For example studies have shown that higher status workers rarely seek advice or assistance from those equal to or lower in status then themselves. Under certain conditions, they may also restrict free and open communication between individuals.

(b) Behaviour is oriented toward preserving status hierarchies—especially by people in high-status positions.

(c) Behaviour is oriented toward improving one's position in the hierarchy—especially by people in lower positions.

(d) Any change perceived as being destructive to the status hierarchy is considered threatening—especially by people in higher positions.

(e) Any change perceived as potentially blocking status equilibrium is perceived as threatening.

(iii) Status Equity

It is important for group members to believe that the status hierarchy is equitable. When inequity is perceived, it creates disequilibrium that results in various types of corrective behaviour.

People expect rewards to be proportionate to costs incurred. If Mannu and Dolly are the two finalists for the head nurse position in a hospital, and it is clear that Mannu has more seniority and better preparation for assuming the promotion, Dolly will view the selection of Mannu to be equitable. However, if Dolly is chosen because she is the daughter-in-law of the hospital director, Mannu will believe an injustice has been committed.

The trappings that go with formal positions are also important elements in maintaining equity. When we believe there is an inequity between the perceived ranking of an individual and the status accoutrements that person is given by the organisation, we are experiencing status incongruence. Our point is that employees expect the things an individual has and receives to be congruent with his or her status.

V. Group Size

Does the size of a group affect the group's overall behaviour? The answer to this question is a definite "Yes," but the effect depends on what dependent variables you look at.

The evidence indicates, for instance, that smaller groups are faster at completing tasks than are larger ones. However, if the group is engaged in problem solving, large groups consistently get better marks than their smaller counterparts. Translating these results into specific numbers is a bit more hazardous, but we can offer some parameters. Large groups—with a dozen or more members–are good for gaining diverse input. So if the goal of the group is fact finding, larger groups should be more effective. On the other hand, smaller groups are better at doing something productive with the input. Groups of approximately seven members, therefore, tend to be more effective for taking action.

One of the most important findings related to the size of a group has been labelled *social loafing*. Social loafing is the tendency for individuals to expend less effort when working collectively than when working individually. It directly challenges the logic that the productivity of the groups as a whole should at least equal the sum of the productivity of each individual in that group.

What causes this social loafing effect? It may be due to a belief that others in the group are not carrying their fair share. If you see others as lazy or inept, you can re-establish equity by reducing your effort. Another explanation is the dispersion of responsibility. Because the results of the group cannot be attributed to any single person, the relationship between an individual's input and the group's output is clouded. In such situations, individuals may be tempted to become "free riders" and coast on the group's efforts. In other words, there will be a reduction in efficiency where individuals think that their contribution cannot be measured.

The research on group size leads us to two additional conclusions: (1) groups with an odd number of members tend to be preferable to those with an even number; and (2) groups made up of five or seven members do a pretty good job of exercising the best elements of both small and large groups.

VI. Composition of Group

Most group activities require a variety of skills and knowledge. Given this requirement, it would be reasonable to conclude that heterogeneous groups—those composed of dissimilar individuals—would be more likely to have diverse abilities and information and should be more effective. Research studies generally substantiate this conclusion.

When a group is heterogeneous in terms of gender, personalities, opinions, abilities, skills, and perspectives, there is an increased probability that the group will possess the needed characteristics to complete its tasks effectively. The group may be more conflict laden and less expedient as diverse positions are introduced and assimilated, but the evidence generally supports the conclusion that heterogeneous groups perform more effectively than do those that are homogeneous.

VII. Group Cohesiveness

Cohesiveness defines the degree of closeness that the members feel with the group. It identifies the strength of the member's desires to remain in the group and the degree of commitment to the group. The extent of cohesiveness depends upon many factors including the compatibility of individual goals with group goals. The more the members are attracted to each other and the more the group goals align with their individual goals, the greater the group's cohesiveness. Similarly, less attraction of members toward each other will lesson the strength of cohesiveness. There may be situations where an individual may become a member of a country club for the sake of his own prestige or career enhancement or for making selective friends for his business interests. These reasons for joining the group will undermine the strength of cohesiveness.

Groups differ in their *cohesiveness,* that is, the degree to which members are attracted to each other and are motivated to stay in the group. For instance, some work groups are cohesive because the members have spent a great deal of time together, or the group's small size facilitates high interaction, or the group has experienced external threats that have brought members close together. Cohesiveness is important because it has been found to be related to the group's productivity.

What can you do to encourage group cohesiveness? You might try one or more of the following suggestions:

(i) Make the group smaller.
(ii) Encourage agreement with group goals.
(iii) Increase the time members spend together.
(iv) Increase the status of the group and the perceived difficulty of attaining membership in the group.
(v) Stimulate competition with other groups.
(vi) Give rewards to the group rather than to members.
(vii) Physically isolate the group.

(i) Features of Cohesive Groups

Those that are high in cohesion are likely to be groups.

(i) That have relatively few members.
(ii) Whose members have similar interests and backgrounds.
(iii) That have a high degree of status within the organisation.
(iv) In which members have ready access to one another so that interpersonal communication is easy to maintain.
(v) That are physically remote or isolated from other groups in the organisation.
(vi) In which the leader rewards cooperative behaviour.
(vii) That are pressured or threatened by some common outside force.
(viii) That have a history of past success.

(ii) What Makes a Group Cohesive?

There are numerous sources of attraction to a group. A number of factors determine the degree to which a group is cohesive :

(i) Size. Other things being equal, small groups have a greater probability of being cohesive than larger one. In larger groups the necessary interactions are inhibited, communication between members is reduced to a feeble walk and there is the danger of formation of sub-groups. Small groups offer frequent interaction opportunities leading to better understanding between members.

(ii) Location. People who work closely together in the same geographical location have numerous opportunities to interact and exchange ideas resulting in highly effective and cohesive groups than do people who are geographically separated.

(iii) Outside Pressure. External threats create higher bonds between members. When the members perceive that the group is threatened by an external force, they strive together to combat the collective threat. In the face of a common enemy, members forget their common differences and become cohesive.

(iv) *Status of the Group.* A high status group that is successful in achieving its goals tends to have greater cohesiveness. Membership in such a group is highly rated than membership in a group widely denounced by all. It is better to be a "big fish in a little pond" or "a little fish in a big pond" than remain unnoticed as a "little fish in a little pond".

(v) *Success.* There is nothing like success to increase group spirit and cohesiveness. A near universal finding is that cohesiveness generally increases with success.

(vi) *Other Reasons.* Other reasons like compatible goals (goals of the group and the members are essentially alike and expressed in a clear language) attractive leaders (the group has a dynamic, energetic leader) collective power (people join groups to obtain personal power) also compel members to seek membership in well-knit groups.

(iii) Factors Contributing to Group Cohesiveness

There are many factors that foster the cohesion of the group. Some of the more important factors are illustrated below :

(i) *Time Together.* It is quite natural that the more time people spend together, the more they will get to know each other and more tendency there will be to get closer to each other, thus strengthening the degree of cohesiveness. This is based upon the assumption that you will spend more time with only those whom you like personally and want to continue interacting with them. These interactions typically lead to common interests and increased attraction. The idea of long courtships or the ideas that couples live together before marriage is primarily to assure that there will be a high degree of cohesiveness in the marriage if the couple gets to know each other well by spending more time together and in close proximity to each other.

(ii) *Group Size.* Since continuous and close interaction among members is a fundamental necessity for cohesiveness, it would be natural to assume that large groups restrict the extent of communication and interaction with each other, thus resulting in the reduction of degree of cohesiveness. Another problem with large size groups is that there is a likelihood of forming small groups within the large groups. This would result in the dilution of the common group goal thus increasing the extent of power politics play. This tends to decrease the overall cohesiveness.

(iii) *Difficulty in Entry.* Some groups are not easy to join. The members are very carefully selected and the selected member feels a sense of pride and accomplishment. The more difficult it is to get into a group, the more cohesive that group becomes. The reason being that in exclusive and elite groups the members are selected on the basis of certain characteristics and these characteristics being common to all adds to the degree of liking and attraction towards each other. The more exclusive the group, the more is the closeness among members. Accordingly, individuals like to join such exclusive groups.

(iv) *Threat and Competition.* Whenever the common group goal is threatened, cohesiveness increases. Also, such cohesiveness increases the importance of the goals. When we fight for a goal then the goal gets the highest priority. For example, when a hostile group wants to take over a corporation, the Board of Directors of the corporation suddenly becomes a united front against the takeover and their cohesiveness reaches its peak. Similarly, management-threats frequently bring together an otherwise disarrayed union. Thus the threatening party will have a less chance of success when faced with a unified force.

(v) *Previous Successes.* When a group achieves a meaningful goal, the cohesiveness of the group increases because the success is shared by all the members and each one feels responsible for the achievement. For example, when a sports team wins an important game, every one in the team congratulates every other member of the team for this success. Specially, if a group has a series of successes, it builds a united team spirit. For this reason, successful companies find it easier to hire new talented employees. Similarly, prestigious universities are never short of applicants for admission. This proves the adage that every one loves a winner.

(vi) *Similarity of Attitudes and Values.* One of the strongest source of group cohesiveness is the similarity in values, morals, beliefs and code of conduct. We enjoy the company of others who hold similar opinions and characteristics as ourselves. That is one reason why interfaith marriages are discouraged. Similarity of interests is specially important when the group's primary goal is that of creating a friendly interpersonal climate. This increases group cohesiveness. This factor may not be so important if the goal is task oriented. For example, if an army unit has to win a strategic battle, then the successful task accomplishment becomes the cohesive factor rather than the similarity of interests because the unit may consists of black soldiers and white solders who may not have much in common.

(iv) Consequences of Cohesiveness

These positive outcomes of group cohesiveness are explained in more details as follows :

(i) *More Participation.* Because group cohesiveness involves close interpersonal relationships, the members consider the group as their own, just like a family and they are motivated to participate actively in group affairs and activities. Members also try to assist and support other members of the group in times of need and this strengthens the bonds of friendship. The turnover rate of members is very low and they look forward to group meetings and group activities as it gives them an opportunity of social interaction in addition to devising strategies for achieving individual and group goals.

(ii) *More Conformity.* While all individuals who are in the group are unique in many ways with their own norms, values, beliefs and attitudes and some times these characteristics may be in conflict with the group norms, the members usually make sacrifices in order to conform to group norms. The cohesive group is generally able to put subtle pressure on the individual member who "deviated" from the group norms in order to bring him back to the mainstream. For example, if a member is working too hard or is playing politics to enhance his personal objectives, the group might put social pressure on him to comply with the group norms. If these pressures do not succeed, then the member may be dropped from the group in order to maintain cohesiveness among other members.

(iii) *More Success.* Success and cohesiveness are interdependent factors. Cohesiveness makes the goal achievement easier and goal achievement adds to cohesiveness.

(v) Effects of Group Cohesion

Research has generally shown that a cohesive group is more productive than a less cohesive group provided the group's attitude aligns with the goals of the organisation. For example if the group norm is a high level of performance, the more cohesive group is likely to influence each member toward higher productivity. On the other hand, if cohesiveness is high but attitudes unfavourable, productivity declines. A highly cohesive group is like a 'time-bomb' in the hands of management. Where the group norms is not supportive of performance, cohesive groups are less productive. Resistance to organisational changes is greater and where proper leadership is not provided, such groups can restrict output soverely. "If management wishes to maximise productivity it must build a cohesive group and give it proper leadership."

VIII. Group Processes

The next component of our group behaviour model considers the processes that go on within a work group—the communication patterns used by members for information exchanges, group decision processes, leader behaviour, power dynamics, conflict interactions, and the like.

Why are processes important to understanding work group behaviour? One way to answer this question is to return to the topic of social loafing. We found that 1 + 1 + 1 does not necessarily add up to three. In group tasks where each member's contribution is not clearly visible, there is a tendency for individuals to decrease their effort. Social loafing, in other words, illustrates a process loss as a result of using groups. But group processes can also produce positive results.

Synergy is a term used in biology that refers to an action of two or more substances that results in an effect that is different from the individual summation of the substances. We can use the concept to better understand group processes.

Social loafing, for instance, represents negative synergy. The whole is less than the sum of its parts. On the other hand, research teams are often used in research laboratories because they can draw on the diverse skills of various individuals to produce more meaningful research as a group than could be generated by all of the researchers working independently. That is, they produce positive synergy. Their process gains exceed their process losses.

Another line of research that helps us to better understand group processes is the social facilitation effect. Have you ever noticed that performing a task in front of others can have a positive or negative effect on your performance? For instance, you privately practice a complex springboard dive at your home pool for weeks. Then you do the dive in front of a group of friends and you do it better than ever. Or you practice a speech in private and finally get it down perfect, but you "bomb" when you have to give the speech in public.

The social facilitation effect refers to this tendency for performance to improve or decline in response to the presence of others. While this effect is not entirety a group phenomenon—people can work in the presence of others and not be members of a group—the group situation is more likely to provide the conditions for social facilitation to occur. The research on social facilitation tells us that the performance of simple, routine tasks tend to be speeded up and made more accurate by the presence of others. Where the work is more complex, requiring closer attention, the presence of others is likely to have a negative effect on performance. So what are the implications of this research in terms of managing process gains and losses? The implications relate to learning and training. People seem to perform better on a task in the presence of others if that task is very well learned, but poorer if it is not well learned.

GROUP TASKS

Imagine, for a moment, that there are two groups at a major oil company. The job of the first is to consider possible location sites for a new refinery. The decision is going to affect people in many areas of the company—production, engineering, marketing, distribution, purchasing, real estate development, and the like—so key people from each of these areas will need to provide input into the decision. The job of the second group is to coordinate the building of the refinery after the site has been selected, the design finalised, and the financial arrangements completed. Research on group effectiveness tells us that management would be well advised to use a larger group for the first task than for the second. The reason is that large groups facilitate pooling of information. The addition of a diverse perspective to a problem-solving committee typically results in a process gain. But when a group's task is coordinating and implementing a decision, the process loss created by each additional member's presence is likely to be greater than the process gain he or she makes. So the size-performance relationship is moderated by the group's task requirements.

POTENTIAL GROUP EFFECTIVENESS + **PROCESS GAINS** – **PROCESS LOSSES** = **ACTUAL GROUP EFFECTIVENESS**

Fig. 2. *Effects of Group Processes.*

The impact of group processes on the group's performance and member satisfaction is also moderated by the tasks that the group is doing. The evidence indicates that the complexity and interdependence of tasks influence the group's effectiveness.

Tasks can be generalised as either simple or complex. Complex tasks are ones that tend to be novel or nonroutine. Simple ones are routine and standardised. We would hypothesise that the more complex the task, the more the group will benefit from discussion among members on alternative work methods. If the task is simple, group members don't need to discuss such alternatives. They can rely on standardised operating procedures for doing the job. Similarly, if there is a high degree of interdependence among the tasks that group members must perform, they'll need to interact more. Effective communication and minimal levels of conflict, therefore, should be more relevant to group performance when tasks are interdependent.

GROUP THINK

Group think is an extreme form of consensus in which the group thinks as a unit rather than as a collection of individuals. It is a kind of consensus-seeking process that goes on in a cohesive group. When a group is too cohesive new ideas may be rejected too quickly. Members are imbued with feelings of "We know best". There is a tremendous desire for unanimity. Seeking consensus becomes an end in itself. Free exchange of ideas is inhibited. Some members in a group may be timid or cowed down by dominating members imposing their ideas on others. At other times, the group members try to promote consensus at the possible expense of arriving at a more defective solution. Lack of critical thinking is at the heart of group think followed by the group's low-risk, conservative traditional and mediocre decisions group members cease to think independently. *Irving Jansis* used the 'group think' to describe the unfortunate situation in which the desire to agree becomes so dominant in a cohesive group that it tends to override realistic appraisal of alternative courses of action. Members try to avoid being too harsh in their judgments of one another's ideas. They adopt a soft line of criticism. At their meetings, all the members are chummy and seek complete agreement on every important issue. As a result of little or no real criticism, the illusion of unanimity is created.

(i) Symptoms of Group Think

Group think is characterised by a "deterioration of mental efficiency, reality testing and moral judgment." The following symptoms have been identified with group think:

(i) Illusions of invulnerability which leads to over optimism. Groups ignore danger signals and take excessive risks.

(ii) Collective efforts at rationalisation so as to discredit warning that might force members to question their policy decisions.

(iii) An unflinching faith in the group's morality, leading members to ignore the ethical or moral consequences of their results.

(iv) Persons or groups with opinions differing from those of the group are stereotyped as weak, stupid or evil.

(v) Conformity pressure is applied very strongly by the group to any member who deviates or even expresses strong arguments against any of the group's thinking.

(vi) Self-censorship develops as members apply pressure to themselves to avoid deviating from the apparent group consensus.

(vii) In the absence of real criticism, the illusion of unanimity is created; the appearance of unanimity tends to keep criticism from being expressed. Each member believes that all other members agree with group standards.

(viii) The emergence of self-appointed mind guards, defined as members who protect the group from information that might shatter their shared complacency about the effectiveness and morality of their decisions.

(ii) The Remedy for Group Think

When group think does occur, positive action must be taken if the group is to be effective in performing its task. As we have seen concurrence-seeking will smoother objective consideration and evaluation of alternatives. The following steps are recommended by Janis to overcome group think tendencies :

(i) Encourage the group members to express doubts and criticisms of proposed solutions to problems. Permit critical evaluation of group ideas by members freely.

(ii) Allow key members to adopt an initial impartial stance on solutions.

(iii) Divide the group into subgroups to stimulate ideas. Then have the subgroups confront one another to examine why they differ.

(iv) Periodically invite qualified outsiders to challenge group views.

(v) Allow atleast one member to play a devil's advocate role to oppose the views of other group members.

(vi) After arriving at a tentative decision in a particular way, allow the group to hold a second chance meeting wherein members fully describe every possible doubt they have about the solution reached.

GROUP SHIFT

It indicates that in discussing a given set of alternatives and arriving at a solution, group members tend to exaggerated the initial positions that they hold. In some situations, caution dominates, and there is a conservative shift. More often, however, the evidence indicates that groups tend toward a risky shift.

In comparing group decisions with the individual decisions of members within the group, evidence suggests that there are differences. In some cases, the group decisions are more conservative than the individual decisions.

What appears to happen in groups is that the discussion leads to a significant shift in the positions of members toward a more extreme position in the direction in which they were already leaning before the discussion. So conservative types become more cautious and the more aggressive types take on more risk. The group discussion tends to exaggerate the initial position of the group.

The groupshift can be viewed as actually a special case of groupthink. The decision of the group reflects the dominant decision-making norm that develops during the group's discussion. Whether the shift in the group's decision is toward greater caution or more risk depends on the dominant prediscussion norm.

The greater occurrence of the shift toward risk has generated several explanations for the phenomenon. It's been argued, for instance, that the discussion creates familiarisation among the members. As they become more comfortable with each other, they also become more bold and daring. Another argument is that our society values risk, that we admire individuals who are willing to take risks, and that group discussion motivates members to show that they are at least as willing as their peers to take risks. The most plausible explanation of the shift toward risk, however, seems to be that the group diffuses responsibility. Group decisions free any single member from accountability for the group's final choice. Greater risk can be taken because even if the decision fails, no one member can be held wholly responsible.

TYPES OF GROUP INTERACTION

There are two principal types of group interaction:

(i) Meetings

(ii) Team

One exists when people come together and discuss ideas and views and is generally called a *meeting*. The other exists when people perform tasks together is called a *team*. Here in this question, we are discussing the meetings and in the next question, the 'teams'.

I. Meetings

Organisational meeting refers to committees conferences and other groups that face to face discuss the various work problems concerning the group in an organisation. Meetings are convened for many purposes, such as :

(i) To give information to group members;

(ii) To seek advice on a particular problem;

(iii) To decide the course of action in performing the specific act by the groups;

(iv) To negotiate the deal with other groups;

(v) To coordinate the various activities of the group to improve the functioning of the group;

(vi) To initiate a creative thinking.

A committee is a special type of meeting in which members in their group role have been delegated authority with regard to problem at hand. The matter is discussed and views are expressed by each members of the committee. Authority is expressed in terms of one vote for each member without considering their status in the formal organisation group. If a supervisor and a worker are the members of the some committee both have equal authority or committee roles. Committee often creates special human problems because people are unable to make role adjustment of this type.

In organisation meetings, size of the meeting should be given first priority because the size of a meeting affects the way of working. The number of member in a committee should not exceed seven otherwise the communication would tend to become centralised because members do not have adequate opportunity to communicate directly with one another. If, anyhow, it is necessary to have a larger meeting to include the representation from all sections of people likely to affect, to special efforts and extra time should be given to ensure good communication. A meeting of five members seemed to be regarded as an ideal meeting for typical situations. A smaller meeting (of less than five members) sometimes develops power conflicts and its functioning becomes difficult. It has been experienced that in a meeting of three persons, two persons make a separate group against the third. If manager in an organisation thinks that a power problem is likely to be critical, he should avoid appointing a committees of two or three persons. The structure of such committees is too sensitive to disagreement.

II. Team

When people perform task together, it is called a team or they act as a team. It is one way of interaction of people and when groups seek to develop a cooperative state called teamwork. Team is a group of persons irrespective of their number. A team may consist of thousands of workers engaged in an organisation or a few say five or ten. But here we use the term to a limited definition, i.e. a small group of members interacting regularly.

Institutional and Operations Team. Teams may be classified as institutional or operation teams. A team of the persons working in an organisation may be called *institutional team.* A small group of persons may be *operation team*. *Keith Davis* has defined the operation team "*as coordinated action by a cooperative small group in regular contact wherein members contribute responsibly and enthusiastically to task achievement*". This kind of genuine teamwork makes the work easier and generally improves the job satisfaction. The difference between the two is only of size. Operation team is a part of institutional team. The *operation team* may further be divided in *traditionally hierarchy team* and the *work team.* These two teams reflect the behavioural difference.

The *hierarchy team* follows chain of command and control. A team consisting of manager, superintendent, supervisor and workers may be called a hierarchy operation team.

A *work-team* is not necessarily to include the hierarchical chain of command. It has multidirectional interaction in terms of the needs of the situation, and the abilities of each member to contribute to those needs. In practice one arrangement overlays the other to reflect both, the way the group is organised and the way its member work together.

A group can work together as a team only when each one knows the role of the other persons with whom he has to interact in the group and each one must be qualified in performing his job effectively. It will promote cooperation among the members of the team. The team member work in cooperation in each operating situation without waiting for some one to give an order. In other words team members works voluntarily to the job situation and take necessary actions to further the team goals.

(I) Types of Teams Based on Their Objective

The three most common forms of teams you're likely to find in an organisation are :

(a) problem-solving teams
(b) self-managed teams, and
(c) cross-functional teams.

(a) Problem-Solving Teams

If we look back 15 years or so, teams were just beginning to grow in popularity, and most of these teams took similar form. These were typically composed of 5 to 12 hourly employees from the same department who met for a few hours each week to discuss ways of improving quality, efficiency, and the work environment. We call these *problem-solving teams.*

In problem-solving teams, members share ideas or offer suggestions on how work processes and methods can be improved. Rarely, however, are these teams given the authority to unilaterally implement any of their suggested actions.

(b) Self-Managed Work Teams

Problem-solving teams were on the right track but they didn't go far enough in getting employees involved in work-related decisions and processes. This led to experimentation with truly autonomous teams that could not only solve problems but implement solutions and take full responsibility for outcomes.

Self-managed work teams are groups of employees (typically 10 to 15 in number) who take on the responsibilities of their former supervisors. Typically, this includes planning and scheduling of work, collective control over the pace of work, making operating decisions, and taking action on problems. Fully self-managed work teams even select their own members and have the members evaluate each other's performance.

(c) Cross-Functional Teams

The Boeing Company used the latest application of the team concept to develop its 777-jet. This application is called *cross-functional teams*. These are teams made up of employees from about the same hierarchical level, but from different work areas, who come together to accomplish a task.

Many organisations have used horizontal, boundary-spanning groups for years. For example, IBM created a large task force in the 1960s—made up of employees from across departments in the company– to develop the highly successful System 360. And a *task force* is really nothing other than a temporary cross-functional team. Similarly, *committees* composed of members from across departmental lines are another example of cross-functional teams.

But the popularity of cross-discipline work teams exploded in the late 1980s. All the major automobile manufacturers—including Toyota, Honda, Nissan, BMW, GM, Ford, and Chrysler—have turned to these forms of teams in order to coordinate complex projects.

TEAMS *VERSUS* GROUPS

Groups and teams are not the same thing. In this section, we want to define and clarify the difference between a work group and a work team.

We defined a *group* as two or more individuals, interacting and interdependent, who have come together to achieve particular objectives. *A work group* is a group that interacts primarily to share information and to make decisions to help each member perform within his or her area of responsibility.

Work groups have no need or opportunity to engage in collective work that requires joint effort. So their performance is merely the summation of each group member's individual contribution. There is no positive synergy that would create an overall level of performance that is greater than the sum of the inputs.

A *work team* generates positive synergy through coordinated effort. Their individual efforts results in a level of performance that is greater than the sum of those individual inputs.

These definitions help clarify why so many organisations have recently restructured work processes around teams. Management is looking for that positive synergy that will allow their organisations to increase performance. The extensive use of teams creates the *potential* for an organisation to generate greater outputs with no increase in inputs. Notice, however, we said "potential". There is nothing inherently magical in the creation of teams that ensures the achievement of this positive synergy. Merely calling a *group* a *team* does not automatically increase its performance. Successful or high-performing teams have certain common characteristics. If management hopes to gain increases in organisational performance through the use of teams, it will need to ensure that its teams possess these characteristics.

GROUP DYNAMICS

The term '*dynamics*' connotes adjustive changes taking place in the group structures as a whole, as caused by changes in any part of the group. Thus, group dynamics refers to *changes which take place within groups and is concerned with the interaction and forces obtained between group members in a social setting.* It is the study of forces operating within a group. When the term group dynamics is employed in the study of organisational behaviour, the stress is on the dynamics of members of informal and formal groups.

The outstanding name in the study of group dynamics is that of *Kurt Lewin* who popularised the term in the 1930's. However, there have emerged different *confusing connotations* over the period of time. According to one viewpoint, group dynamics reveals how a group should be organised and conducted. Here, attempts are made to emphasise democratic leadership, member participation, and overall cooperation. The other view-point considers group dynamics as a set of techniques and equates it with role playing, brainstorming, buzz groups, group therapy, sensitivity training, and allied techniques. To avoid confusion, it would be plausible to discuss group dynamics as visualised by its founder. This necessitates the study as to what kinds of groups tend to change, under what conditions they change, and in what direction the change is likely to occur.

In other words, this involves a discussion of internal and external determinants of a group change and theories of group formation.

INTERNAL DETERMINANTS OF A GROUP CHANGE

It has been found that some groups are more stable than others whereas other groups undergo rapid changes even if there is no marked change in the external situation. Instability stems from conflict among individuals and among sub-groups within the entire group. It emerges from a lack of balance among different forces operating within the group itself. Because of this lack of balance, changes in group structure occur. Usually, these changes are directed toward the reduction of tension, attainment of the balances of the forces and thereby establishment of a stable group structure.

There are numerous changes in a group structure which enhance stability. Sub-grouping may give way to newness accompanied by mutual interaction and adjustment. The deviant elements may be ousted from the group altogether to achieve harmony within the group. The leadership structure may change dramatically replacing the old leaders with the new ones. There may occur ideological shifts to redefine its objectives, beliefs and plans. The degree of stability of the group is determined by the strength of the cohesive and disruptive forces. Groups are bound together because of a common objective of the members and common conception that these objectives can be accomplished through the group. These objectives may be positive or negative in nature. Groups are also held together by emotional bonds, that is, the identification of the member with the group and the other members. Groups sometimes tend to dissolve not because of the prevalence of disruptive forces but because of the low strength of cohesive forces.

EXTERNAL DETERMINANTS OF A GROUP CHANGE

Besides the above internal imbalances and tensions, there are external determinants of a group change. Groups vary in the degree in which they are susceptible to such external influences. The rigid groups tend to disintegrate while flexible groups tend to adapt to exigencies of external changes. The organised groups tend to display different reactions to external influence as compared to unorganised groups. Variations in situations cause variations in the group structure. In the face of external dangers, group unity frequency enhances and inner differences disappear. We find changes in group structure as caused by membership changes. For example, the simultaneous retrenchment of numerous employees will cause restructuring. Group changes may also arise because of socio-economic changes. Thus, the study of how and why groups change provides us an understanding of group dynamics.

THEORIES OF GROUP FORMATION

A recent viewpoint which is akin to *Lewin's* original conception, visualise group dynamics from the standpoint of the internal nature of groups, how they develop their structure and processes and how they influence individual members, other groups, and the organisation.

The most fundamental theory of group formation is ***propinquity theory***, which asserts that people tend to affiliate with one another because of spatial or geographical closeness.

Another comprehensive theory of group formation is the ***social system theory***, founded by *Homans*. It incorporates the interrelated elements of activities, interactions, and sentiments. Individuals tend to interact in a group to solve problems, reduce tension, attain goals, and achieve a balance. Workers in organisational settings interacting in this way tend to form groups.

Still another theory of group formation is the ***balance theory* of Newcomb,** which asserts that individuals are attracted to one another because of their identical attitudes towards some common objects and goals. Attempts are made to maintain a symmetrical balance between the attraction and the common attitudes. If the balance cannot be maintained, the relationship disappears.

The ***exchange theory,*** which is based upon rewards-costs results of interaction, deserves attention. A minimum positive level (i.e. rewards exceeding costs) of a result must be maintained so that attraction occurs. Here, rewards from interaction satisfy needs while costs cause tension.

Along with these theoretical interpretation, there are some practical reasons for group formation. Obviously, employees in work settings tend to form groups for satisfying their economic, security and social needs.

COMMITTEE GROUPS

To provide perspective, several organisations lean heavily on committee management. The committees form the most crucial kind of formal groups obtained in modern organisational settings. Committee groups are increasingly employed with enhanced responsibilities and provide a platform for the exchange of various points of view and information as well as help in major decisions. It has been found that the use of committee groups increases with the increasing size of the organisations.

The committee groups have been defined as groups of people who operate collectively (Haimann and Scott). According to *Koontz* and *O'Donnell,* the committee groups consist of persons to whom, as groups, some matters are committed. Thus, committee groups are those groups which purport to attain specific goals. They operate in either a formal or informal way and have been variously designated as teams, commissions, boards or task forces. They are obtained in all organisational settings and at various levels in them.

TYPES OF COMMITTEE GROUPS

Some companies attempt to elicit group participation by establishing *consultative* committees with a view to improving the two-way communication with the lower levels providing them with opportunity to express their viewpoints directly to top management by passing the intermediate levels. Thus, the management may form joint worker management or union-management consultative committees to work on production problems, collective bargaining, welfare measures and allied issues.

Moreover, some other examples are the board of directors, the finance committee, the grievance committee, and so on. They accomplish numerous functions in various capacities such as *advisory*, *coordinating* and *decision-making*. On account of the tendency to involve several individuals, they are designated as plural executives. Union Carbide represents this trend where the president and three vice-presidents from the central point of management authority. Obviously, this kind of group management is gaining increasing popularity. Committees may be standing, continuing or *ad hoc* for specific assignments only.

BENEFITS OF COMMITTEES

There is an adage that two heads are better than one. Thus committee actions have many advantages over individual actions. Some of these advantages are discussed as follows :

(i) Pooling of Opinions. The members bring in different backgrounds, values, viewpoints and abilities. These wide ranging abilities result in greater knowledge base which results in better quality decisions. Additionally group deliberations generally ensure a thorough consideration

of problems from all angles and alternative points of view before arriving at a decision. This would not have been possible if the same problem was looked at by a single executive.

(ii) Improved Cooperation. The members of the committee usually get to know each other well and thus see each other's point of view with respect. They are willing to cooperate and coordinate, specially when they become aware of their role and how their decisions are going to affect the entire organisation.

(iii) Motivation. From a human standpoint, the biggest advantage of committees may be increased motivation and commitment derived from participation in the committee deliberations and indirectly in the important organisational affairs. Also, when the committee consists of managers and subordinates, it gives the subordinates some degree of recognition and importance. They rightfully feel that they are an integral part of the decision-making process which boosts their morale and motivates them to do better.

(iv) Representation. Since the committee members may have different interests and opinions which may be opposing to each other, the process of committee deliberations gives a critical viewpoint and balanced outcome of these different representations. However, even though, a committee should be highly representative of all interests, capabilities of the members should take precedence over the representation.

(v) Dispersion of Power. While autocratic authority makes decision-making and implementation faster and easier, it may lead to misuse of power and wrong decisions. However, by spreading authority and responsibility over all committee members, this problem can be eliminated.

(vi) Executive Training. The committees provide an excellent training grounds for young executives. They also provide an opportunity for personal development that individuals may not be able to get on their own. In the committees, they learn the value of interaction, human relations and group dynamics. They get exposed to various viewpoints and tend to think in liberal manner and get to understand how collective decisions are made. Such type of exposure and experience enables them to take an integrative view of solving various organisational problems.

(vii) Continuity. Most committees do not replace all of its members at the same time so that some new members join to replace some old members while the other members remain and thus the continuity of operations is maintained. The U.S. Senate works on this basis, so that every two years there is an election for one-third of the total Senate. According to Newman, "There are always some members of the group who know the reasons for previous actions and this tends to promote consistency and continuity of thinking that is difficult to achieve when an executive who has been making decisions by himself has to be replaced."

(viii) Communication. A committee can be an excellent forum for management and workers to have simultaneous communication and discuss matters of common interest in an atmosphere of goodwill and understanding and reach some mutually benefiting conclusions. These conclusions can then be communicated to all members throughout the entire organisation via committee members. This may be a preferred and trusted method for transmitting correct, authentic and prompt information to all.

(ix) *Better Chances of Recommendations to be Accepted.* A committee recommendations is much more likely to be accepted than an individual recommendations. Also, the decisions made on the basis of these recommendations would be easily accepted by membership and such decisions would be easily implemented.

LIMITATIONS OF COMMITTEES

Many management theorists have stressed the negative aspects of committees. Some of the major disadvantages of formal task groups and committees are:

(i) *Time and Cost.* The very structure of the committee is a costly affair in terms of money and time. The nature of the committee is such that every one has an equal chance to speak out and take part in discussions and this can be very time consuming. Each member is involved in cross communication trying to convince others as to the usefulness of his own point of view, thus taking a lot of total time. Also, since it is a matter of prestige to be a member of a committee, there is always pressure to add more members to the committee, thus adding to this problem. Additionally in the course of research for material, there may be committee related travel and staff expenses for preparation and typing of material and final reports. All these activities could be very costly. Accordingly, the usefulness of committee decisions must be measured against the costs involved so that if a problem can be solved by a single executive or a few staff members, then the committees should not be appointed.

(ii) *Compromise.* Usually, there is a tendency to present unanimous decisions and hence a majority viewpoint is taken as representative even when the minority viewpoint is valid. This may result in premature agreements and decisions of medicore quality. The minority may be unwilling to pursue their viewpoints for fear that they will stand out and may be labelled as uncooperative. They may also be willing to compromise for less than optimal solutions because if these solutions turn out to be wrong, they will not be traceable to individuals but the whole committee will get the blame. This shows that a committee decision may not be an optimal one, but merely an acceptable one.

(iii) *Personal Prejudice.* Sometimes, winning an argument or getting back at some body for personal reasons may give the problem as secondary priority, thus diluting the strength of the decision.

(iv) *Logrolling.* This term is coined for wheeling and dealing for political interests and purposes. These political pressures may come from the top management who wants a particular point of view domination in the committee discussions. A case in point is the promotion of and granting of tenure process in colleges. If the president of a college does not want a particular person to be promoted, he will put pressure on committee members to do so. In that respect, it is not really a democratic process but more of a democratic "dictatorship".

(v) *Strain on Interpersonal Relations.* In the committee meetings, there is a tendency that every body wants to please every body else so that any displeasure within the committee can strain working relations outside the committee into personal life. For example, in the college committee meetings for promotions where voting of members is the main contributing factor, anybody voting against the person who is being considered for promotion will not have friendly relations with such voting person, if this voting pattern leaks out. This is a very different and sensitive area and a lot of training in interpersonal competence is needed.

(vi) *Lack of Effectiveness.* Certain issues are better solved by individuals rather than committees. The committees are very useful in handling grievances and interdepartmental problems, but they are not effective in formulating such policies where individual initiative and creativity is involved.

GROUP DECISION-MAKING

Group decision-making is an activity that is based on the old adage that "two heads are better than one". It permits the coming together of people with heterogeneous characteristics who can understand the problems in a better way and hence, develop creative alternatives leading to effective group performance. Most decisions in organisations, no wonder, are made in a group context only. However, group decision-making is different in process and outcome from decision-making done by individuals in the following ways :

(i) *Conformity.* Norms are established by a group as a means of achieving its goals. Over a period of time these norms become standards of conduct accepted by participants in a small group. A group tries to enforce these norms ruthlessly and norm violators are punished in many ways. No wonder, decisions in groups move toward conformity. In other words, the subjects provided answers that they knew were wrong but that were consistent with the answers of other group members.

(ii) *Superiority.* The common sense adage "Two heads are better than one" derives its strength from many sources. Groups have important problem solving abilities. A group, with its faculty drawn from many disciplines, has got the capacity to generate more ideas than individuals. Groups "have better learning and recall, make fewer mistakes and detect mistakes quicker. Group forecasting and judgement likely are more accurate." Heterogeneous people with characteristics can bring a greater amount of information and expertise to bear on a problem, generate more creative alternative solutions and make it more likely that the solution will be understood, accepted and implemented. A number of studies support the view that groups are superior to individuals in problem solving. After reviewing the literature in this area, *B.J. Kolasa* concluded thus "the preponderance of expert opinion is in favour of superiority of the group in problem solving performance."

(iii) *Risky shift.* The average risk-taking score tends to be higher in groups. There is considerable evidence to show that in some situations, groups make riskier decisions than individuals. Why do groups make riskier decisions than individuals? Four explanations can be offered :

(a) Taking moderate risks is something that is highly rated in our society. Moderate risk has a strong cultural value than caution.

(b) Risk taking offers an opportunity for a group member to become the leader. Dominant and influential members generally occupy the leadership 'berths' in a group.

(c) Groups are able to share information in an open environment, Members become more familiar with the problem being discussed. Initially they encourage cautions, go-slow tactics and once the problem is familiarised, they are willing to take adventurous risky decisions.

(d) If a project adopted by a group fails, backpassing is easy and no one individual can be held wholly responsible. Group decisions dilute and thin out responsibility. So whenever managers are forced to solve knotty problems these are turned over to groups.

According to *Gary John*, there are three assumptions that form the basis for this argument. These are:

(i) Groups are more "vigilant" than individuals. Because of natural constraints, any single individual cannot look at all possible angles of a complex problem and thus he may miss an important aspect of the issue. But if there are more members looking at the same problem then it is more likely that someone among the group has thought of or looked at that particular aspect. This is specially important at problem identification and information search stages.

(ii) Groups can generate more ideas and develop more alternative solutions than individuals. Members of the group come from different backgrounds with different experiences and outlooks, so that it is more likely that someone will come up with an idea that others had not thought of before. Also, by listening to each other's ideas, the group members may develop new ideas based upon such information and come up with a unique solution that no single member could conceive.

(iii) Groups can evaluate ideas better than individuals. This again is a result of various and diverse viewpoints presented by the members of the group. Because individuals can sometimes become emotional when making decisions, it is possible that bias would be introduced into the decision if it was made by one person. Different persons can check for bias and evaluate ideas on a more objective basis so that the decisions would be made on the basis of facts and rationality rather than sympathy and emotionalism.

"Groups are valuable when they can maximize the unique contribution of each individual. Moreover, as each individual's contribution is enhanced, his or her commitment to the resulting decision is increased or internalised."

THE NATURE OF DECISION-MAKING

Decision–making is almost universally defined as choosing between alternatives. It is closely related to all the traditional management functions. The classical theorists, however, did not generally present decision-making this way. Classical theorists such as *Fayol* and *Urwick* were concerned with the decision-making process only to the extent that it affects delegation and authority, while *Frederick W. Taylor* alluded to the scientific method only as an ideal approach to making decisions. Like most other aspects of modern organisation theory, the beginning of a meaningful analysis of the decision-making process can be traced to *Chester Barnard*. In *The Functions of the Executive*, Barnard gave a comprehensive analytical treatment of decision making and noted : "The processes of decision . . . are largely techniques for narrowing choice."

Most discussions of the decision-making process break it down into a series of steps. For the most part, the logic can be traced to the ideas developed by *Herbert A. Simon*, the well-known

Nobel Prize-winning organisation and decision theorist, who conceptualises three major phases in the decision-making process :

(i) *Intelligence activity.* Borrowing from the military meaning of "intelligence," *Simon* describes this initial phase as consisting of searching the environment for conditions calling for decision-making.

(ii) *Design activity.* During the second phase, inventing, developing, and analysing possible courses of action take place.

(iii) *Choice activity.* The third and final phase is the actual choice—selecting a particular course of action from among those available.

More empirical basis (that is, tracing actual decisions in organisations), are the stages of decision-making of *Mintzberg* and his colleagues :

(i) *The identification phase*, during which *recognition* of a problem or opportunity arises and a *diagnosis* is made. It was found that severe, immediate problems did not receive a very systematic, extensive diagnosis but that mild problems did.

(ii) *The development phase*, during which there may be a *search* for existing standard procedures or solutions already in place or the *design* of a new, tailor-made solution. It was found that the design process was a grouping, trial-and-error process in which the decision-makers had only a vague idea of the ideal solution.

(iii) *The selection phase*, during which the choice of a solution is made. There are three ways of making this selection : by the *judgment* of the decision-maker. On the basis of experience or intuition rather than logical analysis : by *analysis* of the alternatives on a logical, systematic basis; and by *bargaining* when the selection involves a group of decision-makers and all the political manoeuvring that this entails. Once the decision is formally accepted, an *authorisation* is made.

The essential point is that decision-making is a *dynamic process.* This dynamic process has both strategic and behavioural implications for organisations. Recent empirical research indicates that the decision process which involves making the right strategic choices does lead to successful decisions for the organisation. However, what has become known as behavioural decision-making is especially relevant to the study and application of organisational behaviour.

CHARACTERISTICS OF DECISION-MAKING

The following characteristics of decision-making are noteworthy:

(i) Decision-making is an integral part of planning. Every planner has to make a choice of appropriate solutions or alternatives in a situation of availability of options.

(ii) It aims at choosing a suitable course of action by weighing and weeding out several available alternatives.

(iii) It involves judgement and discretion of the decision-maker. It is not entirely a rational process because decisions are bound to be affected and coloured by personal likes dislikes and whims of the manager.

(iv) Decisions made by the managers involves commitment of the organisation for adopting a specific course of action and utilising resources in a particular manner.

(v) Decision-making is a human and social process implying interference of individual as well as social factors. An intelligent manager will always take into account social and human implications of a decision.

(vi) Decision-making is a propulsive activity because it is directed towards the achievements of goals and objectives.

DECISION-MAKING PROCESS

When a manager makes a decision, it is in effect the organisation's response to a problem. As such, decisions should be thought of as means rather than ends. Every decision is the outcome of a dynamic process which is influenced by multiple forces. This process is presented in Fig. 3. However, this process should not be interpreted to mean that decision-making is a fixed procedure. A process is basically a dynamic concept rather than static. Events and relationships are dynamic, continuous and flexible and must be considered as a whole in which many forces interact; a force affecting others and being affected by others. Therefore, the decision-making process as presented in Fig. 3 should be seen as sequential process rather than a series of steps to enable decision-maker to examine each element in the progression that leads to a decision. Moreover, the process reveals that it is more applicable to non-programmed decisions than to programmed ones. Problems that occur infrequently, are unstructured, and are characterised by a great deal of uncertainty regarding their outcome, require the manager to utilise the entire process. For frequently occurring structured problems, it is not necessary to consider the entire process. If a policy is established or a specific rule or procedure developed to handle such problems, it will not be necessary to develop and evaluate alternatives each time the problem arises.

I. Specific Objectives

The need for decision-making arises in order to achieve certain specific objective. Every action of human being is goal directed. This is true for decision-making also which is an action. Therefore, the starting point in any analysis of decision-making involves the determination of whether a decision need to be made. In fact setting of specific objective itself is an outcome of an earlier decision. However, since the objective setting is an outcome of earlier decision, this may not be considered truly as the first step of decision process but provides framework for the decision.

II. Identification of Problems

Since a particular decision is made in the context of certain given objectives, identification of problem is the real beginning of decision-making process. A problem is a felt need, a question thrown forward for solution. It is the gap between present and desired state of affairs on the subject-matter of decision. It is just like the diagnosis of patient by the doctor. When a doctor makes a diagnosis he has a normal, healthy person and he also has a fairly clear concept of what a healthy person is. With this model as the desired result, he looks for disparities in the patient's actual state of health or factors which indicate that his future health will fall short of normal. In the case of management decision, however, a manager cannot rely on a commonly accepted norm such as healthy person. The objectives, if set precisely and specifically on the subject-matter of decision, will provide clue in identifying the problem and its possible solution. Further in management, a problem exists whenever one faces a question whose answer involves doubt and uncertainty. If there is no solution to the problem, it cannot be treated as problem from decision point of view, though the consequences of not solving this problem may be terrible. A problem can be identified much clearly, if managers go through diagnosis and analysis of the problem.

(i) Diagnosis

The term diagnosis has come from Medical Science where it is used as the process of identifying a disease from its sign and symptoms. A symptom is a condition or set of conditions that indicates the existence of a problem. For example, a patient has certain symptoms on the basis which his disease can be identified. Symptoms occupy an essential place in the problem-solving process for they signal the existence of problem and guide the search for the underlying problem. For example, if an organisation has high turnover of its employees, it indicates that something is wrong with the organisation. The symptom of high turnover may provide the clue to the real problem and managers can overcome the problem by taking appropriate action (decision-making involves in taking action). Often managers fail to diagnose the problem correctly and sometimes they treat symptom as problem. Therefore, they should do this exercise very carefully. Diagnosing the real problem implies knowing the gap between what is and what ought to be, identifying the reasons for the gap, and understanding the problem in relation to higher objectives of the organisation.

(ii) Analysis

While the diagnosis of problem gives the understanding of what should be done in terms of decision-making, analysis of problem takes it a step further. The analysis of the problem requires to find out who would make decision, what information would be needed, and from where the information is available. This analysis may provide managers with revealing circumstances that help them to gain an insight into the problem. The whole approach of analysis of problem should, however, be based around critical factors like the availability of information for making decision, critically of decision, and the time available for making decision. For example, information may be available from external and internal sources and some of the information may not be available at all. Similarly the critically of decision will determine the level at which the decision can be made. Thus diagnosis and analysis of problem requiring decision will clarify what is needed and where the alternatives for doing the thing can be sought.

III. Search for Alternatives

A thorough diagnosis defines both a specific problem and the situation in which the problem exists. With this definition in mind, a decision-maker seeks possible solutions. A problem can be solved in several ways, however, all the ways, cannot be equally satisfying. Further, if there is only one way of solving a problem, no question of decision arises. Therefore, the decision-maker must try to find out the various alternatives available in order to get the most satisfactory result of a decision. Identification of various alternatives not only serves the purpose of selecting the most satisfactory one, but it also avoids bottlenecks in operation as alternatives are available if a particular decision goes wrong. However, it should be borne in mind that it may not be possible to consider all alternatives either because some of the alternatives cannot be considered for selection because of obvious limitation of the decision-maker or information about all alternatives may not be available. Therefore, while generating alternatives, the concept of limiting factor should be applied. A limiting factor is one which stands in the way of accomplishing a desired objective. If these factors are identified, managers will confine their search for alternatives to those which will overcome the limiting factors. For example, if an organisation has limitation in raising sizable finances, it cannot consider projects involving high investment.

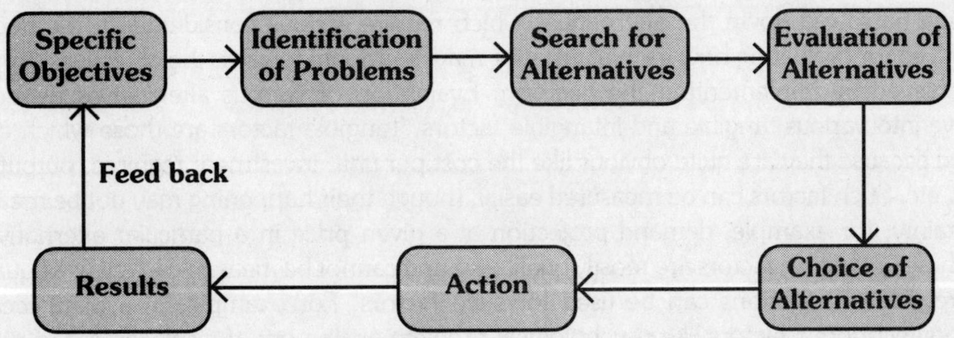

Fig. 3. *Decision-making Process.*

A decision-maker can use several sources for identifying alternatives: his own past experience, practices followed by others, and using creative techniques. Past experience, applied in most cases of decision-making, takes into account the actions taken by the decision-maker in the past with obvious differences between the former challenges and the present one. The successful action of the past may become an alternative for the future. This is very simple approach but has obvious limitations because there may be so much changes in the decision context that old action becomes totally irrelevant. Copying from the experience of other is another way of generating alternatives. Thus alternatives used by successful decision makers can be thought of as alternatives for decision-making. This is also practised by many organisations after making suitable amendments in the light of changed decision context. Importing of technology from foreign countries with suitable changes is good example of this type of alternatives. The third method of generating alternatives is through creative process where various exercises are taken to generate entirely new ideas.

IV. Evaluation of Alternatives

After the various alternatives are identified, the next step is to evaluate them and select the one that will meet the choice criteria. However, all alternatives available for decision-making will not be taken for detailed evaluation because of the obvious limitations of managers in evaluating all alternatives. The energy of managers is limited and psychologically most of them prefer to work on plans that have good prospect of being carried out. In narrowing down the number of alternatives, two approaches can be followed: constraint on alternatives and grouping of alternatives of similar nature. The decision-maker develops a list of limits that must be met by a satisfactory solution. He may treat these limits as constraints, that is, he may check proposed alternatives against limits, and if an alternative does not meet them, he can discard it. In the second approach, various alternatives can be grouped into classes on some specific criteria important to decision-making. A representative alternative from one group may be selected for future analysis. Then having found the group that shows up the best, decision-maker can concentrate on alternatives within this group. This method is very helpful in decision-making regarding the location of plant, warehouse, etc.

Having narrowed down the alternatives which require serious consideration, the decision-maker will go for evaluating how each alternative may contribute towards the objectives supposed to be achieved by implementing the decision. Evaluation of various alternatives dissects an alternative into various tangible and intangible factors. Tangible factors are those which can be quantified because they are quite obvious like the cost per unit, investment required, output to be received, etc. Such factors can be measured easily, though their happening may not be measured with certainty; for example, demand projection at a given price in a particular alternative. As against these, intangible factors are mostly qualitative and cannot be measured in terms of quantity. Therefore, some definitions can be used for such factors. For example, in a plant location, various non-economic factors like psychological problem arising out of displacement of persons from the plant site, ecological balance, etc., have to be taken into account which cannot be quantified. In evaluating an alternative, both these factors have to be taken into account. For determining the impact of a factor, various quantitative techniques have been developed.

V. Choice of Alternative

The evaluation of various alternatives presents a clear picture as to how each one of them contributes to the objectives under question. A comparison is made among the likely outcomes of various alternatives and the best one is chosen. Choice aspect of decision-making is related to deciding the most acceptable alternative which fits with the organisational objectives. It may be seen that the chosen alternative should be acceptable in the light of the organisational objectives. Thus, it is not necessary that the chosen alternative is the best one. This concept is based on the satisfying approach rather than the maximising approach of decision making. In choosing an alternative, the decision-maker can go through three approaches : experience, experimentation, and research and analysis.

(i) *Experience.* Managers can choose an alternative based on their past experience if they have solved similar problem earlier. Reliance on past experience plays a larger part than it deserves in decision-making. Managers rely more on experience than alternative methods of choice. Past experience has some benefits but it has certain limitations that it blocks making correct choice specially when the environmental factors are more flexible.

(ii) *Experimentation.* Experimentation which is generally used in scientific enquiry involves that a particular alternative is put in practice, result is observed, and the alternative giving the best result is selected. For example, many organisations go for test marketing of their products before the products are really introduced in the market. During the test marketing, the actions can be taken to change product features which are not acceptable. Experimentation as a method for choice of an alternative can be used on a limited scale because of cost and time factor.

(iii) *Research and Analysis.* Research and analysis is the most certain method of selecting an alternative, specially when major decisions are involved. This approach entails solving a problem first by comprehending it. This involves a search for relationships between the more critical variables, constraints, and planning premises that bear the objectives sought. In the second stage, the alternative is broken into various components. Their individual impact on objective is evaluated and the impact of all factors of an alternative is combined to find out the total impact of the particular alternative. The one having the most positive impact is chosen. Since this requires making lot of calculations, often the help of computer is taken. In fact, various computer-based models have been developed to make the choice of an alternative easier.

Though various approaches are available for choosing an alternative, the decision-maker's personal values and aspirations affect what alternative will be chosen. In fact, in one way, the decision-making is the translation of one's values and aspirations into action. Thus the rational process of decision-making is considerably affected by the personal factors. Further, managers should take into account the uncertainty of outcome of a decision. Therefore, they should be ready with alternative action if one fails. In order to do this, managers should often be ready with contingency plans.

VI. Action

Once the alternative is selected, it is put into action. Truly speaking, the actual process of decision-making ends with the choice of an alternative through which the objectives can be achieved. However, decision-making, being a continuous and on-going process, must ensure that the objectives have been achieved by the chosen alternative. Unless this is done, mangers will never know what way their choice has contributed. Therefore, the implementation of decision may be seen as an integral aspect of decision.

Once the creative and analytical aspects of decision-making through which an alternative has been chosen are over, the managerial priority is one of converting the decision into something operationally effective. This is the action aspect of decision-making. The basic difference between decision-making as an analytical process and action is that the former requires the use of conceptual skills since it translates the abstract ideas into reality. For example, suppose that there is a change in consumers' tastes. This change is very abstract and cannot be seen unless some specific techniques and measurements are applied. How this change can provide opportunity to the organisation is mostly a conceptual exercise requiring managers to interpret what changes are taking place and what products or services will be preferred in the changed situation. Action, on the other hand, relates to putting a decision into practice so that objectives of decision are achieved. This practice will provide further feedback for evaluating the soundness of the decision and, if need be, a change in the decision.

Implementation of a decision requires the communication to subordinates, getting acceptance of subordinates over the matters involved in the decision, and getting their support for putting the decision into action. The decision should be effected at appropriate time and in proper way to make the action more effective. The effectiveness of action is important because it is only effective action through which organisational objectives can be achieved, and right decisions help in effective action.

VII. Results

When the decision is put into action, it brings certain results. These results must correspond with objectives, the starting point of decision process, if good decision has been made and implemented properly. Thus results provide indication whether decision-making and its implementation is proper. Therefore, managers should take up a follow-up action in the light of feedback received from the results. If there is any deviation between objectives and results, this should be analysed and factors responsible for this deviation should be located. The feedback may also help in reviewing the decision when conditions change which may require changes in decision. Therefore, a successful manager is one who keeps a close look at the objectives and results of the decision and modifies his decision according to the changes in the situations.

POSITIVE AND NEGATIVE ASPECTS OF GROUP DECISION-MAKING

Group decision-making has both positive and negative aspects. Some of these emerge because of the group decision-making process itself, others depend on the nature of the problem and the group members involved.

I. Positive Aspects of Group Decision-Making

Every group decision-making has some positive aspects in terms of better decision, commitment of people towards decision, better communication and commitment but at the same time, has some negative aspects in the form of time consuming and being costly, problem of outcomes, and undue pressure on conformity to norms. These aspects are presented below :

(i) *Pooling of Knowledge and Information.* Since many individuals are involved in group decision-making, more data and information can be brought to bear on the decision. The group provides specialised inputs in defining variables and suggests alternatives that the individual alone is unlikely to come up with. Pooling of such knowledge and information is likely to improve the quality of decisions provided group dynamic factors are positive.

(ii) *Satisfaction and Commitment.* Individual satisfaction and commitment in group decision-making are often enhanced. This may be caused by an attitude change regarding the alternatives as a result of discussion. It may also be caused by the development of group spirit as people discover similarities among themselves. People who share in an important activity like decision-making feel more ownership than when they are excluded from it. Individuals' satisfaction and commitment are important for effective implementation of the decision.

(iii) *Personnel Development.* Group decision-making is a source of development of individuals in the organisation. Learning is enhanced when one observes others. Practices what has been seen, and experiences the positive rewards received for successfully repeating the new behaviour. These three learning factors are present in group decision-making. Individuals can learn to know to gather data, evaluate it, generate alternatives, calculate risks, and choose the best solution by practising with others in group decisions. Thus, the problem of succession in the organisation can be overcome.

(iv) More Risk Taking. Every decision involves some kind of risk because a decision affects future events and one can never be sure about future. Since individuals vary in terms of risk taking aptitudes and capabilities, risk taking increases when these individuals are pooled in a group. Thus the risk taking tends to be higher in group decision-making. Higher risk taking generates in group decision-making because :

(a) Group is able to share information in an open environment; members become more familiar with the problem being discussed; initially they may be cautious about risk and

(b) If the outcome of the decision is negative, it is easy to pass the buck by individuals.

Therefore, when amount of risk involved in a decision is significant, group decision-making is more appropriate.

II. Negative Aspects of Group Decision-Making

Group decision-making has following negative features which may either affect the quality of decision or cost of decision:

(i) Time-Consuming and Costly. Inevitably, groups take more time to reach decisions than individuals. There are several reasons for this:

(a) More ideas and opinions are held by the group members which must be discussed for decision-making.

(b) Arrangements for the group meeting, place, format, and assembly must be made which are time-consuming. In all these things, cost is also involved.

Thus, the total cost of group decision-making would be cost of arrangement and cost of members' time. Therefore, group decision-making should be resorted to only when the matter cannot be decided by individuals separately.

(ii) Individual Domination. Because of the group dynamics prevailing in group interaction, some individuals dominate the group processes and have considerable bearing on decision outcomes. This may be because such individuals may enjoy higher status because of their age, experience, expertise, or other influencing characteristics. Thus, what appears to be a group decision may actually be the individual decision ratified by the group. Domination of such persons may not necessarily improve the quality of decisions.

(iii) Problem of Responsibility. No doubt, group decision brings more commitment from members and its implementation is easier but this is true when the decision implementation outcome is positive. When this outcome is negative, no one can be held responsible. A group decision is no one's decision and no one is held individually responsible for that. In such a situation, groups may come out with ill-conceived or irresponsible decisions.

(iv) Groupthink. Groupthink is a type of thinking that occurs when reaching agreement becomes more important to group members than arriving at a sound decision. Groupthink is more

likely to happen in cohesive groups because there is pressure for conformity to group norms and members avoid being too harsh in their judgements of fellow members. They try to avoid bickering and conflict, which they perceive as a threat to the team spirit. There are five reasons for the happening of groupthink:

(a) There is development of an extraordinarily high sense of group cohesiveness. While cohesiveness is sometimes desirable, it is not desirable when a variety of opinions is as crucial as they are in decision-making.
(b) The group isolates itself from the negative consequences which its decision may have on others outside the group.
(c) There may be unintentional setting of narrow constraints on the acceptability of decisions. Decisions that would affect the norms and structures of the group are unacceptable, even though the basic parameters of the decisions would be otherwise beneficial.
(d) The feeling of high degree of competence, team spirit and agreement may mislead the group to seriously overestimate the collective wisdom and hence not a good decision.
(e) Certain members may take the role of social leader of the group and they may protect the group from any facts, criticisms, or evaluations that might alter the illusion of unanimity and infallibility.

Groupthink not necessarily results into poor decisions but it simply increases the likelihood of such a decision by limiting discussion on various alternatives evaluation of critical facts bearing impact on decisions, and adhering to similar decisions made in the past, though faulty.

HOMANS MODEL

More than three decades ago, in the Human Group, *George Homans* developed a conceptual framework to aid in understanding the complex workings of group behaviours. His model, also called 'the A-I-S model', makes some common sense notions about small groups and is based on three concepts: Activity, interaction and sentiment.

(a) Activity. Activities are the tasks that people perform, like walking to work, assembling a machine, inspecting a component, talking etc.
(b) Interaction. Interactions are the behaviour that occur between people in performing the above tasks. Interaction may involve two or more individuals. It may be verbal or non-verbal.
(c) Sentiment. Sentiments include feelings, values, opinions, and beliefs held by an individual or a group. Sentiments, unlike interactions and activities, are not directly observable in group interaction, rather, they must be determined subjectively by inference for ongoing group activity. Sentiments can be positive, negative or neutral.

Required and Emergent System

Homans uses these three basic systems elements of activity, interaction, and sentiment to define and delineate two basic systems that exist within the group. Homans calls them the required system and the emergent system.

(i) *Required system.* The required system/behaviour includes all activities, interactions, and sentiments that a necessary part of the group function. For instance, a student may have to frequently confer with his professor in order to complete the field assignment. Approaching the professor signifies an activity, having a dialogue indicates interaction and having continued discussions thereafter initiates the A-I-S chain. Together, these required activities, interactions, and sentiments from the required behaviour in the group.

(ii) *Emergent system/behaviour.* The emergent system includes activities, interactions, and sentiments that evolve as a result of the required group function. For example, it is quite possible that in working together within the required system, the members of the group will evolve their own social structure. This social structure may be characterised by status levels, norms of behaviour, friendships and hostile interaction patterns. The emergent system is made up of these elements.

Background and Environmental Factors

According to *Homans*, the distinct features of a group's required and emergent systems will be influenced by a number of background and environmental factors. These factors include the physical aspects of the work to be finished, the organisational policies, practices the political, cultural and economic environment, the personal background factors of members. It is the interaction of these background factors (external system) influencing both the required and emergent systems that will ultimately determine levels of group output in three significant areas: productivity, satisfaction and personal growth.

As can be seen from the above diagram, the external system provides the raw material for forming the internal system, the set of emergent activities, interactions and sentiments and norms for behaviour in the group. The operation of the internal system leads to productivity, satisfaction and growth consequences. These results, then, feedback into stage I to affect the background factors.

Implications

The Homan's model offers managers considerable insight into group behaviour and helps in predicting certain outcomes. For example the model helps in predicting the emergent behaviour in a given situation. Emergent interaction is more likely between members whose given sentiments are similar, whole jobs force them to have a continuous dialogue, who are actually required by the management to interact and so on. Homans pointed out that interaction and inter-personal sentiments are closely related. Favourable sentiments emerge between members who interact frequently and frequent interaction develops between members who like one another. Unfavourable sentiments are directed against members who do not share or who violate the norms generally approved by the group. Managers, according to the model, can increase group cohesiveness by increasing the frequency of interactions among employees who like each other.

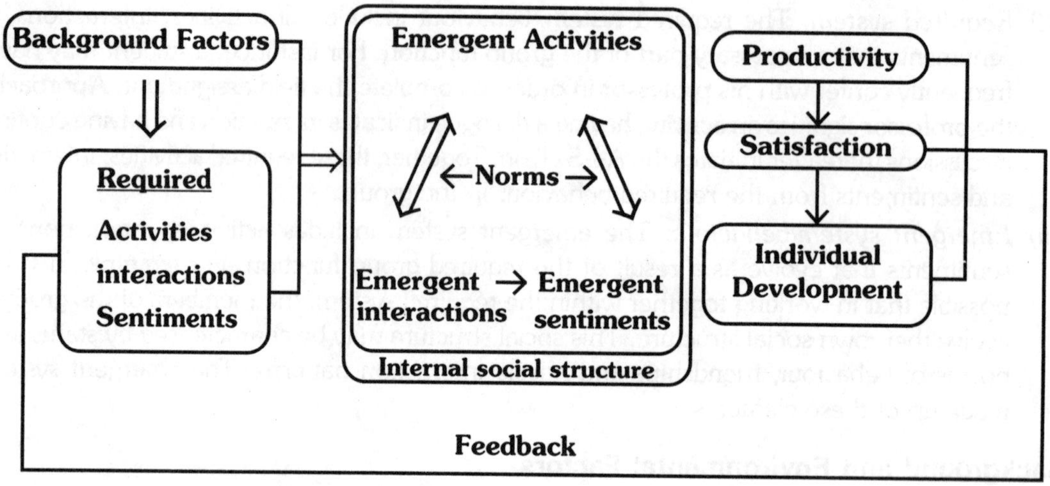

Fig. 4. *Homans Model.*

PARTICIPATIVE DECISION-MAKING TECHNIQUE

I. The Delphi Technique

Although Delphi was first developed many years ago at the *Rand Corporation's think tank*, it has only recently become popularised as a group decision-making technique, for example, for long-range forecasting. Today, numerous organisations in business education, government, health, and the military are using Delphi. No decision technique will ever be able to predict the future completely, but the Delphi technique seems to be as good a crystal ball as is currently available.

The technique, named after the oracle at Delphi in ancient Greece, has many variations, but generally it works as follows :

(i) A group (usually of experts, but in some cases non-experts may deliberately be used) is formed, but, importantly, the members are not in face-to-face interaction with one another. Thus, the expenses of bringing a group together are eliminated.

(ii) Each member is asked to make anonymous predictions or input into the problems decision the group is charged with.

(iii) Each member then receives composite feedback from what the others have inputted. In some variations the reasons are listed (anonymously), but mostly just a composite figure is used.

(iv) On the basis of the feedback, another round of anonymous inputs is made. These interactions take place for a predetermined number of times or until the composite feedback remains the same, which means everyone is sticking with his or her position.

A major key to the success of the technique lies in its anonymity. Keeping the responses of Delphi group members anonymous eliminates the problem of "saving face" and encourages the experts to be more flexible and thus to benefit from the estimates of others. In the traditional interacting group decision-making technique, the experts may be more concerned with defending their vested positions than they are with making a good decision.

Many organisations testify to the success they have had so far with the Delphi technique. McDonnell Douglas Aircraft has used the technique to forecast the future uncertainties of commercial air transportation. Weyerhaeuser, a building supply company, has used it to predict what will happen in the construction business, and Smith Kline Beecham, a drug manufacturer, has used it to study the uncertainties of medicine. TRW, a highly diversified, technically oriented company, has fourteen Delphi panels averaging seventeen members each. The panels suggest products and services that have marketing potential and predict technological developments and significant political, economic, social, and cultural events. Besides business applications, the technique has been used successfully on various problems in government, education, health, and the military. In other words, Delphi can be applied to a wide variety of program planning and decision problems in any type of organisation.

The major criticisms of the Delphi technique centre on its time consumption, cost, and Ouija-board effect. The third criticism implies that, much like the parlour game of that name, Delphi can claim no scientific basis or support. To counter this criticism, Rand has attempted to validate Delphi through controlled experimentation. The corporation set up panels of non-experts who use the Delphi technique to answer questions such as, "How many popular votes were cast for Lincoln when he first ran for president?" and "What was the average price a farmer received for a bushel of apples in 1940?" These particular questions were used because the average person does not know the exact answers but knows something about the subjects. The result of these studies showed that the original estimates by the panel of non-experts were reasonably close to being correct, but with the Delphi technique of anonymous feedback, the estimates greatly improved.

II. The Nominal Group Technique

Closely related to Delphi is the nominal group approach to group decision-making. The nominal group has been used by social psychologists in their research for many years. A nominal group is simply a "paper group." It is a group in name only because no verbal exchange is allowed between members. In group dynamics research, social psychologists would pit a fully interacting group against a nominal group (a group of individuals added together on paper but not interacting verbally). In terms of number of ideas, uniqueness of ideas, and quality of ideas, research has found nominal groups to be superior to real groups. The general conclusion is that interacting groups have certain dysfunctions that inhibit creativity. For example, a recent study found that the performance of participants in interactive groups was more similar, more conforming, than the performance of those in nominal groups. Yet, except for idea generation, the interactive effect of group members is known to have a significant positive effect on other variables.

When the pure nominal group approach is expanded into a specific technique for decision-making in organisations, it is labelled the *nominal group technique* (NGT) and consists of the following steps :

(i) Silent generation of ideas in writing.
(ii) Round-robin feedback from group members, who record each idea in a terse phrase on a flip chart or blackboard.
(iii) Discussion of each recorded idea for clarification and evaluation.
(iv) Individual voting on priority ideas, with the group decision being mathematically derived through rank ordering or rating.

The difference between this approach and Delphi is that the NGT members are usually with one another, have face-to-face contact, and communicate with one another directly in the third step. Although more research is needed, there is some evidence that NGT-led groups come up with many more ideas than traditional interacting groups and may do as well as, or slightly better than, groups using Delphi. A study also found that NGT-led groups performed at a level of accuracy that was equivalent to that of the most proficient members. However, another study found that NGT-led groups did not perform as well as interacting groups whose participants were pervasively aware of the problem given the group and when there were no dominant persons who inhibited others from communicating ideas. A recent study also found that individuals working alone and then formed into nominal groups were superior, but for computer-mediated idea generation, intact groups (such as a regular work group) generated more ideas (with higher quality) than those working in subgroups or than individuals in a nominal group. Thus, as is true of most of the techniques discussed in this text, there are moderating effects.

III. Dialectic Decision Method

One of the common problems in group decision-making is that group members coverage too quickly on one alternative while overlooking others which may be more promising than the one chosen. This may happen because they want to avoid group meetings or they may lack willingness to raise and confront tough issues. In order to overcome this problem, dialectic decision method (DDM) has been evolved. DDM proceeds through various steps as given in Figure 4.

Here, only two alternatives have been proposed for the sake of simplicity. In practice, there may be so many alternatives. The dialectic process begins with a clear statement of a problem to be solved. Based on this statement, alternative proposals are generated and participants identify the explicit and implicit assumptions underlying each proposal. The group then breaks into advocacy subgroups to study the proposals in the light of the problem. The entire group meets after this exercise for the final choice. The choice may be made in terms of a particular proposal based on its pros and cons, or there may be compromise of different proposals, or new alternative/ is may be proposed.

DDM generates better understanding of the proposals, their underlying assumptions, and their pros and cons. The group members are likely to feel more confident about their choices. However, it suffers from one weakness in the form of propensity to forge a compromise. Sometimes, this compromise may not be based on actual pros and cons of a proposal but may be affected by the debating skills of the participants.

THE LEADERSHIP ROLE IN GROUP DECISION-MAKING

While the composition of the group is very important for effective decision-making, the presence and behaviour of a responsible group leader is the key element in steering the group discussion and participation. The group leader is in a critical position to affect the quality and acceptance of the decision. Whether he is elected by the group or appointed by the management, his role is highly responsible in guiding the direction of the group discussion. A good leader of the group would not dominate the discussion but generally guide the members towards the established goals as well as moderate the discussion. He develops a kinship with the members and is always sympathetic to the members input. There are some basic characteristics of a good group leader whose attention and guidance would determine the success of the group function. These basic characteristics fall into two broad categories.

First category consists of *task characteristics* which deals primarily with the operations of the group and the *second* category is that of *maintenance characteristics* which deals with the human aspect of the groups. These characteristics are explained as follows:

I. Task Characteristics

(a) The leader of the group must define the problem clearly and carefully and bring it to the attention of the group members so that each member becomes fully conversant with the issues at hand. He should initiate the discussion and may suggest a procedure for finding a solution.

(b) He should have the ability to make every member feel comfortable about the situation and the problem at hand and should seek relevant information from group members who may not volunteer information unless asked. He must encourage every member to express his opinions freely.

(c) The leader should have the ability and knowledge to provide answers to any questions, clarify interpretations of the data presented and guide the members to the central point of discussion if the discussion becomes tangential from varying interpretations of the same data.

(d) The leader should offer his personal opinions for consideration, but he should not excessively emphasize his viewpoint, or assume the role of a dictator. He should be willing to compromise, if necessary, for the sake of group cohesion.

(e) The leader should remain in continuous touch with the group so as to be aware of the progress at any given moment. At the end of the discussion, a leader should be able to summarise the ideas presented and propose a conclusion to the group to accept, reject or modify.

II. Maintenance Characteristics

(a) The leader should be fair and friendly to all the group members and maintain a rapport with them by showing concern for their contribution and recognition.

(b) He should be skilled in interpersonal relations so that he is able to sense the mood of the

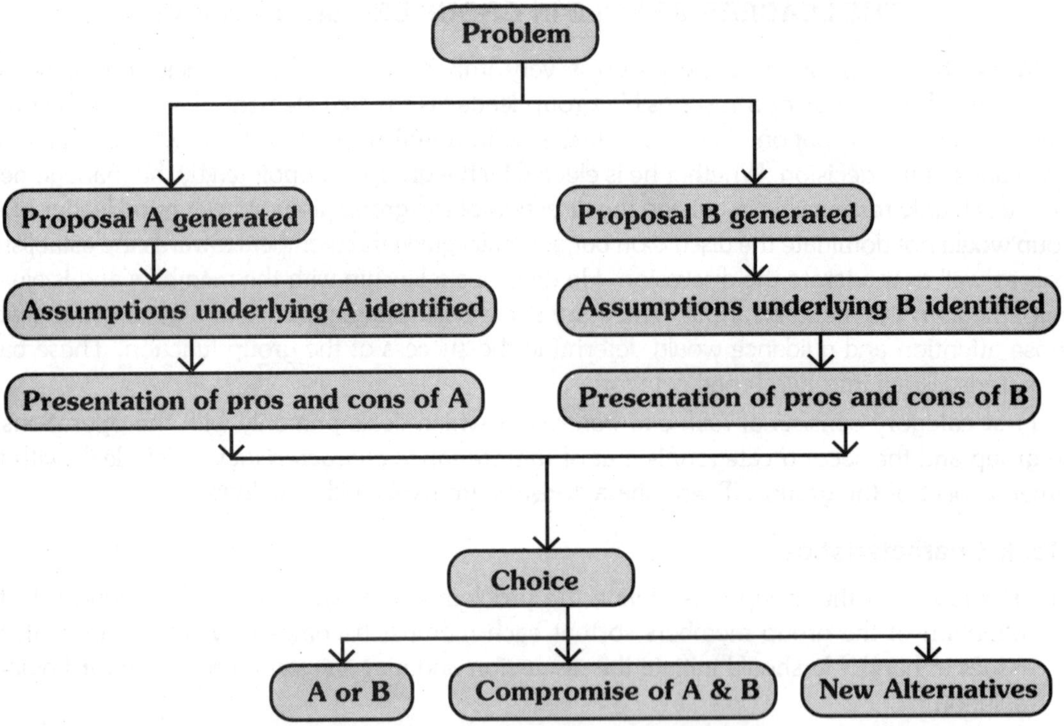

Fig. 5. *Steps in Dialectic Decision-Making.*

group and share in that mood. He should try to settle disagreements in a harmonious manner. This should result in reducing the tension in the group environment.

(c) He must be willing to give in wherever necessary. This would improve group cohesiveness, respect for the leader and maintain an atmosphere of harmony.

(d) The leader should be open minded and flexible. He should keep the lines of communication with members open so that the members are free to express their ideas openly and with confidence, expecting that their ideas would be taken seriously, and these ideas should be considered seriously.

THE RATIONAL DECISION-MAKING PROCESS

The optimizing decision-maker is rational. That is, he or she makes consistent, value-maximising choices within specified constraints. These choices are made following a six-step rational decision-making model. Moreover, specific assumptions underlie this model.

I. The Rational Model

The six steps in the rational decision-making model are listed. The model begins by defining the problem. As noted previously, a problem exists when there is a discrepancy between an existing and a desired state of affairs. If you calculate your monthly expenses and find you're spending $50 more than you allocated in your budget, you have defined a problem. Many poor decisions can be traced to the decision-maker overlooking a problem or defining the wrong problem.

Once a decision-maker has defined the problem, he or she needs to identify the decision criteria that will be important in solving the problem. In this step, the decision-maker determines what is relevant in making the decision. This step brings the decision-maker's interests, values, and similar personal preferences into the process. Identifying criteria is important because what one person thinks is relevant another person may not. Also keep in mind that any factors not identified in this step are considered irrelevant to the decision-maker.

The criteria identified are rarely all equal in importance. So the third step requires the decision-maker to weight the previously identified criteria in order to give them the correct priority in the decision.

The fourth step requires the decision-maker to generate possible alternatives that could succeed in resolving the problem. No attempt is made in this step to appraise these alternatives, only to list them.

Once the alternatives have been generated, the decision-maker must critically analyse and evaluate each one. This is done by rating each alternative on each criterion. The strengths and weaknesses of each alternative become evident as they are compared with the criteria and weights established in the second and third steps.

The final step in this model requires computing the optimal decision. This is done by evaluating each alternative against the weighted criteria and selecting the alternative with the highest total score.

II. Assumptions of the Model

The rational decision-making model we just described contains a number of assumptions. Let's briefly outline those assumptions:

(i) Problem clarity. The problem is clear and unambiguous. The decision-maker is assumed to have complete information regarding the decision situation.

(ii) Known options. It is assumed the decision-maker can identify all the relevant criteria and can list all the viable alternatives. Furthermore, the decision-maker is aware of all the possible consequences of each alternative.

(iii) Clear preferences. Rationality assumes that the criteria and alternatives can be ranked and weighted to reflect their importance.

(iv) Constant preferences. It's assumed that the specific decision criteria are constant and that the weights assigned to them are stable over time.

(v) No time or cost constraints. The rational decision-maker can obtain full information about criteria and alternatives because it's assumed that there are no time or cost constraints.

(vi) Maximum payoff. The rational decision-maker will choose the alternative that yields the highest perceived value.

REVIEW QUESTIONS

1. Define and classify the group. What are the main factors of group formation?
2. Explain fully the characteristics of different types of groups.
3. What is group dynamics? What are the main determinants and functions of group in an organisation?
4. What are the committee group? Explain advantages and disadvantages of committee group.
5. What is group structure ? Explain in detail.
6. What do you mean by team work? Make the difference between team *versus* groups.
7. Explain the various types of team.
8. What do you understand by group decision-making?
9. Explain the process of rational decision-making.
10. What are the characteristics of decision-making? Also discuss the nature of decision-making.
11. What are the positive and negative aspects of group decision-making?
12. Explain advantages and disadvantages of group decision-making.
13. Explain the leadership role in group decision-making.
14. Write short notes on:
    (a) Delphi Technique.
    (b) Fishbowling.
    (c) Didatic Interaction.

REFERENCES

1. *J.W. Thibaut and H.H. Kelley, The Social Psychology of Groups, New York, John Wiley and Sons, 1959.*
2. *A. Zander, Making Groups Effective, Sanfransisco, Jossey Bass, 1982.*
3. *M.E. Shaw, Group Dynamics: The Psychology of Small Group Behaviour, New York, McGraw Hill, 1971.*
4. *I.L. Janis, "Group Think", Psychology Today, Nov., 1971.*
5. *I.L. Janis, Victims of Group Think, Boston, Houghton Mifflin, 1973.*
6. *H.G. Hicks and C.R. Gullett, The Management of Organisations, Tokyo, McGraw Hill, 1976.*
7. *N.R.F. Maier, "Assets and Liabilities in Group Problem Solving", Psychological Review, July, 1967.*
8. *Andrew H. Van de Ven and Andrew L. Delbecq, "The Effectiveness of Nominal, Delphi and Interacting Group Decision-Making Processes", Academy of Management Journal, Dec., 1971.*
9. *L.R. Sayles, Behaviour of Industrial Work Groups, Prediction and Control, New York, John Wiley and Sons, 1958.*
10. *L.N. Jewell and H.J. Reitz, Group Effectiveness in Organisations, Glenview III, Scott, Foresman 1981.*
11. *W.J. Duncan, Organisational Behaviour, Boston, Houghton Mifflin Company, 1978.*

8th CHAPTER

ORGANISATIONAL CULTURE AND CLIMATE INFLUENCES

OVERVIEW

• ***After reading this chapter, you should be able to know:***

- Introduction
- Features of Organisational Cultures
- Generalisations for Change Culture
- Ethical Dimensions of Culture
- Culture is a Descriptive Term
- Consequences and Forms of Organisational Cultures
- Different Forms of Organisational Culture
- Uniformity of Culture
- Organisational Culture and Effectiveness
- National Culture
- History and Culture
- Strong *versus* Weak Cultures
- Culture *versus* Formalisation
- Creating and Maintaining a Culture
- Components of Culture
- Developing Organisational Culture
- Changing Organisational Culture
- Performance and Organisational Culture
- Ethical Behaviour and Organisational Culture
- The Organisational Socialisation Process
- Cross-cultural Training
- Cross-Cultural Research Findings
- Uncertainty Avoidance
- Masculinity-Femininity
- Cross-Cultural Transitions
- Levels of Culture
- Managing Organisational Culture
- How Culture Affects Work?
- Organisational Climate
- Factors Affecting Organisational Climate
- Developing A Sound Organisational Climate

8

Organisational Culture and Climate Influences

INTRODUCTION

Organisational culture is the collection of shared (stated or implied) beliefs, values, rituals, stories, myths, and specialised language that foster a feeling of community among organisation members. The cultural concept has been a main stay in the field of anthropology from its beginnings and even was given attention in the early development of theories of organisational behaviour. As one recent analysis noted : "In the decade since the culture perspective burst on to the organisational studies scene, the perspective has waxed and waned in influence and vitality." Anthropologists have defined culture as *"that complex whole which includes knowledge, belief, art, law, morals, customs, and any capabilities and habits acquired by man as a member of society."*

Culture consists of patterns, explicit and implicit, of and for behaviour acquired and transmitted by symbols, constituting the distinctive achievement of human groups, including their embodiment in artifacts; the essential core of culture consists of traditional (i.e., historically derived and selected) ideas and especially their attached values. When people join an organisation, they bring with them the values and beliefs they have been taught. Quite often, however, these values and beliefs are insufficient for helping the individual succeed in the organisation. The person needs to learn how the particular enterprise does things.

Edger Schein, who is probably most closely associated with the study of organisational culture, defines it as, '. . . a pattern of basic assumptions—invented, discovered, or developed by a given group as it learns to cope with its problems of external adaptation and internal integration—that has worked well enough to be considered valuable and, therefore, to be taught to new members as the correct way to perceive, think, and feel in relation to those problems.'

Organisational culture is quite complex. Although there are a number of problems and disagreements associated with the conceptualisation of organisational culture, most definitions, recognise the importance of shared norms and values that guide organisational participants' behaviour. In fact, there is research evidence that not only are these cultural values taught to newcomers, but newcomers seek out and want to learn about their organisation's culture.

FEATURES OF ORGANISATIONAL CULTURES

Organisational cultures can vary widely from one organisation to the next. Even so, authorities on the subject have identified six common characteristics. Let us briefly examine these common characteristics to gain a fuller understanding of organisational cultures:

(i) *Cultures:* Just as a photographer cannot capture your typical busy day in a single snapshot, it takes intense and prolonged observation to capture the essence of an organisations's culture.

(ii) *Inherently Symbolic*: Actions do, in fact, often speak louder than words. Some words or slogans may have great symbolic meaning. But often we need to read between the lines to discover true cultural messages. For example, at Microsoft, competitive sports are a key feature of the software company's culture. "'It's an intense play-hard, work-hard atmosphere,' says Jon Staenberg, a marketing manager. 'A lot of business is done on the fields.'... [But] Staenberg says after he bested a higher-up in racquetball, the man's attitude toward him completely changed. 'Policially, I probably shouldn't have beaten him,' he says."

(iii) *Historically Based:* Shared experiences, over extended periods of time, bind groups of people together. We tend to identify with those who have had similar life experiences. Trust and loyalty, two key components of culture, are earned by consistently demonstrating predictable patterns of words and actions.

(iv) *Innovation and Risk Taking:* The degree to which employees are encouraged to be innovative and take risks.

(v) *Dynamic:* In the long-term, organisational cultures promote predictability, conformity, and stability. Just beneath this apparently stable surface, however, change boils as people struggle to communicate and comprehend subtle cultural clues. A management trainee who calls the president by her first name after being invited to do so may be embarrassed to learn later that "no one actually calls the president by her first name, even if she asks you to."

(vi) *Collective :* Organisational cultures are social entities. While an individual may exert a cultural influence, it takes collective agreement and action for an organisation's culture to take on a life of its own.

(vii) *Aggressiveness:* The degree to which people are aggressive and competitive rather than easy-going.

(viii) *Emotionally Charged:* People tend to find their organisation's culture a comforting security blanker that enable them to deal with (or sometimes mask) their insecurities and uncertainties. Not surprisingly, people can develop a strong emotional attachment to their cultural security blanket. They will fight to protect it, often refusing to question its basic values.

(ix) *Outcome Orientation:* The degree to which management focuses on results or outcomes rather than on the techniques and processes used to achieve these outcomes.

(x) *Observed Behavioural Regularities:* When organisational participants interact with one another, they use common language, terminology, and rituals related to deference and demeanour.

(xi) *People Orientation:* The degree to which management decisions take into consideration the effect of outcomes on people within the organisation.

(xii) *Team Orientation:* The degree to which work activities are organised around teams rather than individuals.

(xiii) *Stability:* The degree to which organisational activities emphasise maintaining the *status quo* in contrast to growth.

Each of these *characteristics* exists on a continuum from low to high. Appraising the organisation on these characteristics, then, gives a composite picture of the organisation's culture. This picture becomes the basis for feelings of shared understanding that members have about the organisation, how things are done in it, and the way members are supposed to behave.

GENERALISATIONS FOR CHANGE CULTURE

Despite the significant barriers and resistance to change, cultures can be managed and changed over time. This attempt to change culture can take many different forms. The generalisations are as follows :

(i) Assess the current culture.

(ii) Set realistic goals that impact on the bottom line.

(iii) Recruit outside personnel with industry experience, so that they are able to interact well with the organisational personnel.

(iv) Make changes from the top down, so that a consistent message is delivered from all management team members.

(v) Include employees in the culture change process, especially when making changes in rules and processes.

(vi) Take out all trappings that remind the personnel of the previous culture.

(vii) Expect to have some problems and find people who would rather move than change with the culture and, if possible, take these losses early.

(viii) Move quickly and decisively to build momentum and to defuse resistance to the new culture.

(ix) Stay the course by being persistent.

Also, organisations attempting to change their culture must be careful not to abandon their roots and blindly abandon their core, but distinctive, competencies.

ETHICAL DIMENSIONS OF CULTURE

There are many cultural dimensions that differentiate cultures. These cultural dimensions can influence behaviour which can cause misunderstanding, disagreement, or conflict.

I. People's Relationship to Nature

In some countries, people attempt to control their natural environment. Americans and Canadians use human-made fertilisers and insecticides and technologically sophisticated equipment to improve crops and crop yield. Middle Easterners view life as being preordained. When a flood or typhoon wipes out a village, it's seen as good's will. Far Eastern countries attempt to deal with nature on nature's terms, to work in harmony with it.

These three perspective can referred to as dominance, preordained, and harmony. In terms of organisational practices these three perspectives could result in significantly different responses to poor performance. In a culture in which dominance is practiced, poor performance often results in sanctions or punishment. In a preordained culture setting, poor performance is expected from some people. In a harmony-oriented culture, poor performance is likely to be met with recognition that it must be improved.

II. Activity Orientation

In cultures such as the United States, emphasis is placed in taking action. Accomplishing results and being recognised for achievements are considered important. Managers in results-oriented cultures can motivate employees with promotions, merit-based raises, bonuses, and public recognition.

In contrast to a results-oriented culture is a being culture. The being culture emphasises enjoyment, living with the flow, and being gratified for the moment. Employees in a being culture work for today, and when the job becomes troublesome or detracts from their enjoyment, they quit.

Understanding a culture's activity orientation can provide insight into how employees view work and leisure, what is rewarding, and how they make decisions regarding the job. The results-oriented culture suggests that employees work to accomplish specific goals. The being-oriented culture finds employees working to enjoy life more fully.

III. Informality

Americans do not ordinarily have a high regard for tradition, ceremony, and social rules. This informality has caused problems in business dealings and negotiations with people from other cultures. Latin Americans enjoy and respect pomp, circumstances, and ceremony. They tend to like public receptions, lavish meetings, and formal introductions. Americans faced with such events are often ill at ease.

In negotiations, Americans have acquired a reputation around the world for not wanting to chitchat. Americans want to get to the problem, solve it, and get on with business. However, negotiators from the Middle East, Latin America, and Southern Europe find it customary to converse first about unrelated areas and topics. They believe that first some degree of rapport must be established between negotiators. Being blunt and informal is considered impolite and nonprofessional.

IV. Individualism *versus* Collectivism

Americans place a high premium on the concept of individualism that describes the attitude of independence of a person who feels a large degree of freedom in his personal life and decisions. In American culture, individualism may motivate personal accomplishment or striving for self-fulfillment. This focus arises from a historical and religious base known as "the Protestant work ethic."

Germany and Japan are today categorised as communitarian societies. This term reflects a premise that the individual is an integral part of the whole and that his best chance to self-fulfillment is in the context of the nation's goals. In an individualist society, each person is regarded as already fulfilled and her problem is to protect what she has from being taken away by the state.

The organisation charts of firms in individualistic and collective societies differ. For example, in the United States, organisation charts generally specify individual positions by title, job description, and job responsibilities. By contrast, organisation charts in more group-oriented societies only specify sections, units, or departments. In group-oriented societies, assignments are provided in collective terms.

V. Time Orientation

How is time viewed in a society? In many countries, employees are not accustomed to specific scheduling of work on an hourly basis. Time might be considered in terms of seasons rather than in hours or workdays. Americans are meticulous about time-arriving at work, starting a meeting, beginning a sporting event. Being late for a meeting in northern Europe might be considered so disrespectful as to sever a business relationship. On the other hand, in South America or various areas of Africa, being late is considered the norm.

Americans tend to perceive time as a resource that is scarce and must be used wisely. Therefore, this view of time results in impatience about delays plus attempting to fit as many activities as possible in the allotted time. In contrast. Eastern cultures view time as unlimited—an unending, inexhaustible resource. These differences in cultural views of time help explain behavioural differences among people from different societies.

VI. Language

Languages present barriers to conducting global transactions. Culture reflects what the society values in its language. In some European and Asian countries, a number of languages are spoken. It is not correct, however, to conclude that when only one language exists, there will be only one culture. People in the United States and Australia speak English, but both countries have their own culture.

Canada provides a unique case of how language can play a significant role in business. Canada's heated controversy about the English and French languages has resulted in a joint government-industry committee producing typewriter and computer keyboards including accented French letters. Although the Canadian government is officially bilingual, English remains the dominant language. Many English speakers believe that promoting French will cause the disintegration of Canada.

Where many spoken languages exist in a single country, one language usually serves as the focus of communication across cultures. When communication in organisations involves translation from one language to another, the problems of meaning that arise become significant. It is difficult to translate from one language to another. Many managers have been surprised to find that noddings and yes responses to their Japanese counterparts did not mean the deal was accepted. The Japanese word for yes, hai, can also mean "I understand you" or "I hear you".

Examples of language problems in business transactions have filled books. An example that illustrates barriers and misinterpretations involved a Monterey Park, California, medical office building with the numbers 941 - 943 emblazoned in three-foot characters. These are merely the building's address. However, to the many Chinese-Americans who pass by or see the building, the numbers have a different meaning. In Mandarin or Cantonese dialects, they sound like a common Chinese saying : "Nine die; one lives." To the Chinese, a medical building with such numbers suggests that the possibility for surviving is almost zero. Chinese numerology is an amalgam of linguistic interpretation and age-old superstitions that have been brought to America.

VII. Religion

In many cultures, religion is a dominant factor. As such, it can have a significant effect on how and what business is conducted, work schedules, and attitudes about ethics. In Christian societies, Sunday is considered a day of rest, whereas in Islamic countries, it's Friday, while in Israel, it's Saturday.

Islam also forbids "excessive" profit, which is considered exploitive. Islam preaches moderation and the sharing of wealth with others less fortunate. The concept of sharing wealth is manifested in one form called zakat, an annual tax of 2.5 percent collected from individuals and used for the benefit of the community. Banks in fundamentalist Islamic nations take equity in financing ventures, sharing profits as well as losses in the joint ventures.

Muslims are expected to pray facing the holy city of Mecca five times every day. Companies and managers must be aware of this religious ritual and might consider making adjustments that would permit employees to stop working during prayer time. Are American, British, or French managers aware of this ritual and are they willing to provide their Muslim workers with the opportunity to practice this religious ritual?

In certain countries, religion may require its followers to dress in a particular manner that may conflict with organisations' norms of appearance. These customs may have to be examined in terms of the individual, the religion, and the organisation.

CULTURE IS A DESCRIPTIVE TERM

Organisational culture is concerned with how employees perceive the characteristics of an organisation's culture, not with whether or not they like them. That is, it is a descriptive term. This is important because it differentiates this concept from that of job satisfaction.

Research on organisational culture has sought to measure how employees see their organisation. Does it encourage teamwork? Does it reward innovation? Does it stifle initiative?

In contrast, job satisfaction seeks to measure affective responses to the work environment. It is concerned with how employees feel about the organisation's expectations, reward practices, and the like. Although the two terms undoubtedly have overlapping characteristics, keep in mind that the term organisational culture is descriptive, while job satisfaction is evaluative.

CONSEQUENCES AND FORMS OF ORGANISATIONAL CULTURES

Fig. 1 lists major consequences and forms of organisational cultures. To the extent that people in an organisation share symbols, a common language, stories and practices, they will tend to experience the four consequences. The degree of sharing and intensity of the consequences

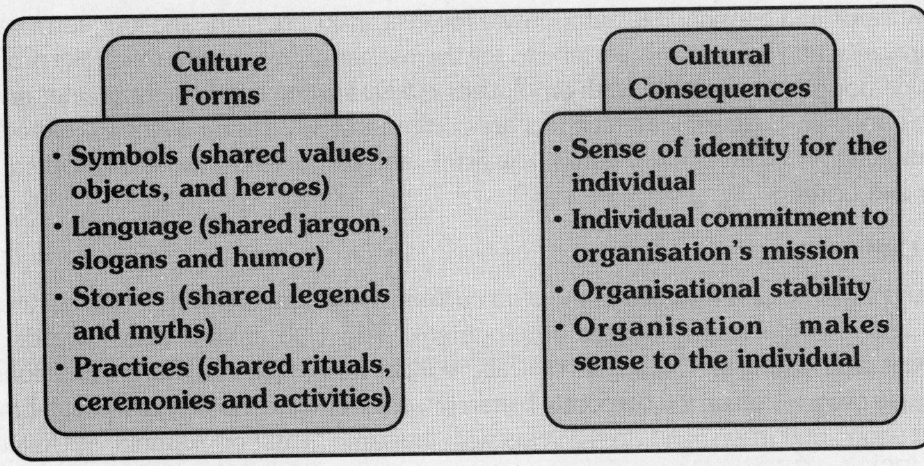

Fig. 1. *Forms and Consequences of Organisational Cultures.*

determine whether the organisation's culture is strong or weak. According to the authors of the best-selling book Corporate Cultures, "... a strong culture has almost always been the driving force behind continuing success in American business." One true test of this statement will be how well IBM deals with its recent radical restructuring. IBM's culture-white shirts, no layoffs, and all—was long admired as one of the strongest. Now that cutbacks, plant closings, and layoffs have severely strained the company's vaunted culture, IBM will soon find out if its "social glue" is the problem or the solution.

Shared values stand out as a pivotal factor in Fig. 1. Organisational values are shared beliefs about what the organisation stands for. For example, McDonald's, works hard to embed the values of its founder *Ray Kroc* into the huge company's culture. Although Kroc, who built the fast-food empire from scratch, died in 1984, his presence is still pervasive. His motto– "quality, service, cleanliness, and value"– is still central to the company's employee training and image. Kroc's office is still as he left it, preserved behind glass in Oak Brook, Illinois; and managers and trainees who attend the company's Hamburger University still "talk with Ray" by way of an interactive video. The McDonald's shrine to founder Ray Kroc is a powerful organisational symbol reinforcing key shared values.

DIFFERENT FORMS OF ORGANISATIONAL CULTURE

One of the most comprehensive and widely known is that by *Deal* and *Kennedy* describes the four basic types of cultural profiles they uncovered. Each is characterised by a combination of two factors: the type of risks managers assume and the type of feedback that results from their decisions.

I. Baseball Team Culture

Organisations with a *baseball team culture* attract entrepreneurs, innovators, and risk takers and pay employees for what they produce. Top performers often receive large salaries or other financial rewards and considerable autonomy. However, risks are high, and long-term security is virtually nonexistent. High performers tend to see themselves as free agents, much like professional athletes. Job hopping is common, with employees readily leaving one firm for greater rewards or freedom at another. Baseball team cultures are common in advertising agencies, biotechnology firms, consulting firms, investment banks, law firms, and computer software developers, such as Microsoft and Lotus.

II. Club Culture

Age and experience are valued in the *club culture*. Organisations with a club culture reward seniority and provide stable, secure employment. The club culture also rewards loyalty, commitment, and "fitting in." Managers typically work at various jobs in different functions during a slow, steady progression up the corporate hierarchy; quick upward mobility is unusual. Employees often start young and may spend 35-40 years with the same firm. For example, at United Parcel Service (UPS), the CEO and his entire top management team began their UPS careers as clerks, delivery drivers, or commercial banks, many utilities (such as the Bell companies), government agencies, and the U.S. military.

III. Academy Culture

Organisations with an *academy culture* also tend to hire recruits early often directly from college—as do those with club cultures. However, academy cultures emphasize training employees to become expert in a particular function. For example, someone hired as a marketing representative would be unlikely to serve a stint in manufacturing. The academy culture stresses continuity of service, functional expertise, and institutional wisdom. Although there is some opportunity for "fast trackers," the academy culture is more likely to appeal to the steady climber who enjoys mastering the job. Academy cultures exist at Coca-Cola, IBM, Proctor & Gamble and many other consumer product firms, the big three U.S. automakers, pharmaceutical companies, and many electronic and office products companies.

IV. Fortress Culture

The *fortress culture* is preoccupied with survival. Organisations with a fortress culture promise little in the way of job security and have difficulty in rewarding employees for good performance. Typically, they may be in the process of downsizing or restructuring, causing the dismissal of many employees. A fortress culture might appeal to individuals who relish the challenge of turning a company around, but wouldn't appeal to those who desire a sense of belonging opportunities for professional growth, or secure future income. Some fortress culture organisations that have fallen on hard times previously had baseball team, club, or academy cultures. Others are firms in businesses that are characterised by periodic boom and bust cycles. Currently, the ranks of fortress companies include some forest products firm, hotel, oil and gas companies, publishers, large retailers, and textile firms.

Most organisations probably cannot be categorised neatly as having a baseball team, club, academy, or fortress culture. Some may be a blend of these types; others may be in transition between types or even be different types at different times.

These cultural types are offered as a way of introducing the concept of culture and understanding some important distinctions among organisations. However, other labels or a categories of cultural types are commonly used.

UNIFORMITY OF CULTURE

A common misconception is that an organisation has a uniform culture. However, at least as anthropology uses the concept, it is probably more accurate to treat organisations "as if" they had a uniform culture. "All organisations 'have' culture in the sense that they are embedded in specific societal cultures and are part of them." According to this view, an organisational culture is a common perception held by the organisation's members. Everyone in the organisation would have to share this perception. However, all may not do so to the same degree. As a result, there can be a dominant culture as well as subcultures throughout a typical organisation.

A dominant culture is a set of core values shared by a majority of the organisation's members. For example, most employees at Southwest Airlines seem to subscribe to such values as hard work, company loyalty, and the need for customer service. Southwest employees take to heart cultural values such as : irreverence is okay; it's okay to be yourself; have fun at work; take the competition seriously, but not yourself; and do whatever it takes for the customer. At Hewlett-Packard, most of the employees seem to share a concern for product innovativeness, product quality, and responsiveness to customer needs. At Wal-Mart stores, the associates—a term Wal-Mart uses for its employees that is very symptomatic of its culture—share a concern for customer service, hard work, and company loyalty. At Arizona Public Services Company, the personnel share a common concern for providing quality service and eliminating rate increases in the foreseeable future. These values create a dominant culture in these organisations that helps guide the day-to-day behaviour of employees.

Important, but often overlooked, are the subcultures in an organisation. A subculture is a set of values share by a minority, usually a small minority, of the organisation's members. Subcultures typically are a result of problems or experiences that are shared by members of a department or unit. For example, after the AT&T break-up several years ago, the consumer products division, which has its own subculture in the huge corporation, was in deep trouble. It was rapidly losing market share of residential phones to innovative competitors. Division losses were in eight-digit figures. Top-level corporate management gave the mandate: either turn the division around quickly or it would be dropped. This obviously spurred the division into action. The division managers felt that it was unthinkable for their company—which grew out of *Alexander Graham Bell's* invention over a hundred years ago—to cease making phones. They slashed the division's bureaucracy, reducing seven layers, to four, moved manufacturing offshore, and, in less than two years, AT&T's consumer products division became the industry's most ferocious competitors.

Subcultures can weaken and undermine an organisation if they are in conflict with the dominant culture and/or the overall objectives. Successful firms, however, find that this is not always the case. Most subcultures are formed to help the members of a particular group deal with the specific day-to-day problems with which they are confronted. The members may also support many, if not all, of the core values of the dominant culture. In the case of AT&T's consumer products division, the subculture became a model for the cultural changes that top-level management were trying to accomplish for the whole corporation.

ORGANISATIONAL CULTURE AND EFFECTIVENESS

The organisational culture of an enterprise operating globally will influence and be influenced by the national cultures in which it operates. Since global firms operate in different countries, they may develop organisation cultures that differ from the culture of any one nation. Nestle, the Anglo-Swiss Condensed Milk Company, was established in 1866 by a pair of American brothers. Today only 2 percent of Nestle's business is done in its home country. Nestle operates 200 units throughout the world. Its organisation culture is different from the culture of any one country.

When referring to an organisational culture, we mean something similar to the culture in a society. An organisation's culture consists of shared values, beliefs, assumptions, perceptions, norms, artifacts, and patterns of behaviour. According to culture experts, culture is to the organisation what personality is to the individual—a hidden, yet unifying theme that provides meaning, direction, and mobilisation. It is the culture in an organisation that helps workers respond to the inevitable uncertainties and chaos of performing a job.

Second, organisational culture is a way of looking at and thinking about behaviour of and in organisations, a perspective to take for understanding what is occurring. In this manner, organisational culture refers to a collection of themes that attempt to explain and predict how organisations and people in them behave in different circumstances.

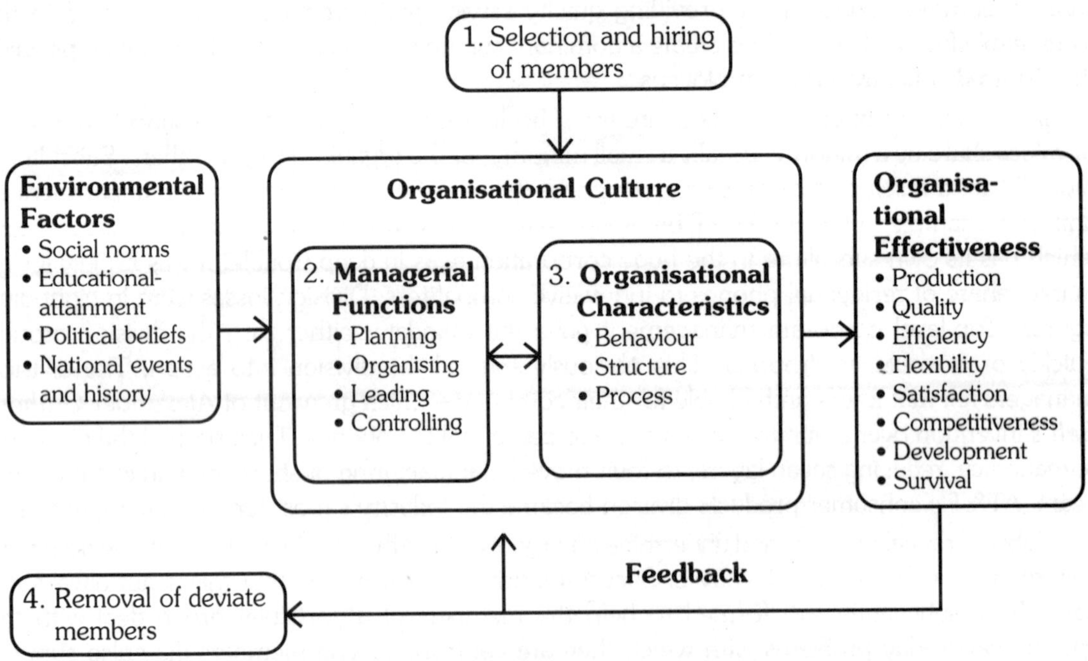

Fig. 2. *Organisational Culture and Effectiveness.*

NAME OF THE CULTURE	TOUGH-PERSON	WORK HARD/ PLAY HARD	GET YOUR COMPANY	PROCESS
Type of risks that are assumed	High	Low	High	Low
Type of feedback from decisions	Fast	Fast	Slow	Slow
Typical kinds of organisations that use this culture	Construction, cosmetics, television radio, venture capitalism, management consulting.	Real estate, computer firms, auto distributors, door-to-door sales operations, retail stores, mass consumer sales.	Oil, aerospace, capital goods manufacturers, architectural firms, investment banks, mining and smelting firms, military.	Banks, insurance companies, utilities pharmaceuticals, financial-service organisations, many agencies of the government.
The ways survivors and/or heroes in this culture behave	They have a tough attitude. They are individualistic. They can tolerate all-or-nothing risks. They are superstitious.	They are super salespeople. They often are friendly, half-fellow-well-met types. They use a team approach to problem solving. They are non-superstitious.	They can endure long-term ambiguity. They always double-check their decisions. They are technically competent. They have a strong respect for authority.	They are very cautious and protective of their own flank. They are orderly and punctual. They are good at attending to detail. They always follow established procedures.
Strengths of the personnel/culture	They can get things done in short order.	They are able to quickly produce a high volume of work.	They can generate high-quality inventions and major scientific break-*throughs.*	They bring order and system to the workplace.
Weaknesses of the personnel/culture	They do not learn from past mistakes. Everything tends to be short-term in orientation. The virtues of cooperation are ignored.	They look for quick-fix solutions. They have a short-term time perspective. They are more committed to action than to problem solving.	They are extremely slow in getting things done. Their organisations are vulnerable to short-term economic fluctuations. Their organisations often face cash-flow problems.	There is lots of red tape. Initiative is downplayed. They face long hours and boring work.
Habits of the survivors and/or heroes	They dress in fashion. They live in "in" places. They like one-on-one sports such as tennis. They enjoy scoring points off one another in verbal interaction.	They avoid extremes in dress. They live in tract houses. They prefer team sports such as touch football. They like to drink together.	They dress according to their organisational rank. Their housing matches their hierarchical position. They like sports such as golf, in which the outcome is unclear until the end of the game. The older members serve as mentors for the younger ones.	They dress according to hierarchical rank. they live in apartments or no-frills homes. They enjoy process sports like jogging and swimming. They like discussing memos.

Organisational culture, in simple terms, in considered to be the "personality" or "feel" of the organisation. Culture influences the way people act within organisations. How they perform, view their job, work with colleagues, and look at the future are largely determined by cultural norms, values, and beliefs. These ingredients constitute the culture.

Despite being an important concept, organisational culture as a perspective from which to observe and understand behaviour within organisations has its limitations. First, it's not the only way to view organisations. We have already discussed the goal and systems view without so much as mentioning culture. Second, as with so many concepts, organisational culture is not defined the same way by any two popular theorists or researchers. Some definitions of culture are :

(a) Symbols, languages, ideologies, rituals, and myths.

(b) Organisational scripts derived from the personal scripts of the organisation's founder(s) or dominant leader(s).

(c) Is a product; is historical; is based on symbols; and is an abstraction from behaviour and the products of behaviour.

(d) "A pattern of basic assumptions invented, discovered, or developed by a group as it learns to cope with its problems of external adaptation and internal integration—that has worked well enough to be considered valid and therefore to be taught to new members as the correct way to perceive, think, and feel in relation to those problems."

Negative cultures are counterproductive to management efforts to improve performance. Consider what can happen in the banking industry. Although exceptions exist, cultures of contemporary banks on the whole emphasise values and beliefs that discourage the behaviour required to compete in the recently deregulated banking industry. Bank cultures that value conservative, *status quo* behaviour are incompatible with the need to be competitive in the marketplace. Some banks have attempted major overhauls in their corporate cultures in an effort to make them more dynamic. First Chicago and Bank of America are among the major banks that have exerted considerable efforts to redirect their cultures.

The realisation that organisational culture is an important cause of organisational effectiveness is widespread in management practice. Not so wide-spread, however, is understanding of how management can change an organisational culture that inhibits organisational effectiveness. Many management practitioners and consultants are experimenting with alternative change approaches. Much more will be learned as managers move toward the 21st century. At this point, however, we can suggest some tentative guidelines for changing culture.

First, you must understand that organisational culture—the system of shared values, beliefs, and norms—is the product of the interaction among the selection process; the managerial functions; the organisation's behaviour, structure, and process; the larger environment in which the organisation exists; and the removal process shown in Fig. 2. Organisational culture encompasses both the managerial functions and organisational characteristics. Management is both a cause of and a part of organisational characteristics. The existing culture of any organisation reflects past and present managerial planning, organising, leading, and controlling activities. For example, a manufacturing plant culture that values operations efficiency (quality of output, customer satisfaction, efficient use of resources) does so because manufacturing managers have stated missions, goals, and objectives in those terms. These managers evaluate employees in terms of accuracy—for example, minimum number of errors—and they publicly proclaim the importance of doing things correctly. Manufacturing executives have created the culture by virtue of their own managerial actions, and they hire and socialise employees to adopt and accept the important beliefs and values of that culture.

Employees who are not well matched with or suited to the organisational culture will exit, voluntarily or involuntarily. Deviants are often isolated or ostracised; they are cut off from communications, are not involved in rituals, and may be simply ignored. In some cases, deviants may be asked to leave or to resign. The deviant can be identified by examining effectiveness measures.

At each of the four points (1, 2, 3, and 4) identified in Figure, management can intervene to alter the organisational culture. While it is correct to state that organisational culture is difficult to change, understanding where to begin the cultural change process appears to be important for managing organisational behaviour. Studies comparing performance of American firms with that of European, Japanese, and other Asian competitors have introduced concepts of culture and changing culture as possible explanations of differences in competitive effectiveness. This line of study suggests that discussing organisational behaviour without including culture as a specific organisational variable is incomplete analysis.

If management can create organisational culture, management should be able to use the same means to change it. But it's not that simple or easy a task. Cultures are self-reinforcing. Once in place, cultures provide stability and certainty for their members. Individuals know what is expected, what is important, and what to do. They quite naturally resist any threatened disruption of the existing culture.

Managers must practice planning, organising, leading, and controlling that are consistent with the beliefs and values of the desired culture. All four functions can contribute to changing the culture, but it is generally agreed that leading is most important. By personal example and behaviour, managers can demonstrate how things should be done. But they must be capable managers and respected leaders.

NATIONAL CULTURE

A national culture is a set of values, attitudes, beliefs, and norms shared by a majority of the inhabitants of a country. These become embodied in the laws and regulations of the society, as well as in the generally accepted norms of the country's social system. People in a society learn what to notice and what not to notice, how to behave with each other, and how to handle responsibility, success, and failure. Most people are unaware of just how their culture has influenced their values, attitudes, beliefs, and norms.

In most countries, a dominant national culture exists. However, even the most homogenous nations such as Japan contain subcultures with distinct characteristics. In the United States, powerful subcultures exist among many groups such as the Amish in Pennsylvania, the Cajuns in Louisiana, the Russian immigrants in Brighton Beach, New York, and the Pueblo Indians in

Colorado. Strong national culture may create a state of conflict with subcultures that undermines the society and subgroups.

ORGANISATIONAL CULTURE *VERSUS* NATIONAL CULTURE

The challenges facing Mazda's new president as he tries to change Mazda's organisational culture. But we also saw how Japan's national culture was closely intertwined with Mazda's corporate culture. Throughout this book we have argued that national differences—that is, national cultures—must be taken into account if accurate predictions are to be made about organisational behaviour in different counties. It seems appropriate at this point, then, to ask the question: Does national culture override an organisation's culture? Is an IBM facility in Germany, for example, more likely to reflect German ethnic culture or IBM's corporate culture?

The research indicates that national culture has a greater impact on employees than does their organisation's culture. German employees at an IBM facility in Munich, therefore, will be influenced more by German culture than by IBM's culture. These findings, incidentally, are consistent with what the new president at Mazda found—that Japan's national culture has strongly shaped this company's organisational culture, and that Japanese employees resist Ford-type cultural values. Our conclusion: As influential as organisational culture is to understand the behaviour of people at work, national culture is even more so.

The preceding conclusion has to be qualified to reflect the self-selection that goes on at the hiring stage. IBM, for example, may be less concerned with hiring the "typing Italian" for it Italian operations than in hiring an Italian who fits within the IBM way of doing things. Historically, Italians who have a high need for autonomy are more likely to go to Olivetti than IBM. Why? Because Olivetti's organisational culture is informal and non structured. It has tended to allow employees considerably more freedom than IBM does. In fact, Olivetti seeks to hire individuals who are impatient, risk taking, and innovative—qualities in job candidates that IBM's Italian operations historically sought to exclude in new hires.

HISTORY AND CULTURE

A country's history provides insight into the development of a national culture. The US culture has been shaped by Native Americans, pioneers, immigrants, its vast size, and a large base of natural resources. The importance of the individual has been embedded in American history and folklore for centuries.

The Atlantic and Pacific Oceans, separating the United States from other continents, have created a tendency toward isolation, a distrust of alliances, and a general lack of concern about political issues and policies in other countries. Americans have viewed their country as an island, separate from world conditions, problems, and politics. However, as the world became more interdependent and transportation systems evolved, Americans were suddenly brought into contact with world problems such as hunger, religious conflict, collapsing regimes, environmental degradation, and territorial disputes.

National culture, subcultures, organisational culture and history all influence behaviour patterns of employees, structures, and processes found in organisations. The complexity of these patterns, structures, and processes requires careful analysis of many different variables. Despite such complexity, it is more important than ever for managers to attempt to unravel the dimensions that differentiate cultures.

Figure 2 presents a model that illustrates how national and organisational culture interact to impact organisational effectiveness. The organisational culture results from the national culture which then effects workplace values, attitudes, beliefs, norms, and goals. The result of these interactions and effects is behaviour in such forms as performance, attendance, satisfaction, and ethical behaviour.

STRONG *VERSUS* WEAK CULTURES

It has become increasingly popular to differentiate between strong and weak cultures. The argument here is the strong cultures have a greater impact on employee behaviour and are more directly related to reduced turnover.

In a strong culture, the organisation's core values are both intensely held and widely shared. The more members who accept the core values and the greater their commitment to those values is, the stronger the culture is. Consistent with this definition, a strong culture will have a great influence on the behaviour of its members because the high degree of sharedness and intensity creates an internal climate of high behavioural control. For example, Seattle-based Nordstrom has developed one of the strongest service cultures in the retailing industry. Nordstrom employees know in no uncertain terms what is expected of them and these expectations to a long way in shaping their behaviour.

One specific result of a strong culture should be lower employee turnover. A strong culture demonstrates high agreement among members about what the organisation stands for. Such unanimity of purpose builds cohesiveness, loyalty, and organisational commitment. These qualities, in turn, lessen employees propensity to leave the organisation.

CULTURE *VERSUS* FORMALISATION

A strong organisational culture increases behavioural consistency. In this sense, we should recognise that a strong culture can act as a substitute for formalisation.

High formalisation in an organisation creates predictability, orderliness, and consistency. Our point is that a strong culture achieves the same end without the need for written documentation. Therefore, we should view formalisation and culture as two different roads to a common destination. The stronger an organisation's culture, the less management need be concerned with developing formal rules and regulations to guide employee behaviour. Those guides will the internalised in employees when they accept the organisation's culture.

CREATING AND MAINTAINING A CULTURE

The ways in which an organisation functions and is managed may have both intended and unintended effects on maintaining or changing organisational culture. Figure 2 shows a basic method of maintaining an organisation's culture: The organisation attempts to hire individuals who, in some sense, fit the organisational culture. In addition, organisations maintain cultures by removing employees who consistently or markedly deviate from accepted behaviours and activities.

Specific methods for maintaining organisational culture, however, are a great deal more complicated than just hiring and firing the right people. The most powerful reinforces of the organisation's culture are:

(1) what managers and teams pay attention to, measure, and control;
(2) the ways managers (particularly top managers) react to critical incidents and organisational crises;
(3) managerial and team role modelling, teaching, and coaching;
(4) criteria for allocating rewards and status;
(5) criteria for recruitment, selection, promotion, and removal from the organisation; and
(6) organisational rites, ceremonies, and stories.

What Managers and Team Pay Attention to one of the more powerful methods of maintaining organisational culture involves the processes and behaviours that managers and teams pay attention to, that is, the things that get noticed and commented on. Dealing with things systematically sends strong signals to employees about what is important and expected of them. For example, a large toy manufacturer installed a management-by-objectives (MBO) performance appraisal system. After a few years, top management discovered that the MBO process was working well in one part of the corporation but not in another. An investigation revealed that MBO was working well where senior management was enthusiastic and committed. These managers perceived real benefits from the program and conveyed these beliefs to others. Where MBO was failing, senior management viewed MBO as just another bureaucratic exercise. Subordinates quickly learned to complete the paperwork but ignore the purpose of the MBO system. The firm's top management concluded that MBO would work only when employees believe that managers care about the results and pay attention to them.

Reactions to Incidents and Crises. When an organisation faces a crisis, the handling of that crisis by managers and employees reveals a great deal about the culture. The manner in which the crisis is dealt with can either reinforce the existing culture or bring out new values and norms that change the culture in some way. For example, an organisation facing a dramatic reduction in demand for its product might react by laying off or firing employees. Or it might reduce employee hours or rates of pay with no work-force reduction. The alternative chosen indicates the value placed on human resources and may reinforce and maintain the current culture or indicate a major change in the culture. Such a situation occurred at Hewlett-Packard early in its history. The company responded to declining demand for its products by reducing hours. It went to a schedule of working nine days every two weeks — a 10% reduction in time with a corresponding cut in pay-rather than fire or lay off employees. Hewlett-Packard thus sent a clear message to its employees about their value to the company. This response became deeply ingrained in the company's folklore and now serve to reinforce this aspect of its culture.

Role Modelling, Teaching, and Coaching aspects of the organisation's culture are communicated to employees by the way managers fulfil their roles. In addition, managers and teams may specifically incorporate important cultural messages into training programs and day-to-day coaching on the job. For example, training films shown to new employees might emphasize customer service. Also, managers might demonstrate good customer or client service practices in their interactions with customers. The repeated emphasis on good customer relations in both training and day-to-day behaviour would help create and maintain a customer-oriented culture throughout the organisation. Arthur Anderson, the large public accounting firm, sends all newly hired accountants to a 15-week training program not only to learn accounting procedures used by the firm, but also to become steeped in the organisation's culture.

Allocation of Rewards and *Status.* The rewards and punishments attached to various behaviours convey to employees the priorities and values of both individual managers and the organisation. Similarly, the organisation's status system maintains certain aspects of its culture. The distribution of perks (e.g., a corner office on an upper floor, carpeting, a private secretary, or a private parking space) demonstrates which roles and behaviours are most valued by the organisation. However, an organisation may use rewards and status symbols ineffectively and inconsistently. If it does, it misses a great opportunity to influence its culture because an organisation's reward practices and its culture appear to be strongly linked. In fact, some authorities believe that the most effective method for influencing organisational culture may be through the reward system.

Recruitment, Selection, Promotion, and Removal. As Figure 2 suggests, one of the fundamental ways that organisations maintain a culture is through the recruitment process. In addition, the criteria used to determine who is assigned to specific jobs or positions, who gets raises and promotions and why, who is removed from the organisation by firing or early retirement, and so on reinforce and demonstrate basic aspects of a culture. These criteria become known throughout the organisation and can maintain or change an existing culture.

Organisational Rites, Ceremonies, and *Stories. Organisational Rites* and *Ceremonies* are organised, planned activities or rituals that have important cultural meaning. Certain managerial or employee activities can become organisational rituals that are interpreted as part of the organisational culture. Rites and ceremonies that sustain organisational culture include rites of passage, degradation, enhancement, and integration. Table contains examples of each of these four types of rites and identifies some of their desirable consequences.

A ceremony used at Mary Kay Cosmetics Company provides a good example of rites of enhancement. During elaborate awards ceremonies, gold and diamond pins, fur stoles, and the use of pink Cadillacs are presented to saleswomen who achieve their sales quotas. The ceremonies are held in a setting reminiscent of a Miss America pageant with all the participants dressed in glamorous evening clothes. The setting is typically an auditorium with a stage in front of a large, cheering audience. The ceremonies clearly are intended to increase the identity and status of high-performing employees and emphasize the rewards for performance.

Many of the underlying beliefs and values of organisation's culture are expressed as legends and stories that become part of its folklore. These stories and legends transmit the existing culture from older to new employees and emphasize important aspects of that culture. Some stories may persist for a long time. For example, a Fortune 500 manufacturer had a factory with a history of hostile labour-management relations, low productivity, and poor quality. The company hired a consultant who started out by talking with the employees in the plant. They eagerly told him about the plant manager, a 300-pound gorilla named Sam with a disposition that made King Kong look like Bonzo the chimp. Employees told a number of outrageous stories about Sam's behaviour. The stunned consultant made an appointment to see the plant manager. When the consultant walked into the manager's office, he saw a slim, pleasant-looking man behind the desk who introduced himself as Paul. "Where Sam?" asked the consultant. Paul, looking puzzled, replied, "Sam has been dead for nine years."

COMPONENTS OF CULTURE

Culture factors manifest themselves in a number of ways in formal organisations. Conveniently, culture can be classified into two parts—material and non-material. Though such a classification seems something like oversimplification, anthropologists resort to the similar categorisation.

I. Material Culture

It comprises of all the things that man produces—artifacts. These man-made objects are created by technology and often referred to as material culture. Food, clothing, housing, tools and transportation devices are all visible items, whereas advancement in science—X-rays, Gama rays, etc., all belong to the category of invisible items. These material aspects of culture have great relevance to the way in which organisations are created and made operative.

In the business organisation, one finds artifacts somewhat similar to those of society. Sometimes, some minor variations can be noticed in organisations with regard to material culture. For example, in Army, the officers are attired in an identifying uniform; similarly in hospitals the nurses have special white uniform, doctors have different uniform from surgeons.

Another important factor of great importance is the tools and equipment used in business organisations. The extensive use of machinery, power, and automated equipment in the recent past by business organisations has resulted in 'industrial culture.'

II. Non-material Culture

Non-material culture refers to the intangible beliefs, philosophies, habits, customs among the members of organisation or society. Non-material cultural aspects also affect the nature of organisations significantly. Rituals, taboos, jargon are the famous examples of non-material culture.

(a) Rituals. One feature of non-material culture is the use of rituals. Rituals are usually associated with the ceremonies and tribal observances requiring a number of people to act in union according to prescribed formulae. These rituals are not limited to religion and religious ceremonies alone, they are followed in our society and very much in business organisations. For instance, in some institutions employees will be asked to come in a particular uniform during some organisational ceremonies (seminars, annual meetings, and annual functions etc.). It is not rare to find rituals in business institutions. Some ceremonies in organisations have definite ritualistic flavour. For example, some organisations make it a practice to treat outgoing employee at the time of retirement; and farewell banquets are held in honour of the occasion.

(b) **Taboos.** Another feature of non-material culture is taboo. Every society has a system of taboos. These taboos represent generally the nature of acceptable human conduct affecting morality. In organisations, for instance, no one calls the president by his first name. It may be wrong to accept gifts from customers or suppliers. In fact, in almost all organisations, groups exist to punish the members for non-compliance of the existing taboos.

(c) **Jargon.** The most important non-material cultural factor is the jargon or the language used by people when they are in a group. For instance, teenagers develop a type of slang that is virtually incomprehensible and unpalatable to many adult members. Further, railroaders have a special language which they use when they join as a group. Similarly, musicians, have special words for ordinary things and deeds of day-to-day life.

DEVELOPING ORGANISATIONAL CULTURE

How does an organisational culture develop? *Edgar Schein* suggests that organisational culture forms in response to two major challenges that confront every organisation: (1) external adaptation and survival; and (2) internal integration.

External adaptation and *survival* has to do with how the organisation will find a niche in and cope with its constantly changing external environment. *External adaptation* and survival involve addressing the following issues:

(i) *Mission and strategy:* Identifying the primary mission of the organisation; selecting strategies to pursue this mission.

(ii) *Goals:* Setting specific goals.

(iii) *Means*: Determining how the pursue the goals; means include selecting an organisational structure and reward system.

(iv) *Measurement*: Establishing criteria to measure how well individuals and teams are accomplishing their goals.

Internal integration concerns the establishment and maintenance of effective working relationship among the members of the organisation. *Internal integration* involves addressing the following issues:–

(i) *Language and concepts:* Identifying methods of communication; developing a shared meaning for important concepts.

(ii) *Group and team boundaries*: Establishing criteria for membership in groups and teams.

(iii) *Power and status:* Determining rules for acquiring, maintaining, and losing power and status.

(iv) *Rewards and punishments*: Developing systems for encouraging desirable behaviour and discouraging undesirable behaviours.

An organisational culture emerges when members share knowledge and assumptions as they discover or develop ways of coping with external adaptation and internal integration issues.

Fig. 2 shows a common pattern in the emergence of organizational cultures. In new companies, a founder, top manager, or a few key individuals may largely determine the organisation's culture. Later in the life of the organisation, its culture will reflect a complex mixture of the assumptions,

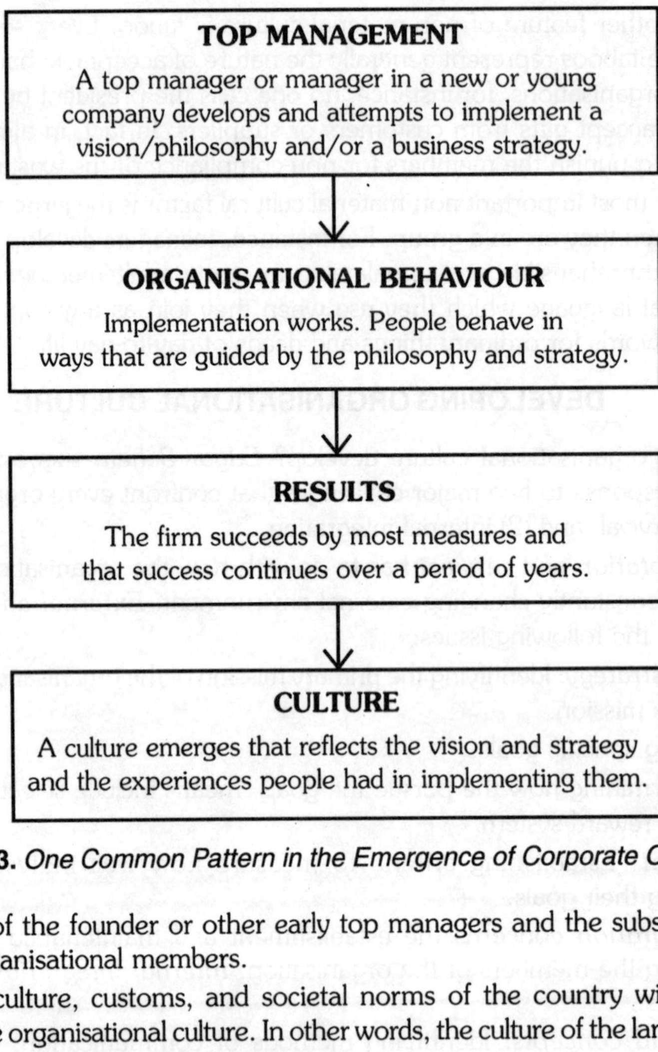

Fig. 3. *One Common Pattern in the Emergence of Corporate Culture.*

values, and ideas of the founder or other early top managers and the subsequent learning and experiences of organisational members.

The national culture, customs, and societal norms of the country within which the firm operates also shape organisational culture. In other words, the culture of the larger society influences the culture of organisations operating within it.

The dominant values of a national culture can be reflected in the constraints imposed on organisations by their environments. For example, the form of government may have a dramatic impact on how an organisation does business in a country. In addition, the members of the organisation have been raised in a particular society and thus bring the dominant values of the society into the firm. For example, individuals learn values, such as freedom of speech or respect for individual privacy, from their societies. The presence or absence of these and other values within the larger society has implications for organisational behaviour. Finally, increased global operations have forced an awareness that differences in national culture may seriously affect organisational effectiveness. Multinational corporations such as IBM, Ford, and GE are discovering that organisational structures and cultures that might be effective in one part of the world may be ineffective in another.

CHANGING ORGANISATIONAL CULTURE

The same basic methods used to maintain an organisation's culture may be used to change it. Culture might be changed by:

(i) changing what managers and teams pay attention to,
(ii) changing how crisis situations are handled,
(iii) changing criteria for recruiting new members,
(iv) changing criteria for promotion within the organisation,
(v) changing criteria for allocating rewards, and
(vi) changing organisational rites and ceremonies.

For example, an organisational culture that tends to punish risk taking and innovation and reward risk avoidance might be deliberately altered through changes in the reward system. Employees could be encouraged to set riskier and more innovative goals for themselves in coaching and goal-setting sessions. In performance appraisal sessions and through merit raises, individuals could be rewarded for attempting more challenging tasks, even if they failed sometimes, than for attaining safe goals that required no innovative behaviour.

Changing organisational culture can be a tricky business, and at least two perspectives suggest caution. One concern is articulated by well-known management expert *Peter Drucker* who has questioned whether the deep, core values of organisational culture are amenable to change. In his view, focusing managerial efforts on changing on effective behaviour and procedures is more meaningful than attempting to change organisational culture. *Drucker* further argues that changing behaviour will work only if it can be based on the existing culture.

A second perspective that suggests caution in culture change considers the difficulties in accurately assessing organisational culture. Most large, complex organisations actually have more than one culture. General Electric, for example, has distinctly different cultures in different corporate units. Sometimes these multiple cultures are called subcultures. Faced with a variety of subculture, management may have difficulty, first, in accurately assessing them and, second, in effecting needed changes.

Despite these concerns, we believe that changing organisational cultures is both feasible and, in the case of failing organisations, sometimes essential. Successfully changing organisational culture requires:

(i) understanding the old culture first because a new culture can't be developed unless managers and employees understand where they are starting from;
(ii) providing support for employees and teams who have ideas for a better culture and are willing to act on their visions;
(iii) finding the most effective subculture in the organisation and using it as an example from which employees can learn;
(iv) not attacking culture head on but finding ways to help employees and teams do their jobs more effectively;
(v) treating the vision of a new culture as a guiding principle for change, not as a miracle worker;

(vi) recognising that significant organisation wide cultural change takes five to ten years; and

(vii) living the new culture because actions speak louder than words.

We cover planned organisational change extensively. Many of the specific techniques and methods for changing organisational behaviours presented in those chapters also may be used to change organisational culture. Indeed, any comprehensive program of organisational change, in some sense, is an attempt to change the culture of the organisation.

We can't overemphasise how difficult changing organisational cultures may be. In fact, the incompatibility of organisational cultures and their resistance to change has been one of the most significant barriers to successful corporate mergers. For a merger to be effective, at least one (one sometimes both) of the merging organisations may need to change its culture. The following Managing in Practice account describes just such a situation.

PERFORMANCE AND ORGANISATIONAL CULTURE

An underlying assumption of cultural change is that an organisation's culture and its performance or effectiveness are directly related. Thus the rationale for attempting cultural change is to create a more effective organisation.

The common theme of a number of popular books is that strong, well-developed culture are an important characteristic of organisations that have outstanding performance records. The term strong culture implies that most managers and employees share a set of consistent values and methods of doing business.

Strong cultures may be associated with strong performance for three reasons. First, a strong culture often provides for a good fit between strategy and culture. This fit is considered essential for successfully implementing corporate strategy. Second, a strong culture may lead to the alignment of goals among employees. That is, the majority of organisational participants share the same goals and have some basic agreement as to how to pursue them. Finally, a strong culture leads to employee commitment and motivation. In this view, culture is crucial for developing the dedication to excellent performance that characterises successful organisations.

Organisational culture and performance clearly are related, although the evidence regarding the exact nature of this relationship is mixed. For example, strong cultures may not always be superior to weak cultures. Some studies indicate that the type of culture may, in fact, be somewhat more important than its strength. A comparison of the cultures of 334 institutions of higher education revealed no differences in organisational effectiveness between those with strong cultures and those with weak cultures. However, the type of culture possessed by these institutions was related to their effectiveness. Colleges and universities that possessed a type of culture whose features matched their market niche and mission were more effective than institutions whose cultures lacked such a match.

Another cautionary note comes from studies showing that the relationship between many cultural attributes (featured in the popular press as being important for performance) and high performance hasn't been consistent over time. Based on what we know about culture-performance relationships, a contingency approach seems to be a good one for managers and organisations to take. Further investigations of this issue are unlikely to discover one "best" organisational culture (either in terms of strength or type).

A four-year study conducted of a large number of organisations resulted in the following conclusions about the relationships between culture and performance:

(i) Organisational culture can have a significant impact on a firm's long-term economic performance.

(ii) Organisational culture will probably be an even more important factor in determining the success or failure of firms in the next decade.

(iii) Organisational cultures that inhibit strong long-term financial performance are not rare; they develop easily, even in firms that are full of reasonable and intelligent people.

(iv) Although tough to change, organisational cultures can be made more performance enhancing.

High degrees of participative management and an emphasis on teamwork often are cited as characteristics of successful organisational cultures. In participative management, managers share decision-making, goal-setting, and problem-solving activities with employees. Of course, high levels of participation do not fit all settings and tasks. Further, changing an organisation from a more traditional management approach to greater collaboration with employees may be extremely difficult. A type of organisational culture designed to foster high performance with high levels of employee involvement is called a high performance-high commitment work culture. As with participative management, cultures that foster high involvement and commitment on the part of employees often exist in organisations that have a record of high performance.

Another type of organisational culture often associated with organisational effectiveness is a total quality culture, which values customers, continuous improvement, and teamwork. Employees in such a culture believe that customers are the key to the organisation's future. Employees expect their jobs to change as they constantly strive to improve and seek better ways of doing things. Moreover, employees in such a culture almost instinctively act as a team. Gillette provides an example of an organisation with a focus on customers, continuous improvement, and teamwork, as the following Managing Quality item demonstrates.

ETHICAL BEHAVIOUR AND ORGANISATIONAL CULTURE

Ethical problems in organisations continue to concern managers and employees greatly. However, researchers are only now beginning to explore the potential impact that organisational culture can have on ethical behaviour. Early findings indicate that organisational culture appears to affect ethical behaviour in several ways.

The ethics component of organisational culture is a complex interplay of formal and informal systems that may support either ethical or unethical organisational behaviour. The formal systems include leadership, structure, policies, reward systems, orientation and training programs, and decision-making processes. Informal systems include norms, heroes, rituals, language, myths, sagas, and stories.

Ethical business practices stem from ethical organisational cultures. For example, a culture emphasizing ethical norms provides support for ethical behaviour. In addition, top management plays a key role in fostering ethical behaviour. Moreover, all authority figures—managers and other professionals—in the organisation can encourage or discourage ethical behaviour. The presence or absence of ethical behaviour in managerial actions both influences and reflects the prevailing culture. The organisational culture may promote taking responsibility for the consequences of actions, thereby increasing the probability that individuals will behave ethically. Alternatively, the culture may diffuse responsibility for the consequences of unethical behaviour, thereby making such behaviour more likely. The following Managing Ethics account demonstrates the impact of organisational culture on ethical practices, including management's behaviours and policies.

THE ORGANISATIONAL SOCIALISATION PROCESS

Organisational socialisation is the process through which outsiders are transformed into accepted insiders. In effect, the socialisation process shapes newcomers to fit the organisational culture.

The culture asserts itself when the taken-for-granted cultural assumptions are in some way violated by the uninitiated and provoke a response. As the uninitiated bump into one after another taken-for-granted assumption, more acculturated employees respond in a variety of ways (tell stories, offer advice, ridicule, lecture, shun, and so forth) that serve to mould the way in which the newcomer thinks about his or her role and about "how things are done around here."

According to the story, an employee accidentally discovered the tape but was unable to get his superiors to buy the idea. Marketing studies predicted a relatively small demand for the new material. Undaunted, the employee found a way to sneak into the board room and tape down the minutes of board members with his transparent tape. The board was impressed enough with the novelty to give it a try and experienced incredible success.

Upon hearing this story, a 3M newcomer has believable, concrete evidence that innovation and persistence pay-off at 3M. It has been said that stories are "social road maps" for employees, telling them where to go and where not to go and what will happen when they get there. Moreover, stories are remembered longer than abstract facts or rules and regulations. How many times have you recalled a professor's colourful story but forgotten the rest of the lecture?

STRENGTHENING ORGANISATIONAL CULTURES

Given the inherent fussiness of organisational cultures, how can managers spot cultural weak spots needing improvement? One respected researcher tells managers to "ask," "Observe," "read," and "feel" when gathering information on organisational cultures, but also cautions:

Reading a culture is an interpretive, subjective activity. There are no exact answers, and two observers may come up with somewhat different descriptions of the same culture. The validity of the diagnosis must be judged by the utility of the insights it provides, not by its "correctness" as determined by some objective criteria.

It is instructive and important to compare intentions with actual behaviour. Taken-for-granted beliefs and values generally need to be inferred from behaviour. Symptoms of a weak organisational culture include the following:

(i) Inward focus : Has internal politics become more important than realworld problems and the marketplace?

(ii) Short-term focus: Is too much time and energy spent on achieving short-term results?
(iii) Morale problems : Is there chronic unhappiness and high turnover?
(iv) Fragmentation / inconsistency: Is there a lack of "fit" in the way people behave, communicate, and perceive problems and opportunities?
(v) Emotional outbursts: Does emotionalism override sound judgment and rational thinking?
(vi) Ingrown subcultures: Is there a lack of communication among subunits?
(vii) Warfare among subcultures: Has constructive competition given way to destructive conflict?
(viii) Subculture elitism: Have organisational units become exclusive "clubs" with restricted entry? Have subcultural values become more important than the organisation's values?

Evidence of these symptoms may encourage a potential recruit to look elsewhere. Each of these symptoms of a weak organisational culture can be a formidable barrier to organisational effectiveness. Organisations with strong cultures, such as United Parcel Service, have done a good job of avoiding these symptoms.

CROSS-CULTURAL TRAINING

In line with our earlier definition, culture is the unique system of values, beliefs, and symbols that foster patterned behaviour in a given population. It is difficult to distinguish the individual from his or her cultural context. Consequently, people tend to be very protective of their cultural identity. Careless defiance of cultural norms or traditions by outsiders can result in grave personal insult and put important business dealings at risk. Cultural sensitivity can be learned, fortunately, through cross-cultural training.

Specific Techniques. Cross-cultural training is defined as any form of guided experience aimed at helping people live and work comfortably in another culture. Following is a list of five basic cross-cultural training techniques, ranked in order of increasing complexity:

(i) *Documentary programs.* Trainees read about a foreign country's history, culture, institutions, geography, and economics. Video-taped presentations also are often used.
(ii) *Culture assimilator.* Cultural familiarity is achieved through exposure to a series of simulated intercultural incidents, or typical problem situations. This technique has been used to quickly train those who are given short notice of a foreign assignment.
(iii) *Language instruction.* Conversational language skills are taught through a variety of methods. Months, sometimes years, of study are required to master difficult languages. But as a cross-cultural communications professor recently noted, "To speak more than one language is no longer a luxury, it is a necessity."
(iv) *Sensitivity training.* Experiential exercises teach awareness of the impact of one's actions on others.
(v) *Field experience.* First-hand exposure to ethnic subcultures in one's own country or to foreign cultures heightens awareness.

Is One Technique Better Than Another? A study of eighty (sixty-three male, seventeen female) managers from a U.S. electronics company attempted to compare the relative effectiveness of different training techniques. A documentary approach was compared with an interpersonal approach. The latter combined sensitivity training and local ethnic field experience. The two techniques were judged equally effective at promoting cultural adjustment, as measured during the managers' three-month stay in South Korea. The researchers recommended a combination of documentary and interpersonal training. The importance of language training was diminished in this study because the managers dealt primarily with English-speaking Koreans.

Considering that 57 percent of American companies have no formal expatriate training programs, the key issue is not which type of training is better, but whether companies have any systematic cross-cultural training at all.

An Integrated Expatriate Staffing System. Cross-cultural training, in whatever form, should not be an isolated experience. Rather, it should be part of an integrated selection-orientation-repatriation process focused on a distinct career path. The ultimate goal should be a positive and productive overseas experience for the employee and his or her family and a smooth professional and cultural re-entry back home.

During the selection phase, the usual interview should be supplemented with an orientation session for the candidate's family. This session gives everyone an opportunity to "select themselves out" before a great deal of time and money has been invested. Experience has shown that, upon arrival at the foreign assignment, family sponsors or assigned mentors are effective at reducing culture shock. Sponsors and menthors ease the expatriate family through the critical first six months by answering naive but important questions and by serving as cultural translators.

Finally, repatriation should be a forethought rather than an afterthought. Candidates for foreign assignments deserve a firm commitment from their organisation that a successful tour of duty will lead to a step up the career ladder upon return. Expatriates who spend their time worrying about being leapfrogged while they are absent from headquarters are less likely to succeed.

Relying on Local Managerial Talent

In recent years, the expensive expatriate failure problem and general trends toward geocentrism and globalism have resulted in a greater reliance on managers from host countries. Foreign nationals already know the language and culture and do not require huge relocation expenditures. In addition, host-country governments tend to look favourably on a greater degree of local control. On the negative side, local managers may have an inadequate knowledge of home-office goals and procedures. The staffing of foreign positions is necessarily a case-by case proposition.

CROSS-CULTURAL RESEARCH FINDINGS

An increasing body of research attempts to empirically investigate cultural variation and its impact on behaviour and styles of management. The research continues to attempt to deal with cultural dimensions that are difficult to reliably and validly measure and that are difficult to translate in various languages. The studies presented in the section are not without their limitations and problems. However, they are major attempts to study cross-cultural issues.

I. Hofstede's Research

Geert Hofstede, a Dutch researcher, decided to study how cultures in countries are similar and different. He developed a survey instrument and administered it to IBM offices in 40 countries. A total of 116,000 survey instruments were returned and analysed. The initial *Hofstede* survey data resulted in four dimensions being identified as explaining differences and similarities in cultures : uncertainty avoidance, masculinity-femininity, individualism-collectivism, and power distance.

Uncertainty Avoidance

This dimension concerns the degree to which people are comfortable with ambiguous situations and with the inability to predict future events with accuracy. People with weak uncertainty avoidance feel comfortable even though they are unsure about future events. Their attitudes are reflected in such statements as :

(i) Life is inherently uncertain and is most easily dealt with if taken one day at a time.
(ii) There should be as few rules as possible, and rules that cannot be kept should be changed or eliminated.

In contrast, strong uncertainty avoidance people are uncomfortable when they are unsure what the future holds. Their attitudes are reflected by such statements as :

(i) The uncertainty inherent in life is threatening and must be fought continually.
(ii) Having a stable, secure life is extremely important.

In cultures characterised by high uncertainty avoidance, behaviour is motivated to some degree by fear of the unknown. People in such cultures attempt to reduce or avoid uncertainty by establishing rules, policies, and procedures. In Japan, for example, where life time employment is somewhat common in large organisations, there is high uncertainty avoidance.

Masculinity-Femininity

Hofstede used the term masculinity to designated the degree to which a culture emphasise assertiveness, dominance, and independence. People in a culture that has a high masculinity orientation believe that :

(i) Sex roles in society should be clearly differentiated; men are intended to lead and women to follow.
(ii) Ambition and assertiveness provide the motivation behind behaviour.

Femininity describes a culture's tendency to favour such values as interdependence, compassion, and emotional openness. People in a culture oriented toward femininity hold the following kinds of beliefs :

(i) Sex roles in society should be fluid and flexible; sexual equality is desirable.
(ii) The quality of life is more important than personal performance and visible accomplishments.

Work in cultures can be divided on the basis of a masculine-feminine dimensions. In masculine cultures, men possess jobs that contain power, authority, and responsibility. In feminine-oriented cultures, the roles of teaching, caring for patients, and helping the less fortunate are valued. There would also be a more equality-based norm between the sexes. Neither men nor women would be expected to be better managers or leaders. Individual talents and skills, and not gender, are the focus for acceptance and recognition in the feminine-oriented national culture country.

II. Power Distance

This refers to the degree to which members of a society accept differences in power and status among themselves. In national cultures that tolerate only a small degree of power distance, norms and values suggest that power differences should be minimal. Such cultures prefer participative management and worker involvement in decision making. Individuals in such cultures believe that :

(i) Superiors should be readily accessible to subordinates.

(ii) Using power is neither inherently good nor inherently evil; whether power is good or evil depends on the purposes for and consequences of its use.

On the other hand, in national cultures characterised by a large degree of power distance, norms and values based on hierarchical distribution predominate. People in these cultures use authority and power to coordinate individual work and behaviours. Individuals in large power distance culture believe that :

(i) Power holders are entitled to special rights and privileges.

(ii) Superiors and subordinates should consider each other to be different kinds of people.

Authoritarian manager styles exist more in a large power distance culture than in a small power distance culture. Decentralisation, participation, and worker involvement are more likely to exist in a small power distance culture than in a large power distance culture.

CROSS-CULTURAL TRANSITIONS

A multinational corporation (MNC) might have operation in different nations but each operation is viewed as a relatively separate enterprise. Key human resources are usually from the company's home offices, and most decision-making remains at corporate headquarters. Thus, although the MNC is largely staffed by people from the nation in which a particular facility is found, managers from the corporation's home country retain most authority. The multinational corporation does not yet see its potential market as the world. Rather, it views each of its foreign operations as a specialised market for a particular product. In other words, each foreign subsidiary concentrates its efforts on the nation in which it is located.

In contrast to an MNC, the global corporation (GC) is structured so that national boundaries disappear and it hires the best persons for jobs irrespective of their national origin. The global corporation sees the world as its labour source as well as its marketplace. Thus, the global corporation will locate an operation wherever it can accomplish its goals in the most cost-effective way. The true global corporation also believes in a world market for essentially similar products. Moreover, the national affiliation of an employee becomes rather unimportant. For example, Mars Inc.-Spain has had an English general manager, a French finance manager, and a Swiss human resource manager.

Perhaps one of the most important tasks for the multinational or global corporation is managing the expatriate adjustment process. An expatriate manager is a manager from the corporation's home nation who is on a foreign assignment. The focus for the company will therefore be on the selection, training, appraisal, and compensation of the expatriate. Significant efforts will also be placed on career management as it relates to the expatriate's return to headquarters.

LEVELS OF CULTURE

According to *Edger Schein,* organisational culture has three levels. These are :

(i) Observable artifacts of culture,

(ii) Shared values, and

(iii) Common assumptions.

If these levels are considered as layers, then the deeper the level, the more difficult it becomes to diagnose and analyse the various aspects of organisational culture at that level. To achieve a comprehensive understanding of an organisation's culture, all three levels must be studied.

I. Observable Artifacts

These are the symbols of culture in the physical and social work environment and are most visible and accessible. Among the artifacts of culture are the following :

(i) *Organisational Heroes.* As a reflection of the organisation's philosophy, this dimension concerns the behaviour of organisational members, specially the behaviour of top management and their leadership styles. These leaders become the role models and a personification of an organisation's culture. They represent what the company stands for and reinforce the values of the culture. Modelled behaviour is a powerful learning tool and such cultural aspects permeate throughout the entire organisation.

(ii) *Ceremonies and Rites.* Ceremonies and rites reflect such activities that are enacted repeatedly on important occasions. Members of the organisation who have achieved success are recognised and rewarded on such occasions. Graduation ceremonies at colleges and universities where diplomas and other symbols of recognition such as special awards are given to students are reflections of culture in educational institutions.

These ceremonies bond organisation members together. Such ceremonies as company picnics, retirement dinners, annual conventions and so on, encourage inter-personal communication and togetherness and thus bring about a common culture bondage.

(iii) *Stories. Lavinson* and *Rosenthal* suggest that stories and myths about organisation's heroes are powerful tool to reinforce cultural values throughout the organisation and specially in orienting new employees. These stories and myths are often filtered through a "cultural network" and remind employees as to "why we do things in a certain way". For example, one of the stories passed down at one of the chemical companies is that its Chief Executive Officer, upon taking office, visited the company cafeteria and upon finding toothpicks at the counter, ordered these to be removed because he thought that it was not keeping with a professional image. Other stories are spread to reinforce customer service. For example, the Japanese car Lexus has enjoyed a reputation for quality and customer service by such stories as the company flying in repairmen to help customers who had problems with their

Lexus cars and could not find local repairmen because of the complexity and sophistication of the automobile.

(iv) *Cultural Symbols*. Symbols communicate organisational culture by unspoken messages. Certain code of dress or a company log can reflect its values and orientations. Many people wear buttons on their jacket lapels suggesting that they are the members of a Rotary Club or International Lions Club, thus reflecting a sense of values about these people. Some of the material artifacts created by an organisation also speak of its cultural orientation and make a statement about the company. These material benefits may range from assigned parking space and larger offices to luxury automobiles given to senior or successful members of the organisation. At Mary Kay Cosmetics, a highly successful cosmetic company in America, top sales performers are awarded a diamond "bumblebee" which has come to be known as a meaningful symbol of culture associated with success.

II. Shared Values

Values are the second an deeper level of culture and are reflected in the way individuals actually behave. Values reflect a person's underlying belief as to what should be and what should be and what should not be. Values are those principles and qualities that shape our thinking and behaviour.

Values can be classified into "instrumental" values and "terminal" values. Instrumental values define such enduring beliefs that certain behaviours are appropriate at all times irrespective of the objectives or outcomes. On the other hand, terminal values are beliefs that certain more tangible objectives are worth striving for and the objectives become more important than the appropriateness of the behaviour in achieving such objectives. For example, when you push a child out of the way of an incoming car, then you have placed a lesser value on politeness and greater value on saving the life of the child.

Values are emotionally charged priorities. These are learned during the human process of socialisation, through family environment of unbringing and through religious influences where values are given a holy tinage. Every culture has defined priorities for every aspect of social life. Values are invoked to justify beliefs and actions that are emotionally prioritised. For example, Mahatma Gandhi, in promoting hand woven "khadi" as against textiles produced by technologically sophisticated machinery, expressed values of human survival as more important than economic progress which would cost some jobs. Contrary to this exercise, Mr. Nehru, India's Prime Minister at the time stated, "You can't get hold of a modern tool and have an ancient mind. It won't work". Nehru was aware that religiously sanctioned beliefs and values generally act as obstacles and inhibitions to technological advancement. For example, even the famous Indian mathematician, Ramanujan had difficulty in going to England because of the religious beliefs that crossing the ocean was not religiously and socially recommended at the time in the early part of this century.

Many management consultants suggest that organisations should develop a "dominant and coherent set of shared values". This way, all members will have a predictable behaviour pattern which is consistent with the organisational philosophy and it will also necessitate and encourage group cohesion.

III. Common Assumptions

Assumptions are at the deepest and most fundamental level of cultural diagnosis. These are deeply held beliefs which are not objectively observable but manifest themselves in the behaviour of people so strongly that any violation of such beliefs would be unthinkable. For example, one steel company in America, Chapparrel Steel, has established values which reflect three basic assumptions. The first assumption is that people are basically good. This assumption is reflected in the company's emphasis on trust. The second assumption is that people are willing to learn, grow and achieve if they are afforded the proper opportunities. This assumption is reflected in the company's extensive training programs. The third assumption rests on the belief that people are motivated by challenges and enjoyable work and this assumption is reflected by the process of common goal setting and goal achievement by participation of members.

These common assumptions, though expressed at organisational level, can be traced to larger social and cultural values held by a particular society or country. For example, in America, the emphasis is mostly on individualised achievement while in Japan, the emphasis is more on collective achievement. Similarly, when IBM opened its operations in Japan in the 1960s, the local Japanese workers were shocked to learn that the company emphasised its goal of highest return on investment to the stockholders. In Japan, the stockholders are considered less important than the employees, because while the stockholders are only interested in profits, the employees are interested in the company and stay with the company for their entire lives.

MANAGING ORGANISATIONAL CULTURE

For any organisation to grow and prosper, it is important that its mission and its philosophy be respected and adhered to by all members of the organisation. Even when an organisation has a strong and established culture, the dynamics of environment may require changes in it or the subcultures may have to be encouraged to support and enhance the organisational culture or countercultures may have to be controlled to minimise its harmful effects.

Since culture is an important aspect of organisational success, it is important that managers play a significant role in keeping values and behaviours of the organisational members under control. This means that the leaders pay continuous attention to maintaining the members as to what is expected of them at all times. This would ensure that any deviations from the norms are caught early so that corrective actions can be taken before any damage is done. Cultural consistency and strong adherence to cultural values become easy when the leaders themselves play strong role models. Employees often emulate leader behaviour and look up to them for guidance. By being strong role models and by guiding, teaching and coaching, leaders reinforce the values that support the organisational culture.

A leader's cultural strength is measured specially by his handling of crisis situations. Emotions are heightened during a crisis. Proper handling of a crisis sends a powerful message about culture. A classic example is Lee Iacocca's handling of financial crisis faced by Chrysler Motor Company during 1970s. He articulated Chrysler's mission as protecting American jobs and asked the government for a bail-out of the crisis situation. The American government is very much against protecting private businesses with government funds but Iacocca was successful in obtaining these funds by emphasising the strong culture of commitment to its employees.

How managers handle their less productive workers or reward their more productive employees also speaks about their ability to maintain a certain strength in their culture. Some managers may simply reassign a less productive worker to another job which may be more suitable to has skills or retrain him instead of firing him. High turnover in any company is an indication of poor cultural standards.

Good managers are able to support and reinforce an existing strong culture by being strong role models and by handling situations that may result into cultural deviations with great diplomacy.

HOW CULTURE AFFECTS WORK?

Even before the employment people have a tendency to develop some basic values by integrating with environment. These basic values will be so ingrained that they become difficult to change. The values influence the level of education he seeks, his level of hard work and his ways of cooperation with fellow-members. Therefore, it should be remembered that the culture-off—the job has a profound influence on the performance of individuals in the organisation. *Keith Davis* points out certain values that affect work viz., freedom, equality, security, and opportunity:

(i) *Freedom*. Autonomy or freedom represents a basic cultural value that affects work in good many organisations. Freedom, not viewed here in absolute sense, refers to freedom from authority and freedom to do as one feels like doing any thing he wants (of course, subject to the constraints imposed by the society). That is to say, this freedom is within some prescribed bonds. Freedom may mean different things to different people. For instance, for an employee freedom may be of have a voice in the general meeting, for another it may mean right to work without restrictions etc. Under freedom, people hold suppressed resistance to strict organisational controls.

(ii) *Equality*. This value states that all people are equal, having equal rights when compared with their neighbours. However, this value gives due recognition to different mental, emotional and social differences and hence different rewards. Another associated idea is equity which states that there should be justice in rewarding performance, i.e., rewards should be based on performance.

(iii) *Security*. People in a dynamic environment seek security. People prefer full employment rather than handout. Some sort of mental tension prevails in the mind of an employee as long as he is economically insecure and he may not contribute effectively to organisational goals. Security is, thus a highly regarded value in culture.

(iv) *Opportunity*. Another value that affects people in work organisations is the opportunity. People expect good many opportunities to climb the ladder in organisations. Modern education, policies of promotion from within and similar factors affect the opportunity of employees.

SUBCULTURES IN ORGANISATIONS

Culture is unique concept. Within any community we can find large variations in culture—known as subcultures. It is quite but natural that within the larger society substantial variations exist in culture, i.e., behaviour patterns and beliefs of one culture are radically different from another culture. It is, of course, possible to classify these subcultures into institutional (or vertical subcultures) and professional (or horizontal) subcultures.

I. Institutional Subcultures

An institutional subculture comprises of the behaviour patterns of a particular group, of a department within the company, of a company as a whole. For example, a company may place tremendous emphasis on the safety and accident prevention. This particular value then is stressed till such a point of time that it is accepted with an almost religious vigour. Personnel who have ingrained such values will not operate equipment without safety equipment or mechanism (say, wearing glasses, or driving a car without safety belt etc.). In this organisation, safety has become a part of firm's subculture. Similarly, in some other organisation, high premium may be placed on the equality of work that is done. Organisation ensures quality by frequently conducting seminars and making employees aware that quality is a very important factor. Thus, quality becomes a part of subculture of the organisation.

A given department within a company may develop its unique culture. The research and development department may not hold to all the company traditions in precisely same manner as the other departments do. For instance, people may feel like working even during the leisure period of time (when their mood permits) and may prefer taking lunch during office working hours. Similarly, sales and engineering departments may hold different beliefs and behavioural patterns with regard to sales in their particular areas.

II. Professional Subcultures

These encompass the customs associated with a particular professional or occupational group within an organisation. Therefore, these are also labelled as horizontal cultures. Some professionals develop certain codes of conduct and ethics applicable to their professions. Doctors and physicians recognise principles that are supposed to be observed by doctors without deviation; accountants have some codes of conduct and they perform their duties and functions irrespective of the consequences to the particular organisation for which they work.

ORGANISATIONAL CLIMATE

All organisational theoreticians and researchers unanimously agree that a sound climate is extremely important for the ultimate achievement of organisational goals. Organisational climate, through abstract in concept, is normally associated with job performance and job satisfaction and morale of the employees.

Climate is commonly experienced phenomenon and often referred to by many expressions as atmosphere, surrounding milieu, environment and culture etc. Organisations like finger prints and snowflakes are always unique. Organisational climate is very important factor to be considered in studying and analysing organisations because it has a profound influence on the outlook, well being and attitudes of organisational members and, thus, on their total performance.

Organisational climate is a relatively enduring quality of the internal environment that is experienced by its members, influences their behaviour, and can be described in terms of the values of a particular set of characteristics of the organisation.

Organisational climate is, thus, the manifestation of the attitudes of organisational members towards the organisation itself. An organisation tends to attract and keep people who fit its climate, so that its patterns are perpetuated at least to some extent.

Organisational climate should be viewed from total system point of view. Some theorists may be of the opinion that there are as may climates as there are people in organisations.

Even though organisational culture and organisational climate are sometimes used interchangeably, some important differences between these two concepts have been recognised. According to *Bowditch* and *Buono*, "Organisational culture is concerned with the *nature* of beliefs and expectations about organisational life, while climate is an *indicator* of whether those beliefs and expectations are being fulfilled". Basically, organisational climate reflects a person's perception of the organisation to which he belongs. It is a set of characteristics and factors that are perceived by the employees about their organisations which serve as a major force in influencing their behaviour. These factors may include job descriptions, organisational structural format, performance and evaluation standards, leadership style, challenges and innovations, organisational values and culture and so on.

Richard M. Hodgetts has classified organisational climate into two major categories. He has given an analogy with an iceberg where there is a part of the iceberg that can be seen from the surface and another part that is under water and is not visible. The visible part that can be observed or measured include the structure of hierarchy, goals and objectives of the organisation, performance standards and evaluations, technological state of the operations and so on. The second category contains factors that are not visible and quantifiable and include such subjective areas as supportiveness, employee's feelings and attitudes, values, morale, personal and social interaction with peers, subordinates and superiors and a sense of satisfaction with the job. Both of these categories are shown below in the form of an iceberg.

While some of the factors are easily measured by quantitative methods, others have to be assessed subjectively simply by asking employees relevant questions as to how they feel about certain factors relating to organisational climate. A number of questions are prepared and the questionnaire is given to the workers to respond. Their responses are generally measured on a scale of 1 to 5 where 1 means generally a strong disagreement with the essence of the question and 5 means a strong agreement. For example, a question such as, "In this organisations, promotions are given entirely on the basis of merit and contribution to the organisation" could elicit a response on the following scale:

(i) Strongly disagree
(ii) Moderately disagree
(iii) Neutral (No opinion)

(iv) Moderately agree
(v) Strongly agree.

These responses can then be tabulated and conclusions can be drawn about how the employees feel about the process of promotion.

Considerable work has been done in this area by *Likert*, who developed a profile of organisational climate by isolating six variables, with each variable having four dimensions and each dimension containing five degrees or levels. For example, one of the variables is decision-making. The question is, "At what levels are decisions made"? The four dimensions to this variable are:

(i) Mostly at the top.
(ii) Policy is set at the top; some delegation occurs.
(iii) Broad policy is set at the top; considerable delegation occurs.
(iv) Decision are made throughout the entire organisation.

Each of these dimensions can be answered on a scale of 1 to 5 as discussed above.

Other organisational variables in this particular profile developed by Likert are: Leadership style, motivation, communication, goal setting and control.

Overt Factors	Hierarchy
	Financial resources
	Goals of organisation
	Skills and abilities of personnel
	Technological state
	Performance standards
	Efficiency measurement
Covert Factors	Attitudes
	Feelings
	Values
	Norms
	Interaction
	Supportiveness
	Satisfaction

Based upon the inputs so received from the employees, the organisation can determine the type and state of the existing climate and the changes that can be undertaken to achieve the desired climate. For example, an organisation with a climate of autocratic leadership might find that the workers are unhappy with the situation and would prefer a more democratic style of management and thus may decide to make changes to make the decision making more participative which is expected to be more conducive to higher productivity.

FACTORS AFFECTING ORGANISATIONAL CLIMATE

In every organisation there exist certain elements that exert profound influence on the existing climate. In some organisations certain factors like structure, or process plays a major role, whereas in others the level of technology may be the major influential factor in climate. *Lawrence James* and *Allan Jones* have tried to identify the factors influencing climate and they grouped these factors under five heads:

(i) Organisational context.
(ii) Organisational structure.
(iii) Process
(iv) Physical environment.
(v) System values and norms.

I. Physical Environment

The external conditions of environment, the size and location of the building in which an employee works, the size of the city, weather or the place—all affect the organisational climate. An employee performing his job in a relatively clean, quiet and safe environment will undoubtedly have a favourable perception of the organisational climate. Office decor, size and space a person has in doing the work are the important factors to be borne in mind, for these affect the climate. Noise has also been considered instrumental in influencing the climate of organisations. High levels of noise brings a bad feeling and leads to frustration, nervousness and aggression and will have a negative effect upon organisational climate. Loud, intermittent noise converts an organisation into a market place.

II. Structure

Structure of the organisation represents another variable that affects climate. It needs no reiteration that structure is a framework that establishes formal relationships and delineate authority and functional responsibility. Further, the actual arrangement of hierarchy is also to be considered, for it affects climate. Highly decentralised structure results in sound climate when the management feels the necessity of high degree of employee input in the total output. In other words, a management that has a strong belief in participative decision-making will promote decentralisation. In a sharp contrast, if the management feels the necessity of maintaining greater degree of consistency in operations regarding decision-making it will be wedded to centralised structure. Thus structure also affects the climate of organisations.

III. System Values and Norms

Every organisation has discernible and fairly evident formal value system where certain kinds of behaviours are rewarded and encouraged and certain kinds of behaviour forces an individual to formal sanctions. The formal value system is communicated to employees through rules, regulations and policies, Although in every organisation informal organisation also exists, the value system of informal organisation is very difficult to ascertain. But from the point of view of organisational climate, both formal and informal groups are very powerful in exerting influence on climate. For instance, the organisation that treats employees with respect to understanding will have certainly a different climate than one which is very cold and impersonal.

IV. Organisational Context

The first and foremost influential factors that affects the climate is the management philosophy. If the company is wedded to such a policy that it effectively utilises its resources both human as well as non-human, then it can be concluded that the climate is good. The manpower philosophy is generally expressed by rules, regulations and policies etc. The point here is that the reactions of the employees and the degrees to which they welcome and accept the managerial philosophy is very crucial to the development of sound and favourable organisational climate. The climate is said to be highly favourable when the existing management techniques are such that employees goals are perfectly matched to the ideals of organisation.

V. Process

In every organisation certain processes are vital so that it runs. Communication, decision-making, motivation, and leadership are some of the very important processes though which the management carries out its objectives. In all these processes, the relationship between superior and subordinate is visible and therefore the supervisor cannot afford to ignore this visible interface. For instance, if we consider leader-follower relationship in leadership process, it is the leader's choice whether to allow subordinates in decision-making, give assignments, does performance appraisals etc. A leader has to be aware of the possible influence of his actions on the climate when deciding about the most appropriate supervisory technique for a given situation. It should be noted that failure to give consideration to the affect on climate would be monumental error that could be reflected adversely on the performance of employees. Furthermore, when a leader mismatches his style to the situation it might abort any hope of attaining organisational objectives.

DEVELOPING A SOUND ORGANISATIONAL CLIMATE

A sound organisational climate is a long-term proposition. The climate of each organisation is set through an organisational behaviour system. However, what should be an organisational behaviour model for a given organisation is not a universal phenomenon. Organisation behaviour philosophy derives from both fact and value premises. Fact premises represent how human beings behave, while value premises represent the view of the desirability of certain goals. Thus, organisational climate should represent the philosophy and goals of those who joint together to create the organisation. Thus, organisational climate exists in a contingency relationship with the organisation, meaning that the type of climate that an organisation seeks is contingent upon the type of people it has, the type of technology, level of education and expectations of people in it.

The organisational climate is contingent on the assumptions of the nature of people in general. In dealing with people, the total men concept should be taken which is essentially a combination of three different concepts about the nature of human beings—economic, social and self-fulfilling. Such a classification is different from an earlier classification of man in the context of decision-making process. The basis of classification of man into three categories derives from the fact that each class of men has different set of thinking, motivation, and hence requires different organisational climate. The economic man is basically motivated by money long-range economic security, and hence the reliance on economic factors to attract, keep and motivate them. For special man, positive social relations and interaction are a must; within his work environment, men seeks an affinity with fellow employees. The creation of a climate where happy family atmosphere prevails is appropriate for him. The self-fulfilling man seeks achievement, accomplishment, and meaning in what he does. The organisational climate with premium on certain degree of freedom is appropriate for him. Thus, each type of man requires a particular climate. In order to build up a sound organisational climate, managers must understand their people in the organisation. The importance must be given to what motivates job performance in general and building an overall climate conducive to motivation, a keen insight into the individual in particular, and tailoring a personal approach to leadership and job design to which the man will respond with commitment. The individual differences suggest that there cannot be any all-purpose organisational climate. Though there are variations in practices, following prescriptions can be taken as features of a sound organisational climate:

1. Absence of political manoeuvring for organisational positions and other personal gains;
2. Linking rewards with performance rather than linking with other consideration such as blood relationship, friendship and social background;
3. High standards of excellence in every area of operation and evaluation;
4. Encouragement for participation and group and its implementation;
5. Encouragement for innovation and freedom to act upon ideas;
6. High value assigned to interpersonal amity and tolerance of individual differences;
7. High standards of moral integrity in dealing with both internal and external matters.

These prescriptions can be achieved on a long-term basis and more by practice and not by prescriptions alone.

REVIEW QUESTIONS

1. Define organisational culture and also explain the main characteristics and components of culture?
2. Write short notes on:
   (a) Is culture a descriptive term?
   (b) Do organisation have uniform culture?
3. Distinguish between:
   (a) Strong *versus* weak cultures.
   (b) Cultures *versus* formalisation.
4. Explain culture's functions and culture as a liability.
5. What do you understand by "organisation climate"? Also give the factors affecting climate of work organisation.

REFERENCES

1. P.C. Smith, LMM. Kendall and C.L. Hulin, "The Measurement of Satisfaction in Work and Retirement: A Strategy for the Study of Attitudes", Chicago, Rand McNally, 1960.

2. *Vroom V.H., Work and Motivation, New York, Wiley, 1964.*
3. *G.A. Forehand and B. Von H. Filmer "Environmental Variations in Studies of Organisational Behaviour", Psychological Bulletin, 62, No. 6, 1964.*
4. *Benjamin Schneider and Rover A. Snyder, "Some Relationships Between Job Satisfaction and Organisational Climate", Journal of Applied Psychology, 60, No. 3, 1975.*
5. *Renate Tagiuri, "The Concept of Organisational Climate", In Renato Tagiuri and George H. Litwin (ed.), Organisational Climate. (Boston, Division of Research, Graduate School of Business Administration, Harvard University, 1968).*
6. *Stevan H. Appelhaum, "The Organisational Climate Study: An Intervention Strategy to Change Department", University of Michigan, Business Review, 28, Sept., 1976.*
7. *Paul Lawrence and Jay W. Lorsch, "Organisation and Environment", Boston, Harvard Graduate School of Business, 1967.*
8. *David McClelland and David H. Burnham, "Power is the Great Motivator", Harvard Business Review, March-April, 1976.*

9th

CHAPTER

OVERVIEW

Leadership Theories and Models

• ***After reading this chapter, you should be able to know:***

- Introduction
- Features of Leadership
- Personal Characteristics of Leaders
- A Model of Leadership
- Theories of Leadership
- Trait Theory
- Behavioural Theory
- Lowa Leadership Studies
- Ohio State Studies
- Managerial Grid
- Tridimensional Grid
- Scandinavian Studies
- Contingency or Situational Theory of Leadership
- Fiedler's Contingency Model
- Path-Goal Theory of Leadership
- Hersey and Blanchard's Situational Theory or Life-cycle Theory
- Leader-member Exchange (LMX) Theory
- Vroom-Yetton Model
- Most recent Approaches for Leadership
- Attribution Theory of Leadership
- Charismatic Leadership Theories
- Transactional and Transformational Leadership
- Transactional Leadership
- Leadership as a Continuum
- Is There a Biological Basis for Leadership?
- Leadership Styles in Indian Organisations

9

LEADERSHIP THEORIES AND MODELS

INTRODUCTION

Leadership is an important element of directing process. To get things done by subordinates, the manager has to lead and guide their activities. Leadership is an influence process. By influencing the working behaviour of subordinates the manager directs it towards the accomplishment of organisational objectives. Leadership is required in every organisation, the success or failure of an organisation to the great extent depends on the quality of leadership particularly on the part of top management. It is true that the manager can manage without having qualities of leadership but if he has leadership qualities he manages efficiently. In this regard *Peter Drucker* has rightly points out that "the managers or business leaders are the basic and scarce resource of any business enterprise and most of the failures of business establishment has been attributed to ineffective leadership." It is because by using leadership qualities the manager develops vision about organisation and directs the activities of members in that direction.

In the words of *Louis A. Allen*, *"A leader is one who guides and directs other people. A leader gives the efforts of his followers a direction and purpose by influencing their behaviour."*

Leadership is a process of influencing the subordinates so that they cooperate enthusiastically in the achievement of group goals. According to *Theo Haimann*, *"leadership is the process by which an executive imaginatively directs, guides and influences the work of others in choosing and attaining specified goals by mediating between the individuals and the organisation in such a manner that both will obtain maximum satisfaction."*

Leadership is a *psychological process* of influencing followers or subordinates and providing guidance to them. It is always related to a situation which means a leader may be effective in one situation while ineffective in another. To be effective, a leader should change his leadership style depending upon the requirements of the situation.

When one individual attempts to affect the behaviour of others in a group without using the coercive form of power, we describe the effort as leadership. More specifically, the handbook of Leadership defines leadership as "an interaction between members of a group. Leaders are agents of change, persons whose acts affect other people more than other people's acts affect them. Leadership occurs when one group member modifies the motivation or competencies of others in the group." There's a growing need to find the best leaders possible to work within institutions. The accompanying Close-Up points out women's growing role in leadership positions.

The leadership definition implies that it involves the use of influence and that all relationships can involve leadership. A second element in the definition involves the importance of being a change agent—being able to affected followers' behaviour and performance. Last, the definition focuses on accomplishing goals. The effective leader may have to deal with individual, group, and organisational goals. Leader effectiveness is typically measured by the accomplishment of one or a combination of these goals. Individuals may view the leader as effective or ineffective according to the satisfactions they derive from the total work experience. In fact, acceptance of a leader's directives or requests rests largely on the followers' expectations that a favourable response can lead to an attractive outcome.

In a *hierarchical organisation*, the appointed manager may direct, instruct, or command; but unless followers have some choice to follow or not follow, there's no leadership. If followers have no choice, there's domination and intimidation. Leadership results when a person influences followers to accept his requests without any apparent exertion of power. Through an ability to influence, the leader creates and uses the power and authority received from followers.

Leadership is an integral part of management and plays a vital role in managerial operations. If there is any single factor that differentiates between successful and unsuccessful organisations, it could be considered as dynamic and effective leadership. Perhaps, it would be a valid assumption to state that the major cause of most business failures would be ineffective leadership. All managers, in a way, are business leaders, even though management primarily relies on formal position power to influence people whereas leadership stems from a social influence process. However, management is an integral component of technical as well as social processes.

Leadership as the ability to influence a group toward the achievement of goals. The source of this influence may be formal, such as that provided by the possession of managerial rank in an organisation. Since management positions come with some degree of formally designated authority, a person may assume a leadership role simply because of the position he or she holds in the organisation. But not all leaders are managers; nor, for that matter, are all managers leaders. Just because an organisation provides its managers with certain formal rights is no assurance that they will be able to lead effective. We find that non-sanctioned leadership—that is, the ability to influence that arises outside the formal structure of the organisation—is often as important or more important than formal influence. In other words, leaders can emerge from within a group as well as by formal appointment to lead a group.

FEATURES OF LEADERSHIP

A leader has certain inherent qualities and traits which assist him in playing a directing role and wielding commanding influence over others. Some of these traits according to *Jago* are :

1. Emotional stability.
2. Sociability.
3. A sense of cooperativeness.

4. Judgement.
5. Personality–height and weight.
6. Initiative.
7. Intelligence.
8. Enthusiasm.
9. Self-confidence.
10. Appearance, presentability.
11. Tact and diplomacy.
12. Moral courage and integrity.
13. Willpower and flexibility.
14. Energy, drive.
15. Knowledge of human relations.

These traits are not universal in nature, nor all the leaders have all these traits. Not all these traits work all the time. While some of these characteristics differentiate successful managers and leaders from unsuccessful ones, it is the behaviour of the leaders, either as a result of these characteristics or otherwise, which is more tangible and obvious and less abstract in nature. The leadership behaviour is directly related to individual and group work activity, loyalty of the group, absences, turnovers and employee morale. These are some of the indicators, which to some degree reflect the effectiveness of leadership behaviour.

Many studies have been conducted in order to identify and separate such characteristics and personal traits that are unique to the behaviour of successful leaders. These traits, then could be set up as standards against which the profiles of leaders could be matched and judged. However, such attempts have not been successful. According to *Ralph Stogdill,* who studied the subject of leadership most extensively, "a person does not become a leader by virtue of the possession of some combination of traits, but the pattern of personal characteristics of the leader must bear some relevant relationship to the characteristics, activities and goals of the followers."

PERSONAL CHARACTERISTICS OF LEADERS

Leadership is an intangible quality and its effectiveness can best be judged by the behaviour and attitudes of followers. Even though, personal backgrounds and personalities differ widely, some of the factors such as education and socio-economic status are poor indicators of judgments of successful leaders. However, some behavioural characteristic may be common to most of the successful and effective leaders. Some of these characteristics are:

(i) *Ability to Inspire Others*. This ability may be due to an internal "charisma" which is an inborn trait and may not be a learnable factor.

(ii) *Problem Solving Skills*. An effective leader has developed the patience and ability to look at the problem from various angles and get down to the cause of the problem and tries to solve the problem from its roots rather than the symptoms of the problem.

(iii) *Emotional Maturity.* Emotional stability and maturity is a major ingredient for effective leadership. It pertains to good adjustment to life, calm, cool and calculated reaction to undesirable situations and obstacles and normal acceptance of success as well as failure. Such leaders are self-confident, rational and are open hearted towards differences in opinions and opposing view points. They generally have a happy family life and have a balanced outlook towards life and the world. They are warm and sensitive and not vindictive in nature.

(iv) *Ability to Understand Human Behaviour.* A leader must understand the needs, desires and behaviour of their subordinates and show respect for such desires. He is emotionally supportive and is careful enough to avoid ego threatening behaviour. He must give credit to subordinates when their efforts are successful.

(v) *Verbal Assertiveness.* A leader must be an effective orator and must be confident of his views and opinions. He must communicate his views honestly and in a straight forward manner without fear of consequences.

(vi) *Willingness to Take Risks.* Routine work, no matter how well-done, never makes a leader. Successful leaders always charter the unknown. They must accept and seek new challenges. However, the risks must be calculated ones and outcomes of actions be reasonably predicted. Should these risks result in failure, a leader must take full blame and responsibility and not shift blame on others, even though they may be operative factors. He must be willing to tolerate frustration and defeat and learn from these failures.

(vii) *Dedication to Organisational Goals.* A leader must demonstrate his dedication and commitment to the organisation's mission, goals and objectives by hard work and self-sacrifice. He must make sure that his followers fully understand the organisational objectives and are equally dedicated and willing to work for these objectives.

(viii) *Skill in the Art of Compromise.* Settling differences is a vital part of leadership and genuine differences must be solved by compromise and consensus. This will induce faith in the fairness of the leader. He must be willing to give in where necessary and must be able to take criticism with grade. However, he must not compromise for the sake of compromising or just smooth sailing only and must be willing to take a stand on controversial issues and accept the consequences of his stand.

A MODEL OF LEADERSHIP

As Fig. 1 suggests, a leader can make a difference in terms of end-result factors: performance, goal attainment, and individual growth and development. However, the degree of difference and the process of using leadership to make a difference are somewhat ambiguous. Some theorists and researchers offer cautious advice about the impact of leadership.

Empirical evidence of the magnitude of the effects of leadership on performance is modest. A number of reasons have been cited for the observed modest effects of leaders on performance and other organisational outcomes. First, those selected as leaders are similar in background, experience, and qualifications. The similarity across selected individuals reduces the range of characteristics exhibited by leaders. The similarity of leaders also can produce a self-selection bias: leaders select individuals similar to themselves. Second, leaders at even the highest levels do not have unilateral control over resources. Major decisions require approval, review, and suggested modification by others. Third, many factors cannot be controlled or modified by a leader. Labour

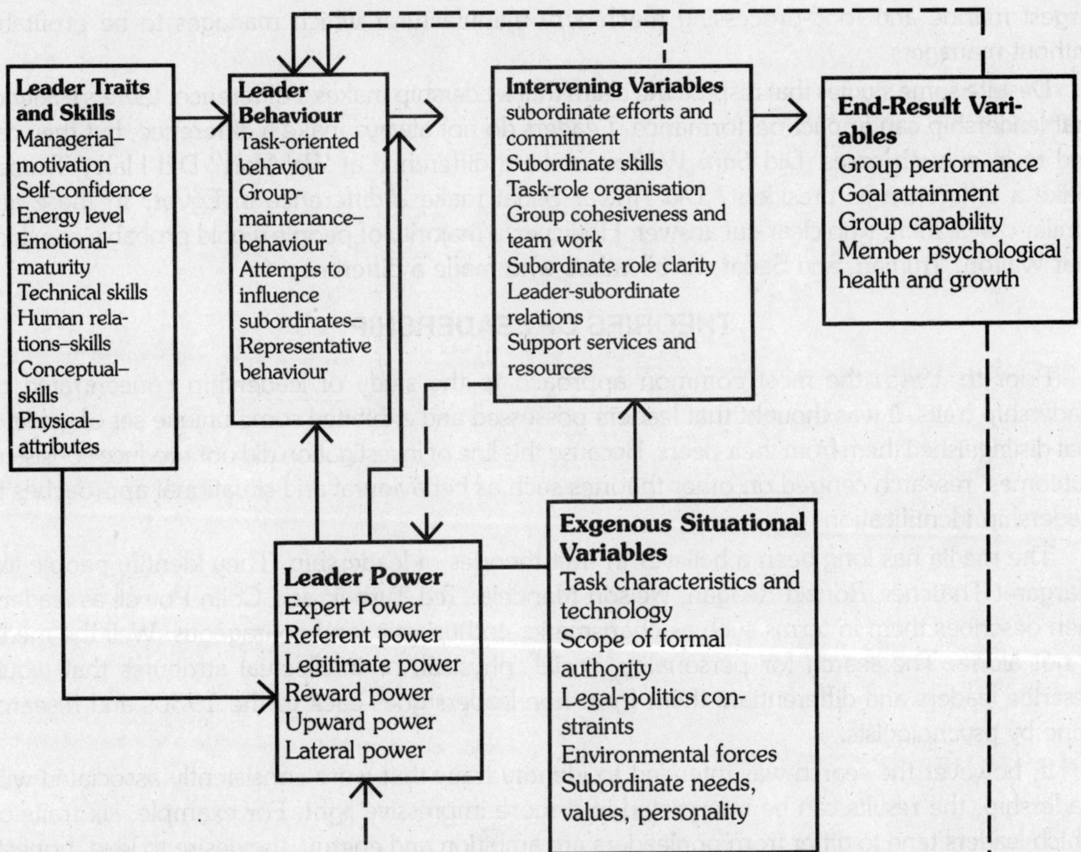

Fig. 1. *Yukl's Overarching Model.*

markets, environmental factors, and policies are often outside a leader's direct control. External factors may be overwhelming and uncontrollable, no matter how astute, insightful, and influential a leader may be in a job situation.

Some research has specified only a modest effect of leadership on performance. One study of 167 firms in 13 industries over a 20-year period found that the administration factor (i.e., a combination of leadership and managership) had a limited effect on sales, profits, and profit margins. Reanalysis of the same data found that leadership accounted for more variance in performance than did many of the other variables studied.

A report by *Sember* on Brazilian managers again raises doubts about the effect of leaders. Sember believes that democracy, profit sharing, and information are more important than a management hierarchy, a power base headed by a leader, or the specialisation of work. Instead, employee involvement, salaries instead of wages, circles instead of management hierarchies, and job rotation make leaders almost unnecessary. Sember refers to the organisation of Brazil's largest marine and food-processing machinery manufacturer which manages to be profitable without managers.

Despite some studies that dispute the claim that leadership makes a difference, there's evidence that leadership can impact performance. Leaders do not always make a difference, but they can and to in enough cases. Did *Sam Walton* make a difference at Wal-Mart? Did Harry Truman make a difference as president? Did Anwar Sadat make a difference in Egypt? In these and similar cases, there's no clear-cut answer. However, a majority of people would probably conclude that Walton, Truman, and Sadat were leaders who made a difference.

THEORIES OF LEADERSHIP

Prior to 1945, the most common approach to the study of leadership concentrated on leadership traits. It was thought that leaders possessed and exhibited some unique set of qualities that distinguished them from their peers. Because this line of investigation did not produce consistent outcomes, research centred on other theories such as behavioural and situational approaches to leadership identification.

The media has long been a believer in trait theories of leadership. They identify people like Margaret Thatcher, Ronald Reagan, Nelson Mandela, Ted Turner, and Colin Powell as leaders, then describes them in terms such as charismatic, enthusiastic, and courageous. Well the media is not alone. The search for personality, social, physical, or intellectual attributes that would describe leaders and differentiate them from non-leaders goes back to the 1930s and research done by psychologists.

If, however the search was intended to identify traits that were consistently associated with leadership, the results can be interpreted in a more impressive light. For example, six traits on which leaders tend to differ from nonleaders are ambition and energy, the desire to lead, honesty and integrity, self-confidence, intelligence, and job-relevant knowledge. Additionally, recent research provides strong evidence that people who are high selfmonitors—that, is are highly flexible in adjusting their behaviour in different situations—are much more likely to emerge as leaders in groups than low selfmonitors. Overall, the cumulative findings from more than half a century of research lead us to conclude that some traits increase the likelihood of success as a leader, but none of the traits guarantee success.

In the earlier studies, the existence of these traits became a measure of leadership. It holds that possession of these traits permits certain individuals to gain position of leadership. Since all individuals do not have these qualities, only those who have them would be considered potential leaders. It was further believed that training individuals to assume leadership roles was not possible and such training would be helpful only to those who had these inborn leadership traits to start with.

According to *B. Solmon*, "History is repeat with non-trained, non-academic Fords, Edisons and Carnegies who could not even claim a grammar school education, yet managed to become leaders who influence was felt around the globe. As for appearance of robust health, need we mention more than the delicate Gandhi or George Washington or Carver, the frail, shrivelled, insignificant little negro who was one of America's greatest scientist and so many more like them. As for high ideals and fine character act, where would Hitler, Capone or Attila the Hun rate here?"

Similarly, if tall people were more inclined to be leaders, how would such short people as Napolean or the most respected Prime Minister of India, Lal Bahadur Shastri have risen to a high leadership position? Accordingly inconsistencies in the trait theory of leadership give rise to a logical criticism against its validity.

According to *behaviour theory*, leadership is shown by a person's acts more than by his traits. The leadership effectiveness is determined in terms of leader-subordinate interaction and outcome. Research studies conducted by *Katz, Maccoby* and *Morse,* suggested that leadership behaviour be defined along employee-centred dimension and production-centred dimension complementing each other so that the employee's performance and productivity is enhanced.

If the behavioural approach to leadership were successful, it would have implications quite different from those of the trait approach. If trait research had been successful, it would have provided a basis for selecting the "right" persons to assume formal positions in groups and organisations requiring leadership. In contrast, if behavioural studies were to turn up critical behavioural determinants of leadership, we could train people to be leaders. The difference between trait and behavioural theories, in terms of application, lies in their underlying assumptions. If trait theories were valid, then leadership is basically in born : You either have it or you don't. On the other hand, if there were specific behaviours that identified leaders, then we could teach leadership—we could design programs that implemented these behavioural patterns in individuals who desired to be effective leaders. This was surely a more exciting avenue, for it meant that the supply of leaders could be expanded. If training worked, we could have an infinite supply of effective leaders.

I. TRAIT THEORY

The traits theory is based on observed characteristics of many leaders—both successful and unsuccessful. The resulting lists of traits—drive, originality, high energy, extraversion, introversion, and so on—are then compared to those of potential leaders to predict their success or failure. There is support those of potential leaders to predict their success or failure. There is support for the notion that effective leaders have interests and abilities and, perhaps, even personality traits that are different from those of less effective leaders. Most researchers, however, believe that the traits approach is inadequate for successfully predicting leadership performance for at least three reasons. First, although more than 100 personality traits of successful leaders have been identified, no consistent patterns have been found. The trait stereotypes of successful leaders in charge of sales people include optimism, enthusiasm, and dominance. Successful production leaders are usually progressive , introverted, cooperative, and genuinely respectful of employees. However, many successful leaders of sales people and production employees do not have all, or even some, of these characteristics. In fact, the list of personality traits never ends, and researchers often disagree over which traits are the most important for an effective leader. Furthermore, two leaders with significantly different traits have been successful in the same situation.

Despite these difficulties, the evidence suggests that most (but not all) successful leaders share four traits. These traits are more likely to be found in middle-level and top managers than in team leaders or first-line supervisors.

- *Intelligence*. Leaders tend to have somewhat higher intelligence than their subordinates.
- *Maturity and breadth*. Leaders tend to be emotionally mature and have a broad range of interests.
- *Inner motivation and achievement drive*. Leaders want to accomplish things; when they achieve one goal, they seek another. They don't depend primarily on employees for their motivation to achieve goals.
- *Employee-centered*. Leaders are able to work effectively with employees in a variety of situations. They respect others and realise that, to accomplish tasks, they must be considerate of others' needs and values.

The second criticism of the traits theory relates physical characteristics such as height, weight, appearance, physique, energy, and health to effective leadership. Most of these factors are related to situational factors that can significantly affect a leader's effectiveness. For example, military or law enforcement people must be a particular minimum height weight, and strength in order to perform certain tasks effectively. Such characteristics may help an individual rise to a leadership position in an organisation, but height, weight, and strength don't correlate highly with leadership performance. Moreover, in educational or business organisations, height, weight, and strength play no role in task performance and thus are not requirements for a leadership position. Then final criticism of the traits model is that leadership itself is complex. A relationship between personality and a person's interest in particular types of jobs could well exist but a study relating personality and effectiveness does not reflect it. For example, one study found that high earners (a measure of success) in small firms were more ambitious, were more open-minded, and described themselves as more considerate than low earners. But in small firms, a leader usually performs numerous jobs. People who like performing multiple jobs may seek out small firms that permit them to do so.

II. BEHAVIOURAL THEORY

The *Lowa, Ohio State, Michigan, Grid and Scandinavian* studies are three of the historically most important leadership studies for the study of organisational behaviour. Unfortunately, they are still heavily depended upon, and leadership research has not surged ahead from this relatively auspicious beginning. Before analysing the current status of leadership research, it is important to look at the theoretical development that has occurred through the years.

(i) Lowa Leadership Studies

A series of pioneering leadership studies conducted in the late 1930s by *Ronald Lippitt* and *Ralph K. White* under the general direction of *Kurt Lewin* at the *University of Lowa* has had a lasting impact. Lewin is recognised as the father of group dynamics and as an important cognitive theorists. In the initial studies, hobby clubs for ten-year-old boys were formed. Each club was submitted to all three different styles of leadership—authoritarian, democratic, and laissez-faire.

The authoritarian leader was very directive and allowed no participation. This leader tended to give individual attention when praising and criticising but tried to be friendly or impersonal rather than openly hostile. The democratic leader encouraged group discussion and decision-making. This leader tried to be "objective" in giving praise or criticism and to be one of the group in spirit. The laissez-faire leader gave complete freedom to the group; this leader essentially provided no leadership.

Unfortunately, the effects that styles of leadership had on productivity were not directly examined. The experiments were designed primarily to examine patterns of aggressive behaviour. However, an important by-product was the insight that was gained into the productive behaviour of a group. For example, the researchers found that the boys subjected to the autocratic leaders reacted in one of two ways : either aggressively or apathetically. Both the aggressive and apathetic behaviours were deemed to be reactions to the frustration caused by the autocratic leader. The researchers also pointed out that the apathetic groups exhibited outbursts of aggression when the autocratic leader left the room or when a transition was made to a freer leadership atmosphere. The laissez-faire leadership climate actually produced the greatest number of aggressive acts from the group. The democratically led group fell between the one extremely aggressive group and the four apathetic groups under the autocratic leaders.

Sweeping generalisations on the basis of the Lippitt and White studies are dangerous. Preadolescent boys making masks and carving soap are a long way from adults working in a complex, formal organisation. Furthermore, from the viewpoint of modern behavioural science research methodology, many of the variables were not controlled. Nevertheless, these leadership studies have important historical significance. They were the first attempts to determine, experimentally, what effects styles of leadership have on a group. Like the *Hawthorne* studies, the lowa studies are too often automatically discounted or at least de-emphasised because they were experimentally crude. The value of the studies was that they were the first to analyse leadership from the standpoint of scientific methodology, and, more important, they showed that different styles of leadership can produce different, complex reactions from the same or similar groups.

(ii) Ohio State Studies

These researchers sought to identify independent dimensions of leader behaviour. They called these two dimensions initiating structure and consideration.

(i) *Initiating structure* refers to the extent to which a leader is likely to define and structure his or her role and those of subordinates in the search for goal attainment. It includes behaviour that attempts to organise work, work relationships, and goals. The leader characterised as high in initiating structure could be described as someone who "assigns group members to particular tasks," "expects workers to maintain definite standards of performance," and "emphasises the meeting of deadlines." *Robert Crandall* and *Paul Kazarian* exhibit high initiating structure behaviour.

(ii) *Consideration* is described as the extent to which a person is likely to have job relationships that are characterised by mutual trust, respect for subordinates' ideas, and regard for their feelings. He or she shows concern for followers' comfort, well-being, status, and satisfaction. A leader high in consideration could be described as one who helps subordinates with personal problems, is friendly and approachable, and treats all subordinates as equals.

Extensive research, based on these definitions, found that leaders high in initiating structure and consideration (a "high-high" leader) tended to achieve high subordinate performance and satisfaction more frequently than those who rated low on either consideration, initiating structure, or both. However, the "high-high" style did not always result in positive consequences. For example, leader behaviour characterised as high on initiating structure led to greater rates of grievances, absenteeism, and turnover and lower levels of job satisfaction for workers performing routine tasks. Other studies found that high consideration was negatively related to performance ratings of the leader by his or her superior. In conclusion, the Ohio State studies suggested that the "high-high" style generally resulted in positive outcomes, but enough exceptions were found to indicate that situational factors needed to be integrated into the theory.

(iii) University of Michigan Studies

In 1947, *Rensis Likert* began studying how best to manage the efforts of individuals to achieve desired performance and satisfaction objectives. The purpose of most leadership research of the Likert-inspired team at the University of Michigan (UM) was to discover the principles and methods of effective leadership. The effectiveness criteria used in many of the studies included :

Productivity per work hour, or other similar measures of the organisation's success in achieving its production goals.

- Job satisfaction of members of the organisation.
- Turnover, absenteeism, and grievance rates.
- Costs.
- Scrap loss.
- Employee and managerial motivation.

Studies were conducted in a wide variety of organisations : chemical, electronics, food, heavy machinery, insurance, petroleum, public utilities, hospitals, banks, and government agencies. Data were obtained from thousands of employees doing different job tasks, ranging from unskilled work to highly skilled research and development work.

Through interviewing leaders and followers, researchers identified two distinct styles of leadership, referred to as job-centered and employee-centered. The job-centered leader practices close supervision so that subordinates perform their tasks using specified procedures. This leader relies on coercion, reward, and legitimate power to influence the behaviour and performance of followers. Concern for people is viewed as an important luxury that a leader cannot always effort.

The employee-centered leader believes in delegating decision making and aiding followers in satisfying their needs by creating a supportive work environment. The employee-centered leader is concerned with followers' personal advancement, growth, and achievement. These actions are assumed to be conductive to group formation and development.

The UM series of studies does not clearly show that one particular style of leadership is always most effective. Moreover, it only examines two aspects of leadership: task and people behaviour.

(iv) Managerial Grid

A graphic portrayal of a two-dimensional view of leadership style was developed by *Blake* and *Mouton*. They proposed a Managerial Grid based on the styles of "concern for people" and "concern for production," which essentially represent the Ohio State dimensions of consideration and initiating structure or the Michigan dimensions of employee oriented and production oriented.

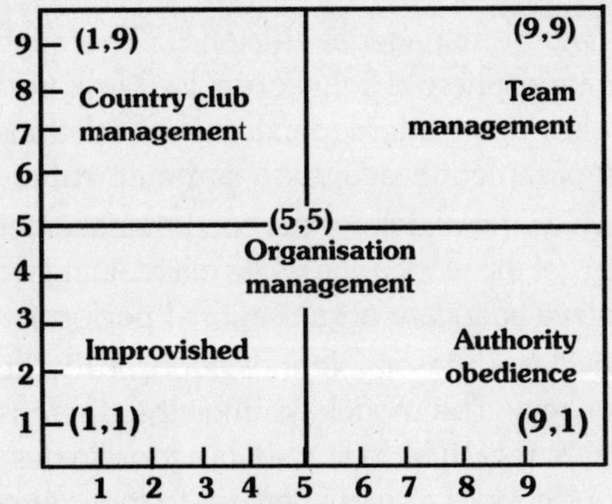

Fig. 2. *The Managerial Grid.*

The grid, has nine possible positions along each axis, creating 81 different positions in which the leader's style may fall. The grid does not show results produced but, rather, the dominating factors in a leader's thinking in regard to getting results.

Based on the findings of Blake and Mouton, managers were found to perform best under a 9,9 style, as contrasted, for example, with a 9,1 (authority type) or 1,9 (country club type) style. Unfortunately, the grid offers a better framework for conceptualising leadership style than for presenting any tangible new information in clarifying the leadership quandary, since there is little substantive evidence to support the conclusion that a 9,9 style is most effective in all situations.

The management grid is built on two axis, one representing the "people" and the other the "task". Both the horizontal, as well as the vertical axis are treated as a scale from 1 to 9 where 1 represents the least involvement and 9 represents the most involvement, so that the coordinates (1,1) would indicate minimum standards for worker involvement and task design, and coordinates (9,9) would indicate maximum dedication of the workers and highly structured operations. Such an involvement would reflect upon the managerial orientation towards tasks and towards workers who are expected to perform such tasks. Blake and Mouton have identified five coordinates that reflect various styles of leader behaviour. The managerial grid figure and these styles are shown as follows:

The managerial grid Fig. 2 as shown above can be interpreted as follows :

(i) Coordinates (1,1). This represents an improvised management and the manager makes minimum efforts to get the work done. Minimum standards of performance and minimum worker dedication.

(ii) Coordinates (9,1). Excellent work design. Well Established procedures. Minimum worker interference. Orderly performance and efficient operations.

(iii) Coordinates (1,9), Personal and meaningful relationships with people. Friendly atmosphere and high morale. Loosely structured work design.

(iv) Coordinates (9,9). Ultimate in managerial efficiency. Thoroughly dedicated people. Trust-worthy and respectable atmosphere. Highly organised task performances. Known as team management style, it relies upon interdependence of relationships based upon trust and respect and work accomplishment based upon commitment of employees.

(v) Coordinates (5,5). Known as the middle-of-the-road management style, it is concerned with balancing the necessity to get the work done while maintaining worker morale at a satisfactory level. The goal is to achieve adequate organisational performance.

This managerial grid provides a reasonable indication of the health of the organisation as well as the ability of the managers. The model assumes that there is one best or most effective style of management, which is the style indicated by coordinates (9,9) also known as *team management style*. It is the objective of all management to move as close to this style as possible, for managers who emphasise both high concern for people as well as productivity are presumed to be more successful. Accordingly, managers should be carefully selected on the basis of their ability to coordinate people and tasks for optimum benefit.

The managerial grid model, however has become controversial on the basis of lack of empirical evidence supporting whether the team management style is the best management style. Even Blake and Mouton offer conceptual, rather than empirical arguments as to why the team management style should be the best style, when conditions are favourable.

(v) Tridimensional Grid

Reddin conceptualised a three-dimensional grid, also known as *3-D management*, borrowing some of the ideas from managerial grid. Three dimensional axes represent task-orientation, relationship-orientation, and effectiveness. By adding an effectiveness dimension to the task-oriented and relationship-oriented behaviour dimensions, Reddin has integrated the concepts of leadership styles with the situational demand of a specific environment.

Task orientations (TO) is defined as the extent to which a manager directs his subordinates' efforts towards goal attainment. It is characterised by planning, organising, and controlling. Relationship orientation (RO) is defined as the extent to which a manager has personal relationships. It is characterised by mutual trust, respect for subordinates' ideas and suggestions, and their feelings. Effectiveness is defined as the extent to which a manager is successful in his position. When the style of a leader is appropriate to a given situation, it is termed as effective; when the

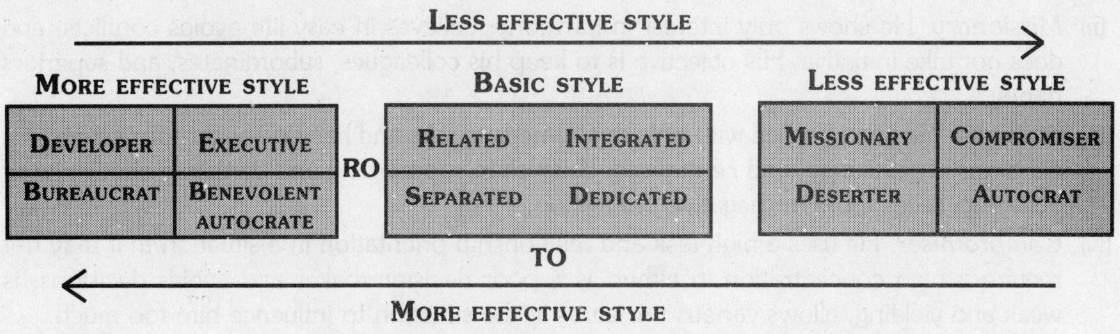

Fig. 3. *Tridimensional Grid.*

style is inappropriate to a given situation, it is termed as ineffective. Thus, the difference between effective and ineffective styles is often not the actual behaviour but the appropriateness of the behaviour to the environment in which it is used.

Either degree of TO or RO, or a combination of both, is used by leaders. On this basis, basically there are four styles as shown in Fig. 4.

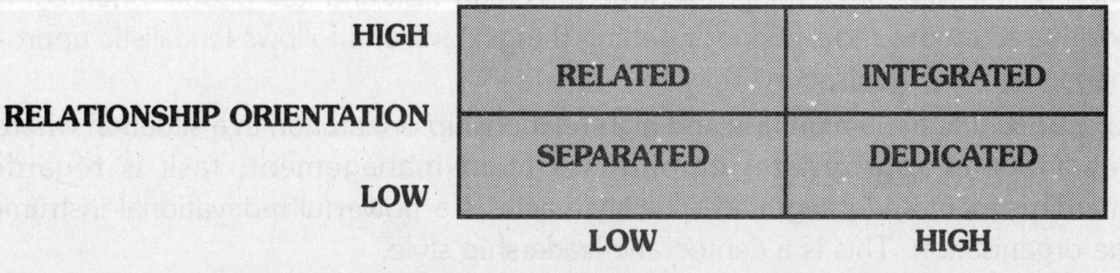

Fig. 4. *Task and Relationship Orientation*

These four styles represent four basic types of behaviour. The separated manager is concerned with correcting deviations. He writes rules and policies and enforces them. The related manager accepts others as he finds them, does not worry about time, sees the organisation as a social system, likes to work with others and obtains co-operation of others by setting examples. Dedicated manager is domineering, interested only in production, and does not identify with subordinates. He cannot work without power. The integrated manager gets himself and his people involved with the organisation. There is free two-way communication and strong identification and emphasis on team work. Any of the styles can be effective in some situations but not in others. Thus, each one of these styles has a less effective as well as a more effective equivalent as shown in Fig. 3. Thus, the four basic styles result into eight styles. These eight styles result from the eight possible combinations of task-orientation, relationship-orientation, and effectiveness as shown in Fig. 4.

According to this, following are ineffective styles :

(i) *Deserter*. He has both low task and low people orientation and is completely alienated from organisational life; avoids involvement; does not want to take responsibility and has low commitment; and believes in minimal output and works to rule.

(ii) *Missionary.* He shows only interest in harmony; believes in easy life avoids conflicts; and does not take initiative. His objective is to keep his colleagues, subordinates, and superiors happy.

(iii) *Autocrat.* He is concerned with only the immediate jobs and has no concern for others; his decisions are unilateral and centralised; believes in suppressing and demands obedience of authority; relies more on negative motivation.

(iv) *Compromiser.* He uses a high task and relationship orientation in a situation that may not require a high concentration in either; is a poor decision-maker and avoids decisions; is weak and yielding, allows various pressures in the situation to influence him too much.

The four corresponding effective styles are as follows:

(i) *Bureaucrat.* He has high orientation towards organisational rules and regulations; is impersonal and less task and relationship-oriented; produces only few ideas and does not take initiative.

(ii) *Developer.* He tends to display implicit trust in people; relies on high relationship orientation and less task orientation; believes in commitment to work, openness, freedom to act, self-expression, and development of subordinates.

(iii) *Benevolent Autocrat.* He is a directive manager who knows what he wants and one often gets it without creating resentment; is high task and less people oriented; adopts positive economic motivation for getting things done and follows feudalistic approach in managing the organisation.

(iv) *Executive.* He has a high task and high relationship orientation in a situation where such behaviour is appropriate; emphasises team management; task is regarded as interdependent and integrated. The style acts as a powerful motivational instrument in the organisation. This is a democratic leadership style.

The three-dimensional model recognises that a manager may use more than one style, and no single style is suggested to be appropriate in all situations. This gives a clear picture of the managerial world. It is assumed that all the styles have an equal chance of occurring and, thus, if a sufficiently large number of managers in a sufficiently diverse number of situations are tested, an equal number of each style would be obtained.

(vi) Scandinavian Studies

The three behavioural approaches we have just reviewed were essentially developed between the late 1940s and early 1960s. These approaches evolved during a time when the world was a far more stable and predictable place. In the belief that these studies fail to capture the more dynamic realities of today, researchers in Finland and Sweden have been reassessing whether there are only two dimensions that capture the essence of leadership behaviour. Their basic premise is that in a changing world, effective leaders would exhibit development-oriented behaviour. These are leaders who value experimentation, seek new ideas, and generate and implement change.

For instance, these Scandinavian researchers reviewed the original Ohio State data. They found that the Ohio State people included development items such as "pushes new ways of doing things," "originates new approaches to problems," and "encourages members to start new activities." But these items, at the time, did not explain much toward effective leadership. It could be, the Scandinavian researchers proposed, that this was because developing new ideas and implementing change were not critical in those days. In today's dynamic environment, this may no longer be true. So the Scandinavian researchers have been conducting new studies looking to see if there is a third dimension-development orientation-that is related to leader effectiveness.

Limitations of the Behavioural Model

The *Ohio* state University research paid attention primarily to relationships between leader and employee. Its principal limitation was that it paid little attention to the situation in which the relationships occurred and its effects on leadership style.

III. CONTINGENCY OR SITUATIONAL THEORY OF LEADERSHIP

After the trait approach proved to fall short of being an adequate overall theory of leadership, attention turned to the situational aspects of leadership. Social psychologists began the search for situational variables that affect leadership roles, skills, behaviour, and followers' performance and satisfaction. Numerous situational variables were identified, but no overall theory pulled it all together until *Fred Fiedler* proposed a widely recognised situation-based, or contingency, theory for leadership effectiveness.

The search for the "best" set of traits or behaviour has failed to discover an effective leadership mix and style for all situations. Thus, situational theories of leadership evolved that suggest leadership effectiveness depends on the fit between personality, task, power, attitudes, and perceptions. A number of situation-oriented leadership approaches have been publicised and researched. Two of the earlier ones are the *Fiedler contingency model* and the *Path-goal theory*.

Only after inconclusive and contradictory results evolved from much of the early trait and personal-behavioural research was the importance of the situation studied more closely by those interested in leadership. Eventually, researchers recognised that the leadership behaviour needed to enhance performance depends largely on the situation; what's effective leadership in one situation may be disorganised incompetence in another. The situational theme of leadership, while appealing, is certainly a challenging orientation to implement. Its basic foundation suggests that an effective leader must be flexible enough to adapt to the differences among subordinates and situations.

Deciding how to lead other individuals in difficult and requires an analysis of the leader, the group, and the situation. Managers who are aware of the forces they face are able to modify their styles to cope with changes in the work environment. Three factors of particular importance are forces within the managers, forces in the subordinates, and forces in the situation. *Tannenbaum* and *Schmidt* state the situational theme in this way:

Thus, the successful manager of men can be primarily characterised neither as a strong leader nor as a permissive one. Rather, he is one who maintains a high batting average in accurately assessing the forces that determine what his most appropriate behaviour at any given time should be and in actually being able to behave accordingly.

As the importance of situational factors and leader assessment of forces became more recognised, leadership research became more systematic, and contingency models of leadership began to appear in the organisational behaviour and management literature. Each model has its advocates and each attempts to identify the leader behaviours most appropriate for a series of leadership situations. Also, each model attempts to identify the leader-situation patterns important for effective leadership.

(i) Fiedler's Contingency Model

More recently, Fiedler and an associate, *Joe Garcia*, reconceptualised the former's original theory to deal with "some serious oversights that need to be addressed." Specifically, they are concerned with trying to explain the process by which a leader obtains effective group performance. They call this reconceptualisation cognitive resource theory.

They begin by making two assumptions. First, intelligent and competent leaders formulate more effective plans, decisions, and action strategies than less intelligent and competent leaders. Second, leaders communicate their plans, decisions, and strategies through directive behaviour. Fiedler and Garcia then show how stress and cognitive resources such as experience, tenure, and intelligence act as important influences on leadership effectiveness.

The essence of the new theory can be boiled down to three predictions :

(i) Directive behaviour results in good performance only if linked with high intelligence in a supportive, non-stressful leadership environment;

(ii) In highly stressful situations, there is a positive relationship between job experience and performance; and

(iii) The intellectual abilities of leaders correlate with group performance in situations that the leader perceives as non-stressful.

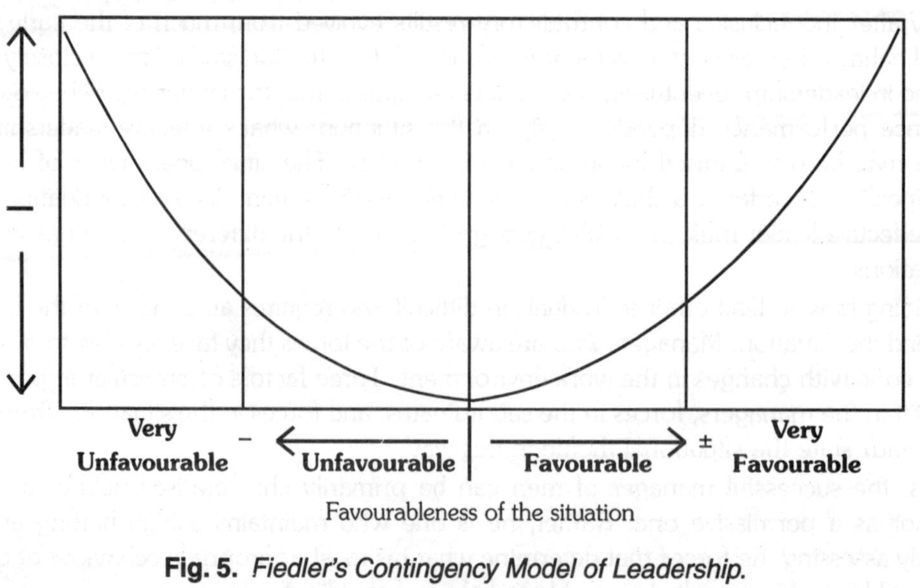

Fig. 5. *Fiedler's Contingency Model of Leadership.*

Fiedler's Contingency Model of Leadership Effectiveness

To test the hypothesis he had formulated from previous research findings, Fiedler developed what he called a contingency model of leadership effectiveness. This model contained the relationship between leadership style and the favourableness of the situation. Situational favourableness was described by Fiedler in terms of three empirically derived dimensions :

(i) The leader-member relationship, which is the most critical variable in determining the situation's favourableness.

(ii) The degree of task structure, which is the second most important input into the favourableness of the situation.

(iii) The leader's position power obtained through formal authority, which is the third most critical dimension of the situation.

Situations are favourable to the leader if all three of the above dimensions are high. In other words, if the leader is generally accepted and respected by followers (high first dimension), if the task is very structured and everything is "spelled out" (high second dimension), and if a great deal of authority and power are formally attributed to the leader's position (high third dimension), the situation is favourable. If the opposite exists (if the three dimensions are low), the situation will be very unfavourable for the leader. Fiedler was convinced through his research that the favourableness of the situation in combination with the leadership style determines effectiveness.

Through the analysis of research findings from all types of situations, Fiedler was able to discover that under very favourable and very unfavourable situations, the task-directed, or hard-nosed and authoritarian, type of leader was most effective. However, when the situation was only moderately favourable or unfavourable (the intermediate range of favourableness), the human relations, or lenient and democratic, type of leader was most effective. Figure 5, summarises this relationship between leadership style and the favourableness of the situation.

Why is the task-directed leader successful in very favourable situations? Fiedler offered the following explanation :

In the very favourable conditions in which the leader has power, informal backing, and a relatively well-structured task, the group is ready to be directed, and the group expects to be told what to do. Consider the captain of an airliner in its final landing approach. We would hardly want him to turn to his crew for a discussion on how to land.

As an example of why the task oriented leader is successful in a highly unfavourable situation, Fiedler cited

. . . the disliked chairman of a volunteer committee which is asked to plan the office picnic on a beautiful Sunday. If the leader asks too many questions about what the group ought to do or how he should proceed, he is likely to be told that "we ought to go home".

The leader who makes a wrong decision in this highly unfavourable type of situation is probably better of than the leader who makes no decision at all. In essence, what Fiedler's model suggests is that in highly unfavourable situations, the effective leader takes charge and makes the decisions that need to be made to accomplish the task without asking for input or trying to keep everyone happy.

Fig. 5, shows that the human relations leader is effective in the intermediate range of favourableness. An example of such situations is the typical committee or unit. In these situations, the leader may not be wholly accepted by the other members of the group, the task may not be completely structured, and some authority and power may be granted to the leader. Under such a relatively unfavourable, but not extremely unfavourable, situation, the model predicts that a human relations, lenient type of leader will be most effective. The same would be true of a moderately favourable situation. Such moderately unfavourable or favourable situations are most common for supervisors and managers. The implication is that in general the human relations, democratic style of leadership would be most effective in managing human resources in the large majority of organisational situations.

Research Support for the Contingency Model

As is true of any widely publicised theoretical development, *Fiedler's* model has stimulated a great deal of research. Not surprisingly, the results are mixed and a controversy has been generated. *Fiedler's* and his students have provided almost all the support for the model over the years. For example, to defend the validity of his theory, he cites thirty studies in a wide variety of teams and organisations (Navy teams, chemical research teams, shop departments, supermarkets, heavy machinery plant departments, engineering groups, hospital wards, public health teams, and others) and concludes that "the theory is highly predictive and that the relations obtained in the validation studies are almost identical to those obtained in the original studies." With one exception, which Fiedler explains away, he maintains that the model correctly predicted the correlations that should exist between the leader's style and performance in relation to the identified favourableness of the situation. As predicted, his studies show that in very unfavourable and very favourable situations, the task-oriented leader performs best. In a moderately favourable and moderately unfavourable situation, the human relations-oriented leader is more effective. Although Fiedler recognises that there is increasing criticism of his conclusions, he maintains that "methodologically sound validation studies have on the whole provided substantial support for the theory." Meta-analytic investigations of the predictions of the model have yielded support, mixed results, and nonsupport. A closer look at the criticisms is needed before applications and conclusions are presented.

Applications of Fiedler's Work

In addition to the conceptual and methodological questions, there is also the criticism of Fiedler's extension of the model of the actual practice of human resource management. On the basis of the model, Fiedler suggests that management would be better off engineering positions so that the requirements fit the leader instead of using the more traditional technique of selecting and developing leaders to fit into existing jobs. With this is mind, Fiedler and his colleagues developed a self-programmed training manual (called Leader Match), which includes a series of questionnaires that identify the person's leadership style and the situational dimensions of his or her job (task structure, leader-member relations, and position power) Then the trainee is given to a series of short problems with several alternative solutions.

Under Fiedler's leadership effectiveness training, the trainee is taught (on the basis of feedback compatible with the contingency model) ways to diagnose the situation so as to change it and optimise the leader style-leader situation match. Some of the suggested ways to modify leader-member relations are spending more (or less) informal time with subordinates and suggesting or effecting transfers of particular subordinates into or out of the unit. To decrease task structure, the leader may ask for new or unusual problems; to increase task structure, the leader may ask for more instructions and prepare a detailed plan. To raise position power, the leader could become an expert on the job, or to lower position power, the leader could call on subordinates to participate in planning and decision-making.

Most of the support for this Leader Match training has again come from Fiedler and his students/colleagues. After a review of five studies conducted in civilian organisations and seven conducted in military settings, Fiedler concluded that all twelve studies yielded statistically significant results supporting Leader match training. He claims that these studies also support "the contested point that leaders are able to modify their leadership situations to a degree sufficient to increase their effectiveness." Other research is critical of Leader Match as not being very constant with what the contingency model should predict.

(i) Fiedler's Contingency Theory in Perspective

Overall, there seems little question that Fiedler has provided one of the major breakthroughs for leadership theory and practice. Although much of the criticism is justified, there are several reasons that Fiedler's model has made a contribution :

(i) It was the first highly visible leadership theory to present the contingency approach.

(ii) It emphasised the importance of both the situation and the leader's characteristics in determining leader effectiveness.

(iii) It stimulated a great deal of research, including tests of its predictions and attempts to improve on the model, and inspired the formulation of alternative contingency theories.

(iv) It led to the development of the Leader Match program that applies the model to actual leadership situations.

At the very least, Fiedler has done and continues to do considerable empirical research, and in recent years he has proposed a new contingency theory.

In the more recent cognitive resource theory (CRT), Fiedler identifies the situations under which a leader's cognitive resources, such as, intelligence, experience, and technical expertise, relate to group and organisational performance. Based on Fiedler and his colleagues' [research, CRT predicts the following:

(i) More intelligent leaders develop better plans, decisions, and action strategies than less intelligent leaders.

(ii) Intelligence contributes more strongly to group performance if the leader is directive and the group members are motivated and supportive of the leader.

(iii) Interpersonal stress distracts the leader from the task and the leader's intelligence will contribute more highly if the leader has relatively stress-free relationships with superiors and subordinates.

As is the case with his original contingency model, CRT has been criticised, but it also will generate more research and, one hopes, make meaningful linkages to practice.

Critical Analysis of the Contingency Model

Although there is probably not as much criticism of Fiedler's work as there is, for example, of *Herzberg's* motivation theory, a growing number of leadership researchers do not wholly agree with *Fiedler's* interpretations or conclusions. For example, Graen and his colleagues initially raised some criticisms of the procedures and statistical analysis of the studies used to support the validity of the model. Schriesheim and his colleagues have been especially critical of the reliability and validity of Fiedler's measurement instrument. Schriesheim and colleagues also recently found that although the model did not hold across the various dimensions of the situations, it did predict better than other models of leadership. Fiedler and his colleagues have answered these criticisms to their satisfaction, but most summaries remain critical. For example, Yukl recently concluded—after reviewing the research—that the model has serious conceptual deficiencies limiting its utility for explaining leadership effectiveness, deficiencies such as its narrow focus on a single leader trait, ambiguity about what is really measured, and the absence of explanatory processes. The intent of these criticisms is not to suggest abandoning Fiedler's model, but, as Schriesheim and colleagues note, to focus on further exploring the model and its predictions and dealing with its shortcomings.

(ii) Path-Goal Theory of Leadership

The other widely recognised theoretical development from a contingency approach is the *path-goal theory* derived from the expectancy framework of motivation theory. Although, Georgopoulos and his colleagues at the University of Michigan's Institute for Social Research used path-goal concepts and terminology many years ago for analysing the impact of leadership on performance, the modern development is usually attributed to Martin Evans and Robert House, who wrote separate papers on the subject. In essence, the path-goal theory attempts to explain the impact that leader behaviour has on subordinate motivation, satisfaction, and performance. The House version of the theory incorporates four major types, or styles, of leadership. Briefly summarised, these are:

(i) Directive Leadership. This style is similar to that of the Lippitt and White authoritarian leader. Subordinates know exactly what is expected of them, and the leader gives specific directions. There is no participation by subordinates.

(ii) Supportive Leadership. The leader is friendly and approachable and shows a genuine concern for subordinates.

(iii) Participative Leadership. The leader asks for and uses suggestions from subordinates but still makes the decisions.

(iv) Achievement-oriented Leadership. The leader sets challenging goals for subordinates and shows confidence that they will attain these goals and perform well.

This path-goal-theory—and here is how it differs in one respect from Fiedler's contingency model-suggests that these various styles can be and actually are used by the same leader in

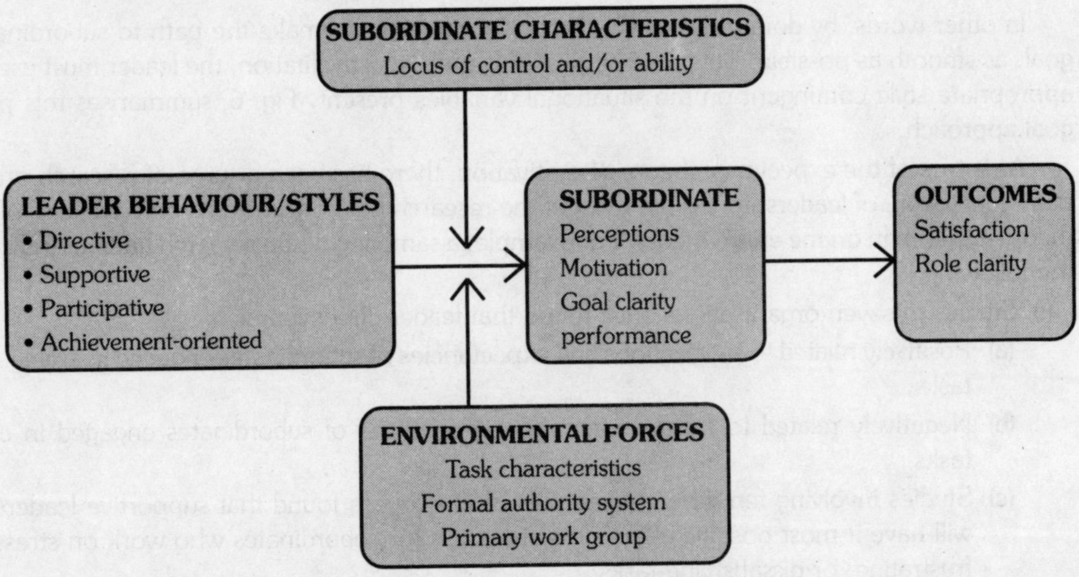

Fig. 6. *Path-Goal Theory of Leadership.*

different situations. Two of the situational factor that have been identified are the personal characteristics of subordinates and the environmental pressures and demands facing subordinates. With respect to the first situational factor, the theory asserts :

Leader behaviour will be acceptable to subordinates to the extent that the subordinates see such behaviour as either an immediate source of satisfaction or as instrumental to future satisfaction.

Leader behaviour will be motivational (e.g., will increase subordinates effort) to the extent that :

(i) It makes satisfaction of subordinate needs contingent on effective performance, and

(ii) It complements the environment of subordinates by providing the coaching, guidance, support, and rewards which are necessary for effective performance and which may otherwise be lacking in subordinates or in their environment.

Using one of the four styles contingent upon the situational factors as outlined above, the leader attempts to influence subordinates' perceptions and motivate them, which in turn leads to their role clarity, goal expectancies, satisfaction, and performance. This is specifically accomplished by the leader as follows :

(i) Recognising and/or arousing subordinates' needs for outcomes over which the leader has some control.

(ii) Increasing personal pay-offs to subordinates for work-goal attainment.

(iii) Making the path to those pay-offs easier to travel by coaching and direction.

(iv) Helping subordinates clarify expectancies.

(v) Reducing frustrating barriers.

(vi) Increasing the opportunities for personal satisfaction contingent on effective performance.

In other words, by doing the above, the leader attempts to make the path to subordinates' goals as smooth as possible. But to accomplish this path-goal facilitation, the leader must use the appropriate style contingent on the situational variables present. Fig. 6, summarises this path-goal approach.

As is true of the expectancy theory of motivation, there has been a surge of research on the path-goal theory of leadership. So far, most of the research has concentrated only on parts of the theory rather than on the entire theory. For example, a sampling of the research findings indicates the following :

(i) Studies of seven organisations have found that leader directiveness is :
   (a) Positively related to satisfactions and expectancies of subordinates engaged in ambiguous tasks.
   (b) Negatively related to satisfactions and expectancies of subordinates engaged in clear tasks.
   (c) Studies involving ten different samples of employees found that supportive leadership will have it most positive effect on satisfaction for subordinates who work on stressful, frustrating, or dissatisfying tasks.

(ii) In a major study in an industrial manufacturing organisation, it was found that in nonrepetitive, ego-involving tasks, employees were more satisfied under participative leaders than under nonparticipative leaders.

(iii) In three separate organisations it was found that for subordinates performing ambiguous, nonrepetitive tasks, the higher the achievement orientation of the leader, the more subordinates were confident that their efforts would pay off in effective performance.

The more recent reviews of the research on the path-goal theory are not as supportive as the above. For example, Schriesheim and Denisi note that only a couple of hypotheses have really been drawn from the theory, which means that it may be incapable of generating meaningful predictions. Another note of pessimism offered by these reviewers is that only one of the two hypotheses has received consistent empirical support. Research has generally substantiated the hypotheses that the higher the task structure (repetitiveness) of the jobs performed by subordinates, the higher the relationship between supportive leader behaviour/style and subordinate satisfaction. On the other hand, the second hypothesis—that the higher the task structure, the lower the correlation between instrumental (directive) leader behaviour and subordinate satisfaction—has received, at best, mixed research support. Schriesheim and Denisi then report results of their own research which indicates that the path-goal theory is capable of producing meaningful and testable predictions beyond the two task structure hypotheses. Also, a comprehensive review of forth-eight studies demonstrated that the mixed results of the individual studies, when cumulated, were transformed into support for continued testing of path-goal theory.

Overall, the path-goal theory, like the other established theories presented in this chapter, seems to need more research, but it certainly warrants further attention in the coming years. One analysis concluded that leaders will be perceived most favourably by their subordinates, and succeed in exerting most influence over them, when they behave in ways that closely match :

(i) The needs and values of subordinates and

(ii) The requirements of a specific work situation.

In other words, the path-goal theory, like the expectancy theory in work motivation, may help better explain the complexities of the leadership process.

Identifying Leadership Style

Fiedler believes a key factor in leadership success is the individual's basic leadership style. So he begins by trying to find out what that basic style is *Fiedler* created the LPC questionnaire for this purpose. It contains 16 contrasting adjectives (such as pleasant-unpleasant, efficient-inefficient, open-guarded, supportive-hostile). The questionnaire then asks respondents to think of all the co-workers they have ever had and to describe the one person they least enjoyed working with by rating him or her on a scale of 1 to 8 for each of the 16 sets of contrasting adjectives. *Fiedler* believes that based on the respondents' answers to this LPC questionnaire, he can determine their basic leadership style. If the least preferred co-worker is described in relatively positive terms (a high LPC score), then the respondent is primarily interested in good personal relations with this co-worker. That is, if you essentially describe the person you are least able to work with in favourable terms, *Fiedler* would label you relationship oriented. In contrast, if the least preferred co-worker is seen in relatively unfavourable terms (a low LPC score), the respondent is primarily interested in productivity and thus would be labelled task oriented. About 16 percent of respondents score in the middle range. Such individuals cannot be classified as either relationship oriented or task oriented and thus fall outside the theory's predictions. The rest of our discussion, therefore, relates to the 84 per cent who score in either the high or low range of the LPC.

Fielder assumes that an individual's leadership style is fixed. As we'll show in a moment, this is important because it means that if a situation requires a task-oriented leader and the person in that leadership position is relationship oriented, either the situation has to be modified or the leader removed and replaced if optimum effectiveness is to be achieved. *Fiedler* argues that leadership style is innate to a person—you can't change your style to fit changing situations!

(iii) Hersey and Blanchard's Situational Theory or Life-cycle Theory

The life-cycle theory of leadership has been developed by *Paul Hersey* and *Kenneth Blanchard*. The model focuses on the "maturity" of the followers as a contingency variable affecting the style of leadership. The "maturity" of the subordinates can be defined as their ability and willingness to take responsibility for directing their own behaviour in relation to a given task. The level of such maturity would determine the leader's emphasis on *task behaviours* (giving guidance and direction) and *relationship behaviour* (providing socio-emotional support). "*Task behaviour*" can be defined as the extent to which the leader engages in spelling out the duties and responsibilities of an individual or group. These behaviours include telling people what to do, how to do it, when to do it, where to do it and who is to do it. Task behaviour is characterised by one-way communication from the leader to the follower and this communication is meant to direct the subordinate to achieve his goal.

Similarly, "*relationship behaviour*" is defined as the extent to which the leader engages in two-way or multi-way communication. The behaviours include listening, facilitating and supportive behaviours.

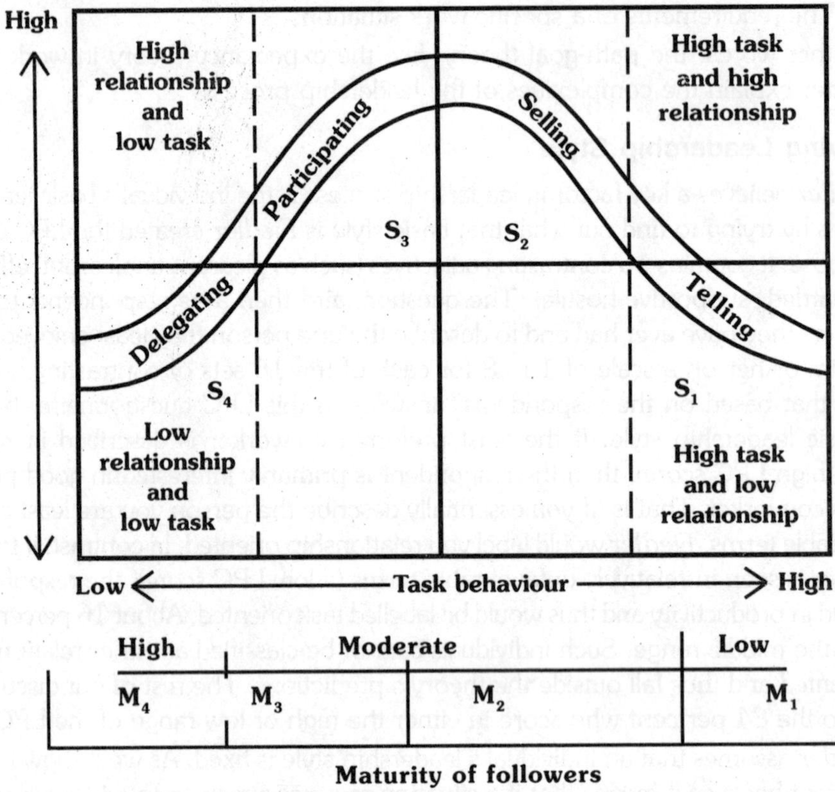

Fig. 7. *Hersey and Blanchard's Situational Leadership Model.*

"Maturity is the crux of the life-cycle theory. It has been defined previously as reflecting the two elements of ability and the willingness on the part of the followers. Ability is the knowledge, experience and skill that an individual or a group has in relation to a particular task being performed and the willingness refers to the motivation and commitment of the group to successfully accomplish such given tasks."

The style of leadership would depend upon the level of maturity of the followers. The following diagram suggests four different styles of leadership for each stage of maturity and a particular style in relationship to its relative level of maturity is considered to be best "match".

These various combinations of leadership styles and levels of maturity are explained in more detail as follows :

(S1) Telling. The "telling" style is best for low follower maturity. The followers feel very insecure about their task and are unable and unwilling to accept responsibility in directing their own behaviour. Thus, they required specific directions as to what, how and when to do various tasks so that a directive leadership behaviour is more effective.

(S2) Selling. The "selling" style is most suitable where followers have low to moderate maturity. The leader offers both task direction and socio-emotional support for people who are unable to take responsibility. The followers are confident but lack skills. It involves high task behaviour and high relationship behaviour.

(S3) Participating. This leadership approach involves high relationship behaviour and low task behaviour and is suitable for followers with moderate to high maturity where they have the ability but are unwilling to accept responsibility requiring a supportive leadership behaviour to increase their motivation. The leader has open door policy with open channels of communication and encourages his followers to perform their tasks well.

(S4) Delegating. Here the employees have both, the high job maturity and high psychological maturity. They are both able and willing to be accountable for their responsibility towards task performance and require little guidance and direction. It involves low relationship and low task behaviour.

The life-cycle theory of leadership requires that leaders attend to the demands of the situation as well as the feelings of the followers, and adjust their styles with the changing levels of maturity of the followers so as to remain consistent with the actual levels of maturity.

(iv) Leader-member Exchange (LMX) Theory

The *leader-member exchange (LMX) theory* argues that because of time pressures, leaders establish a special relationship with a small group of their subordinates. These individuals make up the in-group—they are trusted, get a disproportionate amount of the leader's attention, and are more likely to receive special privileges. Other subordinates fall into the out-group. They get less of the leader's time, fewer of the preferred rewards that the leader controls, and have superior-subordinate relations based on formal authority interactions.

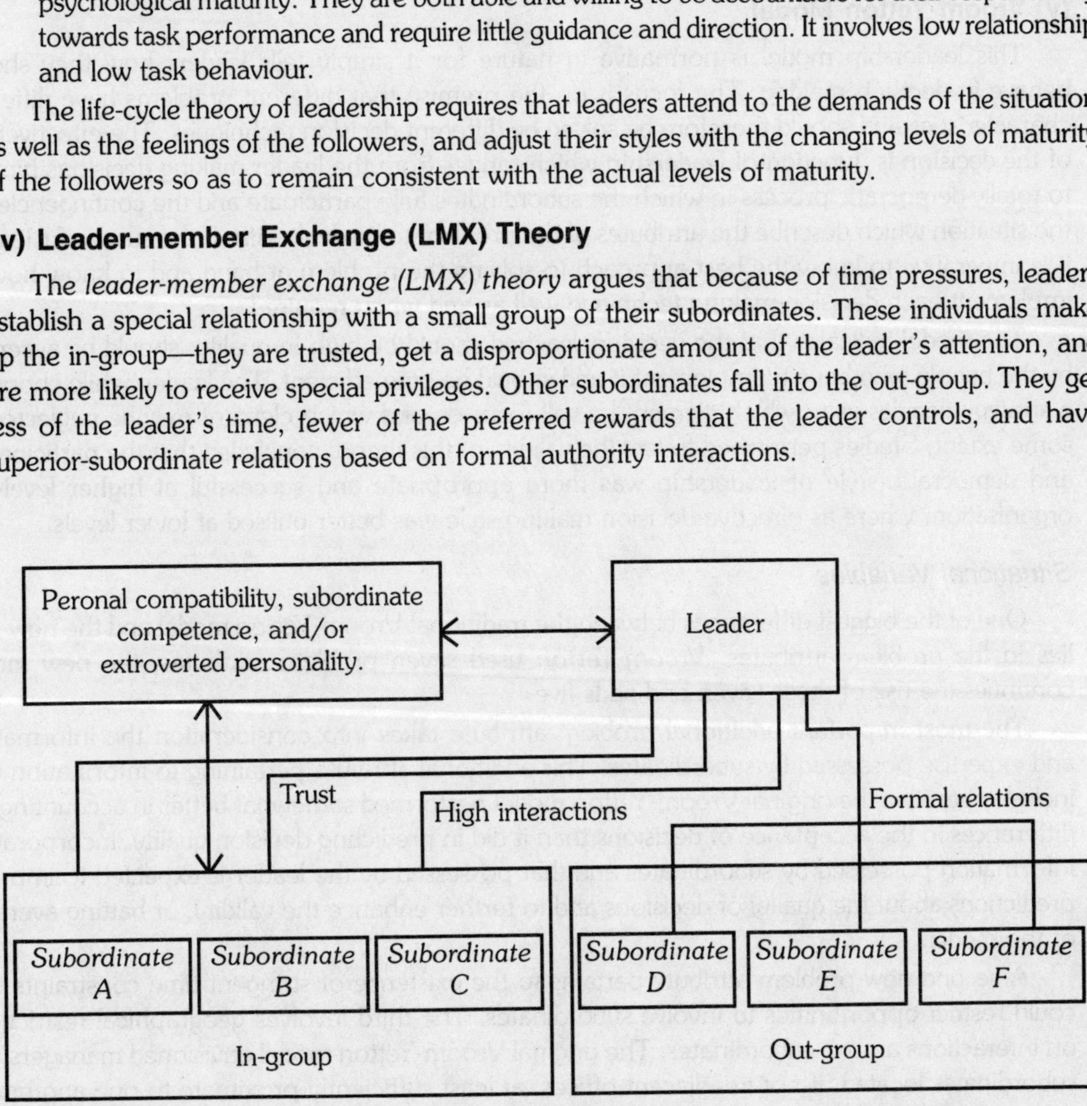

Fig. 8. *Member Exchange Theory.*

The theory proposes that early in the history of the interaction between a leader and a given subordinate, the leader implicitly categorises the subordinate as an "in" or an "out" and that relationship is relatively stable over time. Just precisely how the leader chooses who falls into each category is unclear, but there is evidence that leaders tend to choose in-group members because they have personal characteristics (for example, age, gender, attitudes) that are similar to the leader, a higher level of competence than out-group members, and/or an extroverted personality. (See Fig. 8) LMX theory predicts that subordinates with in-group status will have higher performance ratings, less turnover, and greater satisfaction with their superiors.

(v) Vroom-Yetton Model

This leadership model is normative in nature for it simply tells leaders how they should behave in decision making. The focus is on the premise that different problems have different characteristics and should therefore be solved by different decision techniques. The effectiveness of the decision is function of leadership which ranges from the leader making decisions himself to totally democratic process in which the subordinates fully participate and the contingencies of the situation which describe the attributes of the problem to be dealt with. For a successful leader, it is imperative to know the best approach to solving the problem at hand and to know how to implement each decision-making technique well as and when required.

The model indicates that the decision reached should be high in quality, should be accepted by the people who have to implement it and should be time efficient. The leader, while choosing a strategy decides as to which element he will focus on and which element may be neglected to some extent. Studies performed to test the validity of this theory concluded that the participative and democratic style of leadership was more appropriate and successful at higher levels of organisation, where as directive decision making style was better utilised at lower levels.

Situational Variables

One of the biggest differences between the traditional Vroom-Yetton model and the new one lies in the problem attributes. *Vroom-Yetton* used seven problem attributes; the new model continues the use of these seven and adds five.

The most important additional problem attribute takes into consideration the information and expertise possessed by subordinates. This additional attribute pertaining to information was included because the original Vroom-Yetton model performed somewhat better in accounting for differences in the acceptance of decisions than it did in predicting decision quality. Incorporating information possessed by subordinates and that possessed by the leader is expected to improve predictions about the quality of decisions and to further enhance the validity, or batting average, of the model.

A second new problem attribute pertains to the existence of stringent time constraints that could restrict opportunities to involve subordinates. The third involves geographical restrictions on interactions among subordinates. The original Vroom-Yetton model envisioned managers and subordinates located, if not in adjacent offices, at least sufficiently proximate to one another so that interaction could take place relatively easily. Thus, the Vroom-Yetton model prescribed group meetings of managers separated by thousands of miles. Without denigrating the usefulness of such meetings, the benefits that the Vroom-Yetton model predicted from joint decision-making may not outweigh the costs of assembling far-flung managers in one central location. The revised model addresses this issue by ascertaining not only the existence of geographical constraints but also whether the expected benefits might outweigh the costs.

Finally, the other two new attributes concern the importance of time and development. In the new model, these are not either-or judgments introduced after the fact to guide the choice among equally feasible alternatives. Instead, they are independent judgments obtained simultaneously with judgments of other problem attributes; taken together, they affect the benefits and costs of employing participative methods.

(vi) Vroom-Jago Revised Leadership Model

Vroom and *Yetton* initially developed a leadership and decision-making model that indicates the situations in which various degrees of participative decision-making are appropriate. In contrast to Fred *Fiedler, Vroom* and *Yetton* attempted to provide a normative model (prescriptive) that a leader can use in making decisions. Their approach assumes that no one particular leadership style is appropriate for each situation. Unlike Fiedler, they assume that leaders must be flexible enough to change their leadership styles to fit situations. It was Fiedler's contention that the situation must be altered to fit an individual's leadership style.

In developing their model, Vroom and Yetton made these assumptions :

(i) The model should be of value to leaders or managers in determining which leadership styles they should use in various situations.

(ii) No single leadership style is applicable to all situations.

(iii) The main focus should be the problem to be solved and the situation in which the problem occurs.

(iv) The leadership style used in one situation should not constrain the styles used in other situations.

(v) Several social processes influence the amount of participation by subordinates in problem solving.

Applying these assumptions resulted in the initial model that was concerned with leadership and decision making. The Vroom-Yetton leadership model generated interest among researchers, practitioners, and trainers. However, to improve the accuracy and predictability of the initial model, Vroom and Jago have developed a modified model.

Decision Effectiveness

The new model retains the concept of decision effectiveness (DEff). As shown in the following equation, DEff is dependent on decision quality (DQual) and decision commitment (DComm). Decision quality refers to the technical aspects of a decision. A decision is considered to be of high quality to the extent that it's consistent with the organisational goals to be attained and with potentially available information. Decision commitment refers to the acceptance of decisions by subordinates. Participation in decisions by subordinates tends to produce feelings of commitment and joint ownership.

DEff = DQual + DComm - DTP

However, there is a third term in the equation, DTP (decision time penalty). This term acknowledges that having sound thinking and a committed group to implement the decision is often not all that is needed to produce effective decisions. Decisions must also be made in a timely manner. Many decisions are made under severe time constraints. For example, an air traffic controller has limited time to place airplanes in various zones before increasing the risk of an accident. DTP takes on a value of zero whenever no stringent time constraints limit the process chosen.

Decision effectiveness is the criterion to use if there were no values attached to either time or to development or if those values were completely unknown. However, a more comprehensive criterion called *overall effectiveness* (OEff) is introduced. OEff is greatly influenced by decision effectiveness, but, as shown in the following equation, its values reflect the remaining two criteria affected by degree of participation. Both consequences pertain to effects of the decision process on available "human capital." Independent of the effectiveness of the decisions produced, a decision process can have effects, either positive or negative or both, on the energy and talent available for subsequent work.

OEff = DEff - Cost + Development

Negative effects on human capital occur because decision processes use up time and energy, even in the absence of a time constraint. An executive group meeting including a senior executive and five subordinates and lasting two hours would consume 12 work hours. The value of that time is certainly not zero, although its precise cost varies with the opportunity costs of the meeting. Which other activities did each manager forsake to participate in that meeting? When critically important activities are not carried out because of time spent in meetings, costs are incurred that must, at the very least, be "traded off" against the benefits of the meeting. In the preceding equation, cost represents the value of time lost through use of a given decision process.

On the other hand, participation can contribute to human capital. Participation in decision making can build teamwork, strengthen commitment to organisational goals, and contribute to the development of participants' technical and managerial skills. In the OEff equation, development is intended to represent organisational benefits that extend beyond the individual decision under consideration.

Continuous Scales

The original *Vroom-Yetton* model utilised dichotomous (yes-no) judgments in generating the prescriptions of the model: Do you have enough information to make a high-quality decision?

Of the 12 problem attributes in the new model, 10 have been designed to be expressed as five-point scales. The four attributes dealing with importance (quality, commitment, time, and development) are answered on scales ranging from "no importance" to "critical importance." Another six attributes (leader information, problem structure, commitment probability, goal congruence, conflict, and subordinate information) are expressed as probability estimates. For example, the question "Do you have sufficient information to make a high-quality decision?" Can now be answered no, probably no, maybe, probably yes, or yes. Table (1), shows 1 of the 12 attributes he questions used to measure them, and the permissible responses for each.

Application of the New Model

Using the manager's analysis of the situation represented by that manager's responses to the diagnostic questions, the formulas predict the most appropriate way of handling the situation, the second-best way, and so forth. However, the equations' complexity precludes their pencil-and-paper application.

(Table-1)

How important is the technical quality of this decision?

(1)	(2)	(3)	(4)	(5)
No import	Low import	Average import	High import	Critical import

QR: Quality Requirement

Vroom and Jago offer two alternatives for the application of their new model to actual managerial problems. The first is a computer program that guides the manager through the analysis of the situation and, with speed and accuracy, solves the relevant equations. The second method, more familiar to users of the original Vroom-Yetton model, employs decision trees that represent the operation of the complex equations if certain simplifying assumptions are made.

The first simplifying assumption is that each problem attribute can be given a clear yes or no (or high or low) response. This restricts the application of the model to relatively unambiguous situations. The second simplifying assumption is that 4 of the 12 problem attributes are held constant. Severe time constraints and the geographical dispersion of subordinates (relatively infrequent occurrences) are assumed not to exist. Additionally, it's assumed that the manager's motivation to conserve time and to develop subordinates does not change. Figure depicts what *Vroom* and *Jago* label the "time-driven" decision tree. It's designed for the manager who places maximum weight on saving time and minimum weight on develop subordinates.

Validity of the Vroom-Jago Model

As was the case with the original Vroom-Yetton model when it was first introduced, the revised model currently lacks complete empirical evidence establishing its validity. Certainly, the model is though to be consistent with what we now know about the benefits and costs of participation and represents a direct extension of the original 1973 model. Nonetheless, without extensive evidence that use of the new model can improve decision effectiveness—and, by extension, leadership success—its value as a theoretical contribution and as a practical tool remains open to question.

International Research

A valuable aspect of the Vroom-Yetton and Vroom-Jago approaches to leadership is that research has been conducted both in and outside of the United States. In an increasingly interdependent world it's increasingly important not to reach conclusions about a theory or an approach based solely on domestic samples of leaders.

One study of Austrian managers used real decisions made by the participants. Small discussion groups of managers reviewed each situation and provided :

(i) The decision process used by the manager and

(ii) An analysis of the problem attributes present in the situation.

The study results indicated that small-group judgments were more accurate than a single person's judgments in analysing written descriptions of the situations.

Another study looked at owner-operated cleaning franchises in the United States and Canada. Leadership behaviour of American and Canadian owner-managers was assessed through problem sets. The results indicated that US and Canadian managers who had above-average conformity to what the model prescribes had significantly more profitable businesses and more satisfied employees.

Limitations of the Model

After a thorough review of leadership theories, models, and concepts, one behavioural scientist concluded that the Vroom-Yetton approach is unsurpassed in terms of scientific validity and practical usefulness. Nevertheless, the model has limitations.

The model forces a person to make a definite response. Because it fails to permit a "probably yes" or a "probably no," a yes or no response must be made. Work situations are not that easy to categorise; in many situations, neither yes nor no is accurate.

The model is also criticised for being too complex. It includes decision trees, ratings, and problem sets. Although the model is complex, we believe this criticism is not warranted. The model is precise and specific, which means that some complexity is likely to be needed. Instead of discussing complexity, we might better state that the model, like more leadership explanations, simplifies how managers think and process stimuli.

Finally, organisational life is complex, and the way individual managers think is complex. The model, according to some critics, fails to deal with the realities today's managers face in terms of change, technological advancement, and international competition. Can any model deal with every contingency of leading and remain understandable and useful? Perhaps critics are expecting too much.

MOST RECENT APPROACHES FOR LEADERSHIP

Despite a relative degree of acceptance of the contingency and path-goal theories of leadership and the great (at least relative to other areas in organisational behaviour) amount of research that has been conducted, few would disagree today that leadership is still in trouble. Leadership is currently being attacked on all fronts—in terms of theories relating to it, research methods for studying it, and applications. For example, John Miner was very critical of leadership theory and then proposed that it be dropped altogether, and a recent comprehensive review of the traditional theories concluded that many of the texts concluded to identify moderating effects were judged to be inappropriate and most of the results reported in this domain have not been replicated. The time has come for alternative theories, research methods, and applications for leadership studies.

Besides the established trait, group, contingency, and path-goal theories of leadership, a number of other theories have emerged in recent years. These include the charismatic, transformational, social learning, and substitutes theories of leadership.

I. ATTRIBUTION THEORY OF LEADERSHIP

Attribution theory also has application value as an explanation and analysis of leadership. *Kelley* stresses that attribution theory mainly concerns the cognitive process by which a person interprets behaviour as being caused by (attributed to) certain cues in the relevant environment.

Since most causes of subordinate, or follower, behaviours are not directly observable, determining causes requires reliance on perception. In attribution theory, individuals are assumed to be rational and to be concerned about the casual linkages in their environments.

The attributional approach starts with the position that the leader is essentially an information processor. In other words, the leader searches for informational cues as to "why" something is happening and then attempts to construct causal explanations that guide her leadership behaviour. The process in simple terms appears to be follower behaviour — leader attributions — leader behaviour.

Leader's Attributions

Kelley suggests that the leader's primary attributional task is to categories the causes of follower, or subordinate, behaviour into one of three source dimensions: person, entity, or context.

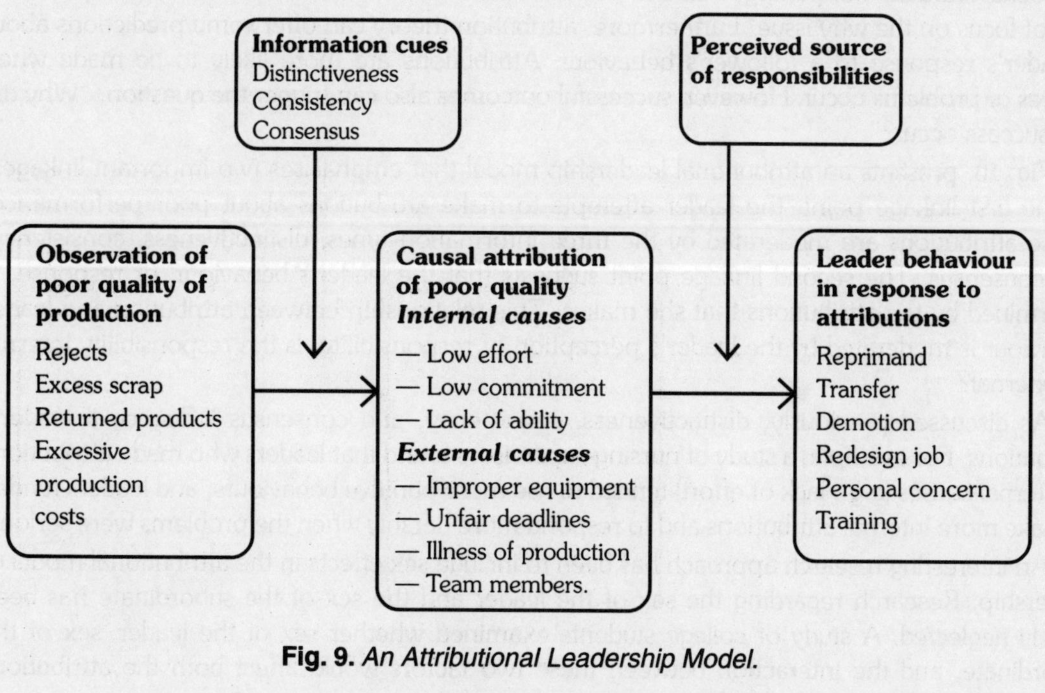

Fig. 9. *An Attributional Leadership Model.*

That is, for any given behaviour, such as poor quality of output, the leader's job is to determine whether the poor quality was caused by the person (e.g., inadequate ability), the task (entity), or some unique set of circumstances surrounding the event (context).

The leader seeks three types of information when forming attributions about a follower's behaviour: distinctiveness, consistency, and consensus. For any behaviour, the leader first attempts to determine whether the behaviour is distinctive to a task—that is, whether the behaviour occurs on this task but not on other tasks. Next, the leader is concerned about consistency, or how frequently the behaviour occurs. Finally, the leader estimates consensus, the extent to which others behave in the same way. A behaviour unique to one follower has low consensus; if it is common to other followers, this reflects high consensus.

Leader's Perception of Responsibility

The judgment of responsibility moderates the leader's response to an attribution. Clearly, the more a behaviour is seen as caused by some characteristic of the follower (i.e., an internal cause) and the more the follower is judged to be responsible for the behaviour, the more likely the leader is to take some action toward the follower. For example, an outcome (e.g., poor performance) may be attributed to factors outside the control of a person (such as not having the tools to do the job well) or to internal causes (such as lack of effort).

Attributional Leadership Model

Attribution theory offers a framework for explaining leader behaviour more insightfully than either trait or personal-behavioural theories. Attribution leadership theory attempts to explain why behaviours are happening; trait and personal-behavioural theories are more descriptive and do not focus on the why issue. Furthermore, attribution theory can offer some predictions about a leader's response to a follower's behaviour. Attributions are more likely to be made when failures or problems occur. However, successful outcomes also can trigger the question, "Why did this success occur?"

Fig. 10, presents an attributional leadership model that emphasises two important linkages. At the first linkage point, the leader attempts to make attributions about poor performance. These attributions are moderated by the three information types: distinctiveness, consistency, and consensus. The second linkage point suggests that the leader's behaviour, or response, is determined by the attributions that she makes. This relationship between attribution and leader behaviour is moderated by the leader's perception of responsibility. Is the responsibility internal or external?

As discussed previously, distinctiveness, consistency, and consensus influence a leader's attributions. For example, a study of nursing supervisors found that leaders who made attributions of internal causes (e.g., lack of effort) tended to use more punitive behaviours, and leaders tended to make more internal attributions and to respond more harshly when the problems were serious.

An interesting research approach has been to include sex effects in the attributional model of leadership. Research regarding the sex of the leader and the sex of the subordinate has been largely neglected. A study of college students examined whether sex of the leader, sex of the subordinate, and the interaction between these two factors would affect both the attributions made for employees' poor performance and the corrective action taken by leaders. The researchers concluded that the sex composition of the leader-subordinate dyad was a critical and neglected variable in attributional research.

Currently, research support for the attributional theory of leadership is limited. There is a need to test the theory in more organisational settings. Understanding the causes of leader behaviour or at least searching for these causes seems more promising for managerial use than does simply adding another trait or descriptive theory to the leadership literature.

II. CHARISMATIC LEADERSHIP THEORIES

Charismatic leadership is a throwback to the old conception of leaders as being those who "by the force of their personal abilities are capable of having profound and extraordinary effects on followers." Although the charismatic concept, or charisma, goes as far back as the ancient Greeks and is cited in the Bible, its modern development is often attributed to the work of Robert House. On the basis of the analysis of political and religious leaders, House suggests that charismatic leaders are characterised by self-confidence and confidence in subordinates, high expectations for subordinates, ideological vision, and the use of personal example. Followers of charismatic leaders identify with the leader and the mission of the leader, exhibit extreme loyalty to and confidence in the leader, emulate the leader's values and behaviour, and derive self-esteem from their relationship with the leader. Superstar *Michael Jorden* has perhaps the best individual skills in the history of basketball. However, he is also known for his charismatic leadership. He explains the effect of his charisma on followers : "I can inspire people to do things I believe in, especially when I see someone with ability who is not trying his hardest." As co-captain of the Chicago Bulls, Jordan sometimes seems to rankle or even infuriate his team-mates, such as Dennis Rodman, but as do all charismatic leaders, he improves the performance of his fellow players and lifts the whole team's level of play to win N.B.A. championships.

Recently, Bass has extended the profile of charismatic leaders by including business leaders such as Lee Iacocca or women who have become top-level executives, discussed in the

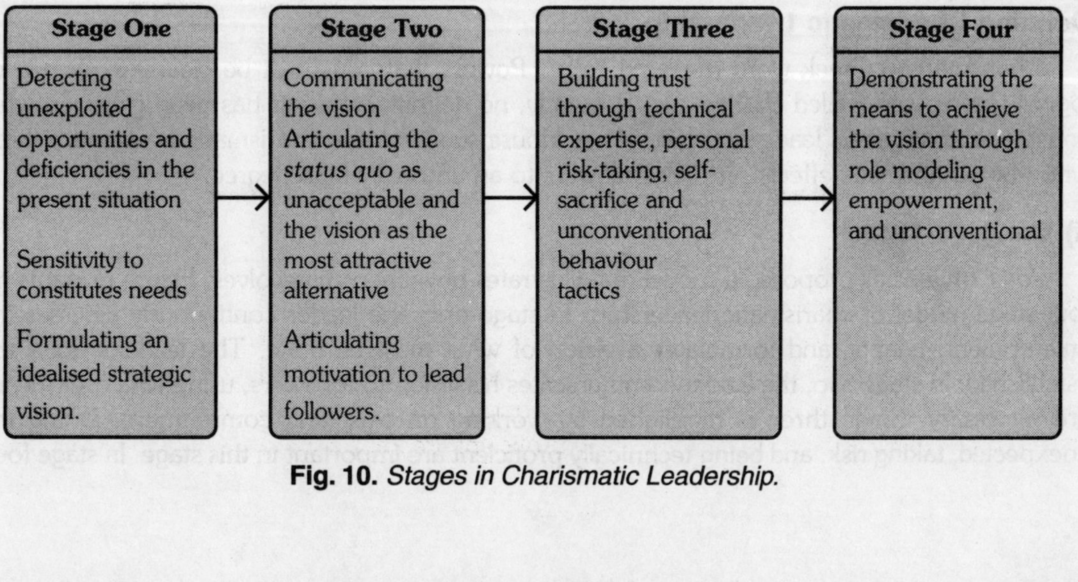

Fig. 10. *Stages in Charismatic Leadership.*

accompanying Managing Diversity in Action: Charismatic Women Leaders in Business. In particular, he notes that charismatic leaders have superior debating and persuasive skills as well as technical expertise and that they foster attitudinal, behavioural, and emotional changes in their followers. A recent Fortune article describes a manager with charisma as follows :

He attended some middling college. Does not have an MBA. But he has an aura. He persuades people-subordinates, peers, customers, even the S.O.B. you both work for—to do thing they'd rather not. People charge over the hill for him. Run through fire. Walk barefoot on broken glass. He does not demand attention, he commands it.

Because of the effects that charismatic leaders have on followers, the theory predicts that charismatic leaders will produce in followers performance beyond expectations as well as strong commitment to the leader and his or her mission. House and his colleagues provide some support for charismatic theory, but as with the other leadership theories, complexities are found and more research is needed. Also extensions of the theory are being proposed. For example, Conger and Kanungo treat charisma as an attributional phenomenon and propose that it varies with the situation. Leader traits that foster charismatic attributions include self-confidence, impression-management skills, social sensitivity, and empathy. Situations that promote charismatic leadership include a crisis requiring dramatic change or followers who are very dissatisfied with the *status quo*.

Included in the extensions of charismatic leadership is also the recognition of a dark side. Charistmatic leaders tend to be portrayed as wonderful heroes, there can also be unethical characteristics associated with charistmatic leaders. With regard to meeting the challenge of being ethical, it has been noted that charismatic leaders :

. . . deserve this lable only if they create transformations in their organisations so that members are motivated to follow them and to seek organisation objectives not simply because they are ordered to do so, and not merely because they calculate that such compliance is in their self-interest, but because they voluntarily identify with the organisation, its standards of conduct and willingly seek to fulfil its purpose.

Defining Charismatic Leadership

Charisma is a Greek word meaning "gift". Powers that could not be clearly explained by logical means were called charismatic. Presently, no definitive answer has been given on what constitutes charismatic leadership behaviour. House suggests that charismatic leaders are those who have charismatic effects on their followers to an unusually high degree.

(i) Conger's Model

Jay Conger has proposed a model that illustrates how charisma evolves. Figure presents his four-stage model of charismatic leadership. In stage one, the leader continuously assesses the environment, adapts, and formulates a vision of what must be done. The leader's goals are established. In stage two, the leader communicates his vision to followers, using whatever means are necessary. Stage three is highlighed by working on trust and commitment. Doing the unexpected, taking risk, and being technically proficient are important in this stage. In stage four, the charismatic leader serves as a role model and motivator. The charismatic leader uses praise and recognition to instill within followers the belief that they can achieve the vision.

A number of empirical studies have examined behaviour and attributes of charismatic leaders, such as articulation ability, affection from followers, ability to inspire, dominating personality, and need for influence. However, no specific set of behaviours and attributes is universally accepted by theorists, researchers, and practitioners.

What Constitutes Charismatic Leadership Behaviour?

What behavioural dimensions distinguish charismatic leaders from noncharismatic leaders? A criticism of the early work on charismatic leadership is that explanations of it lacked specificity. Limited attempts have been made to develop and test specific charismatic qualities such as vision, acts of heroism, and the ability to inspire. However, in most cases, clarifying what specifically constitutes charismatic behaviour has been generally ignored.

Two Types of Charismatic Leaders

Most discussions of charismatic leadership highlight the term vision. It's argued that the first requirement for exercising charismatic leadership is expressing a shared vision of what the future could be. Through communication ability, the visionary, charismatic leader inks followers' needs and goals to job or organisational goals. Linking followers with the organisation's direction, mission, and goals is easier if they're dissatisfied or not challenged by the current situation.

Crisis-based charismatic leaders have an impact when the system must handle a situation for which existing knowledge, resources, and procedures are not adequate. The crisis-produced charismatic leader communicates clearly what actions need to be taken and what their consequences will be.

Crisis management is a growing field of study and inquiry. The crises managers face enable charismatic leadership to emerge. First, under conditions of stress, ambiguity, and chaos, followers give power to individuals who have the potential to correct the crisis situation. The leader is empowered to do what's necessary to correct the situation or solve the problem. In many cases, the leader is unconstrained and is allowed to use whatever she thinks is needed.

A crisis also permits the leader to promote nontraditional actions by followers. The crisis-based charismatic leader has greater freedom to encourage followers to search for ways to correct the crisis. Some methods, procedures, and tactics adopted by followers may be disorderly, chaotic, and outside the normal boundary of actions. However, the charismatic leader in a crisis situation encourages, supports, and usually receives action from followers.

Our knowledge about charismatic leadership is still relatively abstract and ambiguous. Despite *Weber's* concept of charismatic authority, *Conger's* framework of how charismatic leadership evolves, House's definition and propositions about the characteristics of charismatic leaders, and some limited research results, much more theoretical and research work needs to be done. There is a void in understanding about whether charismatic leaders can be harmful in expressing visions that are unrealistic or inaccurate or in the way they attack a crisis problem. Management scholar and writer Peter Drucker claims that "charisma becomes the undoing of leaders". How accurate is Drucker? No one knows at this time. However, evidence suggests that charismatic leaders (e.g., Hitler, Stalin, Jim Jones) can secure greater commitment to failing, personally demeaning, and tragic goals than can the average leader. In the business world, John DeLorean was able to raise hundreds of millions of dollars for his failed automobile venture because of his powers of persuasions and impressions management. He promoted himself as an innovative genius.

III. TRANSACTIONAL AND TRANSFORMATIONAL LEADERSHIP

Each of the leadership theories discussed emphasises that leadership is an exchange process. Followers are rewarded by the leader when they accomplish agreed-upon objectives. The leader helps followers accomplish the objectives.

IV. TRANSACTIONAL LEADERSHIP

The exchange role of the leader has been referred to as transactional. Figure presents the transactional leadership roles. The leader helps the follower identify what must be done to accomplish the desired results: better-quality output, more sales or services, reduced cost of production. In helping the follower identify what must be done, the leader takes into consideration the person's self-concept and esteem needs. The transactional approach uses the path-goal concepts as its framework.

In using the transaction style, the leader relies on contingent reward and on management by exception. Research shows that when contingent reinforcement is used, followers exhibit an increase in performance and satisfaction; followers believe that accomplishing objectives will result in their receiving desired rewards. Using management by exception, the leader won't be involved unless objectives are not being accomplished.

Transactional leadership is not often found in organisational settings. One national sample of US workers showed that only 22 percent of the participants perceived a direct relationship between how hard they worked and how much pay they received. That is, the majority of workers believed that good pay was not contingent on good performance. Although workers prefer a closer link between pay and performance, it was not present in their jobs. Why? There are probably a number of reasons, such as unreliable performance appraisal systems, subjectively administered rewards, poor managerial skills in showing employees the pay-performance link, and conditions outside the manager's control. Also, managers often provide rewards that are not perceived by followers to be meaningful or important.

A small pay increase, a personal letter from the boss, or a job transfer may not be what employees want in the form of a contingent reward. Until managers understand what the employee wants, administer rewards in a timely manner, and emphasise the pay-performance link, there's likely to be confusion, uncertainty, and minimal transactional impact in leader-follower relationships.

V. THE TRANSFORMATIONAL THEME

An exciting new kind of leader, referred to as the transformational leader, motivates followers to work for transcendental goals instead of short-term self-interest and for achievement and self-actualisation instead of security. In transformational leadership, viewed as a special case of transactional leadership, the employee's reward is internal. By expressing a vision, the transformational leader persuades followers to work hard to achieve the goals envisioned. The leader's vision provides the follower with motivation for hard work that is self-rewarding (internal).

Transactional leaders will adjust goals, direction, and mission for practical reasons. Transformational leaders, on the other hand, make major changes in the firm's or unit's mission, way of doing business, and human resource management to achieve their vision. The transformational leader will overhaul the entire philosophy, system, and culture of an organisation.

Names that come to mind when we think about transformational leaders are Michale Eisner at Walt Disney, Jack Welch at General Electric, and, Bill Gates at Microsoft Corporation. Under Eisner's leadership, for example, Disney has moved into live action movies (some R-rated), syndicated a business show for television, introduced a TV channel, developed new cartoon characters, and licensed new apparel products. Eisner took risks and pushed the company along a path that was unheard of for 40 years. He transformed Walt Disney Company from a conservative firm into an assertive, proactive one. Eisner brought in a work ethic, a style, and a vision that has helped put Disney back into the forefront of entertainment.

The development of transformational leadership factors has evolved from research by Bass. He identified five factors (the first three apply to transformational and the last two apply to transactional leadership) that describe transformational leaders. They are :

(i) ***Charisma :*** The leader is able to instill a sense of value, respect, and pride and to articulate a vision. Individual attention. The leader pays attention to followers' needs and assigns meaningful projects so that followers grow personally.

(ii) ***Intellectual stimulation.*** The leader helps followers rethink rational ways to examine a situation. He encourages followers to be creative.

(iii) ***Contingent reward.*** The leader informs followers about what must be done to receive the rewards they prefer.

(iv) ***Management by exception.*** The leader permits followers to work on the task and does not intervene unless goals are not being accomplished in a reasonable time and at a reasonable cost.

One of the most important characteristics of the transformational leader is charisma. However, charisma by itself is not enough for successful informational leadership, as *Bass* clearly states :

The deep emotional attachment which characterises the relationship of the charismatic leader to followers may be present when transformational leadership occurs, but we can distinguish a class of charismatics who are not at all transformational in their influence. Celebrities may be identified as charismatic by a large segment of the public. Celebrities are held in awe and reverence by the masses who are developed by them. People will be emotionally aroused in the presence of celebrities and identify with them in their fantasy, but the celebrities may not be involved at all in any transformation of their public. On the other hand, with charisma, transformational leaders can play the role of teacher, mentor, coach, reformer, or revolutionary. Charisma is a necessary ingredient of transformational leadership, but by itself it is not sufficient to account for the transformational process.

In addition to charisma, transformational leaders need assessment skills, communication abilities, and a sensitivity to others. They must be able to articulate their vision, and they must be sensitive to the skill deficiencies of followers.

VI. VISIONARY LEADERSHIP

The term vision recurred throughout our discussion of charismatic leadership, but visionary leadership goes beyond charisma. In this section, we review recent revelations about the importance of visionary leadership.

Visionary leadership is the ability to create and articulate a realistic, credible, attractive vision of the future for an organisation or organisational unit that grows out of and improves upon the present. This vision, if properly selected and implemented, is so energising that it "in effect jump-starts the future by calling forth the skills, talents, and resources to make it happen."

A review of various definitions finds that a vision differs from other forms of direction setting in several ways : "A vision has clear and compelling imagery that offers an innovative way to improve, which recognises and draws on traditions, and connects to actions that people can take to realise change. Vision taps people's emotions and energy. Properly articulated, a vision creates the enthusiasm that people have for sporting events and other leisure time activities, bringing the energy and commitment to the work-place."

The key properties of a vision seem to be inspirational possibilities that are value centered, realisable, with superior imagery and articulation. Visions should be able to create possibilities that are inspirational, unique, and offer a new order that can produce organisational distinction. A vision is likely to fail if it does not offer a view of the future that is clearly and demonstrably better for the organisation and its members. Desirable visions fit the times and circumstances and reflect the uniqueness of the organisation. People in the organisation must also believe that the vision is attainable. The vision should be perceived as challenging yet doable. Visions that have clear articulation and powerful imagery are more easily grasped and accepted.

First is the ability to explain the vision to others. The leader needs to make the vision clear in terms of required actions and aims through clear oral and written communication. The best vision is likely to be ineffective if the leader is not a strong communicator. Ronald Reagan—the so-called 'great communicator'—used his years of acting experience to help him articulate a simple vision for his presidency; a return to a happier and more prosperous times through less government, lower taxes, and a strong military.

The second skill needed is to be able to express the vision not just verbally but through the leader's behaviour. This requires behaving in ways that continually convey and reinforce the vision. *Herb Kelleher* at Southwest Airlines lives and breathes his commitment to customer service. He's famous within the company for juming in, when needed to help check in passengers, load baggage, fill in for flight attendants or do anything else to make the customer's experience more pleasant.

The third skill is being able to extend the vision to different leadership contexts. This is the ability to sequence activities so the vision can be applied in a variety of situations. For instance, the vision has to be as meaningful to the people in accounting as to those in marketing, and to employees in Prague as well as in Pittsburgh.

VII. PROVIDING TEAM LEADERSHIP

Leadership is increasingly taking place within a team context. As teams grow in popularity, the role of the leader in guiding them members takes on heightened importance. And the role of team leader is different from the traditional leadership role performed by first-line supervisors.

Many leaders are not equipped to handle the change to teams. As one prominent consultant noted, "even the most capable managers have trouble making the transition because all the command-and-control type things they were encouraged to do before are no longer appropriate."

First, team leaders are liaisons with external constituencies. These include upper management, other internal teams, customers and suppliers. The leader represents the team to other constituencies, secures needed resources, clarifies others' expectations of the team, gathers information from the outside, and shares this information with team members.

Second, team leaders are troubleshooters. When the team has problems and asks for assistance, team leaders sit in on meetings and help try to resolve the problems. This rarely relates to technical or operation issues because the team members typically know more about the tasks being done than does the team leader. Where the leader is most likely to contribute is by asking penetrating questions, helping the team talk through problems, and by getting needed resources from external constituencies. For instance, when a team in an aerospace firm found itself short-handed, its team leader took responsibility for getting more staff. He presented the team's case to upper management and got the approval through the company's human resources department.

Third, team leaders are conflict managers. When disagreements surface they help process the conflict. What's the source of the conflict. Who is involved? What are the issues? What resolution options are available? What are the advantages and disadvantages of each? By getting team members of address questions such as these, the leader minimises the disruptive aspects of intra team conflicts.

Finally, team leaders are coaches. They clarify expectations and roles, teach, offer support, cheerlead, and whatever else is necessary to help team members improve their work performance.

LEADERSHIP AS A CONTINUUM

There are, in fact, a variety of styles of leadership behaviour between two extremes of autocratic and free rein. *Tannenbaum* and *Schmidt* have depicted a broad range of styles on a continuum moving from authoritarian leadership behaviour at one end to free-rein behaviour at the other end as shown in Figure. The figure presents a range of leadership behaviour available to a manager. Each type of action represents the degree of authority used by a leader and the degree of freedom which a subordinate enjoys in relationship to his superior. The left side shows a style where control is maintained by a manager and the right side shows the release of control. However, neither extreme is absolute and authority and freedom are never without their limitations. Thus, a question is pertinent: At which point along with the continuum should a manager adopt his behaviour? In fact, there is not readymade answer, but it depends upon three particulars.

(i) Forces in manager, that is, his value system, his confidence in his subordinates, his own leadership inclinations, and his feeling of security in an uncertain situation.
(ii) Forces in subordinates, that is, their need for independence, readiness to assume responsibility for decision-making, level of tolerance for ambiguity, understanding and identifying organisational goals, interest in the problems, knowledge and experience to deal with the problems and learning to expect to share in decision-making.
(iii) Forces in the situation, that is, type of organisation, group effectiveness, the problem itself and the pressure of time.

In 1973, *Tannebaum* and *Schmidt* developed another pattern of choosing leadership behaviour. They feel that because of changes in social system, organisational environment, the old continuum pattern is not longer valid. Organisations do not exist in vacuum, but are affected by changes that occur in the society. Thus, there would be more factors in situational variables affecting the leadership pattern. These forces lie outside the organisation interacting continuously with the organisational environment. Thus, new continuum of leadership pattern is more complex as compared to previous one. In this pattern, the total area of freedom shared by manager and non-manager is constantly redefined by interaction between them and the forces in the environment. The points on the continuum designate the types of manager and manager's behaviour that become possible with any given amount of freedom available to each. This continuum is more complex and dynamic reflecting the organisational and social realities.

A successful leader is one who is keenly aware of those forces which are more relevant to his behaviour at any given time. He accurately understands himself, the individuals and the group he is dealing with, and the organisation and the broader social environment in which he operates.

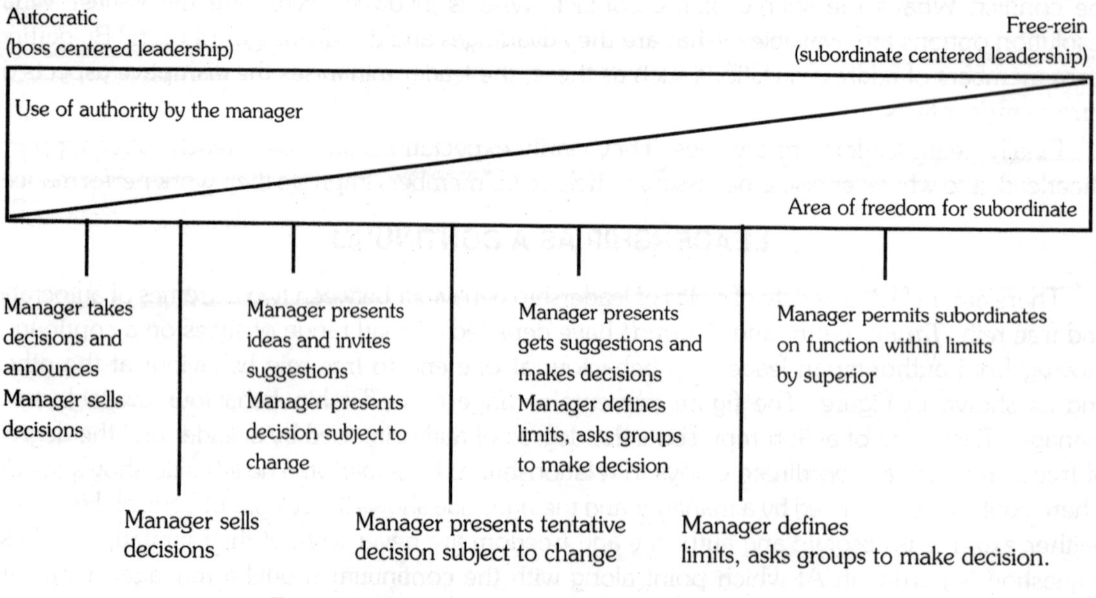

Fig. 11. *Continuum of Leadership Behaviour.*

However, merely understanding these factors correctly is not enough but he can be successful only when he is able to behave appropriately in the light of these perceptions and understanding. Thus, the authors have observed, "the successful manager of men can be primarily characterised neither as a strong leader nor as a permissive one. Rather he is one who maintains a high batting average in accurately assessing the forces that determine what his more appropriate behaviour at any given time should be and in actually being able to behave accordingly. Being both insightful and flexible, he is less likely to see the problem of leadership as a dilemma".

IS THERE A BIOLOGICAL BASIS FOR LEADERSHIP?

Is it possible that leader behaviour lies in the body's harmonies and in the brain's neurotransmitters? While this may take the study of leadership out of the behavioural laboratory and into the chemistry lab, there is increasing evidence indicating that leadership has biological roots.

A growing body of research suggests that the best leaders are not necessarily the smartest, strongest, or more aggressive of a group but rather those who are most proficient at handling social interactions. That finding is not particularly surprising. However, the researchers have found that effective leaders possess a unique biochemical mixture of harmones and brain chemistry that helps them build social alliances and cope with stress.

Two chemicals—serotonin and testosterone—have received most of the attention. Increased levels of the former appear to improve sociability and control aggression. Higher levels of the latter increase competitive drive.

Studies with monkeys find that :

(i) Dominant monkeys—the leaders (whether male or female)—have a higher level of serotonin than do their subordinates; and

(ii) When that leader is removed from the group, the new leader that takes charge shows a marked increase in levels of serotonin.

Researchers believe that high levels of serotonin promote leadership by controlling aggressive and antisocial impulses, as well as reducing overreaction to petty or irrelevant stresses. The direction of causation, however, is not clear : High levels of serotonin may stimulate leadership and/or leadership may result in a rise in serotonin.

Testosterone also seems to play a role in leadership. Studies with baboons find that leaders experience a sudden rise in testosterone levels when legitimate threats appear. In subordinates, the level of testosterone goes down during a crisis.

But enough about monkeys. How about humans? A study in a college fraternity found males in the highest leadership positions had the highest level of serotonin. Researchers have also found that testosterone levels rise in top tennis players before competitive matches. The higher levels seem to make the tennis players more assertive and motivated to win. It's been found that testosterone also rises after status-enhancing achievements such as winning a promotion or earning a degree, and women in professional jobs have higher levels of the hormone.

LEADERSHIP STYLES IN INDIAN ORGANISATIONS

In the first instance, Indian management is generally believed to be autocratic with subordinates closely supervised by their superiors and only a limited degree of participation is allowed to the subordinates. However, the real situation in this context can be appreciated only when a detailed account of various practices is taken for consideration. Fortunately, some empirical studies are variable in this context which do not necessarily support the traditional view rather they present a mixed note.

The review of various studies fails to give a generalised result. The findings are too diverse, sometimes even contradictory. It indicates the absence of a clear-cut direction in the managerial behaviour thereby reflecting a lack of managerial conviction and values. Since, managerial styles are determined by a host of factors such as forces in superiors, subordinates, and situations, it is unlikely to expect a uniform leadership style. Indian work organisations, from this point of view, can be classified into three parts which have some distinctive features and consequently the different leadership styles. Such classification may be :

(i) Family-managed traditional organisations,

(ii) Professionally managed Indian organisations and foreign-owned organisations, and

(iii) Public sector organisations.

In family-managed traditional organisations, the most prevalent style is autocratic. Sons and grandsons of the entrepreneurs are automatically promoted without any consideration to efficiency or overall suitability. Thus, there is management by inheritance or management by chromosomes with the result that these organisations are highly centralised in their organisation structures and are authoritarian in their approach. In many such organisations, a certain amount of the paternalistic attitude prevails. The proprietary character of business and large-scale participation of family members in it have made the attitude of the head of the business, who is also the head of the family, highly paternalistic. The same paternalistic attitude extends to the employees and has developed a set of values in a employer vis-a-vis his employees. At the initial stage, authoritarian style is more suitable which these organisations have followed. However, such style has also been inherited by successors without any appreciable change or modification. On the other hand, there are many organisations in the private sector owned by Indians or by multinationals who have appreciable degree of participation or democratic leadership. The reason is that multinationals do not bring only their technology but also the work culture which is more permissive and conducive towards the application of modern approach of management. As such, the degree of participation is greater in such organisations. The third category of organisations are in public sector. Here, bureaucratic style is more prevalent owing to the work culture inherited by public sector managers. Initially, public sector organisations were manned by civil servants who brought a lot of bureaucratic culture with them. The net results is that the entire organisational processes are governed by bureaucratic model. Its implication is status differentials, class distinctions, and impersonal relationships which work against participative style.

REVIEW QUESTIONS

1. What do you mean by leadership? What are the main characteristics of leadership? Explain.
2. Explain the importance of leadership in an organisation. What are the main functions of leadership?
3. Explain the theories of leadership in details.
4. What do you understand by leadership style? Explain in detail. What are the characteristics of leaders?
5. Describe the most recent approaches to leadership.

REFERENCES

1. *J. Clifton William, "Human Behaviour in Organisations", Cincinnatice South Western Publishing Co., 1978.*
2 *Keity Davis, op. cit., "Human Behaviour at Work", 144. In Fact, Research Evidence Indicates that the Employee-Oriented Leaders Are More Vulnerable to Role Conflict on the Job, Especially When There Are Job Pressures.*
3. *Gary Dessler, Organisation and Management: A Contingency Approach, Englewood Cliffs, NJ Prentice-Hall, Inc., 1976.*
4. *Victor Vroom, "Some Personality Determinants of the Effects of Participation", Journal of Applied Social Psychology, 1959.*
5. *Charles Byrd, "Social Psychology", Appleton-Century-crofts, New York.*
6. *Edwin E. Ghiselli, "Explorations in Managerial Talent", Pacific Palisades, Cal., Goodyear, 1971.*
7. *B. Solomon, Leadership of Youth, Youth Services, New York, 1954.*
8. *Korman, "Consideration and Initiating Structure: A Review", Personal Psychology, 19, Winter, 1966.*
9. *R. Blake and J. Mouton, "The Managerial Grid, Houston Gulf Publishing Co., 1964, Barnes and L. Greiner, "Breakthrough in Organisation Development".*
10. *H.J. Bernardin and Kenneth Alvares, "The Managerial Grid as a Predictor of Conflict Resolution Method and Managerial Effectiveness", Administrative Science Quarterly.*
11. *James V. Spotts, "The Problems of Leadership: A Look at Some Recent Findings of Behavioural Science Research", Kansas Business Review.*
12. *Model of Leadership Effectiveness: A Review of Empirical Findings, Psychological Bulletin, 76, 1971.*
13. *L.S. Ceoke and P.M. Bons, "Manipulating the Situation to Fit the Leader's Style: Two Validation Studies of Leader Match", Journal of Applied Psychology.*
14. *R.W. Rice, "Psychometric Properties of the Esteem for the Least Preferred Co-worker (LPC) Scale", Academy of Management Review, January, 1978.*
15. *B.Garen, K Alvares, J.B. Orris and J.A. Martella, "Contingency Model of Leaderful Effectiveness: Antecedent and Evidential Results", Psychological Bulletin.*
16. *R.P. Vecchio, "An Empirical Investigation of the Validity of Fiedler's Model of Leadership Effectiveness", Organizational Behaviour and Human Performance.*
17. *S.E. Ashour, "The Contingency Model of Leadership Effectiveness: An Evaluation", Organisational Behaviour and Human Performance.*

18. *Mithel, et al., "The Contingency Model; Criticisms and Suggestions".*
19. *Martin G. Evans, "A Leaders' Ability to Differentiate the Subordinate's Performance", Personal Psychology, Vol. 26, 1973.*
20. *Woe E. Stinson and Lane Tracy, "Some Disturbing Characteristics of the LPC Score", Personal Psychology.*

10th

CHAPTER

OVERVIEW

Approaches to Planned Organisational Change

• ***After reading this chapter, you should be able to know:***

- Introduction
- Classification of Forces for Change
- Objectives of Planned Change
- Pressures on Organisations for Change
- Various Forms of Organisational Change
- Basic Forms of Changes Based on the Organisational Culture
- Process of Change
- Steps Included in the Process of Change
- Resistance to Change
- Overcoming Resistance to Change
- Reasons for Resist Change to Employees
- Suggestions for Overcoming Resistance to Change
- Changing Organisations
- Individual Reactions to Change
- Alternative Change Management Approaches
- Depth of Intended Change
- The Essential Stages for Effective Change Management

10

APPROACHES TO PLANNED ORGANISATIONAL CHANGE

INTRODUCTION

In many sectors of the economy, organisations must have the capacity to adapt quickly in order to survive. Often the speed and complexity of change severely test the capabilities of managers and employees to adapt quickly and effectively. When organisations fail to change, the costs of that failure may be quite high. In 1985, 406,000 people worked for IBM worldwide and its profit were $6.6 billion. By 1994, one-third of the people and most of the profits were gone. To a certain extent, all organisations exist in a changing environment and are themselves constantly changing. For example, the world of business is thought to be changing in the following ways :

(i) The average company will become smaller, employing fewer people.

(ii) The traditional hierarchical organisation will give way to a variety of organisational forms, such as networks of specialists.

(iii) Technicians, ranging from computer repairers to radiation therapists, will replace manufacturing operatives as the worker elite.

(iv) The vertical division of labour will be replaced by a horizontal division of labour.

(v) The emphasis of many businesses will shift from making a product to providing a service.

(vi) Work itself will be redefined with more emphasis on constant learning and higher-order thinking.

Increasingly, organisations that emphasise bureaucratic or mechanistic systems are ineffective. Organisations with rigid hierarchies, high degrees of functional specialisation, narrow and limited job descriptions, inflexible rules and procedures, and impersonal management can't respond adequately to demands for change. Organisations need designs that are flexible and adaptive. They also need systems that both require and allow greater commitment and use of talent on the part of employees and managers.

As we know that *change* refers to making things different, innovation is a more specialised kind of change. Innovation is a new idea applied to initiating or improving a product, process, or service. So all innovations involve change, but not all changes necessarily involve new ideas or lead to significant improvements. Innovations in organisations can range from small incremental improvements, such are RJR Nabisco's extension of the Ore product line to include double stuffs and chocolate-covered Ores, up to radical breakthroughs, such as the Amazon.com bookstore on the Internet. Keep in mind that while our examples are mostly of product innovations, the concept of innovation also encompasses new production process technologies, new structures or administrative systems, and new plans or programs pertaining to organisational members.

CLASSIFICATION OF FORCES FOR CHANGE

The forces for change can be classified conveniently into two groups: environmental forces and internal forces. *Environmental forces* are beyond management's control. *Internal forces* operate inside the firm and are generally within the control of management.

I. Environmental Forces

Organisations seldom undertake significant change without a strong shock from their environment. The external environment includes many economic, technological, and social forces that can trigger the change process. Those who have studied and practiced organisational change agree that these environmental triggers are necessary but not sufficient on initiate change. Change also involves managers who are aware of the change and who take action.

The manager of a business has historically been concerned with reacting to changes in the marketplace. Competitors introduce new products, increase their advertising, reduce their prices, or increase their customer service. In each case, a response is required unless the manager is content to permit the erosion of her profit and market share. At the same time, changes occur in customer tastes and incomes. The firm's products may no longer have customer appeal; customers may be able to purchase less expensive, higher-quality forms of the same products.

The enterprise system generally eliminates from the economic scene those firms that don't adjust to market conditions. The manager who's isolated from reality and ignores signals from the market will soon confront the more vocal (and louder) signals of discontented shareholders. By that time, however, the appropriate change may well be dissolution of the firm—the final solution.

Suppliers of the organisation's resources are another market force to be dealt with. A change in the quality and quantity of human resources can dictate changes in the firm. For example, adoption of automated processes can be stimulated by a decline in the supply of labour. The technique of coal mining and tobacco farming have greatly changed during recent years due to labour shortages. McDonald's Corporation recently revised completely its human resource practices to employ greater numbers of older retired individuals as the pool of teenage employees (its traditional source of employees) began to decline.

Changes in the supply of materials can cause the firm to substitute one material for another. Rayon stockings and synthetic rubber tyres were direct outgrowths of war-induced shortages in raw materials. We need not catalogue the whole range of possible changes in resources markets that stimulate organisational change. The potential is great, however, and must be recognised.

The second source of environmental change forces is technology. The knowledge explosion has introduced new technology for nearly every business function. Computers have made possible high-speed data processing and the solution to complex production problems. New machines and new processes have revolutionised how many products are manufactured and distributed. Computer technology and automation have affected not only the technical conditions of work, but the social conditions as well. New occupations have been created, and others have been eliminated. Slowness to adopt new technology that reduces cost and improves quality will show up in the financial statements sooner or later. Technological advance is a permanent fixture in the business worked. As a force for change, it will continue to demand attention.

The third source of environmental change forces is social and political change. Business managers must be tuned in to the great movements over which they have no control but which, in time, influence their firm's fate. Sophisticated mass communications and international markets creates great potential for business, but they are also great threats to managers who can not understand what's going on. Finally, the relationship between government and business becomes much closer as regulations as imposed and relaxed.

These pressures for change reflect the increasing complexity and interdependence of modern living. The banking and transportation industries have in recent times been deregulated and forced to enter into competition with other industries offering the same or similar services and products. Deregulation of these industries has led to tremendous change in organisational strategies and structures.

Corresponding implications of external forces requires organisational learning processes. These processes, now being studies in many organisations, involve the capacity to absorb new information, process that information in the light of previous experience, and act on the information in new and potentially risky ways.

II. Internal Forces

Internal forces for change, which occur within the organisation, can usually be traced to process and behavioural problems. The process problems include breakdowns in decision making and communications. Decisions are not being made, are made too late, or are of poor quality. Communications are short-circuited, redundant, or simply inadequate. Tasks are not undertaken or aren't completed because the person responsible did not get the world. Because of inadequate or nonexistent communications a customer order is an filled a grievance isn't processed, or an invoice isn't field and the supplier is not paid. Interpersonal and interdepartmental conflicts reflect breakdown in an organisational process.

Low levels of morale and high levels of absenteeism and turnover are symptoms of the behavioural problems that must be diagnosed. A wildcat strike or a walkout may be the most tangible sign of a problem, yet such tactics are usually employed because they arouse management to action. A certain level of employee discontent exists in most organisations—it's dangerous to ignore employee complaints and suggestions. But the process of change includes the recognition phase—the point where management must decide to act or not to act.

In many organisations, the need for change goes recognised until some major catastrophe occurs. The employees strike or seek the recognition of a union before the management finally recognises the need for action. Whether it takes a whisper or a shout, the need for change must be recognised by some means; and once that need has been recognised, the exact nature of the problem must be diagnosed. If the problem is not properly understood, the impact of change on people can be extremely negative.

OBJECTIVES OF PLANNED CHANGE

Distinguishing between change that inevitably happens to all organisations and change that is planned by members of an organisation is important. Our focus is primarily on intentional, goal-oriented organisational change. Planned organisational change represents the intentional attempt by managers and employees to improve the functioning of groups, teams, department, divisions, or an entire organisation in some important way.

Because managers and employees cannot control an organisation's environment, they must continually introduce internal organisational changes that allow it to cope more effectively with new challenges. These challenges come from within the firm in terms of the demands and expectations of the work force and from sources outside the firm, such as increased competition, advances in technology, new government legislation and regulations, and pressing social demands. Organisations usually change in response to these pressures, and in some cases, organisations change in anticipation of them.

Planned change efforts always involve specific goals. These goals might include spurring productivity, developing new technology, increasing employee motivation, gaining greater customer satisfaction, or building market share. However, specific goals for improvement are based on two underlying objectives:

(i) To improve the capacity or ability of the organisation to adapt to changes in its environment; and

(ii) To change patterns of employee behaviours.

I. Improving Organisational Adaptability

Organisations need effective approaches and techniques to adapt to changing markets, labour supplies, societal expectations, legal requirements, new ideas, and the like. Organisations typically create departments or specialised teams that plan for and implement needed changes. These adaptive departments or groups often have such names as product research, market research, long range planning strategic, planning research and development, public affairs, or organisation development.

The departments that have traditionally been concerned with issues of organisational change may no longer provide sufficient adaptability. Thus the ability to manage organisational change effectively is no longer the exclusive concern of specialised departments. All parts of the organisation must be challenged to become more adaptive.

II. Changing Individual Behaviours

The second major objective of planned organisational change is to alter the behaviour of individuals within the organisation. An organisation may not be able to change its strategy for adapting to its environment unless its members behave differently in their relationships with one another and their jobs. In the final analysis, organisations survive, grow, prosper, decline, or fail because of employee behaviours—the things that employees do or fail to do.

An example of the importance of changing employee behaviours occurred when the new CEO of an international bank announced a company wide change program. The bank's traditional hierarchical organisation seemed ill suited to respond to serious challenges stemming from deregulation in the United States and increased global competition. The only solution was a fundamental change in how the company operated. The CEO held a retreat with 15 top executives of the bank. They carefully examined the organisations's culture and purpose and drew up a new mission statement. Following the retreat, the bank recruited a new vice-president for human resources from another organisation well-known for its excellent management. In a quick succession of moves, the bank adopted a new organisation design, performance appraisal system and compensation plan, and training programs. The CEO implemented quarterly attitude surveys to track the progress of the change program. All these steps would seem to represent a textbook example of successful organisational change. Unfortunately, there was one principal problem. Two years after the CEO started the change program, virtually no changes in organisational behaviour had occurred. So, what went wrong?

The CEO and his top-management team correctly identified the need for change. But they incorrectly assumed that they alone knew how best to proceed. They believed that simply adopting a new mission statement, new programs, and a new organisation design would achieve the change they desired. However, unless employee behaviours actually change, new programs and structures probably will have little, if any, impact on organisational effectiveness—as the bank's management learned to their chagrin.

Behaviour should be a primary target of planned organisational change. Change programs must have an effect on employee roles, responsibilities, and working relationships. At some fundamental level, all organisational changes depend on changes in behaviour.

PRESSURES ON ORGANISATIONS FOR CHANGE

Both advanced industrialised societies and developing countries are changing in important ways that have significant impacts on organisations. The pressures on organisations for change are accelerating, so in a very real sense, organisations are undergoing several business revolutions—sudden, radical, and complete reorientations of the way business is done—around the world. These business revolutions include :

(i) the globalisation of markets,

(ii) the spread of information technology and computer networks,

(iii) the dismantling of organisational hierarchies, which fundamentally alters management's tasks,

(iv) changes in the nature of the work force employed by organisations.

These revolutions are the result of dramatic forces, or pressures for change, that profoundly affect all organisations and societies. We examine these business revolutions and explore the pressures for change that are affecting organisations. These are not the only pressures for change, but they certainly are among the more dramatic.

I. Globalisation of Markets

Organisations face global competition on an unprecedented scale. Increasingly, the main players in the world's economy are international or multinational corporations. The emergence of these global organisations creates pressures on domestic corporations to redesign and, in turn, internationalize their operations. There is a global market for most products, but in order to compete effectively in it, firms often must transform their cultures, structures, and operations.

II. Information Technology and Computer Networks

A second revolution facing organisation stems from the proliferation of computer networks and the use of sophisticated information technology. *Information technology* comprises complex network of computers, telecommunication systems and remote-controlled devices. Information technology is having a profound impact on organisational operations, power relationships, and development and implementation of strategies. The latest frontier in information technology is a computer application known as virtual reality. *Virtual reality* is created by a display and control technology that surrounds the user with an artificial environment that mimics real life. The user of virtual reality does not passively view a computer screen but rather becomes a participant in a three dimensional setting. Boeing is investigating potential applications of virtual reality to the design and testing of aircraft.

Another new information technology, already in use at some companies, is *electronic data interchange (EDI),* which links an organisation to its suppliers and customers electronically. An organisation can link its manufacturing and inventory functions so that, as soon as the system runs low on a part, a central computer automatically executes an electronic purchase order signalling the suppliers to ship new parts. This technology can save a company millions of dollars in reduced inventory costs and potential downtime from part shortages.

III. Changing Nature of Management

A third business revolution concerns the changing nature of management. Both globalisation and information technology have an impact on organisational management. In adaptive, flexible organisations the roles and practices of managers are being reconceptualised. The old-style manager often told people what to do and how to do it. The new-style manager asks the right questions and helps employees do the job on their own. New-style managers may still be relatively rare.

IV. Changing Nature of the Work Force

The work force continues to grow more diverse in terms of gender and race. Thus equal opportunity pressures on hiring practices and promotion decisions will persist for some time to come. Other trends add to the challenge for organisations. For example, the dual-career family rapidly is becoming the norm, rather than the exception, in many advanced societies. Further, the contingency work force continues to grow as a percentage of all workers. The *contingency work force* includes part-time employees, free-lancers, subcontractors, and independent professionals hired by companies to cope with unexpected or temporary challenges.

Increasingly, the work force is better educated, less unionised, and characterised by changing values and aspirations. Although changing values and expectations will not lessen the motivation to work, they are altering the rewards that people seek from work and the balance they seek between work and other aspects of life. The *quality of work life* represents the degree to which people are able to satisfy important personal needs through their work and is an important goal for many, if not most, working women and men. More than ever before, employees desire pleasant working conditions, more participation in decisions that effect their jobs, and support facilities, such as day care centres for their children. These and other employee expectations put additional pressures on organisations and affect their ability to compete effectively in the labour market.

VARIOUS FORMS OF ORGANISATIONAL CHANGE

Consultant *David A. Nadler* and management professor *Michael L.Tushman* recently developed an instructive typology of organisational change (Fig. 1). On the vertical axis of their model, change is characterised as either anticipatory or reactive. Anticipatory changes are any systematically planned changes intended to take advantage of expected situations. Oppositely, reactive changes are those necessitated by unexpected environmental events or pressures. The horizontal axis deals with the scope of a particular change, either incremental or strategic. Incremental changes involve subsystem adjustments needed to keep the organisation on its chosen path. Strategic changes alter the overall shape or direction of the organisation. For instance, adding a night shift to meet unexpectedly high demand for the company's product is an incremental change. Switching from building houses to building high-rise apartment complexes would be a strategic change. Four resulting types of organisational change in the Nadler-Tushman model are tuning, adaptation, reorientation, and recreation. These types of organisational changes, listed in order of increasing complexity, intensity, and risk, require a closer look.

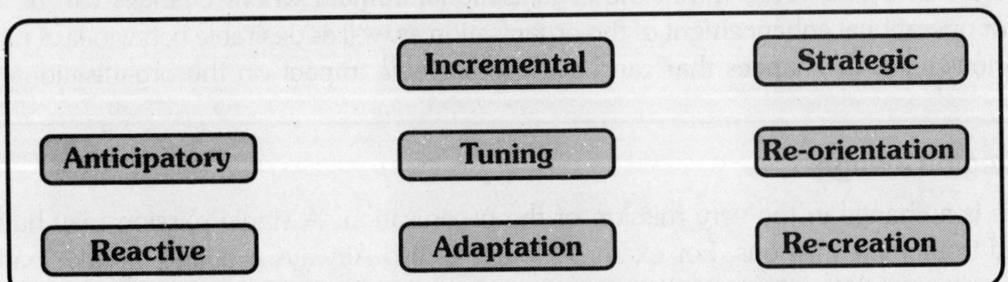

Fig. 1. *Four Types of Organisational Change.*

I. Tuning

This is the most common, least intense, and least risky type of change. Other names for it include preventive maintenance and the Japanese concept of kaizen (continuous improvement). The key to effective tuning is to actively anticipate and avoid problems rather than passively waiting for things to go wrong before taking action. For example, *Du Pont* tuned its marketing efforts by developing an Adopt-a-Customer program. The program "encourages blue-collar workers to visit a customer once a month, learn his needs, and be his representative on the factory floor." This is a refreshing alternative to the traditional practice of waiting for customer complaints and only then trying to figure out how to fix them.

II. Adaptation

Like tuning, adaptation involves incremental changes. But this time, the changes are in reaction to external problems, events, or pressures. For example, after Ford had great success with its aerodynamic styling, General Motors and Chrysler followed suit. In turn, Ford and GM broadened their product lines to complete with Chrysler's trendsetting minivans.

III. Reorientation

This type of change is anticipatory and strategic in scope. Nadler and Tushman call reorientation "frame bending" because the organisation is significantly redirected. Importantly, there is not a complete break with the organisation's past. Fast-food companies, for example, are creatively reaching out to the masses. The food may be the same, but the dining location certainly is not.

IV. Re-creation

Competitive pressures normally trigger this most intense and risky type of organisational change. From a manufacturer of costly luxury cars, he wants it to become an "exclusive, full-line manufacturer" offering high-quality vehicles of all shapes and sizes. *Werner* is pushing Mercedes to expand into two fast-growing segments classified in the US as light trucks: minivans and four-wheel-drive sport-utility vehicles. He also wants Mercedes to have an entry by the mid-1990s in supersmall city cars, a category that scarcely exists today outside Japan.

BASIC FORMS OF CHANGES BASED ON THE ORGANISATIONAL CULTURE

There are various areas within the organisational domain where changes can be brought about for operational enhancement of the organisation as well as desirable behaviour of members. The various types of changes that can have considerable impact on the organisational culture are :

I. Strategic Change

This is a change in the very mission of the organisation. A single mission may have to be changed to multiple missions. For example, when British Airways acquired a major part of US Air, the culture of the entire organisation had to be modified to accommodate various aspects of American organisational culture into the British organisational culture.

II. Structural Change

Decentralised operations and participative management style have seen more recent trends in the organisational structure. Since these structural changes shift the authority and responsibility to generally lower level management, it has a major impact on an organisation's social climate and members have to be prepared to develop a team spirit as well as acquire skills to make on-the-spot decisions at points of operations.

III. Process-oriented Change

These changes relate to technological developments, information processing, automation and use of robotics in the manufacturing operations. This means replacing or retraining personnel, heavy capital equipment investment and operational changes. This would affect the organisational culture and hence changes in the behaviour of patterns of members.

IV. People-oriented Change

Even though, any organisational change affects people in some form, it is important that the behaviour and attitudes of the members be predictable and in accordance with the expectations of the organisation and be consistent with the mission and policies of the enterprise. These changes are directed towards performance improvement, group cohesion, dedication and loyalty to the organisation as well as developing a sense of self-actualisation among the members.

PROCESS OF CHANGE

Once, the need for change and the goals of such a change are recognised and accepted, the management must introduce the change process in such a manner that such change is more or less permanent and the management does not shift back to the original and more familiar ways of doing things. To make the change more lasting, *Kurt Lewin* proposed three phases of the change process for moving the organisation from the present to the future. These stages are :

(i) Unfreezing,
(ii) Changing, and
(iii) Refreezing

I. Unfreezing

The process of unfreezing simply makes the individuals or organisations aware and prepares them for the change. *Lewin* believes that the change should not come as a surprise to members of the organisation. Sudden, unannounced change would be socially destructive. The management must pave the way by "unfreezing the situation", so that members would be willing and ready to accept the change. This way, if there is any resistance to change, it can be neutralised. According to *Schein*, unfreezing is the process of breaking down the old attitudes and behaviours, customs and traditions so that they start with a clean slate. This can be achieved by making announcements, holding meetings and promoting the ideas throughout the organisation via bulletin boards, personal contacts and group conferences. One message to members of the organisation suggested by *Kreitner* is as follows :

"We can all improve the effectiveness of our organisation while increasing our personal satisfaction, if we all cooperate in a comprehensive program of finding out *where* we are, *where* we want to go and *how* we can get there."

The unfreezing process basically cleans the slate so that it can accept new writings on it which can then become the operational style.

II. Changing

Once the unfreezing process has been completed and the members of the organisation recognise the need for change and have been fully prepared to accept such change, their behaviour patterns have to be redefined. *H.C. Kellman* has proposed three methods of reassigning new patterns of behaviour. These are :

(a) *Compliance*. Compliance is achieved by strictly enforcing the reward and punishment strategy for good or bad behaviour. Fear of punishment, actual punishment or actual reward seem to change behaviour for the better. For example, many people have stopped smoking because of warning given by the Surgeon General of United States that smoking causes cancer of the lungs.

(b) *Identification*. Identification occurs when members are psychologically impressed upon to identify themselves with some given role models whose behaviour they would like to adopt and try to become like them. Many public organisations use celebrities as role models in advising young people not to try drugs.

(c) *Internalisation*. Internalisation involves some internal changing of the individual's thought processes in order to adjust to a new environment. Members are left alone to look within themselves and they are given freedom to learn and adopt new behaviour in order to succeed in the new set of circumstances. Sometimes, soul searching brings about a new dimension to the philosophy of existence and thus bring about changes in such behavioural patterns that are not considered socially or professionally redeeming.

III. Refreezing

Refreezing occurs when the new behaviour becomes a normal way of life. The new behaviour must replace the former behaviour completely for successful change to take place. Also, it should be permanent in nature. Accordingly, it must be continuously reinforced so that this new acquired behaviour does not diminish or extinguish.

This must be clearly understood that the change process is not a one time application but a continuous process due to dynamism and ever changing environment. Accordingly, the process of unfreezing, changing and refreezing is a cyclical one and remains continuously in process.

The implementation of this three steps change model can be seen in the case of kidnapping victims or prisoners of war or in deprogramming of some religious cultists. The prisoners of war, for example, may be brainwashed into believing that they are fighting a losing and immoral war and that their enemy is really their friend, by certain shock treatments which involve three steps of unfreezing, changing and refreezing process as explained before. If these prisoners return back to their own country, the process can be repeated to bring them back to their original behaviour.

Another methodology to induce, implement and manage change was also introduced by *Kurt Lewin*, who called it "force-field analysis". This analysis is based upon the assumption that we are in a stable of equilibrium when there is balance between forces that induce change and forces that resist change. To achieve change, we must overcome this *status quo*. The change forces are known as driving forces and the forces that resist change are known as restraining forces as shown below:

DRIVING FORCES — **EQUILIBRIUM** — **RESTRAINING FORCES**

Managers who are trying to implement change must analyse this balance of driving and restraining forces and then strengthen the driving forces or weaken the restraining forces sufficiently so that change can take place.

STEPS INCLUDED IN THE PROCESS OF CHANGE

The first step in the change process is to identify the need for change and the area of change as to whether it is strategic change, process-oriented change or employee-oriented change. This need for change can be identified either through internal factors or through external forces that may be in place. Once this need is identified, the following general steps can be taken to implement such change :

(i) *Develop new goals and objectives:* The managers must identify as to what new outcomes they wish to achieve. This may be a modification of previous goals due to changed internal and external environmental or it may be a new set of goals and objectives.

(ii) *Select an agent for change:* The management must decide as to who will initiate and oversee this change. A manager may be assigned this duty or even outside specialists and consultants can be brought in to suggest the various methods to bring in the change and monitor and change process.

(iii) *Diagnose the problem:* It is important to gather all pertinent data regarding the area or the problem where the change is needed. This data should be critically analysed to pinpoint the key issues. Then the solutions can be focused on those key issues.

(iv) *Select methodology:* Because of natural resistance to change, it is very important to chart out a methodology for change which would be correct and acceptable to all. Member's emotions must taken into consideration when devising such methodology.

(v) *Develop a plan:* This step involves putting together a plan as to what is to be done. For example, if the company wants to develop and implement a flexitime policy, it must decide as to what type of workers will be affected by it or whether flexitime should be given to all members or only to some designated workers.

(vi) *Strategy for implementation of the plan:* In this stage, the management must decide on the "when", "where" and "how" of the plan. This includes the right timing of putting the plan to work, how the plan will be communicated to workers in order to have the least resistance and how the implementation will be monitored.

(vii) *Implementation of the plan:* Once the right timing and right channels of communications have been established, the plan is put into action. It may be in the form of simple announcement or it may require briefing sessions or in-house seminars so as to gain acceptance of all the members and specially those who are going to be directly affected by the change.

(viii) Receive and evaluate feedback: Evaluation consists of comparing actual results to the set goals. Feedback will confirm if these goals are being met so that if there is any deviation between the goals and the actual performance outcomes, then corrective measures can be taken.

RESISTANCE TO CHANGE

Inevitably, change will be resisted, atleast to some extent, by both individuals and organisations. Resistance to change is baffling because it can take so many forms. Overt resistance may be manifested in strikes, reduced productivity, shoddy work, and even sabotage. Overt resistance may be expressed by increased tardiness and absenteeism, requests for transfers, resignations, loss of motivation, lower morale, and higher accident or error rates. One of the more damaging forms of resistance is lack of participation in and commitment to proposed changes by employees, even when they have opportunities to participate.

As Fig. 1, shows previously, resistance to change stems from a variety of sources. Some are traceable to individuals, but others involve the nature and structure of organisations. Managers and employees need to understand the reasons for and sources of resistance to change.

I. Individual Resistance to Change

Fig. 2 shows six important sources of individual resistance to change. Of course, these are not the only reasons why individuals may resist change at work.

(i) Perception

Recall the perceptual error called *perceptual defence*. It is the notion that people tend to perceive selectively those things that fit most comfortably into their current understanding of the world. Once individuals establish their understanding of reality, they resist changing it. Among other things, people may resist the possible impact of change on their lives by (i) reading or

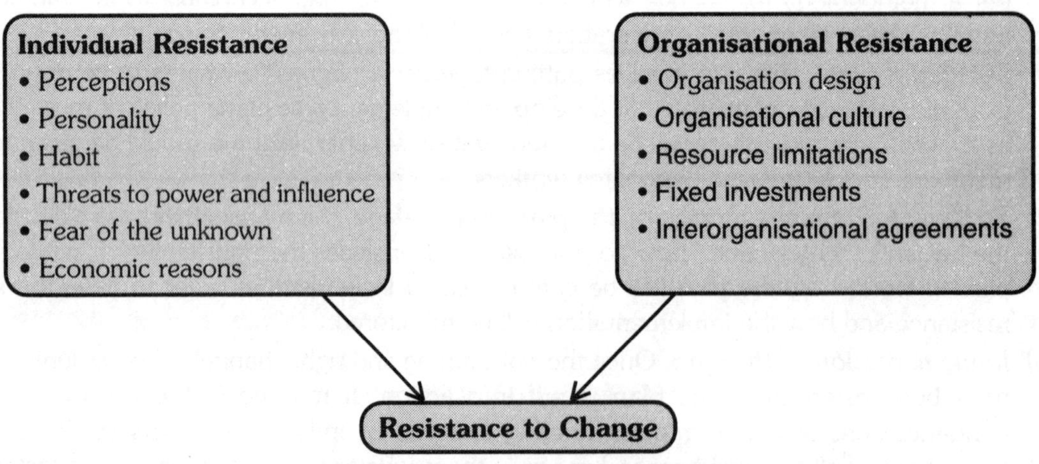

Fig. 2. *Sources of Resistance to Change.*

listening only to what they agree with, (ii) conveniently forgetting any knowledge that could lead to other viewpoints, and (iii) misunderstanding communication that, if correctly perceived, wouldn't fit their existing attitudes and values. For example, managers enrolled in management training programs are exposed to different managerial philosophies and techniques. They may ably discuss and answer questions about these philosophies while carefully segregating in their minds the approaches that they believe wouldn't work from those that they already practice. *Stereotypes* also can serve as a perceptual resistance to change.

(ii) Personality

Some aspects of their personalities (e.g., dogmatism and dependency) may predispose some individuals to resist change. Recall that dogmatism is the rigidity of a person's beliefs. The highly dogmatic individual is close-minded and more likely to resist change than a less dogmatic person. Another example is dependency. If carried to extremes, dependency on others can lead to resistance to change. People who are highly dependent on others often lack self-esteem. They may resist change until those they depend on endorse the change and incorporate it into their behaviour. Employees who are highly dependent on their supervisors for performance feedback probably will not accept any new techniques or methods unless the supervisors personally endorse them and indicate to the employees how these changes will improve performance.

(iii) Habit

Unless a situation changes dramatically, individuals may continue to respond to stimuli in their accustomed ways. A habit may be a source of satisfaction for individuals because it allows them to adjust to and cope with their world. A habit also provides comfort and security. Whether a habit becomes a major source of resistance to change depends, to a certain extent, on whether individuals perceive advantages from changing it. For example, if an organisation suddenly announced that all employees would immediately receive a 20% pay raise, few would object, even though the raise might permit significant changes in their life-styles. However, if the organisation announced that all employees could receive a 20% pay raise only if they switched from working from 9:00 A.M. to 5:00 P.M. to working during the evenings and nights, many would object. Employees would have to change many habits—when they sleep, eat, interact with their families, and so on.

(iv) Threats to Power and Influence

Some people in organisations may view change as a threat to their power or influence. Recall that the control of something needed by other people, such as information or resources, is a source of power in organisations. Once a power position has been established, individuals or groups often resist changes that they perceive as reducing their power and influence. For example, programs to improve the quality of work life (QWL programs) in organisations tend to focus on nonmanagerial employees and often are perceived as increasing their power. As a result, managers and supervisors may resist such programs. Novel ideas or a new use for resources also can disrupt the power relationships among individuals and departments in an organisation and therefore often are resisted.

(v) Fear of the Unknown

Confronting the unknown makes most people anxious. Each major change in a work situation carries with it an element of uncertainty. People starting a new job may be concerned about their ability to perform adequately. Women starting a second career after raising a family may be anxious about how they will fit in with other workers after a long absence from the workplace. An employee may wonder what might happen if he or she relocates to company headquarters in another state. "Would my family like it?" "Will I be able to find friends?" "What will top managers think of me if I refuse to relocate?" Uncertainty in such situations arises not just from the prospective change itself, but also from the potential consequences of the change. In order to avoid both making more demanding types of decisions and the fear of the unknown, some employees may refuse promotions that require relocating or that require major changes in job duties and responsibilities.

(vi) Economic Reasons

Money weights heavily in people's considerations. They certainly can be expected to resist changes that could lower their income. In a very real sense, employees have invested in the status quo in their jobs. That is, they may have learned how to perform the work successfully, how to get good performance evaluations, and how to interact with others. Changes in established work routines or job duties may threaten their economic security. Employees may fear that after changes are made, they will not be able to perform up to their previous standards and subsequently will not be as valuable to the organisation, their supervisor, or their co-workers.

II. Organisational Resistance to Change

To a certain extent, the nature of organisation is to resist change. Organisations often are most efficient when doing routine things and tend to perform more poorly, at least initially, when doing anything for the first time. To ensure operational efficiency and effectiveness, organisations may create strong defences against change. Moreover, change often opposes vested interests and violates certain territorial rights or decision-making prerogatives that groups, teams, and departments have established and accepted over time.

(i) Organisation Design

Organisation need stability and continuity in order to function effectively. Indeed, the term organisation implies that individual, group, and team activities must have a certain structure. That is, individuals must have assigned roles, established procedures for getting the job done, consistent ways of getting needed information, and the like. However, this legitimate need for structure also may lead to resistance to change. Organisations may have narrowly defined jobs; clearly spelled-out lines of authority, responsibility, and accountability; and limited flows of information from the top to the bottom. The use of a rigid design and an emphasis on the hierarchy of authority usually causes employees to use only specific channels of communication and to focus narrowly on their own duties and responsibilities. Typically, the more mechanistic the organisation, the more numerous are the levels of the organisation through which an idea must travel. This organisational design, then, increases the probability that any new idea will be screened out because it threatens the status quo. More adaptive and flexible organisations are designed to reduce the resistance to change created by rigid organisational structures.

(ii) Organisational Culture

Organisational culture plays a key role in change. Recall that cultures are not easy to change and may become a principle source of resistance to needed changes. One aspect of an effective organisation culture is whether the culture has the flexibility to take advantage of opportunities to change. An ineffective organisational culture, from the perspective of our organisational change topic, is one that rigidly socialises employees into the old culture even in the face of evidence that it no longer works.

(iii) Resource Limitations

Some organisations want to maintain the status quo, but others would change if they had the resources to do so. Change requires capital, time, and skilled people. At any particular time, an organisation's managers and employees may have identified changes that could or should be made, but they may have to defer or abandon some of the desired changes because of resource limitations.

(iv) Fixed Investments

Resource limitations aren't confined to organisations with insufficient assets. Wealthy organisation may be unable to change because of fixed capital investments in assets that they can't easily alter (e.g., equipment, buildings, and land). The plight of the central business districts in many cities illustrates this resistance to change most large cities developed before the automobile and can't begin to accommodate today's traffic volumes and parking demands. The fixed investments in buildings, streets, transit systems, and utilities are enormous and usually prevent rapid and substantial changes. Therefore many older central areas are unable to meet the competition of suburban shopping centres.

Fixed investments aren't always limited to physical assets; they also may be expressed in terms of people. For example, consider employees who no longer are making a significant contribution to an organisation but have enough seniority to maintain their jobs. Unless they can be motivated to higher task performance or retrained for other positions, their salaries and fringe benefits represent, from the organisations's perspective, fixed investments that cannot easily be changed.

(v) Interorganisational Agreements

Agreements between organisations usually impose obligations on people that can restrain their behaviours. Labour negotiations and contracts are the most pertinent example. Some ways of doing things that once were considered the prerogatives of managements (the right to hire and fire, assign tasks, promote and demote, and so on) may become subject to negotiation and fixed in the negotiated contract. Other types of contracts also constrain organisations. For example, proponents of change may face delay because of arrangement with competitors, commitments to suppliers and other contractors, and pledges to public officials in return for licenses, permits, or financing.

OVERCOMING RESISTANCE TO CHANGE

Dealing with change is an inescapable part of modern management. Change expert *Ichak Adizes* puts it this way: *Living means solving problems, and growing up means being able to solve bigger problems. The purpose of management, leadership parenting, or governing is exactly that: to solve today's problems and get ready to deal with tomorrow's problems. This is necessary because there is change. No management is needed when there are no problems, and there are no problems only when we are dead. To manage is to be alive, and to be alive means to experience change with the accompanying problems it brings.*

Within the change typology just discussed, organisational change comes in all sizes and shapes. Often it's new and unfamiliar equipment, such as personal computers. It could be reorganisation, a merger, a new pay plan, or perhaps a new performance-appraisal program. Whatever its form, change is like a stone tossed into a still pond. The initial impact causes ripples to radiate in all directions, often with unpredictable consequences. A common consequence of change in organisations is resistance from those whose jobs are directly affected. Both rational and irrational resistance can bring the wheels of progress to a halt. Management faces the challenge of foreseeing and neutralizing resistance to change. The question is, how? To answer that question, we must examine why employees resist change.

REASONS FOR RESIST CHANGE TO EMPLOYEES

Employees resist change for many reasons. Among the most common are the following :

I. Surprise

Significant changes that are introduced on the spur of the moment or with no warning can create a threatening sense of imbalance in the workplace. Regarding this problem, an executive task force at J.C. Penney Co., the well-known retailer, recommended: "Schedule changes in measurable, comfortable stages. Too much, too soon can be counterproductive."

II. Inertia

Many members of the typical organisation desire to maintain a safe, secure, and predictable *status quo*. The byword of this group is, "But we don't do things that way here." Technological inertia also is a common problem. Consider, for example, the history of the standard typewriter keyboard (referred to as the Qwerty keyboard because QWERTY are the first six letters in the upper left-hand corner).

The ungainly layout of the Qwerty keyboard was introduced in 1873 to slow down typists so they wouldn't jam the keys. That design imperative quickly disappeared, yet Qwerty has turned back all attempts—including one by its own inventor—to replace it with something faster. The productivity cost? Undoubtedly billions of dollars.

Thanks to resistance to change, the latest high-tech marvels in personal computing come out of the box today complete with an 1873-style keyboard! Supervisors and middle managers who fall victim to unthinking inertia can effectively kill change programs.

III. Misunderstanding/Ignorance/Lack of Skills

Without adequate introductory or remedial training, an otherwise positive change may be perceived in a negative light.

IV. Emotional Side Effects

Those who are forced to accept on-the-job changes commonly experience a sense of loss over past ways of doing things. For example, consider the following chain of events at Japan's Nissan Motor Company: To consolidate the company's brands worldwide, a headquarters edict jettisoned the high-profile Datsun brand from the US market in favour of the corporate moniker. The changeover dragged on for five years, as frustrated dealers stonewalled the change by refusing to pay for new signs. Once drawn to Datsun for performance and sportiness, customers became confused. Many thought Nissan was a Toyota subsidiary. "Unfortunately, the Nissan name is still weak," Chairman Yutaka Kume concedes.

V. Lack of Trust

Promises of improvement are likely to fall on deaf ears when employees do not trust management. Conversely, managers are unlikely to permit necessary participation if they do not trust their people.

VI. Fear of Failure

Just as most college freshmen have doubts about their chances of ever graduating, challenges presented by significant on-the-job changes can also be intimidating.

VII. Personality Conflicts

Managers who are disliked by their people are poor conduits for change.

VIII. Poor Timing

In every work setting, internal and/or external events can conspire to create resentment about a particular change. For example, Intel's across-the-board salary cut, in response to the electronics industry slump of 1981-82, generated greater-than-expected resentment because "the salary cuts were timed to come just as taxes for social security were reimposed."

IX. Lack of Tact

As we all know, it is not necessarily what is said that shapes our attitude toward people and events. How it is said is often more important. Tactful and sensitive handling of changes is essential.

X. Threat to Job Status/Security

Because employment fulfils basic needs, employees can be expected to resist changes with real or imaginary impacts on job status or job security.

XI. Break-up of Work Group

Significant changes can tear the fabric of on-the job social relationships. Accordingly, members of cohesive work groups often exert peer pressure on one another to resist changes that threaten to break up the group.

These reasons for resisting change help demonstrate that participation is not a panacea. For example, imagine the futility of trying to gain the enthusiastic support of a team of auto assembly line welders for a robot that will eventually take over their jobs. In extreme form, each reason for resisting change can become an insurmountable barrier to genuine participation. Therefore, managers need a broad array of methods for dealing with resistance to change.

SUGGESTIONS FOR OVERCOMING RESISTANCE TO CHANGE

Only in recent years have a management theorists begun to give serious attention to alternative ways of overcoming resistance to change. At least six options, including participation, are available in this area:

(i) *Education and Communication* : This strategy is appealing because it advocates prevention rather than cure. The idea here is to help employees understand the true need for a change as well as the logic behind it. Various media may be used, including face-to-face discussions, formal group presentations, or special reports or publications.

(ii) *Participation and Involvement* : Once again, personal involvement through participation tends to defuse both rational and irrational fears about a workplace change. By participating in both the design and implementation of a change, one acquires a personal stake in its success.

(iii) *Facilitation and Support* : When fear and anxiety are responsible for resistance to doing things in a new and different way, support from management in the form of special training, job stress counseling, and compensatory time off can be helpful.

(iv) *Negotiation and Agreement* : Sometimes management can neutralise potential or actual resistance by exchanging something of value for cooperation. An hourly clerical employee may, for instance, be put on a salary in return for learning how to operate a new computerised work-station.

(v) *Manipulation and Co-optation* : Manipulation occurs when managers selectively withholds or dispense information and consciously arrange events to increase the chance that a change will be successful. Co-optation normally involves token participation. Those who are co-opted with token participation cannot claim that they have not been consulted, yet the ultimate impact of their input is negligible.

(vi) *Explicit and Implicit Coercion* : Managers who cannot or will not invest the time required for the other strategies can force employees to go along with a change by threatening them with termination, loss of pay raises or promotions, transfer, and the like.

CHANGING ORGANISATIONS

Many approaches can be used to diagnose and initiate organisational change. We consider four of the most important and widely used approaches: a systems approach, the process of innovation, the process of action research, and the applied behavioural science called organisation development.

I. A Systems Approach to Change

The systems model of change describes the organisation as six interacting variables that could serve as the focus of planned change: *people*, *culture*, *task*, *technology*, *design*, and *strategy*.

(i) The *people variable* applies to the individuals working for the organisation, including their individual differences—personalities, attitudes, perceptions attributions, problem-solving styles, needs, and motives.

(ii) The *culture variable* reflects the shared beliefs, values, expectations, and norms of organisational members.

(iii) The *task variable* involves the nature of the work itself—whether the job is simple or complex, novel or repetitive, standardised or unique.

(iv) The *technology variable* encompasses the problem-solving methods and techniques used and the application of knowledge to various organisational processes. It includes such things as the use of information technology, robot and other automation, manufacturing processes, tools, and techniques (e.g., computer integrated manufacturing).

(v) The *design variable* is the formal organisational structure and its systems of communication, control, authority, and responsibility.

(vi) Finally, the *strategy variable* comprises the organisation's planning process. It typically consists of activities undertaken to identify appropriate organisational goals and prepare specific plans to acquire, allocate, and use resources in order to accomplish those goals.

A change in any one variable usually results in a change in one or more of the others. For example a change in the organisation's strategic plan might dictated a change in organisation design to an adaptive or network form. This change, in turn, could result in the reassignment of people. At the same time, the redesign may also lead to a change in the technology used, which would affect the attitudes and behaviours of the employees involved, and so on. Any of these changes occur within a particular culture, which might either support or resist them. Moreover, change itself may either modify or reinforce the existing culture. An advantage of a systems approach to organisational change is that it helps managers and employees think through such interrelationships. The systems approach reminds us that we cannot change a part of the organisation without, in some sense, changing the whole.

Organisational change can be introduced by altering these variables singly or in combination, but all six usually are present in an organisation wide change process. However the systems approach to change emphasises the importance of understanding all six variables before making changes in any one of them.

II. Innovation

Innovation is the initiation or adoption of new products, services, processes, procedures, or ideas by an organisation. The capacity to innovate is central to the ability of an organisation to adapt to changes in its environment.

Many critics of U.S. industry argue that its most serious shortcoming in the fact of increased global competition is a lack of innovation. The reasons given for an inability to generate sufficient innovation include :

(1) an overemphasis on short-term profits,
(2) an unwillingness to invest owing to the high cost of capital,
(3) government regulation,
(4) resistance to change,
(5) rigid organisation design and procedures that stifle new ideas, and
(6) reward structures that the central issues involve management philosophy, practices, and culture.

The conclusions stemming from studies of innovation at the Xerox Palo Alto Research Centre (PARC) support the latter view. Investigation of organisational innovation spanning the last 20 years at PARC suggest that effective innovation will occur only by creating "continuously innovating companies." Such an organisation continuously "reinvents" itself and its products or services.

The studies at PARC (Palo Alto Research Centre) also reached the following conclusions regarding innovation:

- Innovation in work practices is as important as innovation in new product development and manufacture.
- Innovation is everywhere in the organisation, not just in research and development labs and research centres.
- Organisations need to learn how to identify these many innovations and share them throughout the system.

Specialised research centres in the organisation cannot just produce innovation, which must be "coproduced." Large numbers of employees must share a vision of the importance of innovation in order for change to occur and be disseminated throughout the organisation.

The organisation's ultimate innovation partner is the customer. Innovation, like everything else the organisation does, must allow the organisation to meet customer needs better.

III. Action Research

Action research is a data based, problem-solving process of organisational change that closely follows the steps involved in the scientific method. It represents a powerful approach to organisational change and consists of three essential steps :

(i) gathering information about problems, concerns, and needed changes from the members of an organisation;

(ii) organising this information in some meaningful way and sharing it with the employees involved in the change effort; and

(iii) planning and carrying out specific actions to correct identified problems.

The action-research sequence often includes an evaluation of the implemented actions. An organisational change program may go through repeated cycles of data gathering, information sharing and action planning before its conclusion.

IV. Organisational Development

Organisational development (OD) is a planned, systematic process of organisational change based on behavioural science research and theory. The goal of OD is to create adaptive organisations capable of repeatedly transforming and reinventing themselves as needed to remain effective. As a field of behavioural science, OD draws heavily from psychology, sociology, and anthropology. Organisation development relies on information from motivation theory, personality theory, and learning theory, and on research on group dynamics, leadership, power, and organisation design. It is based on many well-established principles regarding the behaviours of individuals and groups in organisations. Organisation development isn't a single technique but a collection of techniques that have a certain philosophy and body of knowledge in common.

INDIVIDUAL REACTIONS TO CHANGE

Ultimately, workplace changes of all types become a personal matter for employees. A merger, for example, means a new job assignment for one person and a new boss for another. The first person may look forward to the challenge of a new assignment, while the second may dread the prospect of adjusting to a new boss. Researchers tell us that these two people will tend to exhibit distinctly different response patterns. Specifically, people tend to respond to changes they like differently than they do to changes they *dislike*. Let us explore these two response patterns with the goal of developing a contingency model for managers. Importantly, both models are generic, that is, they apply equally to on- and off-the-job changes.

I. How People Respond to Changes They Like?

A three-stage adjustment is typical when people encounter a change they like as shown in Fig. 3. New college graduates, for instance, often see their unrealistic optimism (stage A) given way to the reality shock (stage B) of earning a living before getting their life and career on track (stage C). Key personal factors—including attitude, morale, and desire to make the change work-dip during stage B. Sometimes the dip is so severe or prolonged that the person gives up as, say,

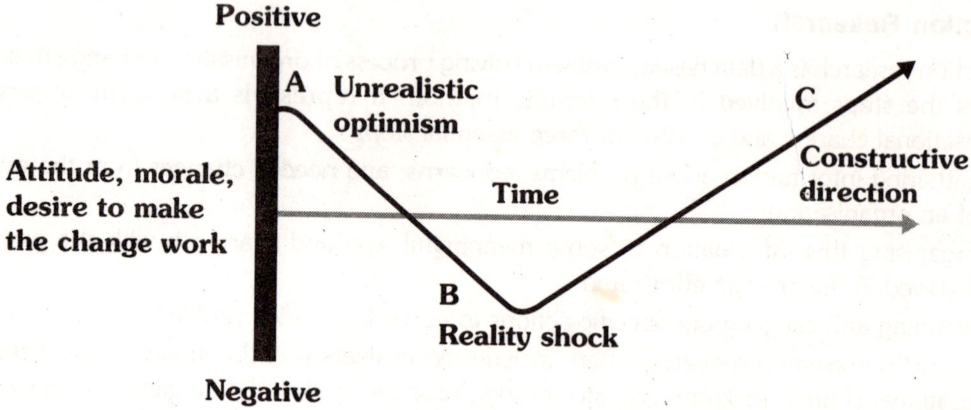

Fig. 3. *How People Tend to Respond to Changes They Like.*

when newlyweds head for the divorce court. Stage B is thus a critical juncture where leadership can make a difference.

II. How People Respond to Changes They Fear and Dislike?

Although exact statistics are not available, the situation in Fig. 4, probably is more common in the workplace than the one in Fig. 3. In other words, on-the-job change generally is more feared than welcomed. Changes, particularly sudden ones, represent the unknown. Most of us fear the unknown. We can bring the model in Fig. 4 to life by walking through it with Maria, a production supervisor at a dairy products cooperative. She and her coworkers face a major reorganisation involving a switch to team-based production.

In stage 1, Maria feels a bit unsure and somewhat overwhelmed by the sudden switch to teams. She needs a lot more information to decide whether she really likes the idea. She feels

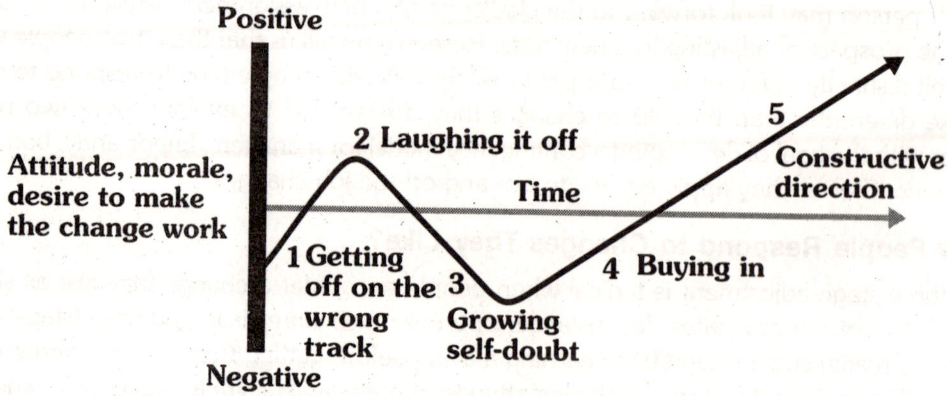

Fig. 4. *How People Tend to Respond to Changes They Fear and Dislike.*

twinges of fear. Stage 2 finds Maria joking with the other supervisors about how upper management's enthusiasm for teams will blow over in a few days, so there's no need to worry. Her attitude, mood, and desire for change improve a bit. After an initial training session on team-based management and participation, Maria begins to worry about her job security. Even if she keeps her job, she wonders if she is up to the new way of doing things. Her morale drops sharply in stage 3. In stage 4, after a stern but supportive lecture from her boss about being a team player, Maria comes to grips with her resistance to the team approach. She resolves to stop criticizing management's "fad of the week" and help make the switch to teams work. Her attitude turns positive, and her morale takes an upswing, in stage 5, as she tries participative management techniques and gets positive results. Additional training and some personal research and reading on team-based management convince Maria that this approach is the wave of the future.

Six months after the switch to teams was announced, Maria has become an outspoken advocate for teams and participative management. Her job security is strengthened by a pending promotion to the training department, where she will coordinate all team training for supervisors. Unknown to upper management, Maria has even toyed with the idea of starting her own consulting business, specializing in team management. Maria's transition from fear to full adaptation has taken months and has not been easy. But the experience has been normal and positive, including a timely boost from her manager between stages 3 and 4.

III. A Contingency Model for Getting Employees through Changes

Contingency managers, once again, adapt their techniques to the situation. The response patterns in Figures (3) and (4) call for different managerial actions. When employees understand that stages 2 and 3 are normal and expected responses, they will be less apt to panic and more likely to respond favourable to managerial guidance through action stages 3 and 4 and 5.

ALTERNATIVE CHANGE MANAGEMENT APPROACHES

Managers can undertake organisational change in various ways. As noted in the opening Issue for Debate, managing change involves important ethical issues that cannot be ignored. No doubt, in many instances the change process occurs at the expense of short-term losses for some in exchange for long-term benefits for the many. One extensive review of the literature identified several approaches that managers can use to manage planned change. Although the terms applied to the different approaches vary from author to author and from proponent to proponent, the underlying theme is the same. Regardless of the terms used, the approaches range from the application of power, in any of its forms, to bring about change the application of reason. Midway between these two extremes is the approach that relies upon re-education.

I. Managing Change through Power

The application of power to bring about change implies the use of coercion. In organisations, managers are generally considered to be the ones who have access to power and who can use their power to coerce nonmanagers to change in the direction they desire. Managers can implement power through their control over reward and sanctions. They can determine the conditions of employment including promotion and advancement. Consequently, through their access to these bases of power, managers can bring to bear considerable influence in an organisation.

The application of power is a manifestation of autocratic leadership and is generally not held in high esteem in contemporary organisations. In times past, autocratic management has been a factor in the rise of labour unions as counterweights to the arbitrary use of managerial power. Except in crises situations when the very existence of the organisation is at stake, power is not a favoured approach for bringing about change.

II. Managing Change through Reason

The application of reason to bring about change is based on the dissemination of information prior to the intended change. The underlying assumption is that reason alone will prevail and that the participants and parities to the change will all make the rational choice. The reason-based approach appeals to the sensibilities of those who take a Utopian view of organisational worlds. But the reality of organisations requires that we recognise the existence of individual motives and needs, group norms and sanctions, and the fact that organisations exist as social as well as work units—all of which means that reason alone won't be sufficient to bring about change.

III. Managing Change through Re-education

The middle ground approach relies upon re-education to improve the functioning of the organisation. Re-education implies a particular set of activities that recognises that neither power nor reason can bring about desirable change. This set of activities has been the subject of much research and application and is generally understood to be the essence of organisational development.

DEPTH OF INTENDED CHANGE

Depth of intended change refers to the scope and intensity of the organisational development efforts. Which likens the organisation to an iceberg. This analogy draws attention to two important components: the formal and informal aspects of organisations. The formal components of an organisation are like that part of an iceberg that's above water; the informal components lie below water, unseen, but are there nevertheless. The formal components are observable, rational, and oriented to structural factors. The informal components are, on the other hand, not observable to all people, affective, and oriented to process and behavioural factors.

Generally speaking, the greater the scope and intensity of the problem, the more likely it is that the problem will be found in the informal components. Thus, depth of intended change refers to how far management must go into the organisation iceberg to solve the problem. At one extreme are problems with the structure of the organisation. Managers can solve such problems by changing job definitions, departmentalisation bases, spans of control, and delegated authority. At the other extreme are problems with the behaviour of groups and individuals. These problems are related to personal views, value orientations, feelings, and sentiments as well as activities, sentiments, and roles within and among groups. And while these behaviours can certainly be affected by changes in structure, they are ordinarily deep-seated and management must confront them more directly. The greater the depth of intervention, the greater the risk of failure and the higher the cost of change.

THE ESSENTIAL STAGES FOR EFFECTIVE CHANGE MANAGEMENT

We can summarise the discussion by presenting an abbreviated, five-stage model for managing change. This model emphasises management's responsibilities to do the essential things that increase the probability that individual, group, and organisational effectiveness will improve. Many consultants and practitioners have contributed to the literature of change management. This chapter's discussion reflects their contributions. The five-stage model can be considered a generally accepted statement of effective change management procedures. Change management has *five stages* :

(i) Initiating the change is typically undertaken by a change agent who may be internal or external to the organisation and who may act alone or with a group who spearhead the program.

(ii) Diagnosing the problem identifies the specific causes and evidence of problems resulting in recognition of target(s) of change.

(iii) Identifying the intervention(s) that, when implemented, will cause the targets to change in the desired direction.

(iv) Implementing the intervention at the appropriate time and scope ensures the highest probability of successful change.

(v) Evaluating the results lots us gauge the magnitude and direction of changes in the targets.

Managers who manage change in the systematic way suggested by the five stages increase the odds that the intended outcome will be the actual outcome.

REVIEW QUESTIONS

1. Explain the different forms of changes.
2. Differentiate between the external and internal forces that induce change in the organisation.
3. Discuss the process of change in organisation. Also explain the objectives and goals of organisational change.
4. Describe in detail the three steps in the change process.
5. What do people resist change and how would you introduce large successfully in an organisation?
6. How to overcome the resistance to change?
7. Write short notes:
   (a) Process of organisational change and important factors.
   (b) Steps involved in organisational change.
8. What are the strategies employed in reducing the resistance to change in an organisation? Explain.

REFERENCES

1. Kurt Lewin, "Frontiers in Group Dynamics, Concept, Methods, Reality in Social Sciences, Social Equilibria and Social Change", Human Relations, No. 1, June, 1947.
2. Edgar H. Schein, "Management Development as a Process of Influence", in (ed.), David R. Hamption, Behavioural Concepts in Management, Belmont: California; Dickinson Publications, 1968.
3. C.B. Ferster and B.F. Skinner, Schedules of Reinforcement, New York, Century Crofts, 1957.
4. Alwin Zander, "Resistance to Change: Its Analysis and Prevention", In Peter B. Schioderbic, "Management Systems", New York, John Wiley and Sons, 1967.
   Also see M. Steward, "Resistance to Technological Change in Industry", Human Organisation, Vol. 16, 1967.
5. William F. Whyte, Men at Work, Homewood III Dorsey, 1961.
6. W. Douglas Seymour, "Restraining for Technological Change", Personnel Management, Dec., 1966.
7. R.M. Hodgets, Modern Human Relations.
8. Alfred J. Marrow, David P. Bowers and Stanley Seashore, Management by Participation, New York, Harper and Row, 1967.
9. John P. Kotter, "Power, Dependence and Effective Management", Harvard Business Review; July-Aug, 1977.
10. Charles Perrow, "Is Business Really Changing", Organisational Dynamics, Summer, 1974.
11. Waston, Goodwin and Edward M. Glasser, "What We have Learned about Planning for Change", Management Review, American Management Association, November, 1965.
12. Alfred Chadler, Strategy and Structure, Cambridge, Mass, MIT Press, 1962.
13. Don Fabun, The Dynamic of Change, Englewood Cliffs, NJ Printice-Hall, Inc., 1967.
14. Richard L. Daft, Organisation Theory and Design, West Publishing Company, New York, 1983.
15. Richard Beckhard, Organisation Development: Strategies and Models, Reading, Mass, Addison-Wesley Publishing Company, 1969.
16. French and Bell, Definition and History of Organisation Development, Academy of Management Proceedings, 1971.
17. W. Warner Burke, Jock Fordyce, and Stanley Jacobson, "What is OD?" News and Reports from NTL Institute of Applied Behavioural Science, Vol. 2, No. 3, June, 1968.